RESEARCH HANDBOOK ON STRATEGIC ENTREPRENEURSHIP

To my academic mentor Daniel Turban for his invaluable guidance and advice, without which I may never have achieved whatever I did; to my niece Navisha and nephew Aarav, maamu loves you more than you (will ever) know. – Vishal K. Gupta

To my family for their love and support: my mother, Semra; my father, Prof. Dr. Deniz Göktan, a prolific academic and author of many books; my husband, Haydar; daughter, Defne; and son, Demir. – A. Banu Goktan

To all my teachers, with gratitude. – Galina V. Shirokova

To my family, for all the support and love you provided throughout my life. – Amit Karna

Research Handbook on Strategic Entrepreneurship

Edited by

Vishal K. Gupta

Professor, Department of Management, Culverhouse College of Business, The University of Alabama, USA

A. Banu Goktan

Associate Professor, School of Business, University of North Texas at Dallas, USA

Galina V. Shirokova

Professor, School of Economics and Management, National Research University Higher School of Economics, St. Petersburg, Russia

Amit Karna

Professor of Strategy, Indian Institute of Management Ahmedabad, India

EE **Edward Elgar**
PUBLISHING

Cheltenham, UK • Northampton, MA, USA

Published by
Edward Elgar Publishing Limited
The Lypiatts
15 Lansdown Road
Cheltenham
Glos GL50 2JA
UK

Edward Elgar Publishing, Inc.
William Pratt House
9 Dewey Court
Northampton
Massachusetts 01060
USA

Paperback edition 2023

A catalogue record for this book
is available from the British Library

Library of Congress Control Number: 2021943513

This book is available electronically in the **Elgar**online
Business subject collection
http://dx.doi.org/10.4337/9781789904444

ISBN 978 1 78990 443 7 (cased)
ISBN 978 1 78990 444 4 (eBook)
ISBN 978 1 0353 2206 0 (paperback)

Printed and bound by CPI Group (UK) Ltd, Croydon, CR0 4YY

Contents

Contributors

Brian S. Anderson is Executive Associate Dean and Associate Professor of Entrepreneurship at the Henry W. Bloch School of Management at the University of Missouri, Kansas City. He is also a visiting professor in the Entrepreneurship and Innovation Group at Ghent University, Belgium. Brian's research centers on entrepreneurial orientation, and causal inference in studying strategic entrepreneurship phenomena. He received his Ph.D. from Indiana University.

Craig E. Armstrong is Associate Professor, Entrepreneurship and Strategic Management, University of Alabama. His research interests include gamification of management research and education; entrepreneurial pitching; lateral thinking, creativity, and problem solving; experiential learning; strategic human capital; new venture financing, environmental management, and entrepreneurial processes. He serves on the editorial boards of the *Journal of Education for Business*, *Journal of the International Council for Small Business*, *Journal of Operations Management*, and *Journal of Small Business Management*.

Florian Bayer is a specialist for digital marketing at Bitkom e.V. and his main research interests include effectuation, entrepreneurial action, and digital marketing. He received his doctoral degree from EBS Universität für Wirtschaft und Recht. His recent research focuses on the conceptual foundation of individual-level entrepreneurial behavior and dyadic social interaction in the context of effectuation.

Nachiket Bhawe is Associate Professor of Strategy at the University of North Carolina-Pembroke. He received his Ph.D. from the University of Minnesota. His research interests include knowledge use by organizations in the gig economy, internal entrepreneurship and policy, and social entrepreneurship in informal economies. His research has been published in the *Journal of Applied Psychology*, *Strategic Entrepreneurship Journal*, *Small Business Economics*, and *Journal of Business Venturing Insights*, among others.

Josie A. Burks is Instructional Assistant Professor, University of Mississippi. Her research interests explore constructs, behavioral mechanisms, and persuasive underpinnings of entrepreneurial venture pitches, support for entrepreneurial innovation and new venture development, as well as entrepreneurial education research regarding venture pitches, mindset, and coachability. Dr. Burks works with entrepreneurs and student teams in preparation for investment opportunities, demo days, and business plan competitions to alleviate challenges incurred due to a lack of understanding associated with persuasive discourse. She received her Ph.D. from the University of Alabama.

Per L. Bylund is Associate Professor of Entrepreneurship and Records-Johnston Professor in the School of Entrepreneurship in the Spears School of Business, Oklahoma State University. He earned his Ph.D. in applied economics from the University of Missouri. His research focuses on institutions, growth, and entrepreneurship as well as strategy and the theory of the firm.

Susanne C. Bylund is President of private equity firm Permanent Equity where she is responsible for the oversight of portfolio companies. Her main areas of expertise are strategic decision-making, organizational design, and change management.

Betsy Campbell is Assistant Professor at Pennsylvania State University where she directs The Cape (Community Advancing Pluralism in Entrepreneurship), a national initiative addressing matters of diversity, inclusion, and belonging in entrepreneurial contexts. Her research focuses on innovative entrepreneurial work from a practice theory perspective. She is a Fulbright Specialist in entrepreneurship and the recipient of the Academy of Management Innovation in Entrepreneurship Pedagogy award. Her advanced degrees are from Harvard and Exeter.

Diego M. Coraiola is Associate Professor of Entrepreneurship at the Peter B. Gustavson School of Business at the University of Victoria, Canada. Diego's research focuses on entrepreneurial action, social change and the strategic uses of the past, Indigenous organizing, and innovation in arts and crafts. His work has been published in several journals such as *Strategic Management Journal*, *Organization Studies*, *Strategic Organization*, *Journal of Management Inquiry*, and *Journal of Business Ethics*.

Riley Doyle graduated in 2020 from the University of Alabama with a degree in management, serving three years as a faculty scholar. During this time, she won an entrepreneurship pitch competition and worked with outstanding professors and researchers Dr. Drnevich, Dr. Armstrong, Dr. Irwin, and Dr. Burks. In addition, Riley presented her work at undergraduate research conferences, and her team's papers were presented at the SMA and USASBE annual meetings.

Paul L. Drnevich is Associate Professor in Entrepreneurship and Strategy, University of Alabama and Visiting Research Scholar at Purdue University. His research interests are new venture creation, value creation/capture, organizational and dynamic capabilities, technology innovation/commercialization, competitive advantage and performance, and cyber security strategy. He has published in the *Financial Times* top 50 research journals. He received his Ph.D. from Purdue University.

Ron Dulek is the John R. Miller Professor of Management at the University of Alabama. He has published eight books and more than 50 refereed academic journal articles in the areas of business strategy and business communication. He is a recipient of the Algernon Sydney Sullivan Award, the university's highest faculty honor, and the Kitty O. Locker Outstanding Researcher Award, the Association for Business Communication's highest research honor. National and international organizations with which Ron has worked extensively include Adtran, AT&T, Chevron, IBM,

Kimberly Clarke Corporation, Mercedes Benz International, OSHA, Procter and Gamble, Spire, Stora Enso, and Volvo.

Mehrsa Ehsani is a Ph.D. student at the Haskayne School of Business, University of Calgary. Her dissertation research is related to the prosperous longevity of firms and evaluating factors affecting the association between decision-making strategies of firms and their survival. For her scholarship, Mehrsa was awarded the Haskayne School of Business Doctoral Scholarship and Alberta Graduate Excellence Scholarship.

A. Banu Goktan is Associate Professor of Management in the School of Business at the University of North Texas at Dallas. Her research interests are in the areas of entrepreneurship, strategy, and national cultural differences.

Elliott Miller Graves is an engineering project manager at Apple Inc. She earned her M.B.A. majoring in strategic management in the Culverhouse College of Business at the University of Alabama. Prior to this, she earned her B.S. in computer science at the University of Alabama. Elliott is passionate about aligning people and technology. In her work, she aims to contribute to a better understanding of the human mind and its interaction with everything in its environment, and to learn how those findings can shape the use and advancement of technology.

Vishal K. Gupta is Professor and Fred and Martha Bostick Faculty Fellow at the University of Alabama. His current research interests are in the areas of corporate entrepreneurship, women's entrepreneurship, and entrepreneurial growth. His research has been published in many prestigious journals, such as the *Academy of Management Journal*, *Academy of Management Review*, *Journal of Applied Psychology*, and *Strategic Management Journal*, among others, receiving multiple awards and honors. He has taught at several leading institutions worldwide, such as the Bahrain Institute of Banking and Finance and Indian Institute of Management. He is the author of *Great Minds in Entrepreneurship Research* (2020).

Yeong Hyun Hong is a doctoral student in management in the Culverhouse College of Business at the University of Alabama. He earned his master's degree in industrial/organizational psychology at Sungkyunkwan University in South Korea, and is the recipient of the Yong Ho Shin Scholarship, Frederic Augustin Brett Scholarship, and Minnie C. Miles Human Resource Management Endowed Graduate Scholarship at the University of Alabama. His research interests include work/non-work interface, employee–organization relationships, and research methodology.

Kris Irwin is Assistant Professor at Old Dominion University. Her research interests include mergers and acquisitions, entrepreneurial start-ups and small and medium-sized enterprises, and strategic human capital. Her work has recently been published in *Human Relations*, *Journal of Small Business Strategy*, and *Journal of Business Research*. She is a recipient of Outstanding Reviewer awards from the Strategic Management and Entrepreneurship Academy of Management divisions and is a section editor at the *Journal of Small Business Strategy*.

Amit Karna is Professor of Strategy at Indian Institute of Management Ahmedabad. He holds a Ph.D. in Management (Strategy). His research focuses on capabilities of the firm, corporate diversification, strategic leadership, and internationalization of emerging market firms.

Christian Landau is Professor of Strategic Management at EBS Business School. Landau previously worked as a research assistant at the Technical University of Berlin and pursued his doctorate degree at the University of Erlangen-Nuremberg. In his research, he focuses on the core issues of strategic management and related questions of innovation and technology management.

Jef Naidoo is Associate Professor of Management and the Derrell Thomas Faculty Fellow in the Culverhouse College of Business at the University of Alabama. Prior to this he was as a consultant at EY Consulting, where he worked on multiple global client engagements that focused on business transformation and process reengineering through technology enablement. His research focuses on leveraging decision modeling to architect intuitive interfaces for communicating data-driven insights to support organizational business intelligence objectives and opening up new perspectives and provoking thought about the pervasive employment of advanced technologies and artificial intelligence in the practice and advancement of management communication processes.

Oleksiy Osiyevskyy is Associate Professor of Entrepreneurship and Innovation and Director of the Global Business Futures Initiative at the Haskayne School of Business, University of Calgary, Canada. In his scholarship, Oleksiy concentrates on the issue of achieving organizational growth and longevity through strategic entrepreneurship and innovation. His research agenda has resulted in over 40 published studies, including articles in premier academic outlets such as the *Strategic Entrepreneurship Journal* and *Journal of Product Innovation Management*.

Anna M. Pastwa is a data science researcher, lecturer at the Warsaw University of Technology, and serves as an artificial intelligence expert at the Kosciuszko Institute. Prior to that, she worked as an assistant professor of entrepreneurship and strategy. She received her doctorate degree in business economics from KU Leuven. Her research interests include corporate entrepreneurship strategy, entrepreneurial finance, and machine learning methods for management research.

Galina V. Shirokova is Professor at the National Research University Higher School of Economics, St. Petersburg. Her research interests include strategic entrepreneurship, entrepreneurship in emerging markets, and student entrepreneurship. Her work has been presented internationally and published within the *Strategic Entrepreneurship Journal*, *Journal of Business Venturing*, *Management and Organization Review*, and *International Small Business Journal*, among others. She is an active member of the Academy of Management.

Kanhaiya Kumar Sinha is Assistant Professor of Entrepreneurship and Innovation at the Labovitz School of Business and Economics, University of Minnesota, Duluth.

In his scholarship, Kanhaiya studies entrepreneurship and innovation practices, performance variability in an entrepreneurial context, governance of innovation, and human capital issues related to new ventures. He holds a Ph.D. from the University of Calgary.

Roy Suddaby is the Winspear Chair of Management at the Peter B. Gustavson School of Business, University of Victoria, Canada and Professor of Management at the Carson School of Business, Washington State University. He is Adjunct Professor at Liverpool University Management School, United Kingdom, Ritsumeikan University, Japan, and at IAE Business School in Argentina and is a Fellow of the Academy of Management.

Fernanda Yumi Tsujiguchi is a post-doctoral research fellow at the Peter B. Gustavson School of Business at the University of Victoria, Canada. Prior to starting her Ph.D. and joining the Gustavson School of Business, Fernanda was a lecturer in a Brazilian university teaching entrepreneurship and innovation. Also in Brazil, she worked as a manager in incubators of technology-based companies connected with public universities and in cooperation with private companies, governmental agents, and other stakeholders.

William J. Wales is the Standish Professor of Entrepreneurship at the University at Albany-SUNY. His research principally explores organizational entrepreneurial orientation, strategy-making processes, and behavior. His work has been published within the *Strategic Management Journal, Journal of Management Studies, Entrepreneurship Theory and Practice, Strategic Entrepreneurship Journal, Journal of Business Research, Journal of Product Innovation Management*, and the *International Small Business Journal*, among others. He is an active member of the Academy of Management.

Shaker Zahra is the Robert E. Buuck Chair of Entrepreneurship and Professor of Strategy and Entrepreneurship at the University of Minnesota. He received his Ph.D. from the University of Mississippi. His research focuses on corporate and international entrepreneurship, dynamic capabilities, social entrepreneurship, and technology strategy and entrepreneurship. His research has appeared in all major journals such as the Academy of Management publications, *Strategic Management Journal, Organization Science*, and *Journal of Business Venturing*.

1. Strategic entrepreneurship research: an introduction

Vishal K. Gupta, A. Banu Goktan, Galina V. Shirokova, and Amit Karna

Organizational researchers have long been interested in the links between strategy and entrepreneurship (Acs & Audtretsch, 2003; Bruton, Filatotchev, Si, & Wright, 2013; Ireland, 2007). For many, strategy and entrepreneurship are two sides of the "economic value" coin, with entrepreneurship researchers delving into value creation and strategy researchers generally gravitating towards value capture (Lepak, Smith, & Taylor, 2007; Pitelis, 2009). Drawing upon Shakespeare's famous play *Romeo and Juliet*, Venkataraman and Sarasvathy (2001) likened entrepreneurship research without a strategic perspective to Romeo without a balcony, and strategy research absent the entrepreneur to the balcony without Romeo.[1] Schendel and Hofer (1979: 6) argued that, the "entrepreneurial choice is at the heart of the concept of strategy." In a similar fashion, strategic thinking is seen as an entrepreneurial imperative (Zabriskie & Huellmantel, 1991).

Given the close affinity between strategy and entrepreneurship research, it is not surprising that there is a significant overlap between the membership of the Academy of Management's entrepreneurship and strategy divisions. For about 50 percent of the members of the entrepreneurship division, their other affiliation is with the strategy division (and vice versa). The close links between entrepreneurship and strategy do not always go down well with scholars (Alvarez & Barney, 2001; Kraus & Kauranen, 2009; Shane, 2012). Some are concerned about strategy's "takeover of the academic field of entrepreneurship" (Baker & Pollock, 2007: 237). For others, there is a real risk – perhaps, even fear – that entrepreneurship may overshadow or overwhelm strategy research (Gupta, 2020). Consider that when entrepreneurship became an independent division of the Academy of Management in 1987, it was originally considered a "spin-off" of the strategy division (Kraus & Kauranen, 2009). At the Strategic Management Society, which is the premier "professional association devoted exclusively to the study of strategic management" (Hambrick & Chen, 2008: 44), the entrepreneurship track now attracts the most submissions, far outpacing the many traditional tracks of strategy research. As a result of this tension between the two fields, there is growing talk about "strategy vs. entrepreneurship" (Meyer, 2009: 346), as if the two fields are competing in a zero-sum game where the survival and growth of one field (and scholars in that field) will come at the expense of the other field.

It was in this zeitgeist – one where strategy and entrepreneurship research came to be seen as rivals, competing for scarce resources and critical legitimacy – that the phrase "strategic entrepreneurship" (SE) was introduced (Kuratko & Audretsch, 2009). Emphasizing the need to explore the intersection of strategic thinking and entrepreneurial mindset, Hitt, Ireland, Camp, & Sexton (2001: 481) define SE as the "integration of entrepreneurial (i.e., opportunity-seeking behavior) and strategic (i.e., advantage-seeking) perspectives in developing and taking actions designed to create wealth." Both strategy and entrepreneurship scholars were interested in understanding how economic actors create and sustain a competitive advantage (Alvarez & Busenitz, 2001). As such, SE was seen as dealing with the combination of "effective opportunity-seeking behavior (i.e., entrepreneurship) with effective advantage-seeking behavior (i.e., strategic management)" (Ireland, Hitt, & Sirmon, 2003: 964). In effect, SE combined the strategic logic of competitive advantage with the entrepreneurial logic of opportunity creation and discovery.

Hitt et al. (2001: 13) introduced the then "new concept (of) strategic entrepreneurship" through an edited book that brought together strategic management and entrepreneurship literatures. Since then, research around SE quickly proliferated, and SE began to be described as an academic field in its own right (Foss & Lyngsie, 2011). Moreover, SE – much like strategy and entrepreneurship research – came to have a scattered and fragmented literature with contributions from scholars across multiple disciplines such as "economics, psychology, sociology, along with other sub disciplines in management including organizational behavior and organization theory" (Hitt, Ireland, Sirmon, & Trahms, 2011: 57).

In 2007, the launch of the *Strategic Entrepreneurship Journal* was a major step that helped the formation, and subsequent expansion of the knowledge base in SE (Ireland, 2007). Over the years, it has seen, along with other journals, a very encouraging discourse around the concept that started as a *strategy versus entrepreneurship* debate and developed into an SE domain with its own identity. Recently, when the Web of Science database was searched for articles that contained the phrase "strategic entrepreneurship" in the text, 259 documents were identified that spanned various research topics, none of which received the sustained in-depth attention needed to advance knowledge in a meaningful fashion (Schröder, Tiberius, Bouncken, & Kraus, 2021). As a result, there is growing concern that the SE concept remains "theoretically under-developed," so that it is unclear "what constitutes opportunity- and advantage-seeking activities" (Zhao, Ishihara, & Jennings, 2020: 2).

While the debate around the definition, domain, and development of SE continues, we decided to mark the 20-year anniversary of Hitt et al.'s (2001) formal introduction of the SE concept with a handbook focused on chapters at the interface of strategy and entrepreneurship. Our thinking was that many scholars are interested in research at the intersection of strategy and entrepreneurship, without being distracted by ongoing discussions about the nature and evolution of the SE label. We wanted to understand what the important topics are at the intersection of strategy and entrepreneurship through the eyes (and minds) of scholars who are working in that space. Of course, we all know the specific topics we are interested in, but where is the collective wisdom of the academic community in terms of the topics that have already been researched and the topics that are worth studying going forward? With this in mind, we put out a call that asked scholars to submit "high-quality ambitious papers that summarize the research on particular topics within strategic entrepreneurship." We were interested in articles pertaining to either theoretical and/or methodological issues in particular areas at the strategy–entrepreneurship interface, or with the interface as a whole. Following Gartner (2014: 13), we asked prospective authors for chapters that help make "sense of the comprehensiveness" of their chosen topic area and "offer a depth of knowledge and insights" into the particular area they chose.

We were particularly happy to note that we received proposals from scholars pursuing a diverse set of studies within the SE domain. Over the last year and a half we worked with each team and were assisted by a very supportive set of reviewers. We completed a double blind review process that resulted in 10 chapters that we are delighted to present as a collection in the form of this *Handbook*. Those who read this *Handbook* cover to cover will find their interest in SE rejuvenated, and several new ideas for future research.

CHAPTERS IN THIS HANDBOOK

Nachiket Bhawe and Shaker Zahra are interested in the structural aspects of the knowledge networks that make up absorptive capacity (ACAP). Their chapter titled "Decomposing the knowledge structures of absorptive capacity" examines the knowledge content of ACAP and how it might affect innovation. Understanding this content can help in addressing the questions about ACAP's antecedents, its evolution, its multi-level nature, and its relationship with innovation. Bhawe and Zahra categorize the different knowledge structures that make up ACAP which enables them to show how ACAP emerges, evolves over time, and the mechanism by which it affects the magnitude and speed of innovation. Their discussion highlights micro foundations of the knowledge content of ACAP and how they can be used across multiple levels of analysis.

Susanne Bylund and Per Bylund define the firm as a vehicle for engaging in, or even a manifestation of, SE. Bylund and Bylund demonstrate that the economic firm is the embodiment of SE necessary for the implementation of entrepreneurial solutions – innovations. This chapter observes the process of the firm formation using a theory of the unhampered market that avoids problems of previous approaches and sheds new light on issues related to the essence of the firm from a Coasean perspective. Bylund and Bylund advance our understanding of the relationship between the markets, organization of the firm, and the function of management and leadership.

Florian Bayer and Christian Landau review 126 articles published within effectuation literature through the lens of SE in their chapter titled "Opportunity-seeking behaviors in strategic entrepreneurship: What do we know from the effectuation literature?" Bayer and Landau consider effectuation and causation as two contrasting perspectives towards entrepreneurial behaviors: causation rooted in the strategic management describing planning and prediction, and effectuation focusing on experimentation and flexibility in creating an entrepreneurial opportunity. This chapter demonstrates how SE and effectuation together advance our understanding of the nature of opportunity-seeking behavior in the entrepreneurial endeavor.

Riley Doyle, Kris Irwin, Josie Burks, Paul Drnevich, and C. E. Armstrong review, integrate, and examine the current state of academic research on incubators, accelerators, and other university-affiliated programs. Their chapter titled "Exploring new venture creation through incubators and accelerators: What value is created and who captures it? Implications for research, teaching, and practice" applies a value creation and capture logic perspective to discern the sources of different types of value created. Doyle et al. also delve into who captures the value created among key stakeholders of the ecosystems in which incubators and accelerators are located.

In their chapter, "Holistic view of strategic entrepreneurship's results: Estimating the implications for performance mean and variability," Oleksiy Osiyevskyy, Kanhaiya Kumar Sinha, Galina Shirokova, and Mehrsa Ehsani emphasize the need to go beyond traditional approaches to evaluating firm performance and analyzing the variance of the performance outcome. Osiyevskyy et al. contend that understanding the performance variability implications of entrepreneurial actions is very important for SE research, because it implies, on one hand, high risk (which is a major driver of business mortality), yet, on the other hand, enables enormously high returns (i.e., explains the possible high-growth outliers). The proposed approach is illustrated using an empirical example of assessing variance implications of two SE constructs – entrepreneurial orientation (an enabler of SE) and exploration (a crucial component of SE).

Diego Coraiola, Fernanda Tsujiguchi, and Roy Suddaby suggest that history can be a source of competitive advantage and foster entrepreneurial action. In their chapter titled "Historical cognition and strategic entrepreneurship," Coraiola et al. define history as cognition that involves perception of the past as an objective, interpretive, and imaginative reality. They suggest that reimagining history in multiple ways may inform alternative paths in the future for SE. Their cognitive perspective of history opens new avenues for future research directions in the SE field.

Betsy Campbell explores ethnomethodology and its potential value to SE in her chapter titled "Making strategic entrepreneurship visible: An ethnomethodology primer." Ethnomethodology and its traditions – including conversation analysis, embodied conversation analysis, membership category analysis, and workplace interaction – can reveal the endogenous ways that strategizing and entrepreneuring are accomplished in practice. Campbell explains what ethnomethodology is, how ethnomethodologically informed studies are done, and why such studies matter to SE.

In their chapter "The eye as a window to the soul: Entering the strategic entrepreneurial mind," Jef Naidoo, Ron Dulek, Elliot Miller Graves, and Yeong Hyun Hong introduce eye tracking as a new methodological approach to studying SE phenomena. The first part of the chapter examines eye movement behavior as a compelling physiological measure for studies in behavioral research. The second part observes the fundamental aspects of eye tracking – from a methodological and technological perspective – and its influence on research in a broad range of disciplines. Finally,

Naidoo et al. conclude that the eye-tracking research approach is viable methodology to advance SE research and offers a potentially promising research agenda for SE inquiry.

Anne Pastwa and William Wales are interested in an important and often over-looked alternative data source for SE research, namely texts. Their chapter "New frontiers? Approaches to computerized text analysis in strategic entrepreneurship research" provide useful guidance to handling texts. Pastwa and Wales summarize several approaches used for textual data sources in SE research, focusing on the most popular and computer-assisted tools for text analyses. The chapter examines the relevance of these tools within the SE research domain. Finally, the authors illustrate the application of topic models with Latent Dirichlet Allocation for explaining the changes in entrepreneurial orientation of publicly listed companies over time.

In his chapter titled "Endogeneity in strategic entrepreneurship research," Brian Anderson focuses on endogeneity problems in SE studies, discussing common threats to causal inference. Anderson suggests an alternative approach to modeling in the SE field and outlines a Bayesian modeling approach to illustrate how entrepreneurship scholars may address multiple endogeneity problems. This chapter helps advance our understanding of the nuances in empirical modeling, providing an alternative to common econometric approaches that may not always be well suited for SE.

Our goal in putting together this *Handbook* was to provide new directions for future SE research. The rich variety of chapters offers a window into the compre-hensiveness of the field and deep knowledge and insights into specific topic areas within SE. Based on our reading of the above chapters, we feel that the book covers fertile ground and represents the growth of the field. Among the chapters, there is evidence of new methods adopted by SE researchers (Anderson, Pastwa/Wales, and Osiyevskyy et al.), introduction of new topics such as effectuation (Bayer/Landau), psychological traits and cognitive approach-based research of SE (Naidoo et al. and Coraiola et al.), and an exploration of SE from a novel perspective (Bylund/Bylund). The eclectic mix of chapters demonstrates the wide range across which SE as a domain has evolved. We believe this not only indicates the richness of the field, but also sets the stage for more researchers from other disciplines (e.g., finance, mar-keting, sustainability) to come forward and draw from and contribute towards this growing field. We hope this *Research Handbook on Strategic Entrepreneurship* will provide useful guidance for traveling new paths not only within the domain of SE research but also across other disciplines, based upon distinct theoretical foundations.

NOTE

1.   Gupta (2020) observed that Venkatarman and Sarasvathy (2001)'s colorful description also points towards a crucial omission in strategy and entrepreneurship literatures: the missing Juliet. Scholars in strategy and entrepreneurship research have generally over-looked women (and femininity), resulting in their relative absence from the literature that comprises the knowledge base of both fields.

REFERENCES

Acs, Z. J., & Audretsch, D. B. (2003). Introduction to the handbook of entrepreneurship research. In *Handbook of Entrepreneurship Research* (pp. 3–20). Springer, Boston, MA.

Alvarez, S. A., & Barney, J. B. (2001). How entrepreneurial firms can benefit from alliances with large partners. *Academy of Management Perspectives, 15*(1), 139–148.

Alvarez, S. A., & Busenitz, L. W. (2001). The entrepreneurship of resource-based theory. *Journal of Management, 27*(6), 755–775.

Baker, T., & Pollock, T. G. (2007). Making the marriage work: The benefits of strategy's take-over of entrepreneurship for strategic organization. *Strategic Organization, 5*(3), 297–312.

Bruton, G. D., Filatotchev, I., Si, S., & Wright, M. (2013). Entrepreneurship and strategy in emerging economies. *Strategic Entrepreneurship Journal, 7*(3), 169–180.

Foss, N. J., & Lyngsie, J. (2011). The emerging strategic entrepreneurship field: Origins, key tenets, and research gaps. In D. Hjorth (ed.), *Handbook on Organisational Entrepreneurship* (pp. 208–225), Edward Elgar, Cheltenham, UK and Northampton, MA, USA.

Gartner, W. (2014). Organizing entrepreneurship research. In A. Fayolle (ed.), *Handbook of Research on Entrepreneurship: What We Know and What We Need to Know* (pp. 13–22). Edward Elgar, Cheltenham, UK and Northampton, MA, USA.

Gupta, V. K. (2020). *Great Minds in Entrepreneurship Research: Contributions, Critiques, and Conversations*. Palgrave Macmillan, Cham.

Hambrick, D. C., & Chen, M.-J. (2008). New academic fields as admittance-seeking social movements: The case of strategic management. *Academy of Management Review, 33,* 32–54.

Hitt, M. A., Ireland, R. D., Camp, S. M., & Sexton, D. L. (2001). Strategic entrepreneurship: Entrepreneurial strategies for wealth creation. *Strategic Management Journal, 22*(6–7), 479–491.

Hitt, M. A., Ireland, R. D., Sirmon, D. G., & Trahms, C. A. (2011). Strategic entrepreneurship: Creating value for individuals, organizations, and society. *Academy of Management Perspectives, 25*(2), 57–75.

Ireland, R. D. (2007). Strategy vs. entrepreneurship. *Strategic Entrepreneurship Journal, 1*(1–2), 7–10.

Ireland, R. D., Hitt, M. A., & Sirmon, D. G. (2003). A model of strategic entrepreneurship: The construct and its dimensions. *Journal of Management, 29*(6), 963–989.

Kraus, S., & Kauranen, I. (2009). Strategic management and entrepreneurship: Friends or foes? *International Journal of Business Science and Applied Management, 4*(1), 37–50.

Kuratko, D. F., & Audretsch, D. B. (2009). Strategic entrepreneurship: Exploring different perspectives of an emerging concept. *Entrepreneurship Theory and Practice, 33*(1), 1–17.

Lepak, D. P., Smith, K. G., & Taylor, M. S. (2007). Value creation and value capture: A multilevel perspective. *Academy of Management Review, 32*(1), 180–194.

Meyer, G. D. (2009). Commentary: On the integration of strategic management and entrepreneurship: Views of a contrarian. *Entrepreneurship Theory and Practice, 33*(1), 341–351.

Pitelis, C. N. (2009). The co-evolution of organizational value capture, value creation and sustainable advantage. *Organization Studies, 30*(10), 1115–1139.

Schendel, D. E., & Hofer, C. W. (1979). Introduction. In D. E. Schendel & C. W. Hofer (eds.), *A New View of Business Policy and Planning* (pp. 1–22). Little, Brown and Company, Boston, MA.

Schröder, K., Tiberius, V., Bouncken, R. B., & Kraus, S. (2021). Strategic entrepreneurship: Mapping a research field. *International Journal of Entrepreneurial Behavior and Research, 27*(3), 753–776.

Shane, S. (2012). Reflections on the 2010 AMR decade award: Delivering on the promise of entrepreneurship as a field of research. *Academy of Management Review, 37*(1), 10–20.

Venkataraman, S., & Sarasvathy, S. D. (2001). Strategy and entrepreneurship: Outlines of an untold story. In M. A. Hitt, R. E. Freeman, & J. S. Harrison (eds.), *The Blackwell Handbook of Strategic Management* (pp. 655–674), Blackwell, Oxford.

Zabriskie, N. B., & Huellmantel, A. B. (1991). Developing strategic thinking in senior management. *Long Range Planning, 24*(6), 25–32.

Zhao, E. Y., Ishihara, M., & Jennings, P. D. (2020). Strategic entrepreneurship's dynamic tensions: Converging (diverging) effects of experience and networks on market entry timing and entrant performance. *Journal of Business Venturing, 35*(2), 105933.

2. Decomposing the knowledge structures of absorptive capacity

Nachiket Bhawe and Shaker Zahra

There is agreement in the literature that common innovations simply involve a rearrangement or a different way of combining existing knowledge (Schumpeter, 1942; Argote, Lee, and Park, 2020; Denford and Ferriss, 2018). For example, the roller bag was a novel idea at its time that used common knowledge such as 'wheels reduce friction and loads are more easily pulled than lifted'. Yet, despite the relative ubiquity of such knowledge, no one saw an opportunity until Bernard Sadow patented his idea of a roller bag in 1972—an innovation that continues to earn rents even now. MTV is an example of an innovation that combined music and television. However, this innovation was not recognized by General Electric despite the company possessing great amounts of knowledge in both sectors (Prahalad and Hamel, 1994). These examples illustrate that having knowledge alone does not confer the ability to know all its implications, especially when it comes to innovation. Even a small-sized knowledge base can have so much potential for innovative recombinations (Denrell, Fang, and Winter, 2003; Fleming and Sorenson, 2004).

A firm's abilities to acquire and use knowledge and employ it in building the capabilities needed for innovation rests on its absorptive capacity (ACAP) (Roberts, Galluch, Dinger, and Varun, 2011). ACAP refers to the 'ability of a firm to recognize the value of new, external knowledge, assimilate it, and apply it to commercial ends' (Cohen and Levinthal, 1990: 128). Differences in ACAP often mirror differences in abilities not only to acquire but also to process and use knowledge. These differences can lead to significant heterogeneity in knowledge resource profiles and innovative outcomes. Toward this end, researchers identify two distinct yet related parts—potential and realized ACAP (Zahra and George, 2002). Potential ACAP refers to a firm's existing repository of knowledge, its prior experience, and investments (Cohen and Levinthal, 1990) that shape a firm's recognition, acquisition, and understanding of new knowledge stimuli. It ensures the flow of external knowledge into the organization. The way a firm's knowledge is structured shapes its habitual responses to new knowledge stimuli (Todorova and Durisin, 2007). Realized ACAP, on the other hand, refers to the firm's competence in making productive use of its knowledge.

The link between ACAP and innovation raises four questions that warrant recognition. First, *does having experience in a knowledge domain increase the firms' ability to gain from knowledge advances in that area?* There is consensus in the literature that ACAP depends in some way on prior related knowledge (Roberts et al., 2011). This makes ACAP domain specific, but how and whether firms can value and use knowledge that may not be directly related to their knowledge base remains unclear. For example, intra- and interindustry advances cannot be valued and integrated if the firm does not have some exposure to the domain knowledge in these industries (Tiwana and McLean, 2005). Yet, having domain knowledge by itself is necessary but not a sufficient condition to be able to use intra- and external knowledge (Bhawe, Zahra, Chao, and Bruton, 2021; Lane, Koka, and Pathak, 2006).

Second, *is the firm's ACAP an additive summation of the firm's constituents?* The literature suggests that ACAP is a multi-level construct and related to knowledge possessed by members of the team, firm, collaboration, or an economic region (Bhawe and Zahra, 2019). However, it is not merely an additive summation of the constituents of ACAP but rather a structural construct that depends on the links between constituents (Cohen and Levinthal, 1990: 133). This makes ACAP a system-level construct as it reflects the network of knowledge in a system.

Third, *is ACAP malleable and how does it evolve over time?* Even though industries evolve over time, there is a general agreement that ACAP may be path dependent in nature. Ironically, the question of how ACAP changes and evolves over time has not been explored. Although experience (which is cumulative) and ACAP are not always linked (Zou, Ertug, and George, 2018), researchers view ACAP both as a stock as well as an ability (Lane et al., 2006). Thus, merely accumulating experience may not be sufficient in developing ACAP since the nature of that experience is important in defining cognitive frames of reference and expectation formation (Roberts et al., 2011). However, by definition, ACAP should change as the flow of external knowledge continues and the firm gains experience in processing and exploiting its knowledge base. In turn this means that the knowledge content of ACAP, and relationships among different components of knowledge, are likely to change over time.

Fourth, *does the concept of ACAP extend across levels of analyses beyond and within firms such as clusters, economic regions, and/or project teams?* Much of the research has operationalized ACAP either as an input such as firm size (Mowery, Oxley, and Silverman, 1996) and research and development intensity (Tsai, 2001) or as an outcome such as patents (Ahuja and Katila, 2001) and a capability usually inferred via surveys (Armstrong and Sambamurthy, 1999). Thus, the operationalization of ACAP is inconsistent and can often confound the measurement with other related and valid constructs such as organizational learning, prior experience, information-processing capabilities, etc. The problem is that these poor measures overlook the structural properties as well as the dynamism of the knowledge content of ACAP.

To address these four shortcomings of the literature, we propose that knowledge content and its structure provides the foundations of ACAP, guiding how new knowledge could be used to conceive and develop innovations of all different types. Specifically, we introduce a conceptualization of ACAP, highlighting the different knowledge structures that underlie it. Further, using Simon's work on decomposability, we link differences in these knowledge structures to show how ACAP evolves over time and how it affects the magnitude and speed of innovation, especially speed and radicalness. We assert that the different ways of linking different knowledge elements underlie heterogeneity in firms' strategic actions as well as how they might perceive their environments (Gavetti, Levinthal, and Rivkin, 2005), value resources (Denrell et al., 2003), and pursue new business opportunities (Grégoire, Barr, and Shepherd, 2010). Our reconceptualization offers a dynamic portrait of the evolution of ACAP, its different structures, and consequences of innovation.

THE STRUCTURE OF KNOWLEDGE

Knowledge structures refer to the web of relationships and links that connect a firm's different domain-specific knowledge and expertise. The nodes in these knowledge structures may be individuals or teams or even divisions which share a common knowledge domain. We refer to this network of relationships between these knowledge nodes as 'knowledge structures'. Companies usually have multiple knowledge bases built around domain-specific knowledge (fields). Typically, each of these domains has multiple knowledge sub*fields* that companies combine and integrate as they build capabilities, develop products, or introduce strategic initiatives (e.g., developing a new product for a new market). The knowledge that makes up these domains and subdomains also has different elements that are combined to give meaning and utility for each piece of knowledge. This has led Cohen and Levinthal (1990: 133) to observe that ACAP rests on 'the links across a mosaic of individual (knowledge) elements'. By considering the links among these domains and subdomains, we can gain a better and more accurate appreciation of the firm's overall knowledge base as well as the potential content of its ACAP and how it might influence different organizational outcomes such as innovation, a key source of strategic heterogeneity among firms.

Focusing on knowledge structures that make up a firm's ACAP, we use Simon's (1962) pioneering work on decomposability to delineate three types of structures that potentially can lead to significant variations in companies' abilities to innovate by exploiting opportunities. *Decomposability refers to the firm's capacity to partition or separate knowledge into its most basic parts or components* (Simon, 1962). Some types of knowledge are amenable to such partitioning (decomposability), but others defy efforts aimed at separating their constituent parts. Partitioning enables firms to use a piece of knowledge, alone or in combination with others, strategically or operationally. Our decomposability-based conceptualization, therefore, provides an explanation for why and how firms differ significantly in their ACAP and how these differences might influence organizational outcomes. In particular, we highlight the crucial role that managers play in combining different types of internal and external knowledge as they build and keep current the knowledge content of their companies' ACAP.

Even though firms' knowledge stocks (i.e., what they have) and flows (i.e., changes in their knowledge stocks) may vary in their size and composition, studying the decomposability of knowledge structures makes it possible to draw broad inferences in the way a firm may use its knowledge through ACAP. It is the web of connections, linkages, and relationships that develop among different knowledge domains (and subdomains) that give firms opportunities to exploit their knowledge reserves. The webs of relationships that exist among different knowledge domains reflect the scientific basis of knowledge as well as the beliefs held about the way in which these domains could be combined or kept independent from each other (Yayavaram and Ahuja, 2008). Some of these knowledge networks develop naturally while others are induced or created by the company. The diversity of science, beliefs, and cognitions—e.g., about which knowledge domains to combine and by how much—underlies the heterogeneity of firms' ACAP and the uses they might drive from it by deploying different resources to gain an advantage.

The heterogeneity of knowledge networks that make up firm knowledge structures can lead to significant differences in the scope and speed of innovations firms undertake primarily due to differences in the rate of evolution of knowledge. There is evidence that domain expertise in one area may lead to incremental innovations with a narrow focus, but this can often blindside on higher-scope innovations (Zhou and Wu, 2010). The learning myopia is an outcome of the way incentives are structured within an organization, often mirroring its emphasis on important knowledge domains—the past exploitation activities in a given domain tend to make further exploitation in that domain even more attractive as the returns are relatively certain and favorable and there is less incentive to search other knowledge bases for alternative options.

Strategically, ACAP should ideally be able to build on domain expertise to give the firm a meta-capability of leveraging knowledge across multiple domains. We address this seeming contradiction by building on the concept of decomposability to show how high ACAP affords greater malleability that promotes and nurtures this meta-capability. In turn, this also helps to explain why 'firms do much less than they know' as well as why firms with similar knowledge stocks may often differ in their innovative ability (Ethiraj and Levinthal, 2009; Fleming and Sorenson, 2004). We also show how firms can reorient their knowledge bases by changing their knowledge structures even without significant external knowledge inflows. In so doing, we draw implications on why and how ACAP can influence the magnitude (i.e., radical versus incremental) and the speed of innovation.

Absorptive Capacity Attributes and Knowledge Decomposability

As noted, ACAP has several key attributes that both define and bound it as a concept. Though ACAP has been applied within specific knowledge domains, some argue that ACAP constitutes a dynamic capability (Zahra and George, 2002); i.e., it is a meta-capability that enables firms to leverage new and existing knowledge across multiple areas and domains (Eisenhardt and Martin, 2000). A dynamic capability refers to 'the capacity of an organization to purposefully create, extend, or modify its resource base' (Helfat, Finkelstein, Mitchell, Peteraf, and Singh, 2007: 4). ACAP gives firms the ability to change or reconfigure their capabilities and quickly adapt their knowledge bases to their changing competitive environments through innovation. Flexibility in deploying these innovation capabilities results from the malleability of firms' knowledge base—a key attribute of ACAP (Lane et al., 2006).

ACAP is also path dependent and idiosyncratic, which makes it a firm-specific capability that is hard to imitate. However, building ACAP is not always a step-by-step incremental process, but a complex set of activities that involves rearranging the networks of relationships that make up the structure of the firm's knowledge base, filling gaps in the firm's knowledge base while exploring new applications. Indeed, the mere acquisition of skills often fails to capture the inter-relatedness of knowledge that emerges from path-dependent development (Baumol, 2010).

ACAP depends not only on the prior knowledge that a firm already has or acquires externally but also the way this knowledge is organized or structured. Having knowledge in a given domain is a prerequisite for recognizing and utilizing new knowledge. Without an initial knowledge base, a firm cannot track and/or develop advances in applied technologies in its domain. Researchers have explored ACAP in various knowledge domains such as semiconductors (Yayavaram and Ahuja, 2008), software development (Tiwana, 2008), and new product development (Pavlou and Sawy, 2010), among others. However, ACAP goes beyond just the sum of a firm's domain-specific knowledge.[1] It depends on 'the links across a mosaic of individual (knowledge) elements' (Cohen and Levinthal, 1990: 133). These links develop based on the science underlying domain-specific knowledge as well as a company's deliberate intent to connect and weave different combinations of knowledge when pursuing specific goals. Moving beyond the sum total of knowledge to the way it is organized in a firm gives us a richer (and perhaps more accurate) depiction of how the content of ACAP can influence the recognition, assimilation, and recombination of knowledge, which is essential for innovation.

Absorptive Capacity Knowledge Structures

Research applying the knowledge-based and learning theories has examined knowledge at multiple levels (Grant, 1996; Nonaka and Takeuchi, 1995; Santos and Eisenhardt, 2005) and has focused on how disparate knowledge elements create knowledge domains and subdomains (Fleming and Sorenson, 2001). Considerable research exists on how the stock; i.e., 'how much you know' (Fleming and Sorenson, 2001), and composition; i.e., 'what you know' (Lane and Lubatkin, 1998), influence a firm's innovation capabilities. Since ACAP refers not just to existing knowledge and prior investments but also embodies the interpretation, transformation, and exploitation of both existing and new knowledge (Zahra and George, 2002)—the structure of a firm's knowledge base—we focus on the knowledge content of firms' ACAP, and the knowledge networks that form their knowledge structures.

The structure of a firm's knowledge base can be thought of as the web of links (networks) that connects its different knowledge fields (domains) within levels in a firm and across organizations as well. These fields and related organizations may differ significantly from the way tasks are divided in the firm (Rivkin, 2000). Each of the firm's knowledge domains may have subdomains, comprising multiple knowledge elements. Repeated and strong interlinks among different knowledge elements may identify them as part of its knowledge subdomain. These subdomains may be connected with other subdomains to develop knowledge domains that are linked to other domains and so on, forming a dense network of relationships. In many complex industries, knowledge may reside beyond the firm's boundaries. Examples include converging industries such as bio-pharmaceuticals, interactive entertainment, telecom, and infrastructure where many different firms specialize in different parts of the value chain and related knowledge. Some of this knowledge lies outside the traditional domains of a firm's knowledge base.

Bringing this external knowledge into the firm usually requires different types of organizations such as project teams that span industry boundaries to allow for the assimilation and integration of this knowledge (Zahra and George, 2002). In addition, firms' knowledge bases may include external networks formed through alliances, supply-chain relationships, as well as the ongoing relationships between subsidiaries and other partners. Thus, much like recent work on ACAP that is performed across levels of analysis—from regional (Zhang, Li, Li, and Zhou, 2010), interfirm (Flatten, Engelen, Zahra, and Brettel, 2011), to even intra-firm (Tsai, 2001)—our reconceptualization of ACAP applies to multiple levels of analysis. Knowledge networks that make up ACAP develop within and across these different levels of analysis.

Knowledge structures have both horizontal and vertical linkages which could have significant strategic consequences. These linkages that connect knowledge domains and subdomains reveal patterns of information exchange as well as the potential for combining and using disparate domain-specific knowledge. They show how changes in one knowledge domain may influence or change other domains. Different structural arrangements of knowledge networks can lead to significant differences in the way firms utilize their knowledge and address changes in their environments. Managers play an important role in restructuring their firm's knowledge networks, identifying various possibilities to combine different knowledge domains. Next, we explain how Simon's concept of decomposability offers a way to study different structural arrangements of firms' knowledge networks.

KNOWLEDGE DECOMPOSABILITY AND ABSORPTIVE CAPACITY

Decomposability is a natural property of any system and defines the relationship between its various components. It describes how different parts of a system affect (and are affected by) the way they are connected with each other (Simon, 1996). Simon (1962) proposes that a system is typically comprised of self-sustaining stable interactions within its elements, which leads to further interactions between these different elements at the next level and so on to represent a near decomposable system. The concept of decomposability is in some ways similar to the concept of modularity. However, there are some conceptual differences primarily in terms of linkage strength across the modules of a system (see Watson and Pollack, 2005).

While modules may be a set of related knowledge nodes with close ties and inter-connections, intermodule connections may be less or more. Unlike pure modular structures where knowledge nodes within knowledge domains may share strong connections and almost little to no intermodule connections, the notion of decomposability allows us to vary the relative strength of within and across module linkages. This resolves the need for coordination often encountered in research on modularity (Marengo, Dosi, Legrenzi, and Pasquali, 2000; Siggelkow, 2003) as the differences in these linkages often point to the balance between incremental advances within a domain to spanning domains for system-level integration of knowledge. Near decomposability arises from the organic evolution of natural systems and is ubiquitous not only in the natural sciences (physics, biology, and chemistry) but also is an integral aspect of social systems—business organizations with departmental hierarchies, federal political systems, and hierarchical markets for labor, components, products, and services.

Absorptive Capacity Evolution and the Scope and Speed of Innovations

Figure 2.1 presents three simple archetype knowledge networks that might develop with similar knowledge domains that differ only in their structural decomposability. The differences stem from the relative differences in the strength of interlinks between knowledge nodes. For purposes of illustration, Figure 2.1 shows only two levels for a firm's knowledge networks but the same ideas apply to any hierarchy of levels such as those within knowledge domains and subdomains themselves. Figure 2.1 also highlights three different configurations for the same knowledge base.

Fully Decomposable Knowledge Structures

A firm's ACAP knowledge structure may be comprised of very strong linkages within different knowledge domains and relatively sparse linkages between domains. This knowledge structure (C in Figure 2.1) may have greater knowledge depth but less breadth (Ahuja and Katila, 2001). We label this a 'fully decomposable' structure, which typically suggests that connections within knowledge domains matter greatly whereas connections between domains have less or insignificant combinatorial potential. As such, beliefs about which different knowledge domains to use and which to ignore get reinforced over time; they may focus executives' attention on particular issues in the environment and how to best address them using familiar knowledge and solutions. This is evident from exploring the implications of this knowledge structure in terms of the magnitude (radicalness and newness) and speed of innovation, as highlighted in Figure 2.2. This is typical of modular structures where emphasis is placed primarily on decentralized knowledge and less on integrating across domains.

A fully decomposable structure usually enhances the depth of knowledge within elements, rather than a breadth across different elements. However, it often lacks the interlinks needed to exploit new knowledge. Within this structure, therefore,

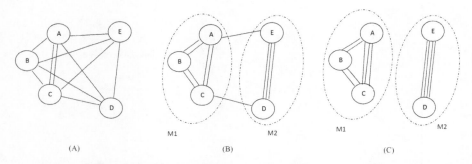

Note: (A), (B), and (C) represent less-decomposable, nearly decomposable, and fully decomposable knowledge structures. Most knowledge structures will fall on a continuum between non-decomposable at one end and fully decomposable at the other. Only two levels of hierarchy are shown for simplicity but in principle this structure can be extended to multiple levels of hierarchy. The connections between elements and the elements themselves are kept the same but the pattern of arrangement varies across different structures. The constraints on connections may be thought of as constraints on number of partners, contracts, interdependencies, etc. The figure illustrates the idea that even for the same size and composition of knowledge many different arrangements are possible. The constraints on connections within and between elements may be relaxed.

Figure 2.1   Different structures for a knowledge base

innovations with a narrow scope are efficient as disparate knowledge elements can be optimized individually without influencing other knowledge domains. A firm's ACAP with a fully decomposable knowledge structure (e.g., C in Figure 2.1) may also become overdependent on one or more knowledge domains. This usually leads to faster knowledge transfer within various domains as well as the efficient optimization of products and services. Since much of the knowledge domain is commensal and comes from a shared lexicon, the ability to value innovations is expedited leading to faster innovation cycles, as noted in Figure 2.2 (C). The efficiency of these innovations enables agile and quick responses to advances in the firm's core knowledge domains.

However, given the lack of breadth of the knowledge domains involved in the firm's ACAP, only incremental innovation is likely to materialize. As new knowledge is added, it is often compartmentalized and utilized within modules rather than across modules. The lack of links that facilitate a system-level integration means that broad-scope innovation that requires sharing and translating across knowledge boundaries becomes a tedious and time-consuming process with uncertain outcomes. The long-term and often uncertain path leading to broad-scope innovation due to the modularized nature of fully decomposable knowledge structures means that quicker turnaround incremental innovation will be preferred. Therefore:

Proposition 1   When firms' ACAP are characterized by fully decomposable knowledge structures, firms have a higher likelihood of (a) incremental innovation and (b) faster rates of innovation.

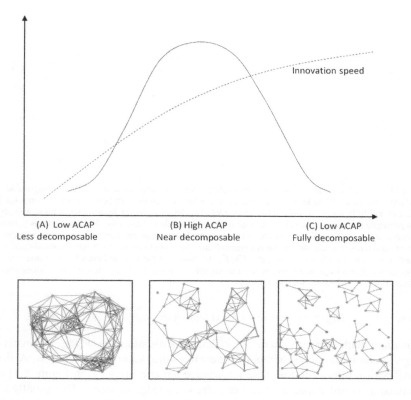

Figure 2.2   Knowledge decomposability and innovation

Less Decomposable ACAP Knowledge Structures

A firm's ACAP knowledge structure may have strong linkages between different knowledge domains but relatively fewer connections within domains (A in Figures 2.1 and 2.2); we label these 'less decomposable' structures. These links may render the knowledge domains themselves less distinct as the relative strength of links blurs domain boundaries. As a result, this knowledge structure may be less decomposable and more integrated, frequently possessing breadth but lacking depth. Given these attributes, this structure (e.g., A in Figures 2.1 and 2.2) enables potentially unlimited combinations between different domains, creating many opportunities but offering no clear way of evaluating new combinations. It allows for the combination of many different knowledge elements because of the potential multiplicity of interlinks among many different knowledge domains that make up ACAP.

As ACAP's knowledge structure becomes less and less decomposable (as A in Figure 2.2), it offers the firm the advantage of building on many different knowledge domains and capitalizing on having a very diverse knowledge base. This knowledge and the innovations built on it are hard to replicate as they often involve idiosyncratic combinations of knowledge from many areas, increasing the potential for radical innovation. Yet, ACAP's breadth may encourage a variety of knowledge recombinations, requiring careful analysis and integration to develop innovations. The process of sifting through these potential combinations to determine which work is often inefficient, tedious, and time consuming (Denrell et al., 2003). The lack of clear boundaries and decomposition into modular knowledge bases with predefined interfaces makes the search and evaluation of optimal combinations slower (Sanchez, 1995). Consequently, the speed by which the firm innovates to adapt to the environment is likely to be slow which may cause the firm to miss important market opportunities or act in sluggish ways in addressing the competitive challenges it faces. Therefore:

Proposition 2   When firms' ACAP are characterized by less decomposable knowledge structures, firms have a higher likelihood of (a) developing radical innovation and (b) slower rates of innovation.

Near Decomposable Knowledge Structures

A nearly decomposable structure (Simon, 1962) usually has strong linkages within different knowledge domains and moderate linkages between domains (B in Figures 2.1 and 2.2). As a result, this structure strikes a balance between the depth and breadth of a firm's knowledge. Nearly decomposable ACAP structures (B in Figures 2.1 and 2.2) enable the firm to absorb new externally generated knowledge, assimilate it, and combine it with other existing knowledge in new ways. As a result, nearly decomposable ACAP structures have the potential to evolve and change at a much faster rate, compared to fully or less decomposable systems (Marengo et al., 2000). Consequently, a nearly decomposable ACAP knowledge structure is strategically better, compared to less decomposable (A in Figures 2.1 and 2.2) or fully decomposable knowledge structures (C in Figures 2.1 and 2.2) (Simon, 1962). Evolutionary changes over time get accelerated in a near decomposable structure as the structure itself is adaptive and malleable allowing itself to be recast to fit with changing conditions (Yayavaram and Ahuja, 2008). Once a near decomposable knowledge structure is created, it requires deliberate upkeep to make sure new knowledge is assimilated using preferential attachment to those modules that show the most promise. This ensures that as new knowledge is brought into the firm, the knowledge structure retains its near decomposability.

Thus, nearly decomposable ACAP knowledge structures (B in Figures 2.1 and 2.2) offer a beneficial tradeoff that enables innovations by promoting and evaluating new combinations across a few knowledge domains. These innovations are often rich in their foci and wide in the scope of applicability, balancing the breadth and depth of a firm's knowledge. In turn, these structures enable a quick evaluation of different combinations and exploitation. Consequently, nearly decomposable structures (B in Figure 2.1) often facilitate the rapid deployment of significant advancements in products, services, and other strategic initiatives. Given the diversity of their knowledge domains and the depth of expertise in these domains, firms can also create idiosyncratic and socially complex inimitable innovation capabilities by developing high ACAP through the creation of nearly decomposable knowledge networks. Therefore:

Proposition 3   When firms' ACAP are characterized by nearly decomposable knowledge structures, firms have a higher likelihood of (a) developing radical innovations and (b) achieving moderate speed of innovation.

DISCUSSION

Our conceptualization of ACAP explains why firms might benefit differently from their knowledge, focusing on the firm's knowledge structure(s) and the decomposability of this knowledge. An important implication of our conceptual reframing is the separation between knowledge accumulation and ACAP. Another important implication is the possibility of fact-free learning, i.e., learning that can be undertaken by rearranging the configurations of knowledge structures—deliberate coupling of certain knowledge elements and modules to create innovative products and services. In addition, our conceptualization has the potential to extend the use of ACAP across levels of analysis when examining differences in knowledge diffusion within firms (Minbaeva, Pedersen, Björkman, Fey, and Park, 2003) as well as across firm boundaries (Zhao and Anand, 2009). Typical firm-level conceptualizations of ACAP emphasize research and development spending and patents. These operationalizations also lead to tautological issues and limit applications across levels of analysis (Volberda, Foss, and Lyles, 2010). Our reframing bridges levels of analysis, within and across firms, while grounding ACAP in knowledge-based theories. Specifically, we show that the knowledge content of ACAP and the organization of this content could (and does) influence important organizational activities such as the types and speed of innovations.

Our discussion also suggests that different ways of organizing knowledge can lead to differences in the scope as well as the speed of innovation. In turn, managers can play an active role in shaping their firm's ACAP—their knowledge networks—by reorganizing and extending the knowledge boundaries of their firm. Although our focus on knowledge content offers theoretical clarity on how knowledge structures have a basis for understanding a firm's ACAP, recognizing and evaluating the way this knowledge may be organized is often a difficult organizational task. Research also highlights a potential tradeoff between knowledge acquisition in one domain and the narrow scope of innovations the firm undertakes (Vasudeva and Anand, 2011). Whereas incremental innovations born from searching and optimizing existing knowledge domains can improve short-term organizational performance (Zhou and Wu, 2010), innovations of greater scope often arise from connecting and combining several different knowledge domains. Innovations that build on well-understood knowledge within existing domains are efficient as well as easier to evaluate and exploit as compared to innovations that build on less-understood connections across different knowledge domains. Figure 2.2 shows the tradeoffs in innovation as a function of decomposability of a firm's ACAP knowledge structure.

Managerial Implications

Our discussion suggests that managers can play an active role in shaping organizational systems and processes that promote creative and effective interlinks between knowledge domains that achieve a balance between the radicalness of innovation and its speed. While knowledge-based theories posit that firms should economize on internal knowledge links to reduce the cost of production, increases in ACAP are usually achieved at the expense of efficiency in incremental innovation.

Managers seeking to introduce strategic initiatives may do well to reorganize their knowledge network by restructuring the links between different knowledge domains. Our discussion hints at how firms may be able to develop new opportunities without infusion of new knowledge into the firm simply by reorganizing the knowledge linkages in the organization. Managers in more mature industries can benefit from such reorganization in generating new knowledge combinations, opening new opportunities for innovation involving new knowledge combinations. In contrast, managers seeking to transition from research and development to streamlined production would do well to minimize interlinks between knowledge domains, focusing instead on developing procedures and standards that ensure the efficient and timely transfer of knowledge within knowledge domains, eschewing interlinks across domains.

Implications for Theory and Future Research

Our discussion suggests several avenues for future research. Our chapter focuses on more established firms that are likely to have several knowledge domains. Younger companies (e.g., start-ups) may have far fewer such domains and the content of their knowledge bases might be different from incumbents. This might have interesting implications for understanding the rivalry between newer firms and incumbents as well as how the two sets of companies develop capabilities, innovate, and initiate strategic action. Research on the implications of these differences for new ventures and their prospect of survival would be informative. Also, we recognize that links among knowledge domains could result from the nature of science underlying them or the deliberate actions managers undertake to make these links possible and viable. How these two types (science-based and deliberate) links among knowledge domains influence the evolution of knowledge structure is another area worthy of exploration. Finally, ACAP makes possible the importation and assimilation of knowledge. However, firms need to develop effective systems that allow for the conversion of incoming knowledge into commercial applications. The types of these systems and their organization deserve close study.

Adopting the structure of decomposability to study ACAP makes it path dependent but also idiosyncratic, meaning it is a capability that is hard to imitate. It gives firms flexibility in responding to changes in their environments. However, building ACAP is not a step-by-step incremental process but rather a complex set of activities that involves rearranging the links in the structure of a knowledge base (Yayavaram and Ahuja, 2008; Argote et al., 2020) and filling in gaps to supplement white spaces. For example, in the late 1990s and 2000s, Malaysia built BioValley in an attempt to emulate Singapore's success in building Biopolis. Despite building and promoting research institutes focused on genomics, pharmaceuticals, and agriculture and imitating policies aimed at promoting bio-pharmaceutical firms, there was very little innovation that emerged from such initiatives. Our reframing can help explain why several attempts to emulate Silicon Valley's success in building a robust ecosystem for innovation have often failed—this is because these attempts fail to recreate the inter-relatedness of knowledge that emerges from path-dependent development (Baumol, 2010). Future empirical studies can look at similar levels of knowledge but differences in knowledge structures to see if these differences manifest in the differences in innovation speed and quality.

Recent empirical work supports the idea that merely adding new knowledge in the local economy (Zhang et al., 2010; Zhou and Anand, 2009; Bhawe and Zahra, 2019) without focusing on building ACAP (by fostering knowledge interlinks to create a near decomposable structure) is less likely to promote innovation. Our focus on the knowledge content of ACAP helps expand the concept beyond firm boundaries while maintaining consistency across levels of analysis. The rise of the gig economy with an emphasis on one-off teams that are comprised of individuals drawn from beyond firm boundaries to work on specific projects makes our reframing of ACAP especially relevant. Using our reconceptualization, we believe future research can extend work on ACAP to the meso-level of projects and teams by analyzing the role structure of knowledge networks in these teams and its effects on innovation.

In conclusion, ACAP is an important concept and has been widely used to explain how firms benefit from the diverse external knowledge to which they are exposed. We have proposed that links among knowledge domains that cut across levels within and across organizations form important knowledge structures that have implications for the ability of the firm to innovate and respond to (or even shape) opportunities in their markets. Future research on the nature of these knowledge structures and how they might change would enrich the literature, especially the knowledge-based view of the firm.

NOTE

1.   Merely possessing knowledge is not a sufficient condition for recognizing opportunities manifest within that knowledge (Denrell et al., 2003; Fleming and Sorenson, 2001). Many common innovations involve not just adding new knowledge but a rearrangement or a different way of combining knowledge. See the MTV example at the beginning of the chapter.

REFERENCES

Ahuja, G., and Katila, R. 2001. Technological acquisitions and the innovation performance of acquiring firms: A longitudinal study. *Strategic Management Journal*, 22(3): 197–220.

Argote, L., Lee, S., and Park, J. 2020. Organizational learning processes and outcomes: Major findings and future research directions. *Management Science*, 67(9).

Armstrong, C. P., and Sambamurthy, V. 1999. Information technology assimilation in firms: The influence of senior leadership and IT infrastructures. *Information Systems Research*, 10(4): 304–327.

Baumol, W. J. 2010. *The Microtheory of Innovative Entrepreneurship*. Princeton, NJ: Princeton University Press.

Bhawe, N., and Zahra, S. A. 2019. Inducing heterogeneity in local entrepreneurial ecosystems: The role of MNEs. *Small Business Economics*, 52: 437–454.

Bhawe, N., Zahra, S. A., Chao, C., and Bruton, G. D. 2021. Protectionist policies and diversity of entrepreneurial types. *Small Business Economics*, 56: 789–807.

Cohen, W. M., and Levinthal, D. A. 1990. Absorptive capacity: A new perspective on learning and innovation. *Administrative Science Quarterly*, 35(1): 128–152.

Denford, J. S., and Ferriss, A. 2018. Absorption, combination and desorption: Knowledge-oriented boundary spanning capacities. *Journal of Knowledge Management*, 22(7): 1425–1441.

Denrell, J., Fang, C., and Winter, S. G. 2003. The economics of strategic opportunity. *Strategic Management Journal*, 24(10): 977–990.

Eisenhardt, K., and Martin, J. 2000. Dynamic capabilities: What are they? *Strategic Management Journal*, 21(10/11): 1105–1121.

Ethiraj, S. K., and Levinthal, D. 2009. Hoping for A to Z while rewarding only A: Complex organizations and multiple goals. *Organization Science*, 20(1): 4–21.

Flatten, T. C., Engelen, A., Zahra, S. A., and Brettel, M. 2011. A measure of absorptive capacity: Scale development and validation. *European Management Journal*, 29(2): 98–116.

Fleming, L., and Sorenson, O. 2001. Technology as a complex adaptive system: Evidence from patent data. *Research Policy*, 30(7): 1019–1039.

Fleming, L., and Sorenson, O. 2004. Science as a map in technological search. *Strategic Management Journal*, 25(8–9): 909–928.

Gavetti, G., Levinthal, D. A., and Rivkin, J. W. 2005. Strategy making in novel and complex worlds: The power of analogy. *Strategic Management Journal*, 26(8): 691–712.

Grant, R. M. 1996. Toward a knowledge-based theory of the firm. *Strategic Management Journal*, 17: 109–122.

Grégoire, D. A., Barr, P. S., & Shepherd, D. A. 2010. Cognitive processes of opportunity recognition: The role of structural alignment. *Organization Science*, 21(2): 413–431.

Helfat, C. E., Finkelstein, S., Mitchell, W., Peteraf, M., and Singh, H. 2007. *Dynamic Capabilities: Understanding Strategic Change in Organizations*. Chichester: John Wiley & Sons.

Lane, P. J., Koka, B. R., and Pathak, S. 2006. The reification of absorptive capacity: A critical review and rejuvenation of the construct. *Academy of Management Review*, 31(4): 833–863.

Lane, P. J., and Lubatkin, M. 1998. Relative absorptive capacity and interorganizational learning. *Strategic Management Journal*, 19(5): 461–477.

Marengo, L., Dosi, G., Legrenzi, P., and Pasquali, C. 2000. The structure of problem-solving knowledge and the structure of organizations. *Industrial and Corporate Change*, 9(4): 757–788.

Minbaeva, D., Pedersen, T., Björkman, I., Fey, C. F., and Park, H. J. 2003. MNC knowledge transfer, subsidiary absorptive capacity, and HRM. *Journal of International Business Studies*, 34(6): 586–599.

Mowery, D. C., Oxley, J. E., and Silverman, B. S. 1996. Strategic alliances and interfirm knowledge transfer. *Strategic Management Journal*, 17(S2): 77–91.

Nonaka, I., and Takeuchi, H. 1995. *The Knowledge-Creating Company: How Japanese Companies Create the Dynamics of Innovation*. Oxford: Oxford University Press.

Pavlou, P. A., and Sawy, O. A. E. 2010. The 'third hand': IT-enabled competitive advantage in turbulence through improvisational capabilities. *Information Systems Research*, 21(3): 443–471.

Prahalad, C. K., and Hamel, G. 1994. Strategy as a field of study: Why search for a new paradigm? *Strategic Management Journal*, 15(S2): 5–16.

Rivkin, J. W. 2000. Imitation of complex strategies. *Management Science*, 46(6): 824–844.

Roberts, N., Galluch, P., Dinger, M., and Varun, G. 2011. Absorptive capacity and information systems research: Review, synthesis, and directions for future research. *MIS Quarterly*, 36(2): 625–648.

Sanchez, R. 1995. Strategic flexibility in product competition. *Strategic Management Journal*, 16(S1): 135–159.

Santos, F. M., and Eisenhardt, K. M. 2005. Organizational boundaries and theories of organization. *Organization Science*, 16(5): 491–508.

Schumpeter, J. A. 1942. *Capitalism, Socialism and Democracy*. New York: Harper.

Siggelkow, N. 2003. Why focus? A study of intra-industry focus effects. *Journal of Industrial Economics*, 51(2): 121–150.

Simon, H. A. 1962. The architecture of complexity. *Proceedings of the American Philosophical Society*, 106(6): 467–482.

Simon, H. A. 1996. *The Sciences of the Artificial*. Cambridge, MA: MIT Press.

Tiwana, A. 2008. Do bridging ties complement strong ties? An empirical examination of alliance ambidexterity. *Strategic Management Journal*, 29(3): 251–272.

Tiwana, A., and McLean, E. 2005. Expertise integration and creativity in information systems development. *Journal of Management Information Systems*, 22(1): 13–43.

Todorova, G., and Durisin, B. 2007. Absorptive capacity: Valuing a reconceptualization. *Academy of Management Review*, 32(3): 774–786.

Tsai, W. 2001. Knowledge transfer in intraorganizational networks: Effects of network position and absorptive capacity on business unit innovation and performance. *Academy of Management Journal*, 44(5): 996–1004.

Vasudeva, G., and Anand, J. 2011. Unpacking absorptive capacity: A study of knowledge utilization from alliance portfolios. *Academy of Management Journal*, 54(3): 611–623.

Volberda, H. W., Foss, N. J., and Lyles, M. A. 2010. Perspective: Absorbing the concept of absorptive capacity: How to realize its potential in the organization field. *Organization Science*, 21(4): 931–951.

Watson, R. A., and Pollack, J. B. 2005. Modular interdependency in complex dynamical systems. *Artificial Life*, 11(4): 445–457.

Yayavaram, S., and Ahuja, G. 2008. Decomposability in knowledge structures and its impact on the usefulness of inventions and knowledge-base malleability. *Administrative Science Quarterly*, 53(2): 333–362.

Zahra, S. A., and George, G. 2002. Absorptive capacity: A review, reconceptualization, and extension. *Academy of Management Review*, 27(2): 185–203.

Zhang, Y., Li, H., Li, Y., and Zhou, L.-A. 2010. FDI spillovers in an emerging market: The role of foreign firms' country origin diversity and domestic firms' absorptive capacity. *Strategic Management Journal*, 31(9): 969–989.

Zhao, Z., and Anand, J. 2009. A multilevel perspective on knowledge transfer: Evidence from the Chinese automotive industry. *Strategic Management Journal*, 30(9): 959–983.

Zhou, K. Z., and Wu, F. 2010. Technological capability, strategic flexibility, and product innovation. *Strategic Management Journal*, 31(5): 547–561.

Zou, T., Ertug, G., and George, G. 2018. The capacity to innovate: A meta-analysis of absorptive capacity. *Innovation*, 20(2): 87–121.

3. The economic firm as a manifestation of strategic entrepreneurship

Susanne C. Bylund and Per L. Bylund

The theory of the firm has invoked numerous important contributions from the points of view of economics (e.g., Alchian & Demsetz, 1972; Coase, 1937; Grossman & Hart, 1986; Jensen & Meckling, 1976; Williamson, 1975), management (e.g., Barney, 1996; Foss, 1994; Nickerson & Zenger, 2004), and entrepreneurship (e.g., Alvarez & Barney, 2007; Casson, 2000; Foss & Klein, 2012; Sautet, 2000; Bylund, 2016a). This literature focuses on three core questions, originally posed (or implied) by Ronald Coase in his groundbreaking article "The Nature of the Firm" (1937): Why are there firms? What are the firm's boundaries? How is the firm's organizational structure determined? (Foss, 1997, p. 175; Foss & Klein, 2008, p. 146; Garrouste & Saussier, 2008, p. 23). The answers tend to be formulated in terms of a cost or coordination rationale for hierarchy, in contrast to a conjectured "pure" market situation that for its coordination relies solely on the price mechanism. To illustrate, Coase theorizes from "atomistic competition" as formalized in neoclassical economic models (Coase, 1937, 1960, 1988), and Transaction Cost Economics (Williamson, 1975, 1985, 1996) adopts a conjecture that "in the beginning there were markets" (1975, p. 20)—to which hierarchy is contrasted.

A pure market conjecture as a starting point for theorizing is not unique to the transaction cost approach to the firm, however. Dating back at least to the scholastics (e.g., Aquinas, [1259] 1953),[1] reasoning from a counterfactual is a useful method for explaining social phenomena. Using this method allows us to explain the firm in terms of its distinctive features and value *contrasted with* the surrounding market (Bylund, 2015a), and clarifies the firm's rationale and boundaries. This helps identify its specific causes, but the starting point for reasoning must be properly balanced. If it is too simplified and streamlined, it can produce conclusions that are unrealistic or inapplicable outside of formal modelling, hence granting explanatory power to potentially irrelevant factors. In other words, the proposed explanation may be spurious correlations rather than, as presumed, causes. In contrast, a too elaborate model makes it difficult if not impossible to distinguish between and analyze real causes. This problem has received notable attention in the law and economics literature since economic explanations for the firm often cannot be separated from legal explanations. This ultimately produces ambiguous explanations for integration in firms, which raises the question of whether there is a firm or if it is simply a "legal fiction" (Alchian & Demsetz, 1972; Jensen & Meckling, 1976). Two examples from the literature help illustrate that this mixing together of explanatory categories is a valid concern: Coase's (1937) firm can be interpreted as a transaction cost-saving device relying on the employment contract's special (legal) status (Bylund, 2014b; Aghion, Bloom, & Van Reenen, 2013), and Williamson's analysis explicitly refers to differences in contract law (Williamson, 1979, 1991). A possible explanation is that too streamlined equilibrium models imply an optimal state that allows for no endogenously caused improvements; consequently, change must have *exogenous* causes. But, as most theories of the firm suggest, firm formation is a response to some market failure or suboptimality (high cost, low productivity, etc.) and thus should take place in disequilibrium. Despite their awareness of the firm's potential "legal fiction" (Masten, 1988), economists have not managed to fully separate economic from legal explanations. Curiously, scholars in strategic management, used to studying distinctly disequilibrium phenomena, as opposed to economists, are comparatively silent on the issue despite being extraordinarily well positioned to separate the firm's economic "being" from its legal status.

Yet it is important to recognize the firm for its actual economic properties, and not simply as a result of or response to specific legal requirements. Strategic entrepreneurship specifically would benefit from this as the economic aspects of what a firm is—how a firm *creates value*—is core to understanding how firms can and do engage in entrepreneurship strategically. Or, as we argue here, that the firm is not the starting point but rather the vehicle for engaging in—even a manifestation of—strategic entrepreneurship, defined by Hitt, Ireland, Camp, and Sexton (2001, p. 480) as "entrepreneurial action with a strategic perspective." Our theoretical investigation of the firm, focusing on what the strategic value of integrated organizing of production might be, finds that the economic (as opposed to the legal) firm *is the embodiment of strategic entrepreneurship*: the establishing of a firm is how actors in a market economy realize new entrepreneurial innovations beyond what is possible through simple contracting. Consequently, as we will show, the economic nature of the firm is the implementation of entrepreneurial solutions—innovations—that cannot be achieved through simple exchange or market contracting.

This chapter thus addresses a foundational issue in strategic entrepreneurship, one that is often overlooked: the role of the firm itself. We also argue that the firm is core to understanding strategic entrepreneurship as it *must*, economically speaking, be carried out through firms. Specifically, our investigation provides a foundation for research on the economic value of the firm by analyzing the firm from a distinctly economic perspective, free from legal bias. We study the firm formation process using a theory of the unhampered market that avoids most (if not all) of the problems of previous approaches. The theory of the economic organism (the economy or economic system) in a stateless society, or market anarchism, explicitly rejects all forms of coercive legal institutions. It therefore provides an analytical benchmark that allows us to study purely economic rationales for integrating production in firms. By portraying a fully decentralized economy, in which economic action is fully embedded in a social context (Granovetter, 1985), the theory contributes realism to our argument well beyond streamlined equilibrium models in economics. This allows us to explain how and whether business firms have a place in the market that is strictly economic yet more realistic than common models. The questions we ask are: What do integrated organizational structures offer in this working market context? What is the value to individual market actors, as well as society as a whole, of organization? How may such structures arise? Why would we expect business organizations ("firms") to be(come) an important part of a stateless market? The answers to all of these questions are relevant to strategic entrepreneurship.

This is to our knowledge the first time this framework, as well as this type of "thick" (fully socially, culturally, and institutionally embedded) conception of society and the economy, has been used in theorizing on the firm. Our analysis therefore sheds new light on a whole set of issues relating to the three Coasean questions regarding the why, what, and how of the firm. Thereby, it also provides a framework and foundation for investigating issues of strategic-entrepreneurial importance. We find that the economic firm does not precede strategic entrepreneurship but rather is a manifestation of it—a means to realize innovations and establish novel production beyond what can be achieved in the open market. This opens new avenues for strategic entrepreneurship research and suggests a new, important perspective. In addition, these conclusions have implications for the study of organizational economics, but potentially change the questions asked in firm management and organizational behavior research. They also have implications for research in entrepreneurship and the entrepreneurial nature of the firm.

The next section discusses the conceptual framework for our analysis, the "anarchist" theory of the workings of the economic organism. We thereafter analyze potential rationales for integration in firms and discuss the possibility of endogenous firm formation within our "thick" market model. The final section discusses our conclusions and suggests issues for future research.

THE "ECONOMIC ORGANISM"

Going back almost two centuries, market anarchism is an intellectual tradition theorizing on voluntarism, the structure of society, and the free market. As the tradition by default rejects political institutions and other coercive means, thinkers in the tradition tend to focus on finding the "natural" mode of interaction and social organizing. They emphasize voluntary and emergent institutions as well as mutual aid, cooperation, and horizontal contracting, and their analysis of society logically coincides with their perception of the market as a social order. Their conception of what we will here refer to as a "thick" market consists of economic and reciprocal exchange embedded in a social context and occurring under the influence of social structures. Actors consider economic as well as social aspects of their behavior and interact horizontally through direct exchange and voluntary contracting under a set of emergent social norms; society and market coincide in the "economic organism." Hence the pure market as here conjectured includes the social structures commonly missing from streamlined neoclassical economic models. We thus assume a social setting in which actors are far more than simple maximizers. They are embedded in the social situation and in this situation they are also affected by each other; they partake in market as well as social, non-economic activities. This order is unaffected by formal political institutions and regulations, which means our analysis of the firm is free from legal bias (there is no state) and the firm therefore is not and cannot be a legal fiction.

Rather than asserting what constitutes a firm, our analysis must proceed without it. The common definitions of the firm are not obviously relevant under a pure market regime. Rather, they specify the firm's rationale prior to analyzing the economic situation, which is too limiting in our analysis. We assert only that in order to distinguish the firm from the market in which it emerges, it must be conceived of as an integrated process.

Voluntary Association and Organization

A common interpretation of anarchism is that it is fundamentally opposed to, prohibits, or can even be defined as the opposite of organization (Meltzer, 1996, pp. 25–26). Yet this misconception is likely based on a narrow and modern definition of organization as a formal structure based on *authority* (Pfeffer, 1981; Bylund, 2014a), the firm as "characterized by coordination through authority relations" (Madhok, 2002, p. 536; cf. Simon, [1945] 1957). But organizations that are libertarian rather than authoritarian, democratic rather than dictatorial, are fully compatible with and can be important parts of the anarchist analysis of society (Meltzer, 1996, pp. 25–26). Anarchism is compatible with organized efforts through the division of labor's voluntary association of specialized workers. It is also compatible with formal and symmetrical cooperation through the exercise of "collective force" as an important source of increased productivity (Proudhon, [1923] 2003, pp. 215–224). Voluntary cooperation through organization can in this sense be an essential part of the economic organism, since even "[t]he smallest fortune, the most insignificant business concern, the most trifling industrial process demands the collaboration of such a wide variety of skills that no one man can suffice" (Proudhon, 1969, p. 43).

Yet organization is not necessarily compatible with the anarchist analysis. Its accepted productive qualities can be undone through use of or reliance on means that are inherently foreign to anarchism, such as formal and oppressive authority, inequality, and dictatorial rule. As Carson (2008, p. 517) notes, "[i]nside an organization, privilege creates a fundamental conflict of interest. It divorces effort from reward, responsibility from authority, and knowledge from power." The forced inequality of institutionalized privilege therefore dissolves the productive bonds of voluntary cooperation through exchange and contract, and allows trustful relationships to degenerate into destructive opportunistic behavior.

While organization under contemporary capitalism is hierarchical and subject to opportunism—both directly and indirectly—and introduces several forms of privilege, productive organization is neither impossible nor unwanted without formal power or the coercive apparatus of the state. Organization can in itself, unaffected by legal privilege, be productive and contribute value to those involved as well as society as a whole. As productivity requires intensive division of labor—and thereby voluntary association for completion of productive processes—even management may be an important part of production. As Tandy ([1896] 1979, p. 165) notes, "[t]he management of a large factory is just as much a trade as the shoeing of horses. It will be to the advantage of everyone concerned to attend to the business to which he has been trained, than to attempt to meddle with that of which he knows little or nothing."

It is such voluntary specialization that facilitates the production of general prosperity in society. By allowing a division of labor into supplying specific, particular services to the economic organism, society as a whole benefits from the productivity increases. As noted already by Adam Smith ([1776] 1976), "[t]he collective force of a hundred workers is incomparably greater than that of one worker multiplied by a hundred" (Proudhon, 1969, p. 46). This productive division of labor and heterogenization of workmanship, which results in differences and hence inequality in terms of skill and profession, is no threat to the voluntary order or equality; as Proudhon (1969, p. 47) notes, "the division of labor, which is harmful neither to society nor to the individual if it is capably managed and co-ordinated, has no disadvantages."

Rather, the division brings men together, since "[t]he wool-grower, the spinner, the weaver, the tailor, all work together to produce a suit of clothes—that is, they co-operate, though there may be no kind of communistic arrangement between them" (Tandy, [1896] 1979, p. 162). It is "[t]hrough the division of labor, which has become a collective force, the relation between the workers is naturally one of association and they are dependent upon each other" (Proudhon, 1969, p. 45). As such, productive organizing—whether through integration, contractual relationships, or exchange—is an important and necessary condition for the thriving of society under anarchism. Carson points to the distinct nature of such association, stating that "[a] voluntary producer cooperative, commune, or mutual aid society is a free market institution. A corporation functioning within the state capitalist system is emphatically not" (2004, p. 378).

Carson's conception of the free market, which in many ways is similar to the economic organism of Proudhon, is "made to order for the purpose of avoiding centralized organization and hierarchy" (Carson, 2004, p. 388) and therefore avoids legal as well as legal-like (coercive) structures. The economic organism in this sense suggests and indeed *requires* equality and freedom, and therefore the absence of formal hierarchy as well as power, through keeping all market transactions and all cooperation voluntary and horizontal. Further, "[w]hen firms and self-employed individuals deal with each other through market, rather than federal relations, there are no organizations superior to them" (Carson, 2004, p. 388). Carson prefers "the workers' and consumers' cooperative, the mutual, the commons, and the voluntary collective to the capitalist corporation as a market actor" (2004, p. 353) and finds "market competition between individuals and voluntary associations, whenever possible, preferable to unnecessary collectivism" (2004, p. 384). This is in essence another way of stating that "[i]t is labor, and labor alone, that produces all the elements of wealth and makes them combine, down to the very last molecule, following a variable but definite law of proportionality" (Proudhon, 1969, p. 42). Economic anarchism, as a decentralized and voluntary market society is therefore "complete individualism" (Tucker, [1897] 2005, p. 38).

This does not disqualify organization, but suggests that association in all its forms—including different types of coordinative organizations, such as the business firm—is both the facilitator of and a limitation to the productive powers of the economic organism. "Social progress is assessed in terms of the development of industry and the sophistication of tools" (Proudhon, 1969, p. 239), which suggests a society highly focused on production for general prosperity and exchange for mutual benefit. Association, where such exists, therefore appears only where in the interest of all the individual persons involved, as well as society at large (by producing greater value), and can never under anarchism be formally and coercively hierarchical:

> Association is not a directing principle, any more than an industrial force. Association, by itself, has no organic nor productive power, nothing which, like the division of labor, competition, &c, makes the worker stronger and quicker, diminishes the cost of production, draws a greater value from materials, or which, like the administrative hierarchy, shows a desire for harmony and order. (Proudhon, [1923] 2003, p. 81)

Without the legal system of the state, which some research suggests may be unnecessary (Ellickson, 1991; Benson, 1990), voluntary association cannot be based on hierarchical relations but must be established through horizontal agreement between free individuals. This makes all productive relationships, associations, and organizations subject to mutual agreement and, consequently, reciprocal contracting. And free contracting without the legal enforcement mechanisms of the state engenders trust (Bohnet, Frey, & Huck, 2001) through social norms, reciprocity, and voluntary enforcement (Fehr, Gächter, & Kirchsteiger, 1997; cf. Benson, 2005). The voluntary agreement or contract is thus a cornerstone of society's economic organism, whether formal and in writing or tacitly understood, through which both prosperity and freedom are strengthened:

> What characterizes the contract is the agreement for equal exchange; and it is by virtue of this agreement that liberty and well being increase; while by the establishment of authority, both of these necessarily diminish ... The contract therefore is essentially reciprocal: it imposes no obligation upon the parties, except that which results from their personal promise of reciprocal delivery: it is not subject to any external authority: it alone forms the law between the parties: it awaits their initiative for its execution. (Proudhon, [1923] 2003, pp. 113–114)

Contract is in this sense "the only moral bond which free and equal beings can accept" (Proudhon, [1923] 2003, p. 171)—the solution to the "problem of opposition of interests and inequality of faculties ... is found in the *organization of economic forces*, under the supreme law of *CONTRACT*" (Proudhon, [1923] 2003, p. 130). Proudhon's view of anarchism is based on "*[c]ommutative justice*, the *reign of contract*, the *industrial* or *economic system*," terms that Proudhon considers synonymous. Anarchist economic thinkers conceive of free society as that which remains when the state, and with it coercion-based societal structures and institutions, has withered away; rather than engaging in subversive rhetoric, these thinkers predict the state's "dissolution in the economic organism" (Tucker, [1897] 2005, p. 104) and a free economic system based on voluntary contract.

Their view of society amounts to simply a free economic system based on industry and production, which has "for its basis the organization of economic forces, in place of the hierarchy of political powers" (Proudhon, [1923] 2003, p. 170). The free market here entails that those means and institutions "that interfere most fundamentally with a free market" are done away with, "and the economic and moral changes that would result from this would act as a solvent upon all the remaining forms of interference" (Tucker, [1897] 2005, pp. 104–105). Without a legal apparatus, coercive hierarchies cannot be sustained against the will of those subjected to it, so all exchange, interaction, and organization are established through voluntary contracts, horizontally between equal parties.

Optionality and Opportunity Cost

A major difference between economic action under anarchism and the state can be explained in terms of opportunity cost (Bylund, 2016b). This concept, core to the study of economics, summarizes the pure logic of choice from the actor's point of view: any course of action taken must, at least subjectively, be perceived as that of highest value. The cost of this choice is the best available alternative that is foregone; opportunity cost is thus the perceived greatest possible value of available fallback options or alternative courses of action (Davenport, [1913] 1968, pp. 58–59). In other words, the higher (lower) the opportunity cost relative to the perceived value of the maximizing choice, the less (more) obvious the choice appears for the individual. If an individual prefers an apple and can choose from many similar apples, choosing one is more difficult (the opportunity cost is higher) than were the choice, with the same preference for apple, between an apple and other kinds of fruit. The latter choice is obvious since the preference is for apple and therefore the value of other fruits is much lower; the former suggests the individual will need to consider other values, of lesser importance, in order to distinguish between the apples (size, color, ripeness, etc.). The former is a case of *optionality*, the degree to which a person has alternative courses of action of value similar to the maximizing choice (Taleb, 2012, pp. 169–262), which means the value lost due to choosing differently (a subpar apple) is relatively small.

Opportunity cost is therefore a function of the optionality of a situation: where the individual has several similar possible courses of action (optionality), the opportunity cost is high and the choice itself (between the comparable options) is less costly in the face of error. This suggests switching costs under optionality should also be relatively low, and it follows that a society in which an individual is restricted from making certain choices, or in which there are restrictions indirectly affecting the individual through making certain choices unavailable, the cost of second-best choices is comparatively high. For this reason, a regulated market *ceteris paribus* has lower opportunity cost (limited optionality) than an unhampered market such as envisioned by the anarchists, and so the loss of value when choosing non-maximizing options is much greater.

Since our conception of the "thick" market is characterized by voluntary association and horizontal contracting, any individual can instead of formal employment in a firm choose exchange with any available trading partners. Choices are overall less costly to reverse should they be in error, due to the comparatively high availability of other similarly valuable courses of action. This optionality, which in many ways has a similar effect on choice-making as would low transaction costs in the Coasean (1937, 1960) sense (see Bylund, 2021), suggests that long-term contracting (especially open-ended, employment-type contracts) should be perceived as comparatively *costly* since temporally extensive contracts exclude alternative and possibly more valuable courses of action for the duration of the regulated period. Tandy ([1896] 1979, pp. 159–160) notes this optionality for workers:

> Free competition will increase the competition among the employers and decrease it among the wage earners. The dream of the old time labor reformers will be realized. The job will search for the laborer, not the laborer for the job. When this takes place wages must necessarily go up rapidly. But the increase of competition among the manufacturers and merchants will also reduce prices. So not only will the wages of the workers be increased as measured in money, but the purchasing power of that money will be increased owing to the cheapening of commodities.

In addition to regulations and other legal requirements, a reason for ubiquitous employment under a state regime may be the regulated market's artificially limited optionality, which reduces workers' opportunity cost (and therefore wages). Carson (2004, pp. 140–144) notes that the failure to realize the import of optionality is at the core of reasoning errors among contemporary market protagonists—what he terms "vulgar libertarianism," or the assumption that voluntary choices denote optimality even if they are made in a regulated or restricted situation. Choice, it must be concluded—even voluntary—is a necessary criterion for optimality but is insufficient unless it is accompanied by unrestricted optionality.[2]

This means that while the economic organism could see both firms and employment, the unrestricted optionality necessitates that any limiting or exclusive contract must be of comparatively greater value than need be under restricted optionality. Its attractiveness consists in the value that it offers to the worker in addition to the second-best option. In other words, employment in the "thick" market must be considerably more valuable (which lowers relative opportunity costs) than under a state regime due to its higher opportunity cost owing to optionality:

> [It is erroneous to assume] that laborers, in order to receive the profits which now go to the employers, *must* become their own employers, and that the *only* way by which they can do this is to assume through their salaried agents the conduct of industry. The Anarchistic solution shows that there is no such *must* and no such *only* … it will make no difference whether men work for themselves, or are employed, or employ others. In any case they can get nothing but that wage for their labor which free competition determines. Therefore

they need not become their own employers. Perhaps, however, they will prefer to do so. (Tucker, [1897] 2005, p. 475)

The decision to be situated inside the "boundaries" of an organization is not necessarily limited to simple preference, as Tucker seems to suggest. There are several conceivable reasons for making such choices, including (very high) risk aversion, a sense of belonging or community, adoration for or kinship with managers or workers part of the organization, etc. (Logan, King, & Fischer-Wright, 2009). There may also be economic reasons if the organization's composition and configuration of factors entails higher productivity and therefore greater overall returns. We will here pursue the latter case.

PRODUCTIVITY AS A REASON FOR ORGANIZING

The extensive optionality that is existent under free competition and voluntary contracting under the type of economic organism discussed above suggests that labor is paid at or very close to its discounted marginal value product (Rothbard, [1962] 2004). In other words, workers enjoy the full "fruit" of their labor—the market value of their contribution to social wants satisfaction. This composes a limit to the possibilities for organizing, since economic benefits from organizing can be accomplished only by generating greater returns to labor and/or capital. To generate such above-normal returns, the organization cannot be a mirror image of the market (as in e.g. Marshall, [1890] 1920 and Coase, 1937), but must exploit some form of innovation or novelty regarding the utilization or division of labor, which has not and cannot be brought about through market contracting (Bylund, 2011, 2016a).

The problem of organization and thus the core issue in the theory of the firm is therefore of establishing the economic value of *integration* as compared to voluntary market contracting. In the "thick" market this amounts to an argument for how integration *overcomes* the impossibility of establishing certain modes of production through simple market contracting. We observe that there is an apparent lacuna in anarchist economic theory regarding what drives economic development and, more specifically, in what sense further development of the economic organism can be brought about. Indeed, while stasis is not assumed, a consequence of the theoretical discussion is a virtual lack of development since labor workers do not actively innovate but passively exploit recognized opportunities. As noted above, anarchist economic theory focuses on the worker's market position and relation with other workers, as well as the freedom and prosperity enjoyed in this position, but the evolution of and change to the market's macro-level productive structure is generally missing from the argument. This means any development of more intensive specialization under the division of labor, which suggests increased productivity, is, as Adam Smith ([1776] 1976) argued, a function of population growth. This makes economic development and growth "very slow and gradual" (Smith, [1776] 1976) and thus subject to what Bylund (2016a) calls the "specialization deadlock." Any achieved significant increase in the productivity of economic processes, therefore, must be the result of reconfiguring and reorganizing resources that are already available (Schumpeter, [1911] 1934) or, in other words, as a result of strategic entrepreneurship. This should then be the object and rationale for establishing an economic organization.

For any collection of existing resources, there exists an optimum in terms of their usage for the production of value, known among economists as the "law of returns" (see Mises, [1949] 1998, pp. 127–130). As the economic organism entails unrestricted (which does not imply unlimited) optionality, it follows that the structure of production should be at or close to this optimum and that resources (factors of production) are used in a maximizing fashion. This is what Tandy ([1896] 1979, p. 160) refers to as meaning "[t]he job will search for the laborer, not the laborer for the job." Where factors of production are combined and used in a maximizing way, the law of returns holds. Comparatively low-productivity processes will hence search for resources, while high-productivity (high-wage) processes enjoy access to labor and capital goods due to the higher compensation they can offer to workers and owners. The market's maximizing equilibrium is where wages equal the discounted marginal value product in labor's most valuable usage. For this reason, the structure of any extra-contractual arrangement such as integration *must provide a means for higher (more valuable) utilization of resources.*

Such productivity gains that make integration economically viable must then defy the law of returns. This means that, to achieve above-normal returns, integration must rely on innovation in production through novel usage of existing or creation of new resources, or innovation in consumer products by creating new markets (Schumpeter, [1911] 1934, p. 66). Innovation, and consequently the extension of the division of labor and development of capital, can provide a means to overcome the limits of the law of returns by finding new and more efficient ways of producing; it hence "enables us to resist the law of diminishing returns" (Lachmann, [1956] 1978, p. 79). Productive innovation, as it increases value creation and therefore wages, must therefore be at the core of what defines a firm (Bylund, 2011, 2015b, 2016a).

To a much more limited extent (and empirically more ambiguously held), this role of the integrated "manufacture" was identified by Karl Marx as a driving force of economic development under industrialization. "That co-operation," writes Marx ([1867] 1906, p. 368), "which is based on the division of labour, assumes its typical form in the manufacture," and is a "method employed ... for ... increasing that labour's productiveness." The division of labor in a manufacture, compared to society at large, "differ[s] not only in degree, but also in kind" ([1867] 1906, p. 389); the "division of labour in manufacture demands, that a division of labour in society at large should previously have attained a certain degree of development. Inversely, the former division reacts upon and develops and multiplies the latter" ([1867] 1906, pp. 387–388). In other words, the division of labor is generally more intensive within the manufacture than is existent in the outside market:

A carriage, for example, was formerly the product of the labour of a great number of independent artificers ... In the manufacture of carriages, however, all these different artificers are assembled in one building, where they work into one another's hands ... The tailor, the locksmith, and the other artificers, being now exclusively occupied in carriage-making, each gradually loses, through want of practice, the ability to carry on, to its full extent, his old handicraft. But, on the other hand, his activity now confined in one groove, assumes the form best adapted to the narrowed sphere of action. At first, carriage manufacture is a combination of various independent handicrafts. By degrees, it becomes the splitting up of carriage making into its various detail processes, each of which crystallizes into the exclusive function of a particular workman, the manufacture, as a whole, being carried on by the men in conjunction. (Marx, [1867] 1906, p. 369)

Marx's analysis of the manufacture's internal structure and utilization of the division of labor suggests a general argument for integration along Schumpeterian lines that is compatible with the economic organism. The economic argument for productivity increasing through the division of labor is valid whether or not this takes place in a regulated market, but Marx fails to realize the effects of the regulatory state on workers' optionality. What is detrimental (to Marx, exploitative) to the employment relation is not employment *per se* (cf. Tucker, [1897] 2005, p. 475), but the restricted optionality that is characteristic for the regulated market. This pushes wages down and makes the utilization of labor a function of capital ownership rather than voluntary contracting (Bylund, 2016b). Exploitation by extracting surplus value is then a result ultimately of the state, not the mode of production. For this reason anarchist economic theorists generally reject the Marxist analysis, its advocacy of certain political means, as well as its conclusions (Kropotkin, [1927] 2002, pp. 169–171; Tucker, [1897] 2005, pp. 1–18).

As Tucker ([1897] 2005, p. 475) notes, in the pure market labor workers "can get nothing but that wage for their labor which free competition determines." We have seen that this approximates the full market value of the fruits thereof—the discounted marginal revenue product. This is true also should workers choose employment in a manufacture, within which their wages must exceed the value of their alternative opportunities: the going free market wage. This means that, in order to make possible this higher wage, *their productivity in the manufacture must also be higher than in the external market.*

Marx's observation thus indirectly offers an answer to the question of integration under anarchism. Integration is a necessary precondition for such innovation that brings about a substantial increase in productivity (Stigler, 1951), which is generally a result of increased specialization through the division of labor and capital, where this cannot be accomplished through horizontal contracting. We should, in other words, see integrated production within the economic organism to the extent that great advances are made in terms of productivity through innovation beyond what is supported by the present market structure and thus the going market level of productivity. As Marx ([1867] 1906, p. 369) points out, an integrated firm brings about the "splitting up" of production "into its various detail processes, each of which crystallizes into the exclusive function of a particular workman" with the production process "being carried on by the men in conjunction."

Thus, under anarchism, the role and result of the integrated business firm must be to raise wages through implementing innovation that increases labor's productivity. This suggests there should also be a role for entrepreneurial foresight, risk-bearing, as well as capital ownership and investment, but while these issues are both important and interesting they are not within the scope of this chapter's discussion. They should be addressed in future research along with analysis of the possible role of the firm in the overall social process of economic development.

THE EMERGENCE AND STRUCTURE OF VOLUNTARY ORGANIZATION

The discussion above suggests that the firm in the economic organism is not simply a means of economizing on transaction costs through instituting hierarchy. Transaction costs should be of relatively limited magnitudes under the anarchist market state since it is organized horizontally and has unrestricted optionality. This entails only scant frictions to voluntary contracting: market prices (and wages) are reflective of real productivity and efficiency in resource allocation, and therefore easily discoverable. Also, opportunism should be a very limited problem under a pure market regime where market reputation and cooperation through voluntary contract are essential. Only limited transaction cost savings should therefore be possible through integration, whereas it is conceivable that high transaction costs (which seems to imply restricted optionality) may push market wages down due to the cost impediments to trade and, consequently, provide the firm an economic rationale in the Marxian sense.

Under unrestricted optionality—free competition—workers are likely to accept extensive contracting or employment only to the extent that the offered above-market wage is more valuable to them than the uneasiness caused by terms and restrictions as well as the length of the contract. The going market wage would be sufficient for leading a contented life—the so-called "iron law"[3] of wages should be applicable only on the regulated market, as noted above. So the choice to accept employment in a firm must appear more satisfactory overall than the state of affairs under voluntary market contracting in the economic organism within which the firm is embedded. There is therefore little (if any) room for exploitation of labor. This further supports Tandy's view of anarchism as a market in which the "job will search for the laborer" rather than vice versa. Indeed, in order to attract labor workers for employment, the firm must offer value to the employee in terms of wages and means to self-fulfillment.

While the firm in the economic organism emerges as an "island of increased productivity" and therefore appears distinct in the market, this conception has implications for our analysis of the firm. It remains to be discussed what factors determine the boundary of the firm, if it is a means toward realizing a productive innovation in addition to such innovation possible through market contracting. We shall also address implications for the role of management, which appears to be primarily one of *serving* employees while coordinating production. The direction-based, hierarchical governance of contemporary business organization (and as elaborated on in the literature on the firm) is in this sense not economically feasible in the pure market; it appears rather to be a result of lacking optionality and therefore, by extension, of market regulation.

Determinants of the Boundary of the Firm

The firm under a pure market regime cannot easily be described as hierarchical, since it consists exclusively of a nexus of horizontal voluntary contracts between contributors to its coordinated goal (cf. Alchian & Demsetz, 1972). Its internal structure is, as was established above, different than productive structures in the market, but it is nevertheless subject to competitive pressure through the unrestricted alternative uses for its resources as well as the market wage-earning uses of workers' labor. While firms could choose to centralize the bearing of risk as a function of its management or leadership, it is possible that a firm may distribute the risk of the venture on those partaking in it. This should only be the case, however, to the extent that employees consider the risk of lesser value than the wage premium obtained within the firm. In rare situations, risk-loving individuals may seek employment in organizations with excessive personal risk for the thrill of it. Yet it is improbable that such choices, which in terms of risk-bearing are economically akin to consumption rather than production, are made long term and as an alternative to earning a wage. Indeed, we should expect workers to find value in employment due to its risk-minimizing effects where risk is borne and managed by the firm's leadership. Some may consider job security and the smoothing of remuneration through employment beneficial, but the unregulated market would scarcely see the levels of involuntary unemployment or wage fluctuations common in the contemporary market.

Whatever major shifts that occur in the structure of the economic organism should be due to sudden and unexpected changes in consumer preferences, which cause realignment by changing and reconfiguring the production structure, or disruptive innovations for increased productivity. Neither of these changes is problematic in the long term as they ultimately bring about increased wants satisfaction throughout society and, consequently, increased prosperity. Realignment of existing production structures is carried out through voluntarily changing productive efforts as well as renegotiating contracts for the benefit of all involved parties. Under anarchism, incentives are aligned throughout the production apparatus via voluntary contracting, as well as with consumer preferences, the ultimate goal of production. Such realignment requires no organizing, but innovation may make the organizing of integrated bodies of production necessary.

The importance and significance of the firm, then, as well as its rationale, are *to produce value through implementing innovative, productive resource structuring and utilization* (cf. Schumpeter, [1911] 1934; Bylund, 2016a). The achieved value must be generated through increased productivity. It will likely be brought about by adopting a more intensive division of labor (Bylund, 2011). This, then, is what distinguishes the firm from the market within which it is embedded. Its boundaries should therefore be a function of the assessed returns on investment, whether this is a decision made by an original entrepreneur (Foss, Foss, & Klein, 2007), an external capitalist investor, or jointly through cooperative decision-making. Firms would employ labor to the extent that doing so is productive, in terms of resource usage and value creation, and as long as labor workers willingly enter them. In other words, workers take part if and when they are offered something in addition to what they can get in the open market. The boundaries of the firm are in this sense a function of its internal scale of production and the relative magnitude of productive improvement.

It then follows that organizing in business firms should be a temporary rather than persistent measure, with the purpose to bring about, experiment with, and test innovative production processes. Successful entrepreneurship in firms suggests market leadership through above-normal returns and comparatively high productivity. These are in turn accomplishments which induce others to emulate the firm's productive solutions and coordinate competing organizations and networks. In other words, successful strategic entrepreneurship makes the firm, not firms that choose (or not) to engage in strategic entrepreneurship. Such competitive pressure ultimately leads to the general adoption of novel and proven successful productive measures, processes, and specialized tasks, and therefore the disintegration of the original firm's boundaries and return to the decentralized market under voluntary contracting. Consequently, new kinds and intensities of the division of labor are established as market standard through the leadership of successful firms and the overall adoption of innovative coordination of resource arrangements that follow. Economic growth then consists of advances made in and by the firm, which are copied and adopted throughout the market.

The boundaries of the firm are determined by the specific productive innovation that it is organized to realize, and specific boundaries should tend to fluctuate with further innovation and learning through continuous experimentation and perfection of the novel production structure. The boundaries persist for as long as the firm's organizing is sufficiently different from that of the economic organism as a whole. This is also the firm's function and value. All parties to the firm have an interest in and are rewarded in accordance with its success. Thus, it is in everyone's interest to act toward coordinating internal efforts to take productivity-improving action, seek, invite, and develop specific competencies that are necessary for success, and to swiftly terminate projects that cause harm, are too risky, or prove to have little chance of success. The firm, in other words, emerges as a vehicle for realizing productivity-improving entrepreneurial innovations, and this is the rationale also for its boundaries (Bylund, 2016a).

Role of Management

The business firm in the economic organism cannot serve as a platform for arbitrary managerial rule or exploitation of workers in the Marxian sense, since it is based on strictly *voluntary* contracting with free workers. Indeed, a business firm's management must be set up through the same horizontal contracting as establishes the firm, and therefore has a leadership role, a delegated coordinative function, tasked with the improvement of overall productivity and increasing chances of success (cf. Alchian & Demsetz, 1972). Management is ultimately a democratic function that aims to improve overall coordination by offering incentives, encouragement, and support. This would then mean that management that lacks workers' respect or that lacks leadership qualities is impotent, as it lacks formal or coercive authority.

The firm's lack of formal authority limits the role of management to one of promotion and service, with the explicit task of motivating workers, guiding and coaching them toward success, and thereby improving the organization's combined output. The distinction between management and leadership (Bertocci, 2009) in present-day organizations becomes unimportant as the function of management is limited to leadership intended to facilitate production. Coordination of production in the business firm can be achieved through leading by example, providing consistent and just guidance, and promoting the common goal of the enterprise. Power exists only as derived from agreed-upon contractual terms and as informal authority to the degree it is accepted. This suggests that such authority must in some sense be considered just by those subject(ed) to it. Such power-like influence would be problematic under restricted optionality due to the very limited number (if any) of satisfactory alternative opportunities for the worker. In the economic organism model, however, the fallback position is the market wage, and workers always retain the power to offer and withdraw consent to leadership. A "manager" has decision-making rights delegated through contract because of his or her foresight or ability to successfully inspire workers, solve problems and conflicts, and otherwise ensure success by coordinating and matching up workers' interests and skills. The manager therefore must be sensitive to employees' passions and values, while being able to figure out how to bring those passions together to create synergies and successfully achieve the organization's stated purpose.

There are two aspects of such leadership pertaining to the short- and long-term coordination of efforts. While there may be a tradeoff in terms of outright maximizing, the pure market setting as we have here adopted should minimize the risk of conflicts between temporally exclusive aims. The long-term aim *facilitates* short-term maximizing through establishing a productive culture and common value base in the firm (Barney, 1986a). This type of strategic leadership is intended to make explicit the set of values, morality, and identity that expedite furtherance of the common aim. The common culture, distinct to the individual firm, can engender and strengthen the trust bonds between members of the organization that prevent unnecessary conflict and empowers them to find productive solutions and overcome obstacles through independently and proactively seeking joint efforts in a decentralized manner. A key task in culture-building is to find and entice the right people for the organization, so that they are fundamentally compatible with the existing organization members' set of values while contributing to the culture. An organization may seek particular skills for its production process, but this may not be the best strategy. Since the firm is different from the market in terms of its division of labor, and therefore its internal tasks are unique specializations, it may be more important to find employees who have the right "attitude." They can then easily become part of the existing team and work to acquire the (new) skills necessary to contribute to the firm as a whole. Skills may in fact be secondary to the firm's building a productive culture.

The task of management is here to align members' interests with that of the organization. This may be done through creating a sense of community around a set of shared values, which is why it is important to find the "right" people. But it should be equally important to fit people in and align their interests with the organization's, especially as the latter changes over time. The undertaking of management is therefore to build support for important firm functions as well as to make it easy for people to do the right thing, from the point of view of the organization as a whole.

This ties directly into the short-term goal of maximizing output through tapping into the power of joint production and a distinct and intensive division of labor. Output is produced through the voluntary efforts of those who have joined the firm, so management should strive for conflict resolution and avoidance in addition to providing overall leadership. Management should ensure the right people are employed and see to the overall alignment of interests. This may pertain to dealing with issues of free-riding or opportunistic and other behaviors that potentially undermine the organization's culture and trust bonds between employees. What matters in the short term is the carrying out of the firm's particular production processes for the benefit of all those involved.

A successful firm taps into, utilizes, focuses, and enables synergies between the passions of its employees. Management is therefore involved in value-based counseling, coaching, and support to help employees identify what they love to do and what they are motivated to contribute—to find out what they are passionate about. Where individuals' passions are obviously in line with the organization's aims, this task is easily accomplished. However, where passions are latent, ill-defined, or poorly formulated, or simply unknown to the individual, management needs to identify their true passion and motivations so that they can be fully fitted with and utilized in the organization. Management, therefore, cannot be a function of authority and rule, as it is often portrayed under the state capitalist system, but must here seek and earn the respect of those employed so that they can be properly and thoroughly served (Carlzon, 1987).

CONCLUDING DISCUSSION

We have seen how using the economic organism for studying organization in the market provides important insights to the value of integration and therefore the business firm. Our analysis relies on a theory of the *economic* functioning of a market without coercive power or hierarchy but including voluntary social institutions and contracting—i.e., a "thick" conception of the pure market as per the market anarchists—to study in detail what could be the rationale for integrating production processes.

The Firm Is Strategic Entrepreneurship

Our theoretical examination suggests the hierarchical business firm may be a result not of market value provision but of lacking optionality, which in turn appears to be a consequence of the political authority of the state. The cause of many of the often assumed problematic characteristics of firms in the present economy may therefore not be economic, but have different origins.

In contrast, under an economic organism under voluntary contract and unrestricted optionality, as we have elaborated in this chapter, the economic incentives for integration must be productivity-based. Thus, the rationale for the firm is to facilitate production that cannot be realized in the regular market. In order to be formed and remain, integrated production in a firm must also directly benefit the employed workers or they would choose to remain free agents earning the standard remuneration in the market. This indicates that the business firm must provide *real value* to those employed by it as well as its other stakeholders and society as a whole. In other words, *the economic firm is a manifestation of strategic entrepreneurship*: the economic firm is itself a result of strategic entrepreneurialism as it emerges out of the undertaking of novel and expectedly highly productive (value-creative) integrated production beyond what can be achieved through regular market exchange.

This conclusion is different from the common assumption that strategic entrepreneurship takes place within firms. While this is certainly true, this is observable for *legal* firms in contemporary markets—not in the pure market situation of the economic organism. Our contribution is not a rejection of the common view, but suggests that there may be several causal explanations. The empirical firm, as our analysis has shown, is formed and operates within a particular context of limited optionality. As economic action can be understood logically, it is also contingent. Limited optionality can therefore have different effects than situations characterized by unrestricted optionality. Our analysis shows this and indicates that the firm plays a different role in a regulated economy than in a pure market context. The empirical firm may therefore be formed for other than productivity reasons (for example, legal benefits such as limited liability), but can—and perhaps even *must*—engage in value-creative entrepreneurship for strategic renewal and sustained profitability.

Empirical reality may thus see a different causal explanation of firm formation than our economic firm. The latter, as it emerges in the pure market context, can have only an economic rationale. The only economic reason to deviate from market-based production is increased productivity, which is achieved through value-creative entrepreneurship. In other words, as we argue above, the firm in the economic organism is a manifestation of strategic entrepreneurship: aiming for value-creative disruption through the adoption of novel production processes.

Specifically, we find that the economic firm is defined by the productive power unleashed by realizing innovation—new production processes, production of new capital goods, or new products—that utilizes a particular division of labor that is (difficult or) impossible to bring about through regular market contracts. The latter impossibility may arise due to the firm's novelty or a lack of exact knowledge of the functioning of the process, which may only be made available (in fact, created) through the implementation process (Bylund, 2015a). In line with these observations, the firm as an economic phenomenon emerges as a vehicle to bring about more intensive specialization that greatly increases the productivity of labor and therefore also its wages. It thereby also contributes to explaining economic growth (Bylund, 2016a).

Seeing the firm as a means to overcome the productive limits of the open market provides important clues to what constitutes its boundaries. While the issue of the boundaries of the firm is frequently discussed in the extant literature on the firm and economic organizing (e.g., Araujo, Dubois, & Gadde, 2003; Cook & Chaddad, 2004; Dosi & Teece, 1998; Jacobides & Winter, 2007; Langlois, 1988), our analysis suggests that the boundaries are less ambiguously identified than is commonly assumed. In fact, the boundaries of the firm in a pure market are dependent only on the extent of a firm's integrated production process, which in turn is limited to what cannot be implemented through voluntary market contracting (and hence requires integration). The firm thereby becomes a temporary means to overcome the impossibility of implementing certain productive innovations through market contracts. The socio-economic value of the firm is to lead the market to improved productivity.

Further, the incentives for integration in a firm appear different in our "thick" conception of the pure market than is commonly recognized. Rather than the vertical relationship between employer and potential employee that is commonly assumed, there appears to be no purely economic need for employment due to optionality. Consequently, the relationship between employer and employee is not vertical with the employer at the top, but is established horizontally through contract but, importantly, with the employer needing to convince the employee. In other words, there can be no room for Marxian exploitation as the firm, in order to be formed, must offer sufficient remuneration for employees to choose employment over free agency earning the market wage.

We therefore also find that the role of management under unrestricted optionality is limited to the empowerment and motivation of the firm's employees—its task is to facilitate the promise of increased productivity. It aims to serve those involved in production so as to preempt and avoid (or, where unsuccessful, resolve) problems, and streamline coordination and collaboration in the organization (Carlzon, 1987). Management's role is here one of leadership, and it serves the value creation in the firm through creating a supportive and enabling culture. It contributes to the overall productive value of the firm by "fitting" employees' passions so that, as far as possible, workers do what they are self-motivated to do, by which the whole organization benefits. This also limits the role of management, since there should be little value in having a "whipping master" or micro-manager of self-motivated employees with aligned passions.

But the role of management is also one of counseling and coaching, by which we mean the "help to self-help" of employees who are in a temporary "low," struggle with personal issues, or are unable to overcome immature professional personalities. In this sense, management has a social function that extends beyond the boundaries of the firm to the extent that employees are empowered and create a sense of confidence and independence. This particular function, while it may be of limited importance or even abrogated under the regulated market's restricted optionality, remains understudied in the literature. This is hardly the traditional role of the manager, but the modern management style is quickly moving toward supportive coaching, culture-building, and with motivational aims rather than authoritarian direction (Parsloe, 1999). Our conclusions suggest that this development is more in line with the nature of the firm *qua* firm—the economic firm rather than the "legal fiction"—than the nature of production as it is carried out in regulated markets. This is a social function of management that contemporary regulated markets often lack.

Limitations and Specific Contributions

The purpose of this chapter was to draft the essence and function of organizing from the point of view of a "thick" conception of the market—the economic organism—as well as outline preliminary conclusions; our analysis is not intended as a full-scale theory of the firm. Instead, we used a novel theoretical framework to provide the firm with a productivity rationale—and thereby find the firm to be a representation or manifestation of strategic entrepreneurship rather than an organization that may engage in such activities. For obvious reasons, then, our specific theoretical findings need further elaboration as well as validation, and should also be contextualized by extending this chapter's limited scope.

The primary contribution of this chapter is the strict separation of the economic rationale for integration of production in the firm from legal influences. This was done by introducing a previously overlooked theory of the economic organism, primarily as imagined by mutualists like Proudhon, Tucker, and Carson. The starting point for our analysis is a "thick" conception of the market, unaffected by coercive institutions or top-down ordering of social organizing, rather than a streamlined and potentially oversimplified equilibrium model of the economy. This theory provides a framework to explain latent and seemingly (but not necessarily) cohesive market phenomena. By using theoretical anarchism as a framework, we were able to analytically eschew many causal factors that may actually be empirically irrelevant or unrealistic, which allows us to uncover the underlying economic logic of firm formation that provides direction for empirical research.

Second is the conclusions of our study and their implications for our understanding of the market and organizing. We identify a productivity rationale for integrating production processes in firms, which may help explain the source of economic development. This rationale is what remains to explain production in firms in an economy that consists entirely of horizontal contractual and trade relationships. Our rather Schumpeterian ([1911] 1934) conclusions, while also in line with what

Bylund (2016a) finds, suggest that the firm, while benefitting from state-dependent privilege and largely structured to exploit the lacking optionality in the contemporary market, has a role to play also under a pure market "regime." The firm here emerges as *a means for entrepreneurial actors to overcome productive limitations* due to the extent of the market and therefore to facilitate a more intensive division of labor, a function that is essentially temporary (since successful implementations are imitated and absorbed by competitors (Barney, 1986b, 1991)) yet is fundamentally strategic and, thus, can be extended and improved using strategic means. As our investigation shows, the firm as a purely economic phenomenon is the embodiment of innovations—a strategic act of entrepreneurship—beyond what could be easily accomplished through regular exchange in the existing market; it is also independent of the legal system (since it is a purely productive measure).

This identification is important as much of the literature asserts hierarchical power as the characteristic mark of the firm (Coase, 1937), and so addresses organizational implications from the point of view of power. Our argument suggests that the firm's primary economic function is *to increase productivity*. It is not one of establishing and maintaining authority and privilege but one of realizing innovations of anticipated higher productivity, or entrepreneurship that provides a strategic advantage that extends significantly through time for the reasons elaborated by Barney (1991). In a sense, the economic firm escapes immediate pressures from the competitive environment by encapsulating through integration a productive innovation. This guards the value-creative qualities of the innovation from being captured by competitors and may also provide a foundation for "internal" tweaking and continued investments in research and development. This, in turn, suggests that firms may invest in continued innovation to extend the strategic value (that is, maintained profitability) of the economic firm by recreating its economic contribution: continuous efforts to innovate can thereby extend the life of the organization through renewed innovativeness contributing to productivity. While more research is needed in this space, strategic entrepreneurship (Ireland & Webb, 2007) has already addressed this issue, but without the foundations we provide here: the nature of the economic as opposed to the legal firm. Our investigation contributes the theoretical platform— the economic rationale for the firm—on which strategic entrepreneurship both as theory and practice could be based. With a sound economic foundation, as opposed to being contingent on specific legal decrees, strategic entrepreneurship provides insight into the structuring of the market as well as indicates processes of economic growth: the economic firm is here a core aspect of the market, whereas the legal firm is a non-market phenomenon that is arguably artificial and necessitates the wielding of an exogenous power for its creation and existence (Oppenheimer, [1914] 1928).

This implication is reproduced in our analysis of the role of management, which without coercive privilege becomes indistinguishable from leadership. Management, in that it is a commonly perceived form of hierarchical or coercive authority, lacks obvious productive value (the opposite of what e.g., Coase (1937) argues) and is therefore unlikely to emerge under voluntary contracting. Leadership, however, is a social, bottom-up phenomenon arising when individuals allow or seek guidance in another's qualities and abilities.

Moreover, these conclusions have important implications for research and practice in strategic entrepreneurship. Defined as "entrepreneurial action with a strategic perspective" (Hitt et al., 2001, p. 480), strategic entrepreneurship here becomes the *rationale* for the firm rather than a strategy to adopt within it. The reason for this is that the firm's productivity rationale is itself necessarily entrepreneurial (innovative). It is also strategic, since this innovative organizing of production is an attempt to (and, in fact, must) outdo the already specialized and so productive market. The result is that our explanation for the firm is the undertaking of strategic entrepreneurship, the organization of integrated production being the manifestation of the attempted productive innovation. This suggests, therefore, that strategic entrepreneurship as it is typically studied either places the cart before the horse (firm first, strategic entrepreneurship second) or inadvertently studies *strategic entrepreneurship as firm renewal*. In both cases, strategic entrepreneurship scholars and practitioners would have much to gain from changing their perspective: to see the firm as a manifestation of strategic entrepreneurship.

Suggestions for Future Research

What remains to be analyzed, which has not been addressed in this chapter, is the issue of ownership and whether and how resources within an integrated structure are allocated *between* projects, and what firm leadership's role in this task may be. It is not obvious how or why a firm in a pure market would integrate several separate production processes, but it is conceivable that there may be synergies from doing so. This should especially be the case if demand for the firm's output fluctuates over time due to, for example, seasonal products or if the firm for other reasons should fail to achieve full resource utilization, in which case switching between projects may offer opportunities for more cost-effective resource use.

Future research can address whether management as bottom-up leadership, based on consent and acquiescence, is sufficient for administering centralized switching between processes, or if some aspects of top-down authoritative management are necessary. It would also be interesting to analyze whether management (as opposed to leadership) can be contractually established in the pure market. Interestingly, while the distinction between management and leadership is prevalent in literatures on organizational behavior and psychology of production, the implications and origins of these concepts are conspicuously absent from the theory of the firm.

In addition, there are several issues only touched on above that require further study. The conception of entrepreneurship, which seems to be the driving force of the market as well as the initiator of firm integration (Mises, [1949] 1998; Spulber, 2008; Bylund, 2016a, 2020), needs to be further elaborated on and studied. Studies of entrepreneurship could provide further details and a more elaborate theory of the firm's boundaries than outlined within the scope of this chapter. Entrepreneurship can also be related to risk-taking and uncertainty-bearing (Knight, [1921] 1985; Cantillon, [1755] 1931), the exact nature of which under the pure market warrants explication.

Related to entrepreneurship, the issue of ownership is central to our understanding of the market as well as modes of production. Tucker defines "the right of ownership" as "that control of a thing by a person which will receive either social sanction, or else unanimous individual sanction, when the laws of social expediency shall have been finally discovered" (Tucker, [1897] 2005, pp. 130–131), but this offers only limited guidance in attempting to understand the market process and delineate the nature and function of integration and organization. The concept is strongly related with production and the structure of civilized society, and should therefore be important to the analysis of the firm, though it was not within the scope of the analysis in this chapter. Resource ownership and control are important extensions of the productivity argument drafted here, however. As Proudhon (1969, p. 243) notes, "it is when man emerges from the state of nature and begins to live in society that property becomes distinct from theft, that exchange is legalized and frees itself from speculation and that labor is organized around the division and the group." It is intricately linked to market structure and institutions such as money, which for Tandy ([1896] 1979, p. 83) "is required to effect the necessary exchange of labor." Ownership is further a basis for understanding specific market action such as investing and risk-taking. While profoundly important, these discussions remain to be addressed in future research.

NOTES

1. The study of political economy has long relied on imaginary states, such as the "state of nature," to identify and explain social phenomena (e.g., Hobbes, [1651] 1994; Locke, [1690] 1962; Mises, 1949; Rawls, 1971). The method has recently seen a resurgence in modern political economy because, when including realistic and imperfect social institutions, it offers a "robust" analysis of comparative political institutions (see e.g., Pennington, 2011).
2. The failure to take into account the economics of optionality lies at the core of the Marxian class analysis, which concludes that workers are exploited by capitalists appropriating the surplus value of labor (Marx, [1867] 1906; Marx & Engels, [1848] 2008). As suggested above, such exploitation is made possible by *restricted* optionality.
3. The "iron law" states that "wages under capitalism are inevitably driven near some physical subsistence level" (Baumol, 1983, p. 303). This, as we note above, is inapplicable in the pure market due to its unrestricted optionality.

REFERENCES

Aghion, P., Bloom, N., & Van Reenen, J. (2013). Incomplete Contracts and the Internal Organization of Firms. *Journal of Law, Economics, and Organization*. doi: 10.1093/jleo/ewt003.

Alchian, A. A., & Demsetz, H. (1972). Production, Information Costs and Economic Organization. *American Economic Review, 62*(5), 777–795.

Alvarez, S. A., & Barney, J. B. (2007). The Entrepreneurial Theory of the Firm. *Journal of Management Studies*, *44*(7), 1057–1063.

Aquinas, T. ([1259] 1953). *Disputed Questions on Truth*. Chicago, IL: Henry Regnery.

Araujo, L., Dubois, A., & Gadde, L.-E. (2003). The Multiple Boundaries of the Firm*. *Journal of Management Studies*, *40*(5), 1255–1277.

Barney, J. B. (1986a). Organizational Culture: Can It Be a Source of Sustained Competitive Advantage? *Academy of Management Review*, *11*(3), 656–665.

Barney, J. B. (1986b). Strategic Factor Markets: Expectations, Luck, and Business Strategy. *Management Science*, *32*(10), 1231–1241.

Barney, J. B. (1991). Firm Resources and Sustained Competitive Advantage. *Journal of Management*, *17*(1), 99–120.

Barney, J. B. (1996). The Resource-Based Theory of the Firm. *Organization Science*, *7*(5), 469.

Baumol, W. J. (1983). Marx and the Iron Law of Wages. *American Economic Review*, *73*(2), 303–308.

Benson, B. L. (1990). *Enterprise of Law: Justice without the State*. San Francisco, CA: Pacific Research Institute for Public Policy.

Benson, B. L. (2005). Spontaneous Evolution of Cyber Law: Norms, Property Rights, Contracting, Dispute Resolution and Enforcement without the State. *Journal of Law, Economics and Policy*, *1*, 269.

Bertocci, D. I. (2009). *Leadership in Organizations: There Is a Difference between Leaders and Managers*. Lanham, MD: University Press of America.

Bohnet, I., Frey, B. S., & Huck, S. (2001). More Order with Less Law: On Contract Enforcement, Trust, and Crowding. *American Political Science Review*, *95*(1), 131–144.

Bylund, P. L. (2011). Division of Labor and the Firm: An Austrian Attempt at Explaining the Firm in the Market. *Quarterly Journal of Austrian Economics*, *14*(2), 188–215.

Bylund, P. L. (2014a). The Firm and the Authority Relation: Hierarchy vs. Organization. In G. L. Nell (Ed.), *Austrian Theory and Economic Organization: Reaching beyond Free Market Boundaries* (pp. 97–120). New York: Palgrave Macmillan.

Bylund, P. L. (2014b). Ronald Coase's "Nature of the Firm" and the Argument for Economic Planning. *Journal of the History of Economic Thought*, *36*(3), 305–329.

Bylund, P. L. (2015a). Explaining Firm Emergence: Specialization, Transaction Costs, and the Integration Process. *Managerial and Decision Economics*, *36*(4), 221–238.

Bylund, P. L. (2015b). Explaining Firm Emergence: Specialization, Transaction Costs, and the Integration Process. *Managerial and Decision Economics*, *36*(4), 221–238.

Bylund, P. L. (2016a). *The Problem of Production: A New Theory of the Firm*. New York: Routledge.

Bylund, P. L. (2016b). *The Seen, the Unseen, and the Unrealized: How Regulations Affect Our Everyday Lives*. Lanham, MD: Lexington Books.

Bylund, P. L. (2020). Finding the Entrepreneur-Promoter: A Praxeological Inquiry. *Quarterly Journal of Austrian Economics*, *23*(3–4), 355–389.

Bylund, P. L. (2021). The Firm vs. The Market: Dehomogenizing the Transaction Cost Theories of Coase and Williamson. *Strategic Management Review*, *2*(1), 79–118.

Cantillon, R. ([1755] 1931). *Essai sur la Nature du Commerce en Général* (C. B. Henry Higgs, Trans.). London: Macmillan & Co.

Carlzon, J. (1987). *Moments of Truth*. Cambridge, MA: Ballinger Publishing.

Carson, K. A. (2004). *Studies in Mutualist Political Economy*. Fayetteville, AR.

Carson, K. A. (2008). *Organization Theory: A Libertarian Perspective*. Booksurge.

Casson, M. C. (2000). An Entrepreneurial Theory of the Firm. In N. J. Foss (Ed.), *Competence, Governance and Entrepreneurship: Advances in Economic Strategy Research*. New York: Oxford University Press.

Coase, R. H. (1937). The Nature of the Firm. *Economica*, *4*(16), 386–405.

Coase, R. H. (1960). The Problem of Social Cost. *Journal of Law and Economics*, *3*(1), 1–44.
Coase, R. H. (1988). The Nature of the Firm: Origin. *Journal of Law, Economics and Organization*, *4*(1), 3–17.
Cook, M. L., & Chaddad, F. R. (2004). Redesigning Cooperative Boundaries: The Emergence of New Models. *American Journal of Agricultural Economics*, *86*(5), 1249–1253.
Davenport, H. J. ([1913] 1968). *Economics of Enterprise*. New York: Augustus M. Kelley.
Dosi, G., & Teece, D. J. (1998). Organizational Competencies and the Boundaries of the Firm. In R. Arena & C. Longhi (Eds), *Markets and Organization* (pp. 281–302). New York: Springer.
Ellickson, R. C. (1991). *Order without Law: How Neighbors Settle Disputes*. Cambridge, MA: Harvard University Press.
Fehr, E., Gächter, S., & Kirchsteiger, G. (1997). Reciprocity as a Contract Enforcement Device: Experimental Evidence. *Econometrica: Journal of the Econometric Society*, 833–860.
Foss, K., Foss, N. J., & Klein, P. G. (2007). Original and Derived Judgment: An Entrepreneurial Theory of Economic Organization. *Organization Studies*, *28*(12), 1–20.
Foss, N. J. (1994). The Theory of the Firm: The Austrians as Precursors and Critics of Contemporary Theory. *Review of Austrian Economics*, *7*(1), 31–65.
Foss, N. J. (1997). Austrian Insights and the Theory of the Firm. In P. J. Boettke & S. Horwitz (Eds), *Advances in Austrian Economics*, Volume 4 (pp. 175–198). Greenwich, CT: JAI Press.
Foss, N. J., & Klein, P. G. (2008). The Theory of the Firm and Its Critics: A Stocktaking and Assessment. In É. Brousseau & J.-M. Glachant (Eds), *New Institutional Economics: A Guidebook* (pp. 425–442). Cambridge: Cambridge University Press.
Foss, N. J., & Klein, P. G. (2012). *Organizing Entrepreneurial Judgment: A New Approach to the Firm*. Cambridge: Cambridge University Press.
Garrouste, P., & Saussier, S. (2008). The Theories of the Firm. In É. Brousseau & J.-M. Glachant (Eds), *New Institutional Economics: A Guidebook* (pp. 23–36). Cambridge: Cambridge University Press.
Granovetter, M. S. (1985). Economic Action and Social Structure: The Problem of Embeddedness. *American Journal of Sociology*, *91*(3), 481–510.
Grossman, S. J., & Hart, O. D. (1986). The Costs and Benefits of Ownership: A Theory of Vertical and Lateral Integration. *Journal of Political Economy*, *94*(4), 691–719.
Hitt, M. A., Ireland, R. D., Camp, S. M., & Sexton, D. L. (2001). Strategic Entrepreneurship: Entrepreneurial Strategies for Wealth Creation. *Strategic Management Journal*, *22*, 479–491.
Hobbes, T. ([1651] 1994). *Leviathan*. Indianapolis, IN: Hackett Publishing.
Ireland, R. D., & Webb, J. W. (2007). Strategic Entrepreneurship: Creating Competitive Advantage through Streams of Innovation. *Business Horizons*, *50*(1), 49–59.
Jacobides, M. G., & Winter, S. G. (2007). Entrepreneurship and Firm Boundaries: The Theory of a Firm. *Journal of Management Studies*, *44*(7), 1213–1241.
Jensen, M. C., & Meckling, W. H. (1976). Theory of the Firm: Managerial Behavior, Agency Costs, and Capital Structure. *Journal of Financial Economics*, *3*(4), 305–360.
Knight, F. H. ([1921] 1985). *Risk, Uncertainty and Profit*. Chicago, IL: University of Chicago Press.
Kropotkin, P. A. ([1927] 2002). *Anarchism: A Collection of Revolutionary Writings*. Minneola, NY: Dover Publications.
Lachmann, L. M. ([1956] 1978). *Capital and Its Structure*. Kansas City, MO: Sheed Andrews and McMeel.
Langlois, R. N. (1988). Economic Change and the Boundaries of the Firm. *Journal of Institutional and Theoretical Economics*, *144*, 635–657.
Locke, J. ([1690] 1962). *Second Treatise of Government*. Indianapolis, IN: Hackett Publishing.

Logan, D., King, J., & Fischer-Wright, H. (2009). *Tribal Leadership*. London: HarperCollins.

Madhok, A. (2002). Reassessing the Fundamentals and Beyond: Ronald Coase, the Transaction Cost and Resource-Based Theories of the Firm and the Institutional Structure of Production. *Strategic Management Journal, 23*(6), 535–550.

Marshall, A. ([1890] 1920). *Principles of Economics. 8th Edition* (8th edn). New York: Macmillan.

Marx, K. ([1867] 1906). *Capital: A Critique of Political Economy*, Volume 1 (S. Moore & E. Aveling, Trans). New York: Charles H. Kerr & Company.

Marx, K., & Engels, F. ([1848] 2008). *The Communist Manifesto*. New York: Pathfinder.

Masten, S. E. (1988). A Legal Basis for the Firm. *Journal of Law, Economics, and Organization, 4*(1), 181–198.

Meltzer, A. (1996). *Anarchism: Arguments for and Against*. San Francisco, CA: AK Press.

Mises, L. v. (1949). *Human Action: A Treatise on Economics*. New Haven, CN: Yale University Press.

Mises, L. v. ([1949] 1998). *Human Action: A Treatise on Economics. The Scholar's Edition*. Auburn: Ludwig von Mises Institute.

Nickerson, J. A., & Zenger, T. R. (2004). A Knowledge-Based Theory of the Firm? The Problem-Solving Perspective. *Organization Science, 15*(6), 617–632.

Oppenheimer, F. ([1914] 1928). *The State: Its History and Development Viewed Sociologically*. New York: Vanguard Press.

Parsloe, E. (1999). *The Manager as Coach and Mentor*. London: CIPD Publishing.

Pennington, M. (2011). *Robust Political Economy: Classical Liberalism and the Future of Public Policy*. Cheltenham, UK and Northampton, MA, USA: Edward Elgar Publishing.

Pfeffer, J. (1981). *Power in Organizations*. Boston, MA: Pitman.

Proudhon, P.-J. ([1923] 2003). *General Idea of the Revolution in the Nineteenth Century*. Minneola, NY: Dover Publications.

Proudhon, P.-J. (1969). *Selected Writings of P.-J. Proudhon* (E. Fraser, Trans., S. Edwards, Ed.). Garden City, NY: Anchor Books.

Rawls, J. (1971). *A Theory of Justice*. Cambridge, MA: Harvard University Press.

Rothbard, M. N. ([1962] 2004). *Man, Economy, and State with Power and Market. Scholar's Edition*. Auburn, AL: Ludwig von Mises Institute.

Sautet, F. E. (2000). *An Entrepreneurial Theory of the Firm*. New York: Routledge.

Schumpeter, J. A. ([1911] 1934). *The Theory of Economic Development: An Inquiry into Profits, Capital, Credit, Interest, and the Business Cycle*. Cambridge, MA: Harvard University Press.

Simon, H. A. ([1945] 1957). *Administrative Behavior: A Study of Decision-Making Processes in Administrative Organization* (2nd edn). New York: MacMillan Company.

Smith, A. ([1776] 1976). *An Inquiry into the Nature and Causes of the Wealth of Nations*. Chicago, IL: University of Chicago Press.

Spulber, D. F. (2008). *The Theory of the Firm: Microeconomics with Endogenous Entrepreneurs, Firms, Markets, and Organizations*. Cambridge: Cambridge University Press.

Stigler, G. J. (1951). The Division of Labor Is Limited by the Extent of the Market. *Journal of Political Economy*, 185–193.

Taleb, N. N. (2012). *Antifragile: Things That Gain from Disorder*. New York: Random House.

Tandy, F. D. ([1896] 1979). *Voluntary Socialism: A Sketch*. Brooklyn, NY: Revisionist Press.

Tucker, B. R. ([1897] 2005). *Instead of a Book: By a Man Too Busy to Write One*. New York: Elibron Classics.

Williamson, O. E. (1975). *Markets and Hierarchies, Analysis and Antitrust Implications: A Study in the Economics of Internal Organization*. New York: Free Press.

Williamson, O. E. (1979). Transaction Cost Economics: The Governance of Contractual Relations. *Journal of Law and Economics, 22*(2), 233–261.

Williamson, O. E. (1985). *The Economic Institutions of Capitalism*. New York: Free Press.
Williamson, O. E. (1991). Comparative Economic Organization: The Analysis of Discrete Structural Alternatives. *Administrative Science Quarterly*, *36*(2), 269–296.
Williamson, O. E. (1996). *The Mechanisms of Governance*. Oxford: Oxford University Press.

4. Opportunity-seeking behaviors in strategic entrepreneurship: what do we know from the effectuation literature?

Florian Bayer and Christian Landau

How, why, and when do individuals, organizations, and stakeholders engage in value creation processes associated with strategic entrepreneurship (SE)? While the SE literature offers sound theoretical explanations of the phenomenon, ambiguity remains as to how firms can implement appropriate opportunity-seeking behavior (Mazzei, 2018; Simsek, Heavey, & Fox, 2017). Today firms face a dynamic environment characterized by uncertainty, complexity, ambiguity, and volatility (Sirmon, Hitt, & Ireland, 2007). The ever changing environment requires firms to adapt their opportunity-seeking behavior. Accordingly, scholars see high potential for SE research in devoting more attention to the context as a boundary condition of entrepreneurial activity (Schindehutte & Morris, 2009; Welter, 2011).

Mazzei, Ketchen, and Shook (2017) advocate investigating SE from different theoretical perspectives to gain additional practical and conceptual insights into the phenomenon and its interrelationships. We see a highly relevant perspective to inform SE in effectuation, since its phenomenon of interest of new opportunity creation occurs similarly to value creation in dynamic environments, between multiple actors, and across different levels of analysis (Hitt, Ireland, Sirmon, & Trahms, 2011; Kerr & Coviello, 2020; Wright & Hitt, 2017; Sarasvathy, 2001). This literature stream makes a contrasting comparison of the entrepreneurial behaviors termed effectuation and causation. Causation is rooted in strategic management and describes a planning and prediction-oriented behavior that is particularly successful in certain and stable environments. On the contrary, effectuation describes entrepreneurial behavior that is preferable in uncertain environments and fosters the creation of new opportunities.

The purpose of this chapter is to examine the body of knowledge of effectuation research and to integrate the findings with SE. By viewing effectuation through the lens of SE, we contribute to the question of how firms can manifest and implement opportunity-seeking behaviors considering the contextual conditions (Mazzei, 2018). In alignment with previous articulations in the SE literature (Mazzei, 2018; Wright & Hitt, 2017), we organize our findings in the categories content, context, inputs, processes, and outcomes. In this way, our review gives insights on contextualized who, what, how, and why questions that relate to opportunity creation.

RELEVANCE OF EFFECTUATION FOR OPPORTUNITY-SEEKING BEHAVIOR IN STRATEGIC ENTREPRENEURSHIP

The effectuation literature focuses on behavioral models describing how entrepreneurs create new business opportunities through the assembly of available resources with a logic of control (Read, Sarasvathy, Dew, & Wiltbank, 2016; Sarasvathy, 2001). Effectuation research shares a great overlap in key themes with SE, which led us to consider effectuation being highly relevant for SE. Table 4.1 provides an overview of the main constructs, key articles, and their findings in effectuation research, which we consider highly relevant for SE research. Our effectuation literature review will point out the multiplicity of contributions in these areas. For the following reasons, we consider the research on the effectuation phenomenon particularly suitable to gain insights into the manifestation of opportunity-seeking behavior.

Multilevel Phenomenon

First, we determine the different origins of both streams. SE has been primarily perceived as an organization-level phenomenon (Simsek et al., 2017) associated with more formal and structured processes in mature, complex organizations (Miller & Le Breton-Miller, 2017). SE can be defined as the simultaneous pursuit of explorative opportunity-seeking and exploitative advantage-seeking behaviors of firms (Ireland, Hitt, & Sirmon, 2003). The focus of the concept was on the organizational level in order to foster construct clarity (Simsek et al., 2017). Nevertheless, phenomena of value creation such as SE demand a multilevel perspective (Lepak, Smith, & Taylor, 2007; Wright & Hitt, 2017), since the involved decision-makers and processes operate across different levels, situations, and multifaceted environments. Therefore, the central question in SE research is how new value can be created for and at the level of individuals, organizations, and other stakeholders such as the society at large (Hitt et al., 2011).

Effectuation was originally conceptualized on the individual level and is particularly relevant in the early start-up phase of new venture creation (Sarasvathy, 2001). Nevertheless, the effectuation literature offers meaningful contributions beyond the individual level at the level of the organization (Dew, Read, Sarasvathy, & Wiltbank, 2008) and the society (Dew & Sarasvathy, 2007). To name some examples, Wiltbank, Dew, Read, and Sarasvathy (2006) offer effectuation as a transformative, control-oriented firm strategy for organizations to face uncertain environments. Brettel, Mauer, Engelen, & Küpper (2012) define characteristics of effectual behavior on the organizational level in the corporate context and show a positive relationship to research and development (R&D) project outcomes in highly innovative contexts. Consequently, effectuation offers valuable contributions to entrepreneurial behavior on the organizational level. Beyond that effectuation as multilevel phenomenon particularly addresses the participation of stakeholders in the entrepreneurial process.

Table 4.1   *Main constructs, key articles, and findings in effectuation*

Constructs	Key articles	Findings
Stakeholder networks	Dew & Sarasvathy (2007) in JBE	Examination of positive benefits and negative externalities of innovation and integration of stakeholder theory and effectuation along elements such as pre-commitments and contractarianism.
	Engel et al. (2017) in JBV	Dynamic processes in entrepreneurial networking based on distinctive elements such as altruism, pre-commitments, serendipity, and co-creation.
	Kerr & Coviello (2019) in IJMR	By the systematic review of effectuation literature the authors "present alternative perspectives on constructs and assumptions surrounding networks in effectuation, integrate network theory into effectuation, and generate important trajectories for future research."
	Kerr & Coviello (2020) in JBV	Development of a "multilevel, multi-theoretical reconceptualization of effectuation that provides for distributed agency and collective cognition of network members."
Uncertainty	Jiang & Tornikoski (2019) in JBV	The authors "take temporality and different types of perceived uncertainty (state, effect, response) (Milliken, 1987) into consideration and map out how the three types of perceived uncertainties and two behavioral logics evolve and develop in a new venture creation context."
	Packard et al. (2017) in Organ. Sci.	Development of "a novel typology of uncertainty that defines and delineates different types of uncertain contexts." Uncertainty transitions and shifts over time through the judgment-based decision-making process of entrepreneurs.
	Townsend et al. (2018) in AMA	"Review the multiple research streams that together constitute the literature on knowledge problems to identify critical boundary conditions of uncertainty as an analytical construct."
Resources	Chiles et al. (2008) in Organ. Stud.	The authors believe there is strong agreement between Lachmannian and effectual approaches to entrepreneurship in the areas of resources and institutions. Furthermore, effectuation may rather be based on Penrosean intersubjectivity.
	Politis et al. (2012) in ISBJ	"Student entrepreneurs have developed a resource logic that favours both effectual reasoning and the use of bootstrapping methods."
	Sarasvathy & Dew (2008b) in Organ. Stud.	The authors clarify conceptual confusion between Lachmann's and Sarasvathy's understanding with respect to: (1) the problem of knowledge (strategies), (2) the problem of resources (players), and (3) the problem of institutions (rules).
	Sarasvathy & Dew (2013) in RAE	Expertise in entrepreneurial decision-making "embodies procedural knowledge that is adaptive in the absence of substantive knowledge, i.e. without judgment." When the authors say effectuators take means as "given" they mean that the entrepreneurs "work with what is readily available and do not necessarily go searching for the 'right' resources for building their venture."

Constructs	Key articles	Findings
Internationalization	Chetty et al. (2015) in EJM	"Entrepreneurs differentiate between foreign market selection and foreign market entry during their internationalization process, potentially using different decision-making processes in them. They tend to interweave effectuation and causation logics as substitutes in their decision-making. Uncertainty during foreign market entry is not always a barrier because it can provide opportunities depending on the logic used."
	Evers et al. (2012) in JIM	"Different stakeholder groups (allied, cooperative, neutral, and entrepreneur) can influence the learning processes (single, double, and triple loop) of the firm and can determine the nature of dynamic marketing capabilities (incremental, renewing, and regenerative) needed to create and sustain international competitive advantage."
	Gabrielsson & Gabrielsson (2013) in IMM	The decision-making logic moderates the impact of opportunities, resources and capabilities, entrepreneurial orientation, and learning on growth phases and survival.
	Galkina & Chetty (2015) in MIR	"The findings show how entrepreneurs network with interested partners, instead of carefully selecting international partners according to predefined network goals. Entrepreneurs who network effectually enter markets wherever an opportunity emerges, and commit to network relations that increase their means."
	Kalinic et al. (2014) in IBR	Entrepreneurs can follow an effectual rather than causal logic when increasing international activities. "Switching from causal to effectual logic allows firms to rapidly increase the level of commitment in the foreign market and could assist in overcoming liabilities of outsidership and, therefore, successfully increase the level of commitment in the foreign market."
	Karami et al. (2020) in SBE	This study systematically reviews the small and medium-sized enterprises internationalization literature covering "the central topics of limited resources, networking, and an unplanned approach, which connect effectuation with extant internationalisation research."
	Nummela et al. (2014) in MIR	"The decision-making of born global firms seems to be characterised by alternating periods of causation- and effectuation-based logics. Triggers for amending the logic include, for example, change of key persons and the search for external funding. Co-existence of the two decision-making logics is possible, due to different degrees of uncertainty in market and technology or multiple decision-makers involved."
	Prashantham et al. (2019) in ISBJ	"An effectual approach to network-building is positively associated with initial entry speed and international scope speed, but negatively associated with international commitment speed, while a causal approach is negatively associated with initial entry speed and international scope speed, but positively associated with international commitment speed."
	Sarasvathy et al. (2014) in ET&P	"An effectual approach can help to resolve four central conflicts and knowledge gaps identified in two recent comprehensive reviews of IE." Furthermore, the authors integrate the Uppsala model with effectuation theory and provide a future research agenda.

Constructs	Key articles	Findings
Expertise	Dew et al. (2009) in JBV	Entrepreneurial experts frame decisions using an effectual logic, whereas novices use a predictive frame and tend to "go by the textbook." These differences result from domain-specific differences in general and entrepreneurial expertise.
	Dew et al. (2015) in JBVI	Entrepreneurial expertise yields significant decision-making improvements in the situational use of control strategies, which are conceptually associated with uncertain new ventures, products, and markets.
	Engel et al. (2014) in JBVI	"The results provide support for the conclusion that novices higher on ESE, compared with a control group and with the low ESE group, used effectual logic to a larger extent, and that this was as a consequence of them framing an uncertain situation as an opportunity."
	Ranabahu & Barrett (2019) in SBE	"Both effectual and causal logics (but not effectuation alone) facilitate deliberate practice." Furthermore, "one effectuation principle—acknowledging and leveraging the unexpected—impacted all five elements of deliberate practice, suggesting that learning to manage uncertainty is a central task—perhaps the central task—in becoming an entrepreneur."
Venture performance	Cai et al. (2017) in JSBM	Effectuation has a positive effect on new venture performance in transitional economies. Exploratory learning has a fully mediating role in the relationship between effectuation and new venture performance.
	Deligianni et al. (2015) in ET&P	Effectuation moderates the diversification–performance relationship, such that diversified new ventures using the effectuation processes of experimentation, flexibility, and pre-commitments perform better than others.
	Laskovaia et al. (2017) in SBE	Both venture cognitive logics effectuation and causation "have positive effects on new venture performance and serve as mediators in the culture–performance relationship."
	Read et al. (2009) in JBV	This meta-analysis supports that the effectuation principles of means, contingency, and partnership positively and significantly relate to new venture performance.
	Smolka et al. (2018) in ET&P	Causation and effectuation both have positive main effects on venture performance. The "combined use further enhances positive venture outcomes. In particular, entrepreneurs who experiment with available means while also engaging in planning activities tend to realize significantly better venture performance."
Innovation	Berends et al. (2014) in JPIM	The canon of best practices in product innovation needs to differentiate between large firms and small firms. Small firms' product innovation processes follow effectuation logic, especially during the earlier development phases, in combination with causation logic, especially in later stages.
	Brettel et al. (2012) in JBV	Effectual dimensions such as affordable loss, preference for partnerships, and acknowledging the unexpected are inclined to be positively related to research and development performance when innovativeness is high. The causal dimensions goal-driven projects, expected returns, and overcoming the unexpected, in contrast, show to be performance drivers in research and development projects with low innovativeness.

Constructs	Key articles	Findings
Innovation	Coviello & Joseph (2012) in JOMar	Deconstruction of the concept of customer participation into ten distinct customer roles, each of which is linked to a new product development activity. Summarization of these roles and activities in an empirically derived taxonomy to enhance the understanding of how and when customers contribute to new product development.
	Futterer et al. (2018) in LRP	"Both behaviors lead to BMI [business model innovation] in situations of moderate industry growth while effectuation (causation) is more effective in high (low) industry growth settings. Furthermore, the results point out that BMI in turn enhances corporate venture performance."
	Reymen et al. (2017) in R&DM	In business model development, effectual decision-making logic is used dominantly to generate a viable value proposition for a specific customer segment. Causal logic is then used dominantly to define the other business model components in relation to the value proposition and customer segment. When a shortage of resources emerges, causal logic is replaced by an increase in effectual decision-making again.
	Sitoh & Yu (2014) in IEEE TEM	Identification of four decision-making configurations with unique modes of interplay between business models and tactics: (1) effectuation centric, (2) discovery centric, (3) causation centric, and (4) tactic centric. Effectuation and causation processes can co-exist and the configurations differ at the various phases of new product creation.
	Szambelan et al. (2020) in EMJ	"Effectual contingency and effectual means orientation are negatively associated with market-based innovation barriers, which are in turn negatively associated with a firm's innovation performance."
	Velu & Jacob (2016) in R&DM	"The presence of entrepreneurs as owner-managers positively influences the degree of innovation: this relation is stronger in less competitive environments but is weaker (and may even reverse) in highly competitive environments."
Marketing	Cui et al. (2019) in IMM	"Decision makers adjust their decision making logics depending on the stage of the servitization process and associated risk patterns. As the servitization process evolves into a more sophisticated stage, decision makers will change their decision making logics from a causation dominant logic to an effectuation dominant logic in order to cope with the increased risks."
	Lam & Harker (2015) in ISBJ	Effectual entrepreneurship "is neither ends-driven nor means-driven, but is a consequence of interplay between actors and social context through ongoing enactment." The means such as social networks, resources, capital, or opportunities emerge from the interaction of entrepreneurs with their customers in marketing activities.

Constructs	Key articles	Findings
Marketing	Mort et al. (2012) in EJM	Identification of "the four key strategies of entrepreneurial marketing as comprising opportunity creation, customer intimacy-based innovative products, resource enhancement and importantly, legitimacy. These core strategies of EM [entrepreneurial marketing] are identified by mapping to enhanced performance."
	Parida et al. (2016) in JBR	Subjective interpretations influence strategic decision-making. Perceived gains in the environment strengthen the positive relationship between effectuation and initial venture sales. Greater likelihood of initial sales is related to causation (albeit at low to medium levels) and to a greater perception of control.
	Read & Sarasvathy (2012) in MT	The independent streams of research, effectuation, and service-dominant logic build on co-creation as the common theoretical ground. Provision of ten specific research questions to advance the co-creation perspective.
Social value	Akemu et al. (2016) in JMS	Effectual entrepreneurial agency is co-constituted by distributed agency, the proactive conferral of material resources, and legitimacy to an eventual entrepreneur by heterogeneous actors.
	Corner & Ho (2010) in ET&P	Identification of four patterns across actors who see a social need and prospect ideas that could address social value creation. The patterns involve interaction of multiple actors: (1) Opportunity development, (2) collective action, (3) experience corridors, and (4) spark.
	Johannisson (2018) in E&RD	Identified core process practices in social enterprises that are similar to effectuation. Instead of profit-making, the "necessity effectuation" logic orients towards supporting people with social needs.
	Newbert (2012) in JPP&M	Social entrepreneurs are less likely than commercial entrepreneurs to implement several best marketing practices, such as considering market data critical to the start-up effort and changes to the market and product.
	Servantie & Rispal (2018) in E&RD	Social entrepreneurs combine effectuation, causation, and bricolage, which overlap and can occur both sequentially and concurrently. The combination changes over a particular venture's life cycle depending on the context of action, the members of the entrepreneurial team, and the stakeholders.
	York et al. (2016) in JMS	The "findings suggest that environmental entrepreneurs: (1) are motivated by identities based in both commercial and ecological logics, (2) prioritize commercial and/or ecological venture goals dependent on the strength and priority of coupling between these two identity types, (3) and approach stakeholders in a broadly inclusive, exclusive, or co-created manner based on identity coupling and goals."

Note: AMA: *Academy of Management Annals*; E&RD: *Entrepreneurship & Regional Development*; EJM: *European Journal of Marketing*; EMJ: *European Management Journal*; ET&P: *Entrepreneurship: Theory and Practice*; IBR: *International Business Review*; IEEE TEM: *IEEE Transactions on Engineering Management*; IJMR: *International Journal of Management Reviews*; IMM: *Industrial Marketing Management*; ISBJ: *International Small Business Journal*; JBE: *Journal of Business Ethics*; JBR: *Journal of Business Research*; JBV: *Journal of Business Venturing*; JBVI: *Journal of Business Venturing Insights*; JIM: *Journal of International Marketing*; JMS: *Journal of Management Studies*; JOMar: *Journal of Marketing*; JPIM: *Journal of Product Innovation Management*; JPP&M: *Journal of Public Policy & Marketing*; JSBN: *Journal of Small Business Management*; LRP: *Long Range Planning*; MIR: *Management International Review*; MT: *Marketing Theory*; Organ. Sci.: *Organization Science*; Organ. Stud.: *Organization Studies*; R&DM: *R&D Management*; RAE: *Review of Austrian Economics*; SBE: *Small Business Economics*

Social Interaction

Second, both research streams effectuation and SE increasingly take the perspective that the associated phenomena occur in a social world. That means the world is constantly changing and is in an in-the-making process, which bases social on interactions (Agarwal, Dushnitsky, Lumpkin, Wright, & Zott, 2017; Mazzei, 2018; Read et al., 2016; Reuber, Fischer, & Coviello, 2016). This view shifts the focus of the investigations from "who interacts" to a broader spectrum of how, when, why, and where the interactions in forms of processes, events, and structures occur across several levels of analysis (Schindehutte & Morris, 2009). Effectuation addresses the pragmatic applicability of entrepreneurship for the "real world" by recognizing the importance of social construction processes. More precisely, effectual entrepreneurship describes processes, which result in opportunity creation through actions, decisions, and behaviors with a focus on resource use. Resource-related human behavior and decision-making under uncertainty are essential parts in the multiplicity of management disciplines. Therefore, effectuation has already been recognized to hold great potential to inform other research streams (Packard, Clark, & Klein, 2017; Reuber et al., 2016). Accordingly, the insights from studying effectuation helps to draw conclusions for intrinsically dynamic, complex, and uncertain social phenomena such as value creation in SE (Garud & Gehman, 2016).

Strategic Behavior

Third, opportunity-seeking behavior in SE is strategic behavior. Therefore, effectuation needs to qualify as a strategic behavior to create value in order to proceed with integrating the findings from the effectuation literature. Behavior can be considered strategic, if it helps to identify the most appropriate opportunity to exploit, the actions are characterized by intents, and include a high level of commitment (Simsek et al., 2017). Experimentation and flexibility build the foundation for effectuation. Both target at identifying the most appropriate opportunity. Furthermore, effectual entrepreneurs consider all available means with the intent to create new means–end relationships. While committing their own means entrepreneurs even go further and deliberately seek to collect pre-commitments from other stakeholders. These exemplary activities in effectual behavior follow a logic with an observable consistency and clearly differentiate from the absence of strategy or a non-strategic approach (Hauser, Eggers, & Güldenberg, 2019).

Contextual Perspective

Finally, firms today face dynamic business environments characterized by uncertainty, complexity, ambiguity, and volatility (Sirmon et al., 2007). Ongoing change and flux are inherent in the real world and have been neglected in SE research in their pluralistic, complex scope. The major challenges for SE lie in exploring the influence of the dynamics of context (Paek & Lee, 2018; Schindehutte & Morris, 2009;

Wright & Hitt, 2017) and its impact on the appropriate use of opportunity-seeking and advantage-seeking behavior (Mazzei, 2018; Uotila, Maula, Keil, & Zahra, 2009). Schindehutte and Morris (2009) referred to effectuation as a promising concept to describe the concrete manifestation of opportunity-seeking behavior that explicitly considers the context. Similarly, Hitt et al. (2011) acknowledged the importance of effectuation as an entrepreneurial approach that incorporates the ability of entrepreneurs to operate under conditions of uncertainty. For these reasons, we see effectuation particularly suitable to inform the understanding of entrepreneurial intentions, decision-making processes, cognition, and capabilities across multiple levels of analysis in SE.

METHOD

We perform an extensive literature review of effectuation following Tranfield, Denyer, and Smart (2003) and Denyer, Tranfield, and Van Aken (2008). Their methodological guidelines postulate transparency, clarity, focus, reliability, alignment of research and practitioner interests, and synthesis, which allow for replicability. We evaluate this as particularly suited to perform an extensive literature review and identify integration potentials while limiting bias (Cook, Mulrow, & Haynes, 1997; Mulrow, 1994). We use the search term "effectuation" in titles, abstracts, and keywords and cover the period from the origin of the concept in 2001 (Sarasvathy, 2001) up to April 2020. We conduct the search in the three search engines EBSCO, Scopus, and ScienceDirect. We include only articles in the English language, published in peer-reviewed journals, and listed in the subject areas business, economics, psychology, and social sciences. Furthermore, we set the search boundary to academic journals listed in the ranking of the Association of Business Schools (2018, charteredabs. org) with a minimum score of 3 to ensure quality (see Table 4.2 for included articles by journals).

After reviewing abstracts, we first excluded eight articles. Afterwards we read all papers and then excluded three additional articles. All these did not refer to effectuation as entrepreneurial behavior or merely mentioned it as an interesting research concept without further investigation. The cross-reference search led to inclusion of further relevant articles. As shown in Figure 4.1, the final scope for the synthesis contains 126 articles.

To synthesize the paper evidence base, we employ an inductive procedure of iteratively reading, coding, and regrouping the reviewed articles (Hsieh & Shannon, 2005). We apply the constant comparison technique by analyzing the individual articles in relation to one another in an effort to identify important concepts, themes, and variations within the articles (Glaser & Strauss, 1967). This technique (Strauss & Corbin, 1990) provides us with an analytical tool to systematically analyze the evidence base of effectuation. In the iterative reading and coding process, we develop first-order codes, which we then further cluster in second-order themes. Scholars organize the knowledge about SE in an input-process-output model (Hitt et al.,

Table 4.2   Scope of the literature review by academic journals

Domain	Journal	# of articles	Association of Business Schools rank
Entrepreneurship and small business management	*Journal of Business Venturing*	12	4
	Entrepreneurship Theory and Practice	12	4
	Strategic Entrepreneurship Journal	7	4
	Small Business Economics	17	3
	Entrepreneurship and Regional Development	11	3
	International Small Business Journal	8	3
	Journal of Small Business Management	1	3
General management, ethics, social responsibilities, and strategy	*Academy of Management Review*	7	4+
	Strategic Management Journal	1	4+
	Journal of Management Studies	2	4
	British Journal of Management	1	4
	Journal of Business Research	7	3
	Long Range Planning	2	3
	Journal of Business Ethics	1	3
Marketing	*Journal of Marketing*	2	4+
	Industrial Marketing Management	6	3
	European Journal of Marketing	2	3
	Journal of International Marketing	1	3
	Journal of Public Policy and Marketing	1	3
	Marketing Theory	1	3
Other disciplines	*Organization Studies*	4	4
	Journal of Product Innovation Management	1	4
	Technological Forecasting and Social Change	3	3
	International Business Reviews	3	3
	R&D Management	2	3
	Management International Review	2	3
	Technovation	1	3
	IEEE Transactions on Engineering Management	1	3
	Journal of Economic Behavior and Organization	1	3
	Journal of Institutional Economics	1	3
	Information Technology and People	1	3
	Journal of Development Studies	1	3
	Management Learning	1	3
	Journal of International Management	1	3
	American Review of Public Administration	1	3
Total		126	

2011; Tavassoli, Bengtsson, & Karlsson, 2017), which has recently been extended to include the categories of content and context (Mazzei, 2018). Schindehutte and Morris (2009) for example point out the fundamental role of the context for SE and its influences on the other model categories. Therefore, we use the extended multilevel SE model from Wright and Hitt (2017) to reflect the findings of effectuation as illustrated in Figure 4.2.

For each category, we explicate prominent research contributions, key constructs, and processes, and propose key questions for future research avenues. The first category (content) specifies the nature and relevance of effectuation and describes its constituting principles. Furthermore, we explicate the multilevel character of the phenomenon. This helps to get a clear understanding of the phenomenon and what potential it offers to SE. Second, we elaborate on the role of the context by linking the success of effectuation with the uncertain condition in the organization's internal and external environment. Third, we examine the input factors serving as antecedents of effectuation, including means or resources, experience, cognition, and identity. Next, we address the actions and processes of effectuation on the levels of the individual, the firm, and the stakeholders. Thereby we mainly focus on the orchestration of resources, goals, and entrepreneurial principles. Finally, we examine outcomes of effectuation, which include opportunities, innovation, and more specifically business model innovation, growth, and creation of value for the organization and the society. By the category inputs and outputs, we explicate relationships with other related concepts within the nomological network.

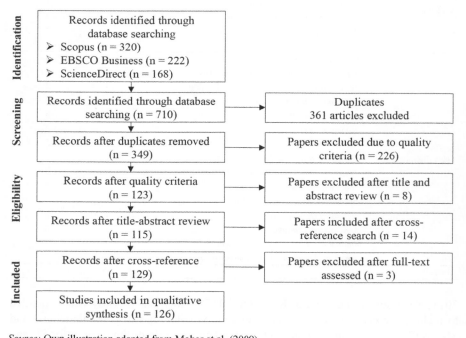

Source: Own illustration adapted from Moher et al. (2009).

Figure 4.1   *Systematic search of the relevant literature*

CONTENT

Mazzei, Ketchen, and Shook (2017) advocate investigating SE from different theoretical perspectives to gain additional practical and conceptual insights into the phenomenon and its interrelationships. We see the emerging theory of effectuation as a highly relevant perspective for informing SE. Both the entrepreneurial behavior of effectuation and the opportunity-seeking behavior of SE occur at multiple levels involving single entities such as individuals and companies and multiple entities such as teams, stakeholder groups, and networks. The actions, behaviors, and capabilities at any level can affect the extent and type of variables at another given level.

Individual Level

In the context of new venture creation, Sarasvathy (2001) investigated the decision-making of experienced entrepreneurs, which differed from prevailing practices. Sarasvathy termed the predominant planning-oriented entrepreneurial behavior

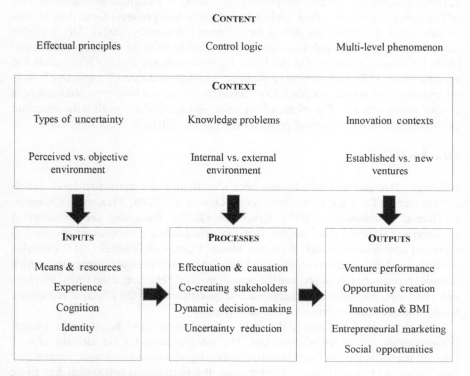

CONTENT		
Effectual principles	Control logic	Multi-level phenomenon

CONTEXT		
Types of uncertainty	Knowledge problems	Innovation contexts
Perceived vs. objective environment	Internal vs. external environment	Established vs. new ventures

INPUTS	PROCESSES	OUTPUTS
Means & resources	Effectuation & causation	Venture performance
Experience	Co-creating stakeholders	Opportunity creation
Cognition	Dynamic decision-making	Innovation & BMI
Identity	Uncertainty reduction	Entrepreneurial marketing
		Social opportunities

Source: Own illustration adapted from Wright (2017).

Figure 4.2   Effectuation findings in the strategic entrepreneurship framework

Table 4.3   Principles of effectuation

Principle	Meaning
Means	Entrepreneurs start with their available means such as who they are, what they know, and whom they know.
Affordable loss	Entrepreneurs limit their risks and downsides by considering what they can afford to lose.
Contingencies	Entrepreneurs see contingencies as positive surprises or potentials to leverage.
Partnerships	Entrepreneurs seek partnerships with self-selecting stakeholders to engage in co-creation.
Control	Entrepreneurs focus on activities within their control.

Source: Sarasvathy (2009).

causation. Causation relies on the predictable aspects of the future. By this view, the market is assumed to exist independently of the entrepreneurial individual, the firm, and the stakeholders. The entrepreneurial task then consists in accurately predicting the future opportunity and gaining as much market share as possible, e.g. through a business plan.

On the other hand, Sarasvathy (2001) termed the identified, opposing decision-making logic of the entrepreneurs effectuation. Effectuation consists of a set of five concrete principles (see Table 4.3). Effectual entrepreneurs focus their actions on issues that they think are within their control (Sarasvathy, 2001). The available resources, means, and capabilities serve as the starting point for decision-making and guide the courses of action. On this basis, the entrepreneurs develop future ends and specific goals. Effectuation aims to shape the environment through proactive behavior and thus does not require predictions about the future and long-term consequences of one's own actions. Therefore, effectuation fits particularly well with uncertain environments, in which correct predictions would be difficult, if not impossible.

Firm Level

Although effectuation originally has been identified at the individual level, scholars transferred the logic to the firm level (Dew et al., 2008; McKelvie, Chandler, DeTienne, & Johansson, 2019). Randerson (2016), discussing the construct of entrepreneurial orientation, argues that the effectuation principles in themselves represent firm-level behavior. Werhahn, Mauer, Flatten, and Brettel (2015) extended the firm-level effectuation construct and defined it as the strategic orientation, which includes the mindset to emphasize the entrepreneurial behavior of the firms' employees. Hereafter, we address the adoption and specification of the effectual principles, taking into account the firm-specific conditions.

First, firms need to identify the truly relevant means and acquire new means, if the relevant means are non-existent. The starting point for the identification of relevant means is the intersection between existing resource equipment, employees' capabilities, and firm strategy. Furthermore, the partnership orientation has to be implemented throughout the organization in order to promote serendipities. This does not only mean that the top management team has to anchor aspects of partnership in the strategy, but also to strive responsibly for understanding at the levels of the middle management and employees. In addition, firms need to develop the mindset to promote contingencies and convert them into serendipities. For example, contingencies can arise as a result of the interaction and negotiation process with stakeholders. From an effectuation perspective, the opportunity creation process unfolds as emergent, evolutionary, and contingent rather than linear and pre-planned. This clearly advocates the benefits of embedding flexibility throughout the organization (Chandler, DeTienne, McKelvie, & Mumford, 2011). Finally, effectuation research developed a good understanding of affordable loss in terms of economic loss. The decision-makers choose actions by committing in advance to what they are willing to lose through affordable experiments and thus design intelligent failures to learn over time (Arend, Sarooghi, & Burkemper, 2015). Such an approach helps to avoid overspending, to keep control over risk and costs, and, therefore, to minimize the likelihood of failure. In addition to physical resources, the affordable loss can also relate to intangible resources of investments, for example, the time affordability in social interaction (Fischer & Reuber, 2011). Furthermore, research started to adopt a more holistic perspective including economic, social, and ecological dimensions of loss. For example, firms should consider loss in reputation and trust in the brand as critical factors when making decisions.

Multiple Entities

Although research preferably models decisions of single entities, natural decision-making in new ventures or firms involves multiple entities. Effectual logic includes the core principle of constantly being open for partnerships with self-selecting stakeholders. The entrepreneur allows for stakeholders to buy into the emergent venture idea and to drive the design of new goals in a co-creating process. The goals evolve and the original business idea constantly adjusts with new stakeholder inputs. Effectuation offers a dynamic process model of effectual networking that challenges assumptions from networking literature (Engel, Kaandorp, & Elfring, 2017; Kerr & Coviello, 2019). Under conditions of uncertainty and goal ambiguity, entrepreneurs do not act exclusively as heroic, goal-oriented network architects who seek, plan, and pursue targeted relationships to stakeholders. Additionally, the networking process alternates between elements such as altruism, pre-commitments, serendipities, and co-creation. Pre-commitments of stakeholders as an essential element does not only provide resources but also stakeholders' engagement in negotiation with other stakeholders to determine roles and relationships in the growing network (Dew & Sarasvathy, 2007). Stakeholders contribute physical resources, advice, new information, and legitimacy to the new venture. Thus, building new partnerships shares risks, reduces uncertainty, and restricts or facilitates entrepreneurial agency (Akemu, Whiteman, & Kennedy, 2016). As the participating stakeholders of this ongoing process are ex-ante unknown, the exact shape of the future outcome is not foreseeable.

Main internal stakeholders include the chief executive officer, co-founders, board members, the middle management, and investors, all of whom may significantly participate in the venture's decision-making processes. In addition, the research highlights the role and relationships of family members of the key decision-makers. The family members influence the behavior of the founders of new ventures by contributing valuable resources such as experience and tacit knowledge across generations (Jones & Li, 2017). Furthermore, external stakeholders such as potential customers and suppliers may actively engage in the value creation by pre-commitments instead of being reactive. Finally, engaging in a community of people who support the entrepreneur with feedback and testing the offer has a significant impact on venture emergence and growth (Fisher, 2012).

CONTEXT

The literature emphasizes the fundamental importance of context in entrepreneurship and the need for a more contextualized view of entrepreneurial phenomena (Welter, 2011). Following Wright and Hitt (2017), we consider the context as a superordinate category that, in addition to its function as an input factor, strongly influences orchestration processes and outcomes. In SE, highly relevant contextual factors include, for example, organizational form, institutional and cultural environment, ownership and governance, technological change, product market fragmentation, and product market emergence (Mazzei, 2018; Wright & Hitt, 2017). The changes arising from dynamic, complex environments strongly influence value creation and thus require firms to adapt their behaviors.

Uncertainty

The basic concept commonly linked to dynamic environments is uncertainty. Uncertainty is the boundary condition of entrepreneurship in general and of effectuation in particular. Effectuation offers a mechanism to transition uncertainty by closing the sets of potential options (i.e. given means) before dealing with the open set of future outcomes. By effectuation entrepreneurs generate new goals and new environments based on their subjective interpretations. Adhering to the control principle leads to reduced perceived uncertainty (Kuechle, Boulu-Reshef, & Carr, 2016). Overall, effectuation represents a behavior that is suitable to face uncertain environments whereas causation is particularly useful in stable environments. Uncertainty is a complex, multidimensional construct that has been conceptualized in various forms (Knight, 1921; Milliken, 1987). Therefore, the type and characteristics of uncertainty differ fundamentally across studies in effectuation.

Sources

The effectuation literature identifies internal and external sources from which uncertainty may arise. The lack of information on internal developments comprises a source of uncertainty. For example, new ventures are rather small and young while in the process of seeking growth and stability. The lack of resources and changing roles within the venture team constitute factors for changing conditions of the venture. In the corporate context, a similar effect arises if the staffing of project teams or the number of included decision-makers is obscure. In the home-based online business environment, entrepreneurs associate uncertainty with their own capabilities and reference to a perceived lack of knowledge and experience (Daniel, Domenico, & Sharma, 2015).

On the other hand, technology- and market-related uncertainty act as significant external drivers for innovativeness in R&D projects (Brettel et al., 2012). Firms face technological uncertainty in the form of disruptiveness or radicalness of new offerings, which strongly depend on the hitherto unknown acceptance of customers. In addition, firms face market uncertainty resulting from changes in customer behavior, competition, or regulation in either new or existing markets. In this sense, the process of internationalization is intrinsically characterized by uncertainty. Industry growth comprises another driver for environmental uncertainty (Futterer, Schmidt, & Heidenreich, 2018). In accordance, Cai, Guo, Fei, & Liu (2017) find that transitional economies exhibit higher environmental uncertainty than mature economies due to the emerging state of the market and undeveloped system of institutions. Finally, the complex coordination of cross-country international research teams holds uncertainty due to the unpredictable and dynamic nature of different environments and thus encourages the use of effectuation (Chetty, Partanen, Rasmussen, & Servais, 2014).

Specific Contexts

Scholars studied effectuation beyond the initial context of new ventures in other types of organizations such as corporates, family firms, or social enterprises. The research primarily involves future-oriented innovative settings such as new product development (NPD) (Berends, Jelinek, Reymen, & Stultiëns, 2014; Coviello & Joseph, 2012), R&D (Brettel et al., 2012), product diversification (Deligianni, Voudouris, & Lioukas, 2015), and business model innovation (Chesbrough, 2010; Sitoh, Pan, & Yu, 2014; Velu & Jacob, 2016). For example, small firms differ from mainstream best practices in NPD due to the need for flexibility, resource constraints, and short-term development (Berends et al., 2014). Small firms leverage their resources and creatively overcome limitations in innovation potential compared to large firms. Furthermore, customer participation and the development of marketing capabilities, effectual in nature, are the key to the creation of successful major innovations in NPD processes (Coviello & Joseph, 2012). Family businesses comprise another context, in which effectuation successfully occurs. Effectuation expands the array of perceived opportunities arising from economic and non-economic objectives (Jones & Li, 2017; Miller, Steier, & Le Breton-Miller, 2016). Finally, effectuation relates positively to R&D output and efficiency in highly innovative contexts. Contrary to existing R&D literature, Brettel et al. (2012) emphasize human action within the organization to deal with uncertainty.

Prospects

The term "uncertainty" is not easy to grasp and very heterogeneous (Townsend, Hunt, McMullen, & Sarasvathy, 2018). The exact characteristics of the uncertainty construct remain underspecified in effectuation research. The work of Jiang and Tornikoski (2019) indicates that the constituting subdimensions of the uncertainty construct might have different impacts on the behaviors and interact with them. Furthermore, even though the differentiation between objective and perceived uncertainty is theoretically recognized and discussed, empirical examinations miss the distinction of real changes in the level of uncertainty compared to changes in the entrepreneur's perception.

Internationalization remains a major challenge of firms and thus is of high relevance in SE research. Comparisons between different culture and industry contexts, as well as between transitional economies and mature economies, provide deep insights into effectual behavior and its outcomes. To date, such research studies are scarce. Furthermore, we see a lack of specificity of the context. For example, a business-to-consumer context might represent a quite different setting than a business-to-business context. In accordance, recent research addresses the context of servitization investigating effectuation and causation as mechanisms to manage strategic, organizational, and operational risks (Cui, Su, Feng, & Hertz, 2019). In addition, the consideration of situational and temporal context is important to draw meaningful conclusions for companies in practice. Examples comprise the existence of time pressure or of economic crisis.

Lastly, the firms' environment is not only characterized by uncertainty, but other dynamics such as complexity, ambiguity, and volatility. Townsend et al. (2018) make an effort to distinguish the different facets of knowledge problems. These facets, which have been generally described as "uncertainty" in the literature, encompass ambiguity, complexity, equivocality, and uncertainty. While effectuation comprises a potent behavior to successfully create new opportunities under uncertainty, the research stream lacks attention in other dynamic environments.

INPUTS

The SE literature classifies inputs into environmental factors (e.g. munificence, dynamism, and interconnectedness), organizational resources (e.g. culture and top leadership), and individual resources (e.g. financial, social, and human capital) (Hitt et al., 2011). The entrepreneurial firm creatively recombines and develops these inputs in order to explore new paths to value creation. The individuals within an organization are the main source of entrepreneurial opportunities (Covin & Slevin, 2002). Accordingly, scholars investigated the important role of entrepreneurial leaders and their knowledge, motivation, abilities, and skills in the development of an entrepreneurial culture and mindset both at the level of the individual and the organization (e.g. Tavassoli et al., 2017). Similarly, one core principle of effectuation is the focus on available means by the individual entrepreneur. The value and use of means are closely linked to the subjective imagination of the entrepreneur.

Relevance of Characteristics

Effectuation draws on Penrose (1959), who highlights the concept of versatility and use of resources (Sarasvathy & Dew, 2005, 2008a). Versatility describes the range of potential services that resources offer. The entrepreneurial individual or firm continuously recombines resources in novel ways to find more productive applications or services. This process necessitates imaginative capabilities, which are highly dependent on subjective perceptions and characteristics of the decision-makers. Sarasvathy (2001) refers to characteristics of the entrepreneurs in terms of *who they are*, *what they know*, and *whom they know* as the primary set of means. *Who they are* includes their identity, more specifically their own traits, tastes, and abilities. *What they know* includes the knowledge corridors they are in. *Whom they know* includes their social network. On the organizational level, information and physical, human, and financial resources may comprise means. On the level of the economy, demographics, current technology regimes, and sociopolitical institutions (such as property rights) comprise potential means. Overall, those resources, characteristics, and capabilities with the potential to drive value and opportunity creation constitute effectual means.

We identified three clusters of antecedents to effectual behavior. Our classification into experience, cognition, and identity is intended to serve as the frame for developing the effectuation mindset within individuals and firms. On the basis of these characteristics, firms can compile entrepreneurial teams that are more likely to use effectuation successfully. Beyond the following insights, individuals and their behavior must always be seen in the broader social context with its strong influences, for example through the organizational culture or the values in the individual's community or country.

Experience

Entrepreneurs with more start-up experience tend to favor an effectual resource acquisition orientation (Politis, Winborg, & Dahlstrand, 2012). Similarly, student entrepreneurs have a higher preference for using effectual resource logic compared to non-student entrepreneurs. In contrast, decision-makers with general business experience are able to adopt causation-based logics faster than inexperienced managers (Nummela, Saarenketo, Jokela, & Loane, 2014). Furthermore, decision-makers have to evaluate the appropriateness to use effectuation in the specific decision.

Entrepreneurial expertise significantly improves situational decision-making capabilities and thus acts as a catalyst for effectuation (Dew, Read, Sarasvathy, & Wiltbank, 2015). In the angel investor context, emphasis on the use of non-predictive control strategies is associated with a reduction in investment failures without a reduction in the number of successes (Wiltbank, Read, Dew, & Sarasvathy, 2009).

Cognition

In addition, cognition based on knowledge, past experiences, abilities, and capabilities determines the entrepreneur's behavior (Chiles, Gupta, & Bluedorn, 2008). Individuals with high entrepreneurial self-efficacy are more likely to frame an uncertain environment as an opportunity, which aligns with effectuation (Engel, Dimitrova, Khapova, & Elfring, 2014). Even though tending towards predictive logics, novice entrepreneurs may apply effectuation solely as a consequence of feeling more confident about their entrepreneurial abilities. This supports the view that effectuation is more a part of general human reasoning than a pure expert logic. Furthermore, the perceived venture conditions influence the choice of effectual (decrease in venture's resource position, increase in perceived uncertainty) or causal (increase of stakeholder pressure) behavior (Reymen et al., 2015). In addition, personal preferences, professional career beliefs, sets of values, and sociocultural backgrounds have high impacts on the entrepreneurs' cognitive processes. For example, socially supportive cultures rely more on effectuation as dominant cognitive logic among young entrepreneurs, as opposed to causation in performance-based cultures (Laskovaia, Shirokova, & Morris, 2017).

Identity

Finally, identity constitutes a cognitive frame for interpreting experiences and behavior options. Both the competitive and success-oriented attitude (Darwinian identity) and the non-profit-oriented attitude (Missionary identity) connect to a higher likelihood to engage in causal behavior (Alsos, Clausen, Hytti, & Solvoll, 2016). In contrast, the community-oriented attitude (Communitarian identity) is connected with effectual behavior. Furthermore, linear (hierarchy orientation) and expert (occupation orientation) career motives have a strong association with a higher preference for causation. In contrast, spiral (occasional job variation) or transitory (consistent job variation) career motives are affiliated with a higher preference for effectuation (Gabrielsson & Politis, 2011). Social identity coupling as the combination of formulating venture goals and incentivizing stakeholders forms the basis for social and environmental entrepreneurship (Akemu et al., 2016; York, O'Neil, & Sarasvathy, 2016).

At this point we want to take a critical look at implicit assumptions of effectuation and hardly treated issues. With regard to the strategic development of entrepreneurial behaviors and cultures, research does not clearly show which facets of effectuation can be learned or are born. Entrepreneurship research tries to connect personality traits with entrepreneurial behavior. The proponents of effectuation emphasize the pragmatic roots and applicability of effectuation as behavior. Recent research links effectuation and causation to the concept of deliberate practice and learning to manage uncertainty (Ranabahu & Barrett, 2019). Furthermore, there is the fundamental question of who in an organization needs to apply effectuation to achieve best performance. Is it all about the top management team, specific departments, or a company-wide culture? Maybe not all employees have to be able to apply effectuation. In light of diversity literature, a team may consist of people with different behavioral approaches. Our presumption would be that all team members need some basic understanding of effectuation, but heterogeneous mindsets could lead to more creative results.

PROCESSES

At the heart of SE are the processes of resource orchestration that enable value creation based on the inputs. Resource orchestration includes actions that "leaders take to facilitate efforts to effectively manage the firm's resources" (Hitt et al., 2011, p. 64). These actions build the basis of the firm's capabilities to structure the resource portfolio, bundle resources, and provide value to customers (Sirmon et al., 2007). While SE literature has developed a profound theoretical understanding of types of capabilities, inarticulacy exists on "exactly how it manifests within organizations" and "in what contexts it is most effective" (Mazzei, 2018, p. 658). Our insights provide guidance on how to translate opportunity-seeking behavior in sequential actions and processes.

Effectuation Process

Scholars attribute pragmatic and process theoretic roots to effectuation (Garud & Gehman, 2016; Steyaert, 2007; Watson, 2013). In the process perspective, the focus is on the emergence and unfolding of the phenomenon, i.e. the temporal ordering and sequential interactions of events and activities (Mohr, 1982). The effectuation process describes the successive application of the principles.

When deciding to engage in the process, entrepreneurs start by assessing their means (see Figure 4.3). Based on the means (1), entrepreneurs begin determining the courses of action depending on what they can afford to lose (2). At the heart of the process are interaction and negotiation with potential stakeholders (3), which might result in further contingencies and pre-commitments (4). In effectuation, stakeholders self-select to participate in the process. Through commitments and contributions, they increase the means (5) while at the same time they determine the manifestation of new goals (6). The focal results, such as effects or artifacts, new information about recently realized gains and losses, market conditions, and mutual needs change the means and goals and thus feed back into the continuous process for the next decision cycle. Effectuation recognizes and interprets exogenous unexpected contingencies in a beneficial way, which means that these contribute to the means and the possible courses of action (7). The effectual process is actor-centric and depends on quantity, timing, and yet unknown self-selecting stakeholders and their types of pre-commitments (Read et al., 2016; Sarasvathy, Kumar, York, & Bhagavatula, 2014). Consequently, the manifestation of the final outcome such as new opportunities (8) is inherently uncertain at the beginning.

At the organizational level, the implementation of effectuation processes comprises a major challenge, as we need to consider existing structures, routines, and habits of employees. Furthermore, the process involves multiple organizational actors as well as external stakeholders. Therefore, the firm needs to develop capabilities to integrate stakeholders as an actively engaging entity in the process. So far, we have few insights on whether effectuation can be implemented more effectively in a top-down or bottom-up approach. Entrepreneurial leaders who anticipate, envision, maintain flexibility, and empower others to create strategic change are essential to institutionalize the entrepreneurial dominant logic of effectuation in particular (Covin & Slevin, 2002).

Dynamic Capabilities

Against the backdrop of dynamic environments and the process nature of change (Schindehutte & Morris, 2009), the entrepreneurial leaders' task is to question the dominant logic, i.e. to challenge the appropriateness of effectuation. This facilitates the development of entrepreneurial capabilities to shift and adapt the firm's behavior dependent on the specific context and situation.

Although Sarasvathy (2001) conceptualized effectuation and causation as opposing logics, she acknowledges that the actual processes may exhibit a sequential use or a combination of both. In general, new businesses tend to effectual approaches in the start and development phase and move to more causal approaches when the growth of the business begins to exceed the entrepreneurs' management abilities. In addition, perceived contextual changes in relation to uncertainty or stakeholder pressure drive the use of effectuation or causation (Gabrielsson & Politis, 2011; Reymen et al., 2015). Critical trigger events for alternation of behaviors are the change of key persons and the search for external funding (Nummela et al., 2014).

We need to pay special attention to the relationship between uncertainty and both behaviors. Uncertainty exists in various forms with multiple dimensions, which in turn has different impacts. If the relationships are seen as linear ones, higher uncertainty will most likely lead to effectuation (Yang & Gabrielsson, 2017). In fact, we find a more diversified picture with complex relationships due to the transition of uncertainty over time during the entrepreneurial process (Packard et al., 2017). Recent work suggests an "integrative relationship" between uncertainty, effectuation, and causation (Jiang & Tornikoski, 2019). The relationships evolve over time depending on the maturity phase of the business, the level of environmental uncertainty, the perceptions of the entrepreneurs about the uncertainty, and the occurrence of unanticipated consequences. The interdependence of these constructs may lead to

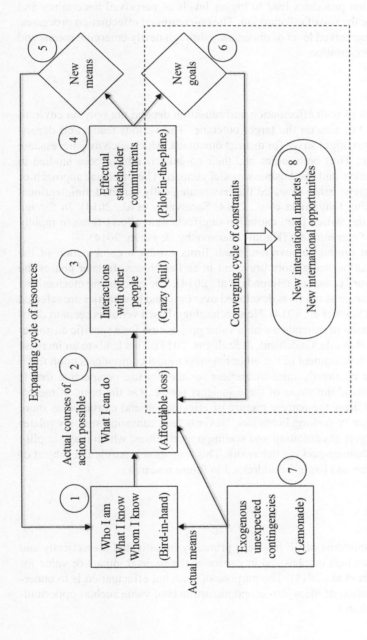

Source: Own illustration adapted from Sarasvathy et al. (2014).

Figure 4.3   *The effectuation process*

the result that causation-related actions may establish conditions that trigger effectuation and vice versa. Especially, the existence of unanticipated consequences that may follow causation processes lead to higher levels of perceived uncertainty and therefore encourage the use of effectuation. The co-creational effectuation processes, in turn, reduce the perceived level of uncertainty through newly emerging means and goals, which favors causation.

Co-existence

The (dis)advantages of both effectuation and causation depend not only on environmental conditions, but also on the target outcome. The various teams and departments within the firm might strive for distinct outcomes, which each may necessitate a different behavior. Thus both logics and their co-existence have been studied in the internationalization and the business model context. The effectual approach of international entrepreneurship revealed the less strategically oriented, unintentional aspects of networking (Nummela et al., 2014; Sarasvathy et al., 2014). In foreign market expansion, the switch from causation to effectuation allows firms to rapidly increase the level of commitment (Kalinic, Sarasvathy, & Forza, 2014).

In the process of product innovation, small firms exhibit a combination of the logics, with effectuation being more prevalent in earlier phases. In later phases the emphasis shifts toward causation (Berends et al., 2014). The co-existing mechanisms influence how the business model is developed over time and how tactics are selected at different phases (Sitoh et al., 2014). New technology-based ventures seem to dominantly use effectuation to generate a viable value proposition for a specific customer segment (Reymen, Berends, Oudehand, & Stultiëns, 2017). This leads to an increase of causation in the development of the other business model components upon this.

At this point we cautiously raise awareness for the holistic perspective that is necessary to understand the value of these insights for SE. On the basis of the literature, our review drew the narrow picture of effectuation and causation as more autonomous opportunity-seeking behaviors. Nevertheless, causation strongly relates to behavior that targets at exploiting and scaling opportunities, which may simplify the transition to advantage-seeking behaviors. This transition is hardly the subject of effectuation literature and has to be addressed in future research.

OUTCOMES

Value as the main outcome of SE has been primarily investigated theoretically and conceptually. Researchers emphasized in particular the societal impact or value for society at large (Hitt et al., 2011). The purpose of studying effectuation is to understand the transformation of ideas into economic artifacts of value such as opportunities and firm formation.

Firm Performance

The majority of empirical research in SE has been on firm financial performance (Mazzei, 2018). Similarly, effectuation research mainly focused on new venture performance across different contexts. In their meta-analysis of studies in the *Journal of Business Venturing*, Read, Song, and Smit (2009) link a detailed inventory of performance variables with the effectual principles. The findings implicated empirical support for a positive and significant relationship between the effectual principles of means (what I know, who I am, and whom I know), partnership, and leverage contingency and new venture performance. Effectuation has been shown to induce greater variance in performance and thus increases the probability of achieving very high performance (Cai et al., 2017). Exploratory learning takes a fully mediating role in this relationship. Furthermore, research shows significant positive moderating effects of effectual components on the relationship between product diversification (Deligianni et al., 2015) as well as national culture (Laskovaia et al., 2017) and new venture performance. Beyond that, research indicates that effectual and causal logic hold synergistic potential (An, Rüling, Zheng, & Zhang, 2019). Their combined use has a greater impact on venture performance than the sum of the distinct main effects. For example, experimentation as an integral approach of effectuation significantly strengthens the relationship between causation and performance (Smolka, Verheul, Burmeister-Lamp, & Heugens, 2018).

Marketing Outcomes

Although new venture performance is the main indicator of successfully created opportunities, researchers continuously move forward in the exploration of other outcomes, for example in the fields of marketing and innovation. The greater use of effectuation is associated with diverse marketing outcomes, such as market creation, value co-creation, resource leveraging, foreign market entry, and initial venture sales (Parida, George, Lahti, & Wincent, 2016; Yang & Gabrielsson, 2017). Perceiving gains in the environment strengthens the influence of effectuation on initial venture sales. On the other hand, perceiving the environment as controllable strengthens the influence of causation on initial venture sales. Effectual and causal behaviors are particularly relevant for internationalization as this context may hold conditions of high uncertainty and goal ambiguity. In these conditions, the switch from causation to effectuation allows overcoming liabilities of outsidership and thus to rapidly and successfully increase the level of commitment in a foreign market (Kalinic et al., 2014).

Innovation Outcomes

Another focus also highly relevant for SE is on innovation outcomes (Covin & Slevin, 2002). Effectuation scholars investigate these mainly in corporate settings. The firm's effectual control orientation has a positive effect on innovation performance (Szambelan & Jiang, 2019) as well as more specific outcomes such as the R&D project performance and business model innovation. In highly innovative contexts representing a high degree of uncertainty the principles of affordable loss, partnerships, and acknowledging the unexpected are positively related to success in R&D projects (Brettel et al., 2012). On the other hand, causation is more beneficial in projects with low levels of innovativeness. Furthermore, business model innovation inherently contains conditions of technological and market uncertainty favoring effectuation. The presence of entrepreneurs as owner-managers, who are presumably more likely to apply effectual logics, has a positive influence on the degree of innovation of the business model (Velu & Jacob, 2016). Similarly, effectuation (respective causation) is more effective to create business model innovation in high (low) industry growth settings (Futterer et al., 2018).

Research into the relationship between effectuation and business model development and innovation is still in its infancy. Insufficiently addressed issues are the different, singular effects of each principle of effectuation and causation. Fine-grained analyses of these effects on specific outcomes such as the degree of innovation (incremental versus radical) and the type of business model may provide crucial insights. Further outcomes might be artifacts such as technology or ideas (Dew & Sarasvathy, 2007). Finally, negative outcomes of the behaviors have been neglected in the literature so far and thus might be subject to a "survivor bias." Failed business opportunities are of great importance for entrepreneurial firms in terms of learning (Arend et al., 2015). Failure management may range from keeping losses of the firm under control to ending the exploration of the business opportunity.

Social Value Creation

The orientation towards social value questions the assumption of economic profitability as the only driver of opportunity-seeking behavior. Effectuation represents not a profit-oriented behavior, but a value-creating behavior. Therefore, scholars highlight the relevance of effectuation in the creation of societal value outcomes (e.g. Corner & Ho, 2010; Newbert, 2012). These processes strongly build on the partnership principle with elements such as stakeholder support and collective action (Akemu et al., 2016). Social entrepreneurs and the stakeholders actively shape and enact opportunities in complex social interaction processes. Furthermore, "hybrid organizations" employing environmental entrepreneurship combine an ecological logic with the commercial logic of economic efficiency and profits (York et al., 2016). The interdependence of the entrepreneur's identity and the economic, social, and ecological goals is crucial for creating societal value through entrepreneurial processes. There exists a potentially conflicting relationship between economic, social, and ecological goals. The effectuation process offers a mechanism for the continuous development of coordinated goals incorporating the stakeholders. The role of goal orientation as the originator of tangible actions has been neglected in effectuation and mainly associated with causation processes. Assessing the role of high-level goals within effectuation remains to be addressed in order to get a more comprehensive understanding (Arend et al., 2015; Read et al., 2016).

CONCLUSION

To further advance the field of SE, scholars advocate considering the complex multi-level phenomenon from different theoretical perspectives. We examine the literature stream of effectuation and integrate the findings with SE in order to inform our understanding of opportunity-seeking behavior. As is common in SE, our discussion of the identified themes and contributions follows the structure of content, context, inputs, processes, and outcomes.

First, we contribute to the growing stream of SE literature by systematically describing the manifestation of the opportunity-seeking behavior of effectuation. We depict the functionality and the temporal execution of the effectuation principles. Effectuation offers mechanisms to create economic opportunities as well as social and ecological value.

Second, both phenomena effectuation and SE entail complex and dynamic processes. The process evolves across a variety of decisions, in each of which stakeholders may be involved in different contexts and environments. We contribute to SE by presenting effectuation as behavior to successfully face uncertain environments. Nevertheless, dynamic environments entail various knowledge problems such as ambiguity, complexity, and equivocality that necessitate different behavioral responses. Therefore, research needs to further examine the multifaceted dynamic environments relevant to SE.

Third, we contribute to the effectuation literature by discussing the interrelationships and results of effectuation with a multilevel perspective, while interpreting the relevance of the findings with a focus on the firm. In addition, we propose fruitful implications in the intersection of SE and effectuation. Future research might drive the endeavor to establish effectuation as a valuable theoretical lens for corporate entrepreneurship.

We see at the same time big challenges and an extraordinary contribution value in SE and effectuation. Both fields aspire to shift research to a new paradigm. The phenomena are characterized by complex dynamics that take place in systems across different levels, units, and contexts. The inherent complexity in the concepts challenges assumptions of dominant paradigms such as environmental stability and rationality of human actors. For this reason, SE and effectuation as emerging concepts resemble much more than the actual human behavior in the real world. Both offer a great opportunity for the ongoing development of practice-oriented social theories. Critiques of effectuation warn in particular that effectuation scholars have so far missed to clearly highlight the added value of the concept. We agree that it is of high importance to recognize the differences to established literature streams and to unequivocally express the unique contribution value. Despite these legitimate objections, we want to encourage scholars to become more aware of integrative potentials of their stream with other literature streams. We see the culmination of research achievement and the greatest potential for further development in the laudable efforts of integrating existing knowledge.

REFERENCES

Agarwal, R., Dushnitsky, G., Lumpkin, G. T., Wright, M., & Zott, C. (2017). Strategic Entrepreneurship Journal at 10: Retrospect and prospect. *Strategic Entrepreneurship Journal, 11*(3), 197–199.

Akemu, O., Whiteman, G., & Kennedy, S. (2016). Social enterprise emergence from social movement activism: The Fairphone case. *Journal of Management Studies, 53*(5), 846–877.

Alsos, G. A., Clausen, T. H., Hytti, U., & Solvoll, S. (2016). Entrepreneurs' social identity and the preference of causal and effectual behaviours in start-up processes. *Entrepreneurship and Regional Development, 5626*(April), 234–258.

An, W., Rüling, C.-C., Zheng, X., & Zhang, J. (2019). Configurations of effectuation, causation, and bricolage: Implications for firm growth paths. *Small Business Economics*, 1–22.

Arend, R. J., Sarooghi, H., & Burkemper, A. C. (2015). Effectuation as ineffectual? Applying the 3E theory-assessment framework to a proposed new theory of entrepreneurship. *Academy of Management Review, 40*(4), 630–651.

Berends, H., Jelinek, M., Reymen, I., & Stultiëns, R. (2014). Product innovation processes in small firms: Combining entrepreneurial effectuation and managerial causation. *Journal of Product Innovation Management, 31*(3), 616–635.

Brettel, M., Mauer, R., Engelen, A., & Küpper, D. (2012). Corporate effectuation: Entrepreneurial action and its impact on R&D project performance. *Journal of Business Venturing, 27*(2), 167–184.

Cai, L., Guo, R., Fei, Y., & Liu, Z. (2017). Effectuation, exploratory learning and new venture performance: Evidence from China. *Journal of Small Business Management*. Jilin: Blackwell.

Chandler, G. N., DeTienne, D. R., McKelvie, A., & Mumford, T. V. (2011). Causation and effectuation processes: A validation study. *Journal of Business Venturing, 26*(3), 375–390.

Chesbrough, H. (2010). Business model innovation: Opportunities and barriers. *Long Range Planning, 43*(2/3), 354–363.

Chetty, S. K., Partanen, J., Rasmussen, E. S., & Servais, P. (2014). Contextualising case studies in entrepreneurship: A tandem approach to conducting a longitudinal cross-country case study. *International Small Business Journal*, 818–829.

Chetty, S., Ojala, A., & Leppäaho, T. (2015). Effectuation and foreign market entry of entrepreneurial firms. *European Journal of Marketing, 49*(9/10), 1436–1459.

Chiles, T. H., Gupta, V. K., & Bluedorn, A. C. (2008). On Lachmannian and effectual entrepreneurship: A rejoinder to Sarasvathy and Dew (2008). *Organization Studies, 29*(2), 247–253.

Cook, D. J., Mulrow, C. D., & Haynes, R. B. (1997). Systematic reviews: Synthesis of best evidence for clinical decisions. *Annals of Internal Medicine, 126*(5), 376–380.

Corner, P. D., & Ho, M. (2010). How opportunities develop in social entrepreneurship. *Entrepreneurship: Theory and Practice, 34*(4), 635–659.

Coviello, N. E., & Joseph, R. M. (2012). Creating major innovations with customers: Insights from small and young technology firms. *Journal of Marketing, 76*(6), 87–104.

Covin, J. G., & Slevin, D. P. (2002). The entrepreneurial imperatives of strategic leadership. In M. A. Hitt, R. D. Ireland, S. M. Camp, & D. L. Sexton (eds), *Strategic Entrepreneurship: Creating a New Mindset*. Oxford: Blackwell.

Cui, L., Su, S.-I. I., Feng, Y., & Hertz, S. (2019). Causal or effectual? Dynamics of decision making logics in servitization. *Industrial Marketing Management, 82*, 15–26.

Daniel, E. M., Domenico, M. Di, & Sharma, S. (2015). Effectuation and home-based online business entrepreneurs. *International Small Business Journal, 33*(8), 799–823.

Deligianni, I., Voudouris, I., & Lioukas, S. (2015). Do effectuation processes shape the relationship between product diversification and performance in new ventures? *Entrepreneurship: Theory and Practice, 41*(3).

Denyer, D., Tranfield, D., & Van Aken, J. E. (2008). Developing design propositions through research synthesis. *Organization Studies, 29*(3), 393–413.

Dew, N., Read, S., Sarasvathy, S. D., & Wiltbank, R. (2008). Outlines of a behavioral theory of the entrepreneurial firm. *Journal of Economic Behavior and Organization, 66*(1), 37–59.

Dew, N., Read, S., Sarasvathy, S. D., & Wiltbank, R. (2009). Effectual versus predictive logics in entrepreneurial decision-making: Differences between experts and novices. *Journal of Business Venturing, 24*(4), 287–309.

Dew, N., Read, S., Sarasvathy, S. D., & Wiltbank, R. (2015). Entrepreneurial expertise and the use of control. *Journal of Business Venturing Insights, 4*, 30–37.

Dew, N., & Sarasvathy, S. D. (2007). Innovations, stakeholders and entrepreneurship. *Journal of Business Ethics, 74*(3), 267–283.

Engel, Y., Dimitrova, N. G., Khapova, S. N., & Elfring, T. (2014). Uncertain but able: Entrepreneurial self-efficacy and novices' use of expert decision-logic under uncertainty. *Journal of Business Venturing Insights, 1*(1–2), 12–17.

Engel, Y., Kaandorp, M., & Elfring, T. (2017). Toward a dynamic process model of entrepreneurial networking under uncertainty. *Journal of Business Venturing, 32*(1), 35–51.

Evers, N., Andersson, S., & Hannibal, M. (2012). Stakeholders and marketing capabilities in international new ventures: Evidence from Ireland, Sweden, and Denmark. *Journal of International Marketing, 20*(4), 46–71.

Fischer, E., & Reuber, A. R. (2011). Social interaction via new social media: (How) can interactions on Twitter affect effectual thinking and behavior? *Journal of Business Venturing, 26*(1), 1–18.

Fisher, G. (2012). Effectuation, causation, and bricolage: A behavioral comparison of emerging theories in entrepreneurship research. *Entrepreneurship: Theory and Practice, 36*(5), 1019–1051.

Futterer, F., Schmidt, J., & Heidenreich, S. (2018). Effectuation or causation as the key to corporate venture success? Investigating effects of entrepreneurial behaviors on business model innovation and venture performance. *Long Range Planning, 51*(1), 64–81.

Gabrielsson, P., & Gabrielsson, M. (2013). A dynamic model of growth phases and survival in international business-to-business new ventures: The moderating effect of decision-making logic. *Industrial Marketing Management, 42*(8), 1357–1373.

Gabrielsson, J., & Politis, D. (2011). Career motives and entrepreneurial decision-making: Examining preferences for causal and effectual logics in the early stage of new ventures. *Small Business Economics, 36*(3), 281–298.

Galkina, T., & Chetty, S. (2015). Effectuation and networking of internationalizing SMEs. *Management International Review, 55*(5), 647–676.

Garud, R., & Gehman, J. (2016). Theory evaluation, entrepreneurial processes, and performativity. *Academy of Management Review, 41*(3), 544–549.

Glaser, B. G., & Strauss, A. (1967). *The discovery of grounded theory.* London: Weidenfield and Nicolson, 1–19.

Hauser, A., Eggers, F., & Güldenberg, S. (2019). Strategic decision-making in SMEs: Effectuation, causation, and the absence of strategy. *Small Business Economics*, 1–16.

Hitt, M. A., Ireland, R. D., Sirmon, D. G., & Trahms, C. A. (2011). Strategic entrepreneurship: Creating value for individuals, organizations, and society. *Academy of Management Perspectives, 25*(2), 57–75.

Hsieh, H.-F., & Shannon, S. E. (2005). Three approaches to qualitative content analysis. *Qualitative Health Research, 15*(9), 1277–1288.

Ireland, R. D., Hitt, M. A., & Sirmon, D. G. (2003). A model of strategic entrepreneurship: The construct and its dimensions. *Journal of Management, 29*(6), 963–989.

Jiang, Y., & Tornikoski, E. T. (2019). Perceived uncertainty and behavioral logic: Temporality and unanticipated consequences in the new venture creation process. *Journal of Business Venturing, 34*(1), 23–40.

Johannisson, B. (2018). Disclosing everyday practices constituting social entrepreneuring: A case of necessity effectuation. *Entrepreneurship and Regional Development, 30*(3–4), 390–406.

Jones, O., & Li, H. (2017). Effectual entrepreneuring: Sensemaking in a family-based start-up. *Entrepreneurship and Regional Development*, 1–33.

Kalinic, I., Sarasvathy, S. D., & Forza, C. (2014). "Expect the unexpected": Implications of effectual logic on the internationalization process. *International Business Review, 23*(3), 635–647.

Karami, M., Wooliscroft, B., & McNeill, L. (2020). Effectuation and internationalisation: A review and agenda for future research. *Small Business Economics, 55*(3), 777–811.

Kerr, J., & Coviello, N. E. (2019). Formation and constitution of effectual networks: A systematic review and synthesis. *International Journal of Management Reviews, 21*(3), 370–397.

Kerr, J., & Coviello, N. E. (2020). Weaving network theory into effectuation: A multi-level reconceptualization of effectual dynamics. *Journal of Business Venturing, 35*(2).

Knight, F. H. (1921). The place of profit and uncertainty in economic theory. *Risk, Uncertainty and Profit*, 3–21.

Kuechle, G., Boulu-Reshef, B., & Carr, S. D. (2016). Prediction- and control-based strategies in entrepreneurship: The role of information. *Strategic Entrepreneurship Journal, 10*(1), 43–64.

Lam, W., & Harker, M. J. (2015). Marketing and entrepreneurship: An integrated view from the entrepreneur's perspective. *International Small Business Journal, 33*(3), 321–348.

Laskovaia, A., Shirokova, G., & Morris, M. H. (2017). National culture, effectuation, and new venture performance: Global evidence from student entrepreneurs. *Small Business Economics*, 1–23.

Lepak, D. P., Smith, K. G., & Taylor, M. S. (2007). Value creation and value capture: A multilevel perspective. *Academy of Management Review, 32*(1), 180–194.

Mazzei, M. J. (2018). Strategic entrepreneurship: Content, process, context, and outcomes. *International Entrepreneurship and Management Journal, 14*(3), 657–670.

Mazzei, M. J., Ketchen, D. J., & Shook, C. L. (2017). Understanding strategic entrepreneurship: A "theoretical toolbox" approach. *International Entrepreneurship and Management Journal, 13*(2), 631–663.

McKelvie, A., Chandler, G. N., DeTienne, D. R., & Johansson, A. (2019). The measurement of effectuation: Highlighting research tensions and opportunities for the future. *Small Business Economics*, 1–32.

Miller, D., & Le Breton-Miller, L. (2017). Sources of entrepreneurial courage and imagination: Three perspectives, three contexts. *Entrepreneurship Theory and Practice, 41*(1).

Miller, D., Steier, L., & Le Breton-Miller, I. (2016). What can scholars of entrepreneurship learn from sound family businesses? *Entrepreneurship: Theory and Practice, 40*(3), 445–455.

Milliken, F. J. (1987). Three types of perceived uncertainty about the environment: State, effect, and response uncertainty. *Academy of Management Review, 12*(1), 133–143.

Moher, D., Liberati, A., Tetzlaff, J., Altman, D. G., & Group, P. (2009). Preferred reporting items for systematic reviews and meta-analyses: The PRISMA statement. *PLoS Med, 6*(7).

Mohr, L. B. (1982). *Explaining Organizational Behavior* (Vol. 1). San Francisco, CA: Jossey-Bass.

Mort, G. S., Weerawardena, J., & Liesch, P. (2012). Advancing entrepreneurial marketing: Evidence from born global firms. *European Journal of Marketing, 46*(3/4), 542–561.

Mulrow, C. D. (1994). Rationale for systematic reviews. *British Medical Journal, 309*(6954), 597.

Newbert, S. L. (2012). Marketing amid the uncertainty of the social sector: Do social entrepreneurs follow best marketing practices? *Journal of Public Policy and Marketing, 31*(1), 75–90.

Nummela, N., Saarenketo, S., Jokela, P., & Loane, S. (2014). Strategic decision-making of a born global: A comparative study from three small open economies. *Management International Review, 54*(4), 527–550.

Packard, M. D., Clark, B. B., & Klein, P. G. (2017). Uncertainty types and transitions in the entrepreneurial process. *Organization Science, 28*(5), 781–964.

Paek, B., & Lee, H. (2018). Strategic entrepreneurship and competitive advantage of established firms: Evidence from the digital TV industry. *International Entrepreneurship and Management Journal, 14*(4), 883–925.

Parida, V., George, N. M., Lahti, T., & Wincent, J. (2016). Influence of subjective interpretation, causation, and effectuation on initial venture sale. *Journal of Business Research, 69*(11), 4815–4819.

Penrose, E. (1959). *The Theory of the Growth of the Firm.* New York: John Wiley & Sons.

Politis, D., Winborg, J., & Dahlstrand, Å. L. (2012). Exploring the resource logic of student entrepreneurs. *International Small Business Journal, 30*(6), 659–683.

Prashantham, S., Kumar, K., Bhagavatula, S., & Sarasvathy, S. D. (2019). Effectuation, network-building and internationalisation speed. *International Small Business Journal, 37*(1), 3–21.

Ranabahu, N., & Barrett, M. (2019). Does practice make micro-entrepreneurs perfect? An investigation of expertise acquisition using effectuation and causation. *Small Business Economics*, 1–23.

Randerson, K. (2016). Entrepreneurial orientation: Do we actually know as much as we think we do? *Entrepreneurship and Regional Development, 28*(7/8), 580–600.

Read, S., & Sarasvathy, S. D. (2012). Co-creating a course ahead from the intersection of service-dominant logic and effectuation. *Marketing Theory, 12*(2), 225–229.

Read, S., Sarasvathy, S. D., Dew, N., & Wiltbank, R. (2016). Response to Arend, Sarooghi, and Burkemper (2015): Cocreating effectual entrepreneurship research. *Academy of Management Review, 41*(3), 528–536.

Read, S., Song, M., & Smit, W. (2009). A meta-analytic review of effectuation and venture performance. *Journal of Business Venturing, 24*(6), 573–587.

Reuber, A. R., Fischer, E., & Coviello, N. E. (2016). Deepening the dialogue: New directions for the evolution of effectuation theory. *Academy of Management Review, 41*(3), 536–540.

Reymen, I., Andries, P., Berends, H., Mauer, R., Stephan, U., & van Burg, E. (2015). Understanding dynamics of strategic decision making in venture creation: A process study of effectuation and causation. *Strategic Entrepreneurship Journal, 9*(4), 351–379.

Reymen, I., Berends, H., Oudehand, R., & Stultiëns, R. (2017). Decision making for business model development: A process study of effectuation and causation in new technology-based ventures. *R&D Management, 47*(4), 595–606.

Sarasvathy, S. D. (2001). Causation and effectuation: Toward a theoretical shift from economic inevitability to entrepreneurial contingency. *Academy of Management Review, 26*(2), 243–263.

Sarasvathy, S. D. (2009). *Effectuation: Elements of Entrepreneurial Expertise.* Cheltenham, UK and Northampton, MA, USA: Edward Elgar Publishing.

Sarasvathy, S. D., & Dew, N. (2005). New market creation through transformation. *Journal of Evolutionary Economics, 15*(5), 533–565.

Sarasvathy, S. D., & Dew, N. (2008a). Effectuation and over-trust: Debating Goel and Karri. *Entrepreneurship: Theory and Practice, 32*(4), 727–737.

Sarasvathy, S. D., & Dew, N. (2008b). Is effectuation Lachmannian? A response to Chiles, Bluedorn, and Gupta (2007). *Organization Studies, 29*(2), 239–245.

Sarasvathy, S. D., & Dew, N. (2013). Without judgment: An empirically-based entrepreneurial theory of the firm. *Review of Austrian Economics, 26*(3), 277–296.

Sarasvathy, S. D., Kumar, K., York, J. G., & Bhagavatula, S. (2014). An effectual approach to international entrepreneurship: Overlaps, challenges, and provocative possibilities. *Entrepreneurship: Theory and Practice, 38*(1), 71–93.

Schindehutte, M., & Morris, M. H. (2009). Advancing strategic entrepreneurship research: The role of complexity science in shifting the paradigm. *Entrepreneurship Theory and Practice, 33*(1), 241–276.

Servantie, V., & Rispal, M. H. (2018). Bricolage, effectuation, and causation shifts over time in the context of social entrepreneurship. *Entrepreneurship and Regional Development, 30*(3–4), 310–335.

Simsek, Z., Heavey, C., & Fox, B. C. (2017). (Meta-) framing strategic entrepreneurship. *Strategic Organization, 15*(4), 504–518.

Sirmon, D. G., Hitt, M. A., & Ireland, R. D. (2007). Managing firm resources in dynamic environments to create value: Looking inside the black box. *Academy of Management Review, 32*(1), 273–292.

Sitoh, M. K., Pan, S. L., & Yu, C.-Y. (2014). Business models and tactics in new product creation: The interplay of effectuation and causation processes. *IEEE Transactions on Engineering Management, 61*(2), 213–224.

Smolka, K. M., Verheul, I., Burmeister–Lamp, K., & Heugens, P. P. (2018). Get it together! Synergistic effects of causal and effectual decision-making logics on venture performance. *Entrepreneurship Theory and Practice, 42*(4), 571–604.

Steyaert, C. (2007). "Entrepreneuring" as a conceptual attractor? A review of process theories in 20 years of entrepreneurship studies. *Entrepreneurship & Regional Development, 19*(6), 453–477.

Strauss, A., & Corbin, J. M. (1990). *Basics of Qualitative Research* (Vol. 15). Newbury Park, CA: Sage.

Szambelan, S. M., & Jiang, Y. D. (2019). Effectual control orientation and innovation performance: Clarifying implications in the corporate context. *Small Business Economics*, 1–18.

Szambelan, S., Jiang, Y., & Mauer, R. (2020). Breaking through innovation barriers: Linking effectuation orientation to innovation performance. *European Management Journal, 38*(3), 425–434.

Tavassoli, S., Bengtsson, L., & Karlsson, C. (2017). Strategic entrepreneurship and knowledge spillovers: Spatial and aspatial perspectives. *International Entrepreneurship and Management Journal, 13*(1), 233–249.

Townsend, D. M., Hunt, R. A., McMullen, J. S., & Sarasvathy, S. D. (2018). Uncertainty, knowledge problems, and entrepreneurial action. *Academy of Management Annals, 12*(2), 659–687.

Tranfield, D., Denyer, D., & Smart, P. (2003). Towards a methodology for developing evidence-informed management knowledge by means of systematic review. *British Journal of Management, 14*(3), 207–222.

Uotila, J., Maula, M., Keil, T., & Zahra, S. A. (2009). Exploration, exploitation, and financial performance: Analysis of S&P 500 corporations. *Strategic Management Journal, 30*(2), 221–231.

Velu, C., & Jacob, A. (2016). Business model innovation and owner-managers: The moderating role of competition. *R&D Management, 46*(3), 451–463.

Watson, T. J. (2013). Entrepreneurial action and the Euro-American social science tradition: Pragmatism, realism and looking beyond "the entrepreneur." *Entrepreneurship and Regional Development, 25*(1/2), 16–33.

Welter, F. (2011). Contextualizing entrepreneurship: Conceptual challenges and ways forward. *Entrepreneurship Theory and Practice, 35*(1), 165–184.

Werhahn, D., Mauer, R., Flatten, T. C., & Brettel, M. (2015). Validating effectual orientation as strategic direction in the corporate context. *European Management Journal, 33*(5), 305–313.

Wiltbank, R., Dew, N., Read, S., & Sarasvathy, S. D. (2006). What to do next? The case for non-predictive strategy. *Strategic Management Journal, 27*(10), 981–998.

Wiltbank, R., Read, S., Dew, N., & Sarasvathy, S. D. (2009). Prediction and control under uncertainty: Outcomes in angel investing. *Journal of Business Venturing, 24*(2), 116–133.

Wright, M., & Hitt, M. A. (2017). Strategic entrepreneurship and SEJ: Development and current progress. *Strategic Entrepreneurship Journal, 11*(3), 200–210.

Yang, M., & Gabrielsson, P. (2017). Entrepreneurial marketing of international high-tech business-to-business new ventures: A decision-making process perspective. *Industrial Marketing Management, 64*, 147–160.

York, J. G., O'Neil, I., & Sarasvathy, S. D. (2016). Exploring environmental entrepreneurship: Identity coupling, venture goals, and stakeholder incentives. *Journal of Management Studies, 53*(5), 695–737.

5. Exploring new venture creation through incubators and accelerators: what value is created and who captures it? Implications for research, teaching, and practice

Riley Doyle, Kris Irwin, Josie A. Burks, Paul L. Drnevich, and Craig E. Armstrong

Entrepreneurs may dream big about creating new solutions and/or improving existing solutions to pressing business and consumer problems. However, to develop a successful new venture they often face a major roadblock: Where will they obtain the resources and legitimacy needed to launch, implement, and grow their dreams? Entrepreneurial support organizations (ESOs) (e.g., Breznitz, Clayton, Defazio, & Isett, 2018; Markley, Lyons, & Macke, 2015; Roundy, 2017) such as incubator and accelerator programs were designed to reduce or remove this roadblock by providing resource support, training, and mentoring to entrepreneurs to help them turn their ideas into profitable businesses. Incubator and accelerator programs are a relatively new type of hybrid organization that has sprung up only recently on college campuses (e.g., Schawbel, 2012), yet they actually began emerging and evolving over the past several decades. Incubators were originally established around 1950 but have changed significantly over time and became much more commonplace over the past decade (Grimaldi & Grandi, 2005).

In contrast, accelerators are a newer concept that did not become popular until circa 2005 with the establishment of Y Combinator (Goswami, Mitchell, & Bhagavatula, 2018). Y Combinator was the first organization to create the now widely copied model of focusing on "batches" of companies that are admitted for a three-month period in residence that culminates in a "Demo Day" on which the teams pitch their venture ideas to hundreds of potential investors (Stross, 2013). However, incubator and accelerator programs world-wide now number well into the thousands (Inc. com, 2020). Moreover, the number of startups that are backed by such programs has increased by at least 20 times (Lyons & Zhang, 2018). However, there is very little published academic research on the effectiveness of incubators and accelerators (Albort-Morant & Ribeiro-Soriano, 2016). Do they really work, and if so, for whom do they work best? Growth in this increasingly popular phenomenon without standard terminology usage, practices, performance outcome evaluation, etc. typically causes much confusion in both practice and the research of the phenomena. For one example of this confusion, many people (including those operating the programs) tend to use the words "incubator" and "accelerator" interchangeably, and/or confuse the objectives and distinctions among the types of programs. To help alleviate some of this confusion, our objectives and intended contributions through this study are: (1) to provide a comprehensive review and clearer definitions for the different programs and, perhaps more importantly, (2) to discern how, where, and under what types of condition value is created through incubator and accelerator programs, and which of the stakeholders in the process are most likely to capture that value.

For the purpose of this chapter, we define incubators as organizations focused on nascent or very early-stage ventures designed to assist those who are just beginning to take the leap into entrepreneurship (Dutt et al., 2016; Kemp & Weber, 2012; Phan, Siegel, & Wright, 2016; Rothaermel & Thursby, 2005). Incubators train and equip young and/or novice entrepreneurs to take their ideas and turn them into small businesses by providing space, resources, mentors, and other services needed to enter the business world (Aernoudt, 2004; Finer & Holberton, 2002; Rothaermel & Thursby, 2005; Kolympiris & Klein, 2017). Incubator participants tend to remain in the programs from one to five years (Cohen, 2013).

While accelerators may offer many of the same services, such as mentoring and office space, they differ from incubators in that accelerators usually target established and operating businesses in the early stages of growth (beyond formation) and offer a coordinated cohort program lasting from three to six months (Miller & Bound, 2011; Yusubova & Clarysse, 2016). Accelerators focus on operating as fixed-term, cohort-based programs that offer mentorship and educational components and that culminate in a public pitch event, often referred to as "demo-day," to connect accelerator startups with investors (Cohen & Hochberg, 2014; Stross, 2013; Yusubova & Clarysse, 2016). In sum, incubator programs are usually geared towards helping more novice entrepreneurs plan, form, and establish early-stage new ventures, while accelerators tend to focus on helping more established ventures with more experienced entrepreneurs grow their ventures and attract the financial and relational capital to do so. As such, education, training, mentoring, and coaching may play a much larger role in incubators while the development and deployment of both relational and financial capital seem to play a bigger role in accelerators.

Beyond reviewing and providing some clarification of the concepts, terminology, and domains of incubators and accelerators, the larger, more pertinent question becomes: To what extent are incubators and accelerators effective? Are these programs effective or merely a waste of resources such as time, talent, and money at a substantial opportunity cost to all stakeholders involved, most particularly the entrepreneur? Most scholars and practitioners are likely to assume these types of programs are (perhaps highly) productive and helpful to the entrepreneur and value enhancing for all stakeholders (cf. Pfeffer & Fong, 2002); however, Dane Stangler of the Kauffman Foundation has declared that incubators are not effective in helping to create businesses (Kauffman Foundation, 2014). This statement challenges the common widely held assumptions of incubator/accelerator program effectiveness and value, and motivates the need for further examination and refinement of our collective knowledge of these phenomena and their implications.

We offer such a further examination and refinement in this chapter and, through doing so, make three contributions to the literature. First, we clearly identify and delineate the roles and objectives of the private sector for profit incubators, accelerators, and similar university-based programs through a detailed review of the current research. Second, we assess these program types, their effectiveness, and what value is created and captured through each program. Third, we identify implications of these findings for both academic research and entrepreneurial practice and provide a suggested agenda of future research opportunities.

The remainder of this chapter is organized in the following way: First we examine sources of value in incubators and accelerators, how they differ, and who benefits from the value created. Second, we describe the method of selecting journals as sources of data for our analysis and the coding logic we applied. Third, we summarize the patterns and processes of value creation and contextual factors relevant to incubators versus accelerators. Fourth and finally, we present a discussion summarizing our findings with recommendations and implications for future research and practice.

THEORETICAL BACKGROUND

Value in Incubators and Accelerators

How exactly is value created in incubators and accelerators? Ideally, value is ingrained through the services they offer aspiring and established entrepreneurs. Value is determined through the usefulness and variety of resources provided to entrepreneurs during their time within an incubator or accelerator. These programs help entrepreneurs gain access to prized mentorship and the opportunity to network with like-minded, creative individuals. Further, incubator participants report that reduced business costs are one of the best features of an incubator (Lange, 2018). Accelerator participants note that the chance to obtain funding at the onset of the program and access to capital following it is vital (Lange, 2018).

Across incubators and accelerator programs, the types of value created include reputational capital, legitimacy, resources, mentoring, and networking (see Table 5.1). The best way to differentiate them from each other might be to point out who captures the value offered by the Entrepreneur Support Organization (ESO) type. Typically, incubator programs are designed for entrepreneurs who are just launching their businesses and are geared towards more novice entrepreneurs who need mentoring and skills training. Consider, for example, Codebase, which is one of the most successful incubators for startups in Europe (Coara.co, 2020). Codebase offers startup mentorships in dozens of cities across the United Kingdom and "pre-accelerator" skills training for startups designed to help startups get started. One would not expect a more seasoned startup to benefit as much from this emphasis on "starting to start." Studies also appear to support this distinction in that they tend to show that experienced entrepreneurs do not seem to derive as much value from an incubator

Table 5.1   Value creation

Program	Value created?	Who captures?	Who doesn't capture?
Incubator	Reputational capital, legitimacy, resources, networking, financial capital	*Novice* entrepreneurs, students, faculty, "at-large" community members	*Experienced* entrepreneurs, technology transfer offices
Accelerator	Reputational capital, legitimacy, resources, mentoring, networking, *financial capital*	*Experienced* and competitive teams of entrepreneurs, community, specifically investors	Non-competitive, individual entrepreneurs
University incubator	Reputational capital, legitimacy, resources, *mentoring, networking*	University, students, faculty, and staff	University (divert resources and decrease patent quality)

as opposed to novice entrepreneurs (Lyons & Zhang, 2018). Further, despite serving as a relatively cost-effective method of stimulating economic activity, it remains far from clear whether or not incubators add value to their host economies and communities (Kemp & Weber, 2012). For these reasons, we conclude that incubators serve to create value solely for early-stage, nascent entrepreneurs, with some potential value created for incubators over a greater time horizon to build reputational capital.

Conversely, accelerator programs are designed for more experienced entrepreneurs and/or those who have established and are growing their business and are geared towards those that have (ideally, but not exclusively) demonstrated some validated demand and problem-solution fit for their products or services. Accelerators help entrepreneurs to demonstrate the efficacy of their business models and to attract outside investments from the community. For these reasons, both the entrepreneur and the community can capture value from an accelerator program. These forms of value capture are enhanced by the requirement most accelerators have that their cohort companies must relocate, at least temporarily, to the accelerator's headquarter facilities, where they have more opportunities to interact with the community. Y Combinator is an example of an accelerator that requires relocation to its facilities in Silicon Valley to provide resources of business development and know-how along with the financial resources of early-stage investors who are part of that community. This model rewards startups who participate in the accelerator with privileged access to resources that are valuable to their growth and the investors in the community who help to finance that growth.

Codebase and Y Combinator provide useful examples of private-sector incubators and accelerators and whom they primarily benefit. However, do university-affiliated programs operate in the same way or differently from private-sector programs? For instance, in university programs, are the programs aligned in the same manner? How is value created and captured when the university is the operator and its participants are employees and students?

University incubators offer students a place to develop their early-stage ideas and receive the mentorship needed to launch their business. While students may benefit from participation in university incubator programs, they must overcome additional obstacles including lack of confidence, experience, and knowledge and resources to start a business (Ahsan, Zheng, DeNoble, & Musteen, 2018). As a result, many students who might be ideal participants in university incubators might not be aware of or might shy away from opportunities to take part.

Faculty and staff with business ideas may also benefit from the opportunity to participate in the incubator program and create a startup if they are aware of the program. Anecdotal evidence suggests that students, faculty, and staff may not be capturing value from incubators on their campuses simply because they don't know how to participate. By extension, it should not be surprising that the value universities might capture from offering incubator programs may be overestimated (Levie & Autio, 2008; Feola, Vesci, Botti, & Parente, 2019; Kolympiris & Klein, 2017). In multi-stakeholder settings like university campuses, incubators actually may divert resources away from other campus services that are in place for the purpose of innovation and creation (Kolympiris & Klein, 2017). As such, university incubator programs may have the unintended effect of undermining overall knowledge generation and even lead to a decrease in university patent volume, quality, and licensing revenue (Kolympiris & Klein, 2017) because the intended audience is not making full use of incubator resources.

Those students, faculty, and staff who do participate in university incubators do derive value. They tend to view their experience in the incubators positively, with mentoring and networking opportunities shown as the most vital features (Ahsan et al., 2018; Yusubova & Clarysse, 2016). We conducted informal, open-ended interviews with participants in many of the incubators and accelerators we studied. In one interview with the founders of a recently acquired medical device firm, we learned that the incubator process helped them to truly build a business development plan; it encouraged them to plan, organize, define, and locate missing skill-sets for their business. This specific example points to a wider-spread satisfaction with the networking and mentoring opportunities that university incubators provide. This points to the "less tangible" value participants can gain from university incubators. In one testimonial we found during our literature review, an incubator participant pointed out that, "The mentors, their knowledge, and resources have been the most valuable. It's one thing to be able to read a book, but it's more important for me to be able to ask questions and get an answer" (Lange, 2018: 87). Entrepreneurs share that the benefits of an incubator or accelerator program are so extremely vital that even if their business failed, they are still thankful they underwent the process (Lange, 2018).

In terms of university-based accelerators, we were hard pressed to find a useful example to use for illustrating any differences between the private and public models for accelerators. The main reason for our difficulty was the consistent conflation of the terms "incubator" and "accelerator" used by the universities themselves in the descriptions of their programs on their own websites. We view this as evidence that supports in part our assertion that the value propositions of the two types of models are not well differentiated, even among the individuals who are assigned to develop and operate them on campuses.

METHOD

We conduct an integrative review of the literature in which we selected a representative sample of the published research on incubators or accelerators (based on keywords and abstract) in the top entrepreneurship and management research journals. The journals included *Academy of Management Journal, Entrepreneurship Theory and Practice, Journal of Business Venturing, Journal of Small Business Management, Strategic Entrepreneurship Journal,* and *Strategic Management Journal* over a ten-year period (2010–2019). This listing of journals does not include all of the quality outlets for research in entrepreneurship, but it is representative of the types of articles appearing in the academic literature.

We coded articles from these journals with regard to capturing different characteristics of the articles such as paper demographics and structure, the paper's purpose/objective and methodology, theoretical grounding, research questions, findings, and practical implications. This approach is similar to one outlined in a similar review effort conducted for the *Academy of Management Journal* (Judge, Cable, Colbert, & Rynes, 2007) and other reviews that adopt Judge and colleagues' journal selection process (e.g., Denk, Kaufmann, & Roesch, 2012; López-Duarte, Vidal-Suárez, & González-Díaz, 2016; Sutter, Bruton, & Chen, 2019). However, while Judge and colleagues' (2007) objective was to identify which factors about the articles themselves caused them to be cited, our objective here is to use similar criteria to identify which articles on incubators and accelerators might be most influential in shaping opinions on this topic. Articles were coded by two or three raters with the target of each article coded by at least two different people. During our articles search we observed that there are now several thousand research articles listed on Google Scholar with the topic "incubator" or "accelerator," ranging across a variety of subject domains (e.g., public policy, research and development, innovation, and management) and multiple levels of geography (international, national, regional, etc.). Research on incubators and accelerators indeed seems to be tracking with the exponential growth of such organizations over the past decade. For the purposes of this chapter, we acknowledge that there are many levels and vantage points of analysis in the burgeoning research; yet for the sake of our intended audience of entrepreneurship researchers, teachers, and others we focus here on the top journals of the management discipline for our analysis. Future research could certainly benefit from a broadening of the scope of journals and topical areas related to incubators and accelerators.

We also conducted interviews as part of an exploratory study to provide some more tangible context for our integrative review. Participants were identified through the networks of this chapter's authors and selected based on having participated or currently participating in an incubator, accelerator, or university program. We asked open-ended questions regarding the decisions to participate in the program(s), benefits and challenges of the programs, and lessons learned. Those who participated in more than one program were also asked to compare and contrast their experiences in the programs. We found these interviews to be particularly relevant to our discussion section and have incorporated them as the section entitled "Experience, Need, and Fit."

REVIEW AND INTEGRATION

We begin our review and integration assessment of the literature on incubators and accelerators by examining and discussing the literature on each of the different categories of venture development organizations. In Table 5.2, we provide an overview of this literature on private incubators and accelerators, as well as university-based incubator and accelerator programs. We then review and assess the literature in these categories in the sections that follow.

Incubators

Incubators help push entrepreneurs forward as they seek to establish their company. Incubators provide vital resources including mentorship (McAdam & Marlow, 2011), legitimacy (Tötterman & Sten, 2005), and a broader social network (Armanios, Eesley, Li, & Eisenhardt, 2017) that many entrepreneurs would lack if they had not participated in the program. The networking aspect of participation in an incubator is one of the most vital and beneficial features (McAdam & Marlow, 2011). The mentorship opportunities in incubator programs are also a prized resource. With mentors helping to support and guide, aspiring entrepreneurs and young entrepreneurs are able to understand better what is needed to start a business, develop their ideas and service, and receive the confidence boost to push forward with their ambitious designs (Ahsan et al., 2018).

   As a business owner, entrepreneurs desire credibility and legitimacy. If a business is not deemed legitimate by potential customers, is there really a need to launch that particular business? Quite frankly, no. It will be a frustrated misuse of time and money. Studies show that incubators provide a source of legitimacy for a startup firm through their process of selection and backing of the startup (Tötterman & Sten, 2005). A startup is able to increase its legitimacy as an organization by being vetted as reliable, authentic, and resilient through participation in an incubator program (Tötterman & Sten, 2005; Partanen, Chetty, & Rajala, 2014).

   Lyons and Zhang (2018) even suggest that incubators help to enlarge the scope of entrepreneurs entering the marketplace as incubators tend to cater towards new entrepreneurs who are just beginning to infiltrate the world of business. Without participating in an incubator, these fresh entrepreneurs may not have had very much exposure or knowledge about how to even succeed with their business. However, as entrepreneurs finish incubator programs, they are much better equipped to enter the corporate work sphere. Moreover, through experiments, one group of scholars showed that incubators may help grow the diversity in the entrepreneurial community (Armanios et al., 2017). For example, incubators offer an open door for "new arrivals (i.e., returnees) and the talented (i.e., local elites)" to create their own startup

Table 5.2   Entrepreneurial support organizations literature review

Cite	Focus	Perspective	Topic	Findings
Ahsan, Zheng, DeNoble, & Musteen, 2018	University incubator	Student entrepreneurs	Mentorship from student to entrepreneur	Positive
Armanios, Eesley, Li, & Eisenhardt, 2017	Incubators and accelerators	Entrepreneurs, located in China	Incubators and accelerators; gain public resources	Positive
Breugst, Patzelt, & Rathgeber, 2015	Incubator	Entrepreneurial teams	Equity; entrepreneurial teams	Positive and negative
Dutt, Hawn, Vidal, Chatterji, McGahan, & Mitchell, 2016	Incubator	Intermediaries	Incubators resolve issues	Positive
Ebbers, 2014	Incubator	Entrepreneurs	Behavior and relationships; incubators	Positive
Feola, Vesci, Botti, & Parente, 2019	University incubator	Student entrepreneurs	Factors contribute to young researchers	Positive
Giudici, Reinmoeller, & Ravasi, 2018	Incubators and venture associations	Entrepreneurs	Open- and closed-system orchestration	Positive
Goswami, Mitchell, & Bhagavatula, 2018	Accelerator	Accelerator graduates, managers, ecosystem stakeholders	Accelerators; Banaglore, India	Positive
Grimes, 2017	Incubator	Founders/entrepreneurs	Creative revision process and optimal distinctiveness	Positive and negative
Hughes, Morgan, Ireland, & Hughes, 2014	Incubator	Entrepreneurial firms	Social capital relationships; absorptive capacity	Positive
Kolympiris & Klein, 2017	University incubator	University innovation	Innovation quality	Negative
Lyons & Zhang, 2018	Other entrepreneurship programs	Entrepreneurs	Who does not gain from entrepreneurship programs?	Positive, negative, and non-significant
Marlow & McAdam, 2015	Incubator	Women (technology ventures, business owners)	Tech incubator; gender	Positive and negative
Marvel, Sullivan, & Wolfe, 2018	Incubator (tech business)	Founders in high-tech sector	Increase sales; startup ventures	Positive
Partanen, Chetty, & Rajala, 2014	Small firms	Four small firms	Innovation types and network relationships	Positive
Shankar & Shepherd, 2018	Accelerators (corporate)	Corporations and entrepreneurial ventures	Pathways for corporate accelerators	Positive
Tocher, Oswald, & Hall, 2015	Incubators, small business development centers	Entrepreneurs	Opportunity creation	Positive
Uy, Foo, & Ilies, 2015	Incubator	Early-stage entrepreneurs	Entrepreneurial work effort; goals	Positive
Uy, Sun, & Foo, 2017	Incubator	Early-stage startup entrepreneurs	Factors affecting beginning entrepreneurs	Negative

(Armanios et al., 2017); this attracts a variety of entrepreneurs rather than only the highly educated or those who have high status within a community. It seems that the establishment of incubator programs and benefits has led to a greater number and variety of people seeking to be entrepreneurs (Aernoudt, 2004; Armanios et al., 2017; Baskaran, Chandran, & Ng, 2019; Feola et al., 2019; Guerrero, Urbano, & Gajón, 2020).

Concerning whether or not incubators are effective, scholars find that incubators are more effective when "focusing on connecting new organizations with collaborative opportunities with incumbent firms and external resource providers" (Amezcua, Grimes, Bradley, & Wiklund, 2013: 1644). Incubators target two different orchestrations: open system and closed system. Within an open-system orchestration, entrepreneurs are able to better define who they are as entrepreneurs. They can hone in on why their business stands out among other businesses in the world market. On the other hand, entrepreneurs in closed systems base their goals more on what other people are doing; they are reliant on making their business better based upon what competitors are doing as opposed to continuously focusing on themselves and just how to make themselves better without putting so much emphasis on the actions of others.

Incubator programs encourage entrepreneurs to share their ideas with other entrepreneurs. By discussing with one another their visions, entrepreneurs and their mentors help fine-tune ideas or throw out ideas in place of a better one. However, by sharing their ideas with others who are also seeking to start a business and make a profit, it can potentially be easy for people to steal ideas. Such observations are well highlighted in experiments on and interviews with individuals in incubator programs, like this quote from an entrepreneur about his time in the setting:

> I honestly can't imagine a better environment for learning the science behind entrepreneurship. I've learned so much from [the individuals in charge] and from all of the other teams. There's a real sense of camaraderie. I mean, I know at the end of the day we're sort of competing for investment, but it's like any sport, where you're cheering for your own team to win, but you also just want the sport to thrive. And … in some ways I'm just excited about becoming a better overall competitor. (Grimes, 2017: 38)

However, in contrast to positive reviews of incubators, other studies have suggested that incubators may actually hinder new venture creation due to fears of intellectual property theft of entrepreneurs' secret ideas (Tocher, Oswald, & Hall, 2015). Even though there may be a chance of someone stealing an idea, more often than not, incubators are a place of everyone working together as a team to encourage one another as each group pursues their individual interests. There is also the additional colloquialism that (entrepreneurial) success is something like 1 percent inspiration and 99 percent perspiration (i.e., success is largely based on the execution more than the ideas and intellectual property). Great new companies rise out of the hard work that their founders invest rather than merely their ideas.

Accelerators

A chief aspect and purpose of accelerators is improving upon something that already exists in the world or the invention of something brand new (Shankar & Shepherd, 2018). While people may go through accelerator programs in order to better understand how to grow their business, profit is not always the central focus. Many people think business is all about profit but it is not always the primary focus. At an accelerator, an additional focus includes making entrepreneurs excited and helping them innovate. Early-stage profitability is often put on the back burner as this type of accelerator strives to increase passion and joy in their product (Shankar & Shepherd, 2018). One accelerator executive said, "In our accelerator, it is not to find the next big investment opportunity. Basically, it is innovation. How quickly we can get access to something that is new, exciting and promising for the future of our company" (Shankar & Shepherd, 2018: 10). So, in this particular accelerator, they desire to build excitement among their team. They want them to have a passion for innovation and an enthusiasm for making things better than they already are, rather than just for a high profit.

Hallen, Bingham, and Cohen (2014) show that accelerators are, indeed, useful. When the venture is in its beginning phases, participating in an accelerator can really provide the necessary benefits that the venture needs to kick off (Hallen et al., 2014). Furthermore, ventures participating in accelerators tend to attain their key milestones faster than ventures that do not. Interestingly, though, Hallen et al. (2014) say that their research did not find a universal acceleration effect.

Three success factors of accelerators include the selection process and criteria, business support services, and networks (Yusubova & Clarysse, 2016). These factors focus on bringing the right people into the accelerator (screening process through applications), assigning accelerator staff to perform admin and para-legal tasks for them (providing support services) and introducing them to an already vetted community of supportive professionals (networks). The emphasis is on helping the teams apply their optimal levels of existing human capital and work ethic with the levers of social and relational capital.

Regarding the selection process and criteria, Yusubova and Clarysse (2016) found that accelerators' selection process is strong. Applicants to accelerators must complete an online application and when choosing which businesses are to participate in accelerators. The focus of these applications is at least as strong on the experience and skills of the venture team as it is on other factors such as market potential or product type. Y Combinator, for example, asks applicants to describe the best non-software "hack" they ever created (Stross, 2013). This particular approach of screening applicants helps Y Combinator to ensure it is not accepting any cohort companies who don't already have a "hacker's mindset" and helps "select in" some cultural aspects that Y Combinator values.

Mentoring, workshops, weekly evaluations, and financial and legal backing are all examples of support services that accelerators offer (Yusubova & Clarysse, 2016). Y Combinator, for example, is well known for its Tuesday night "all hands" dinners with meals served by co-founder Paul Graham and guest speakers such as Peter Thiel and Mark Zuckerberg (Stross, 2013). Another well-known practice Y Combinator provides is office hours for its venture teams. Unlike office hours one might expect with a college professor, though, Y Combinator conducts office hours with at least two mentors at any time and each cohort team on a stage for all Y Combinator teams to witness (Stross, 2013). The open nature of their office hour sessions allows other venture teams to observe the back and forth of questions and answers and to learn vicariously from the examples of every other team's open mentoring sessions.

Similar to incubators, networking during the participation in an accelerator is plentiful. Accelerators connect entrepreneurs to customers, partners, and potential future investors as well as have ventures go through Demo Day, at which entrepreneurs demonstrate their products or services to an audience of hundreds of potential investors and get the chance to form relationships with future resource providers (Stross, 2013).

University Programs

Incubators and accelerators are not solely for aspiring business community-based entrepreneurs. Many incubators (and some accelerators) are located on college campuses and/or in college towns. Several of these university-affiliated incubators cater to students, staff, and faculty and provide them an outlet and support to pursue their startup ideas. We discuss *university programs* separately from the public and private forms of incubators and accelerators because of their unique focus on education. In the university environment professors may integrate participation in incubators or accelerators as part of student course work. Or student teams that win university-sponsored pitching or business plan competitions may receive office space as part of their award. Regardless of the form of participation, we would expect universities to focus on students completing all of their degree requirements before committing to becoming a full-time entrepreneur in a new venture.

Some studies, for example, point out how students with promising ideas are encouraged to take their ideas to an academic incubator and possibly to a university technology transfer office for commercialization to advance their educational and developmental goals (Levie & Autio, 2008; Feola et al., 2019). Universities tend to be the step in a student's life before they enter the "real" business world; universities are in place to prepare students for that next stage in life, so establishing an incubator or accelerator that encourages student participation is an example of another way in which universities can to set their students up for success. Moreover, one of the institutional traditions of universities is to provide opportunities for and recognize academic achievement and excellence. Thus, if universities are actively encouraging their students to start businesses and chase their interests, students are more likely to do exactly that. For student entrepreneurs, the most important factor encouraging entrepreneurial behavior is university support (Feola et al., 2019; Leydesdorff & Etzkowitz, 1996).

Somewhat relatedly, another study discovered that students were more eager to create their own startup based upon the resources, such as an academic incubator at their university (Ahsan et al., 2018). A big difference between student entrepreneurs and older entrepreneurs is that, beyond financial limitations, oftentimes, students are more afraid and lack the confidence needed to jump into starting a business (Ahsan et al., 2018). As students, they often feel as if they are too young to begin a business; they do not have the wisdom or the know-how. Most of what they know regarding business is from sitting in a classroom and taking notes. As far as real-world application goes, they typically have very limited, largely consumer-based, experience. While it was found that university incubators do not provide students with more real-world, practical training, they do provide many counseling services (Dutt et al., 2016). These issues offer a reason why university incubators are so important to the growth of students who seek to be entrepreneurs. They provide the resources, mentorship, and support students need to chase their goals immediately instead of waiting until they feel like they are old enough to do something as adventurous as starting a business.

While university incubators and accelerators can likely be useful for these and other factors, studies indicate that the usefulness and value of incubators and accelerators on university campuses may be overstated (Kolympiris & Klein, 2017). Universities with incubators saw a trend of a decrease in patent quality; "our results suggest that university incubators may not generate net benefits for campus innovation" (Kolympiris & Klein, 2017: 22). Incubators may be causing competition between other campus programs which seek to "foster innovation and generate revenue" (Kolympiris & Klein, 2017: 21). Perhaps university incubators are in fact not actually a good fit for college students, staff, and faculty, particularly if they detract from other campus activities and the resources required to both advance innovation and bring in additional grant and licensing money for the school (Kolympiris & Klein, 2017). One question that arises: Is there a difference between university incubators and regular incubators and accelerators? While some studies find that university incubators do not provide students with more real-world, practical training (Dutt et al., 2016), they are effective at offering consulting services (Dutt et al., 2016), even if such resource investments may undermine their overall knowledge production, patent volume/quality, and license revenue potential (Kolympiris & Klein, 2017).

DISCUSSION

We promised in our title to discuss our findings with respect to research, teaching, and practice. We present that discussion in this section. We also discuss three points we feel are particularly relevant to any conversation on incubators and accelerators, namely, entrepreneurial experience, entrepreneurial need, and program fit, in the context of value creation and capture. Finally, we offer suggestions for future research. But first we lead with a summary description of our findings as we progressed through the review of panel articles.

Summary Description of Review Findings

Our selection criteria yielded a total of 19 articles on incubators and accelerators in our panel of target journals. With regard to topical focus in publications, we observed a trend in the articles addressing the *types of entrepreneurs* who use incubator and/or accelerator services (Ahsan et al., 2018; Armanios et al., 2017; Breugst et al., 2015; Ebbers, 2014; Feola et al., 2019; Giudici, Reinmoeller, & Ravasi, 2018; Goswami et al., 2018; Grimes, 2017; Hughes, Morgan, Ireland, & Hughes, 2014; Lyons & Zhang, 2018; Marlow & McAdam, 2015; Marvel, Sullivan, & Wolfe, 2018; Partanen et al., 2014; Uy, Foo, & Ilies, 2015; Uy, Sun, & Foo, 2017; Shankar & Shepherd, 2018; Tocher et al., 2015). Second, we observed that a smaller number of articles focused on the *breadth of scope* of incubator and accelerator operations (e.g., Partanen et al., 2014; Shankar & Shepherd, 2018), indicating the need to identify common roles of incubators and accelerators across different application contexts and locations and to study further the effectiveness of these roles in serving stakeholder needs. Taken together, these two trends in topical focus suggest that the study of incubators and accelerators is still in its early stages of scholarly development.

With regard to temporal trends in publications in our panel journals and the broader literature, we did not find any particular trends in the number of articles published per year in our panel, likely due to a small population of articles. However, we did find an increase in number of articles each year, indicating increasing interest in this phenomenon and its antecedents and outcomes. We interpret the absence of trends in the articles published by our panel of journals to be a function of the relatively small number of articles in our panel overall and as evidence that different journals are assessing the suitability of fit for these articles for their audiences.

We looked for trends regarding number of articles in each of the journals and authors who are publishing in the area. We identified four articles in the *Journal of Business Venturing*, three articles in the *Journal of Small Business Management*, *Entrepreneurship Theory and Practice*, and *Strategic Entrepreneurship Journal*, and two each in the *Academy of Management Journal* and *Strategic Management Journal*. We did not observe any trends in author publication.

Implications for Research, Teaching, and Practice

Implications for research
In applications of institutional theory (e.g., DiMaggio & Powell, 1983) on universities, researchers have found that universities compete with one another and tend to imitate their geographic peers; the level of imitative intensity tends to increase with closer proximity (Rey, 2001). We suspect similar relationships may exist between university incubators and accelerators with regard to competition and imitation. Researchers should examine the extent to which the tendency toward isomorphism (DiMaggio & Powell, 1983) affects these organizations and how they are affected. This research question is important for policy makers and operators of university-affiliated incubators and accelerators because resources are limited

within universities, and these limitations may actually lead to a reduction in the level of innovations (Kolympiris & Klein, 2017). Further, because entrepreneurial ecosystems may involve several universities, policy makers would probably prefer not to duplicate efforts across the incubators and accelerators of those institutions. Boston, for example, has a robust entrepreneurial ecosystem in large part because each of the city's nine major universities plays a distinctive yet complementary role in contributing to innovative output (Judge, 1997). For example, while MIT and Harvard tend to receive the most accolades for innovation, schools like Boston University have made substantial contributions to the ecosystem's expertise port-folio in photonics technologies. Given the intensive amount of resources needed to launch a university-affiliated incubator or accelerator, as well as the economic needs and other contextual factors of the university's ecosystem, researchers may find an inverted U-shaped relationship between competition and cooperation.

Another aspect of university-affiliated incubators and accelerators that shows promise for future research is the relationship between the mission of the university and the potential benefits its incubators and accelerators can offer. Universities generate, accumulate, and confer knowledge for the benefit of their graduates and broader society. Students develop not only their human capital – knowledge, skills, and abilities that will allow them to earn a living as adults (Becker, 1964) – but also develop relational capital with fellow students and professors that can provide them with learning advantages throughout their careers.

Graduates build careers, companies, and economies out of the foundational knowledge and relational capital they develop as students. These societal benefits of universities are much the same as those expected from university-affiliated incuba-tors and accelerators. In terms of research, incubators and accelerators offer scholars a rich context for the study of human capital, social capital, and social networks. Do these university-affiliated organizations "incubate" and "accelerate" the knowledge, skills, and abilities of their customers? What forms of organizing, structuring, and investing work the best? How do the "products" of these organizations help society? In terms of linking incubator and accelerator functions to these outcomes, this may be the most important question for universities to address.

Implications for teaching
Incubators and accelerators provide environments for slow and accelerated intensive learning, respectively. In terms of the learning model of universities in general and their incubators and accelerators specifically, we now have three models for teaching and learning. The traditional university model focuses on the four-year undergrad-uate degree, of course, with a foundation in social sciences, humanities, and natural sciences followed by a concentration in a chosen major. Incubators, with their focus on helping nascent entrepreneurs address the "liabilities of newness" (Stinchcombe, 1965) that nearly every early-stage startup faces, provide their participants with access to entrepreneurial networks and resources to assist them in commercializing their business ideas. In contrast, accelerators provide entrepreneurs with an envi-ronment to rapidly further develop their entrepreneurial skills and to gain market

acceptance for these ideas and ventures. We believe that incubators and accelerators in business, and possibly for other educational contexts, provide valuable and novel complements to the traditional learning models of the university. In turn these different contexts will demand different teaching and training skills, different types of "pedagogies" used to deliver knowledge, and different types of roles for the expert specialists who provide the teaching.

Different learning contexts often require different approaches to teaching and learning. We expect this to be true in incubators and accelerators. The learning model in incubators is a balance between learning approaches that nurture young fragile ventures in the present and support growth prospects for the future (Patton & Marlow, 2011). Pedagogies for teaching and training in incubators should likely be more oriented toward the classroom model and content should likely be more uniform across the cross-section of participants because of the shared inexperience of their participants. Instructors and expert specialists would be expected to be more nurturing in terms of helping these entrepreneurs develop skills to grow their early-stage ventures.

In accelerators participants develop their mastery of the entrepreneurial skills they'll use to grow their new ventures, learning as much about those skills and the needs of their customers as possible in, usually, the span of a semester. Much of the learning in accelerators is directed toward gaining traction for their business ideas so that they can pitch those ideas effectively to investors at Demo Day. In this learning environment, teachers and trainers should likely be much more focused on the growth process and, ideally, have taken their own startups through their own growth processes. Other expert specialists would likely be selected based on the usefulness of their experience to the specific ventures of a particular cohort. For this reason, other experts would likely join accelerators on an ad hoc or limited "in-residence" basis and, by extension, should lead to different types of available expertise and mentors to accelerator entrepreneurs depending on their specific needs. Incubators would therefore tend to be staffed by experienced generalists who would be expected to be part of the "team" for years rather than months. In contrast, accelerators should be staffed by expert specialists who themselves have recently undergone the growth process in their own ventures. Because these specialists would be brought into the accelerator based on the idiosyncratic needs of the members of the cohort and, perhaps, due to the high opportunity costs these specialists incur by not growing their own ventures, they would be expected to be on the team for weeks or months rather than years.

Implications for practice

By the term "practice," we are referring to the operation of university-affiliated incubators and accelerators. We have pointed out some of the differences that should characterize each of these models based on their learning emphasis and the people they need to facilitate that learning. We believe administrators of university-affiliated incubators and accelerators should closely examine the goals they ultimately hope to achieve for their stakeholders in deciding between the incubator and accelerator models. These decisions should also consider the types and availability of resident experts (long term or temporary, generalist versus specialist) they need to run them effectively, as well as what deployment of these resources does to other university-based innovation efforts (e.g., Kolympiris & Klein, 2017).

Experience, Need, and Fit

As we mentioned in the Method section, we also conducted interviews to provide some more tangible context for our integrative review. As we discussed the transcripts of participant interviews with one another, we converged on three main types of benefits of incubators and accelerators for further discussion. These topics are *experience, need,* and *fit.*

Entrepreneurial experience

One young entrepreneur in our study made the observation: "Incubators are typically more geared towards beginners, entrepreneurs just starting out. Most people who are a part of incubators do not yet understand basic business ideas." In contrast, this young man said that accelerators tend to be more useful for more experienced entrepreneurs (people who have already taken the initial steps to build their business). Starting a business is not limited to being an adult in their 30s or older. It can include anyone, such as college students. Incubators have been created specifically for the purpose of reaching out to aspiring college entrepreneurs. Such observations appear to have support in the literature. For example, one study shows that for student entrepreneurs, the most important factor encouraging entrepreneurial behavior is university support (Feola et al., 2019; Leydesdorff & Etzkowitz, 1996). The reason why college students tend to not start businesses, despite lower opportunity costs, compared to when they may be older is because they lack confidence in themselves or their idea or both (Ahsan et al., 2018), as well as resources. Therefore, by creating university incubators, students can acquire the necessary skills and resources needed so that they may feel more confident, and have better access to the resources required to launch their business earlier instead of waiting.

Entrepreneurial need

Entrepreneurial need (e.g., network, money, etc.) will depend on which program is a better fit. For example, what do you need access to? Do you need lots of people or is a small group sufficient? For example, Y Combinator may generally have 100 companies participate in each cohort which provides a diverse group to interact with and learn from through multiple networking opportunities in the program. On the other hand, smaller, regional accelerators such as Velocity in Birmingham, AL operated with targeted cohorts of 8 to 12 firms which offers the opportunity to form deeper connections and be more community development based (essentially a much different mission than investment vehicle type large corporate accelerators; Velocity Accelerator, n.d.). Across research studies, two of the most beneficial aspects of participating in an incubator or accelerator are the availability of mentorship and the opportunity to toss around ideas with other entrepreneurs. Incubators and accelerators create an expansion in the entrepreneurial group (Armanios et al., 2017). Often, entrepreneurs just starting out do not know where to begin or how to get their business built, so the mentorship provided through incubator and accelerator programs can be immensely helpful.

Program fit
Through our supplemental interviews with entrepreneurs and discussions with program operators, we identify that fit with the program (in terms of personality, industry focus, objectives, and business model, among other factors) is very important. While the location of the accelerator program allows for the co-location of resources, the drawback requires relocation or frequent travel to the location. For example, as part of Y Combinator entrepreneurs were provided with access to Silicon Valley's highly sought-after tech ecosystem upon exiting the program. The Silicon Valley location serves as an "epi-center for entrepreneurial opportunities" and this co-location was appreciated based on "the community in this environment and the access provided there." However, if an entrepreneur prefers a more structured curriculum, then a smaller program like Velocity, mentioned previously, may be a better fit than Y Combinator.

While people are apt to perceive the quality of an accelerator program on the success of participating companies, most such observations will likely not provide an accurate judgment. Rather, studies suggest "government policy makers should judge accelerators based on their expertise; namely, their expertise in building connections, developing founders, coordinating mentorship, and selecting participants (both founders and mentors)" (Goswami et al., 2018: 130).

In summary, an entrepreneur trying to choose between an incubator and an accelerator has several important factors to consider when making the decision. These factors include: (1) business stage, (2) what the entrepreneur is looking for and what the incubator's or accelerator's goals are, (3) how the incubator/accelerator chooses participants and what their graduation policies are, (4) what the incubator/accelerator has to offer and which one better fits the needs of the entrepreneur, and (5) networking opportunities availability (Isabelle, 2013).

FUTURE RESEARCH

In light of the similarities and differences we have pointed out across private and public incubators and accelerators in terms of value creation and capture, we now offer suggestions for future research. In Table 5.3, we provide an overview of the suggestions for future research offered in the literature on incubators, accelerators, and university programs. We then discuss these suggestions from the literature in the categories of additional programs, broader scope, and entrepreneurial effectiveness, along with our own assessment and suggestions in the sections that follow.

Table 5.3   *Entrepreneurial support organization literature's future research*
              suggestions

Cite	Category	Future research
Ahsan, Zheng, DeNoble, & Musteen, 2018	Mentorship	Factors that influence mentors affect the new venture context; impact on mentoring relationships and venture outcomes
Armanios, Eesley, Li, & Eisenhardt, 2017	National differences	Analyze and compare results from China to that of other countries
Breugst, Patzelt, & Rathgeber, 2015	Relationships	Study the relationship of trust between the starting entrepreneurial team and the overarching trust in the firm and its employees
Dutt, Hawn, Vidal, Chatterji, McGahan, & Mitchell, 2016	Longitudinal	Changes of incubators as time passes
Ebbers, 2014	Relationships	Contracting relationships as well as structural network characteristics
Feola, Vesci, Botti, & Parente, 2019	National differences	Research on Ph.D. students from all over the United States/world
Giudici, Reinmoeller, & Ravasi, 2018		How open-system orchestration affects new business models and effective leadership
Goswami, Mitchell, & Bhagavatula, 2018	National differences	Study incubators outside of India
Grimes, 2017	Relationships	Research on creativity, innovation and entrepreneurship, needs to study group optimal distinctiveness and how that in turn affects outcomes over time
Hughes, Morgan, Ireland, & Hughes, 2014	Relationships	Performance of beginning entrepreneurial firms affected by social capital and network-based learning
Kolympiris & Klein, 2017	University differences	Differences between types of university incubators
Marlow & McAdam, 2015	Diversity	Research on women from various backgrounds
Marvel, Sullivan, & Wolfe, 2018	Entrepreneurial actions	Domain planning and effect on entrepreneurial startups
Partanen, Chetty, & Rajala, 2014	Breadth of scope	Tests via quantitative study; similar studies should be in variety of fields and industries
Shankar & Shepherd, 2018	Breadth of scope; national differences	Ways that corporate accelerators can be designed and tested; study other parts of the world
Tocher, Oswald, & Hall, 2015	Entrepreneurial actions	Do ideas that are actually feasible and viable get dumped?
Uy, Foo, & Ilies, 2015	Stage of entrepreneur	Study teams and entrepreneurs who are in later stages
Uy, Sun, & Foo, 2017	Demographic differences; stage of entrepreneur	Research various backgrounds; differences between serial and novice entrepreneurs?

Broader Scope

One common theme from our review of the academic literature is the need for future research to have a broader scope. Often, research was limited to a certain country and population or a certain gender or very specific accelerator programs (e.g., Armanios et al., 2017; Goswami et al., 2018). Thus, it would be beneficial to initiate research that studies entrepreneurs and programs on a bigger scale. Also, further research is needed to understand the differences between types of university incubators, such as science oriented versus engineering focused (Kolympiris & Klein, 2017). Moreover, as incubators and accelerators are developing, they can change as time passes as they transform and grow, and thus more longitudinal studies are needed to understand those changes more fully (Dutt et al., 2016).

Effectiveness by Entrepreneur

Lastly, scholars should continue to study the performance and success of incubators and accelerators so that entrepreneurs may better understand their effectiveness. Conducting in-depth qualitative and mixed-method studies with entrepreneurs who have participated in various incubator and accelerator programs is needed to obtain a better understanding of the effectiveness of these programs. Additionally, it would be useful to interview people who not only have gone through the same incubator or accelerator but also to interview people who have gone through different incubators and accelerators, ranging from top-notch to smaller and less-ranked ones, so that we may understand if the size or other factors determine business success as well.

It would likely be beneficial to conduct further research to determine the value that incubators and accelerator programs believe they are creating and compare that to what entrepreneurs say is the value they are receiving. Do these line up with one another? In the end, additional insights will benefit both incubator and accelerator programs by showing them the linkage and disconnect between what value they think they create and what value entrepreneurs gain. As a result, incubator and accelerator programs could also learn to better structure their programs so that they can more effectively help the entrepreneurs. Another reason for continuing further value determination is to help entrepreneurs answer questions about the effectiveness of incubator and accelerator programs and determine if it is worth their time to participate in such programs. We summarize the future research questions we identified in the Appendix.

CONCLUSIONS

Through this integrative review we provided a detailed overview of the full scope and current state of the published academic research on incubators and accelerators, with the objective of discerning the nuances of their contributory roles, effectiveness, and value. From this review, we offer a better understanding of the current state of research on these subjects in terms of what questions have been asked, current findings, and implications for research and practice on incubators and accelerators. Further, we contribute to the literature by offering a detailed agenda for future research on these topics in articulating what we still do not know as a field, and what the benefits could be gained from addressing some of the numerous gaps remaining in this emerging field of inquiry.

We also offer some implications for entrepreneurship education and pedagogy from this study. One opportunity is in the design and execution of a university semester-long new venture formation course. Course objectives of learning about starting a business and competing in business plan competitions by the end of each semester offer students real-world pitch experience and mentoring opportunities, which directly address students' needs. These teams also have the opportunity to continue with their ventures, and move into incubator and accelerator programs at the host university, within the region, and/or national/international programs. Therefore, the implications of this research study are directly applicable to refining this course and related courses, and designing new courses, as well as enhancing the evaluation abilities, participation levels, and success rates of student-led new ventures in incubator/accelerator programs.

REFERENCES

Aernoudt, R. 2004. Incubators: Tool for entrepreneurship? *Small Business Economics*, 23(2): 127–135.

Ahsan, M., Zheng, C., DeNoble, A., & Musteen, M. 2018. From student to entrepreneur: How mentorships and affect influence student venture launch. *Journal of Small Business Management*, 56(1): 76–102.

Albort-Morant, G., & Ribeiro-Soriano, D. 2016. A bibliometric analysis of international impact of business incubators. *Journal of Business Research*, 69(5): 1775–1779.

Amezcua, A., Grimes, M., Bradley, S., & Wiklund, J. 2013. Organizational sponsorship and founding environments: A contingency view on the survival of business incubated firms, 1994–2007. *Academy of Management Journal*, 56: 1628–1654.

Armanios, D. E., Eesley, C. E., Li, J., & Eisenhardt, K. M. 2017. How entrepreneurs leverage institutional intermediaries in emerging economies to acquire public resources. *Strategic Management Journal*, 38(7): 1373–1390.

Baskaran, A., Chandran, V. G. R., & Ng, B.-K. 2019. Inclusive entrepreneurship, innovation and sustainable growth: Role of business incubators, academia and social enterprises in Asia. *Science, Technology and Society*, 24(3): 285–400.

Becker, G. 1964. *Human Capital*. Chicago, IL: University of Chicago Press.

Breugst, N., Patzelt, H., & Rathgeber, P. 2015. How should we divide the pie? Equity distribution and its impact on entrepreneurial teams. *Journal of Business Venturing*, 30(1): 66–94.

Breznitz, S. M., Clayton, P. A., Defazio, D., & Isett, K. R. 2018. Have you been served? The impact of university entrepreneurial support on start-ups' network formation. *Journal of Technology Transfer*, 43(2): 343–367.

Coara.co. 2020. 19 Best incubators for startups worldwide 2020. https://coara.co/blog/best -incubators-for-startups, accessed March 1, 2021.

Cohen, S. 2013. What do accelerators do? Insights from incubators and angels. *Innovations: Technology, Governance, Globalization*, 8(3–4): 19–25.

Cohen, S., & Hochberg, Y. V. 2014. *Accelerating Startups: The Seed Accelerator Phenomenon.* SSRN Scholarly Paper no. ID 2418000. Rochester, NY: Social Science Research Network.

DiMaggio, P. J., & Powell, W. W. 1983. The iron cage revisited: Institutional isomorphism and collective rationality in organizational fields. *American Sociological Review,* 48: 147–160.

Denk, N., Kaufmann, L., & Roesch, J. F. 2012. Liabilities of foreignness revisited: A review of contemporary studies and recommendations for future research. *Journal of International Management,* 18(4): 322–334.

Dutt, N., Hawn, O., Vidal, E., Chatterji, A., McGahan, A., & Mitchell, W. 2016. How open system intermediaries address institutional failures: The case of business incubators in emerging-market countries. *Academy of Management Journal,* 59(3): 818–840.

Ebbers, J. J. 2014. Networking behavior and contracting relationships among entrepreneurs in business incubators. *Entrepreneurship Theory and Practice,* 38(5): 1–23.

Feola, R., Vesci, M., Botti, A., & Parente, R. 2019. The determinants of entrepreneurial intention of young researchers: Combining the theory of planned behavior with the Triple Helix Model. *Journal of Small Business Management,* 57(4): 1424–1443.

Finer, B., & Holberton, P. 2002. Incubators: There and back; Good ideas don't always translate into profits, as the experience of for-profit incubators shows. *Journal of Business Strategy,* 23(3): 23–26.

Giudici, A., Reinmoeller, P., & Ravasi, D. 2018. Open-system orchestration as a relational source of sensing capabilities: Evidence from a venture association. *Academy of Management Journal,* 61(4): 1369–1402.

Goswami, K., Mitchell, J. R., & Bhagavatula, S. 2018. Accelerator expertise: Understanding the intermediary role of accelerators in the development of the Bangalore entrepreneurial ecosystem. *Strategic Entrepreneurship Journal,* 12(1): 117–150.

Grimaldi, R., & Grandi, A. 2005. Business incubators and new venture creation: An assessment of incubating models. *Technovation,* 25(2): 111–121.

Grimes, M. 2017. The pivot: How founders respond to feedback through idea and identity work. *Academy of Management Journal,* 61(5): 1692–1717.

Guerrero, M., Urbano, D., & Gajón, E. 2020. Entrepreneurial university ecosystems and graduates' career patterns: Do entrepreneurship education programmes and university business incubators matter? *Journal of Management Development,* 39(5): 753–775.

Hallen, B. L., Bingham, C., & Cohen, S. 2014. Do accelerators accelerate? A study of venture accelerators as a path to success? *Academy of Management Annual Meeting Proceedings,* 1: 12955–12955.

Hughes, M., Morgan, R. E., Ireland, R. D., & Hughes, P. 2014. Social capital and learning advantages: A problem of absorptive capacity. *Strategic Entrepreneurship Journal,* 8(3): 214–233.

Inc.com. 2020. Business incubators. February 6. www.inc.com/encyclopedia/business -incubators.html, accessed March 18, 2021.

Isabelle, D. 2013. Key factors affecting a technology entrepreneur's choice of incubator or accelerator. *Technology Innovation Management Review,* 3(2): 16–22.

Judge, P. 1997. Boston's Route 128: Complementing Silicon Valley. *BusinessWeek,* August 13.

Judge, T. A., Cable, D. M., Colbert, A. E., & Rynes, S. L. 2007. What causes a management article to be cited – article, author, or journal? *Academy of Management Journal,* 50(3): 491–506.

Kauffman Foundation. 2014. Kauffman sketchbook – myth-busting entrepreneurship. September 16. https://youtu.be/K8rdum5DFHk, accessed March 18, 2021.

Kemp, P., & Weber, P. 2012. Business incubators: Their genesis, forms, intent and impact. In R. A. Blackburn & M. T. Schaper (Eds), *Government, SMEs and Entrepreneurship Development: Policy, Practice and Challenges,* 141–155. New York: Routledge.

Kolympiris, C., & Klein, P. G. 2017. The effects of academic incubators on university innovation. *Strategic Entrepreneurship Journal*, 11(2): 145–170.

Lange, G. S. 2018. The value of business incubators and accelerators from the entrepreneur's perspective. Dissertation, Georgia State University.

Levie, J., & Autio, E. 2008. A theoretical grounding and test of the GEM model. *Small Business Economics*, 31(3): 235–263.

Leydesdorff, L., & Etzkowitz, H. 1996. Emergence of a Triple Helix of university-industry-government relations. *Science and Public Policy*, 23(5): 279–286.

López-Duarte, C., Vidal-Suárez, M. M., & González-Díaz, B. 2016. International business and national culture: A literature review and research agenda. *International Journal of Management Reviews*, 18(4): 397–416.

Lyons, E., & Zhang, L. 2018. Who does (not) benefit from entrepreneurship programs? *Strategic Management Journal*, 39(1): 85–112.

Markley, D. M., Lyons, T. S., & Macke, D. W. 2015. Creating entrepreneurial communities: Building community capacity for ecosystem development. *Community Development*, 46(5): 580–598.

Marlow, S., & McAdam, M. 2015. Incubation or induction? Gendered identity work in the context of technology business incubation. *Entrepreneurship Theory and Practice*, 39(4): 791–816.

Marvel, M. R., Sullivan, D. M., & Wolfe, M. T. 2018. Accelerating sales in startups: A domain planning, network reliance, and resource complementary perspective. *Journal of Small Business Management*, 57(3): 1086–1101.

McAdam, M., & Marlow, S. 2011. Sense and sensibility: The role of business incubator client advisors in assisting high-technology entrepreneurs to make sense of investment readiness status. *Entrepreneurship and Regional Development*, 23(7–8): 449–468.

Miller, P., & Bound, K. 2011. The startup factories. *NESTA*. www.nesta.org. uk/library/documents/StartupFactories.pdf, accessed September 22, 2021.

Partanen, J., Chetty, S. K., & Rajala, A. 2014. Innovation types and network relationships. *Entrepreneurship Theory and Practice*, 38(5): 1027–1055.

Patton, D., & Marlow, S. 2011. University technology business incubators: Helping new entrepreneurial firms to learn to grow. *Environment and Planning C: Government and Policy*, 29(5): 911–926.

Pfeffer, J., & Fong, C. T. 2002. The end of business schools? Less success than meets the eye. *Academy of Management Learning and Education*, 1(1): 78–95.

Phan, P., Siegel, D. S., & Wright, M. 2016. Science parks and incubators: Observations, synthesis and future research. In P. A. Phan, S. A. Mian, & W. Lamine (Eds), *Technology Entrepreneurship and Business Incubation: Theory Practice Lessons Learned*, 249–272. London: Imperial College Press.

Rey, E. D. 2001. Teaching versus research: A model of state university competition. *Journal of Urban Economics*, 49(2): 356–373.

Rothaermel, F. T., & Thursby, M. 2005. University–incubator firm knowledge flows: Assessing their impact on incubator firm performance. *Research Policy*, 34(3): 305–320.

Roundy, P. T. 2017. Hybrid organizations and the logics of entrepreneurial ecosystems. *International Entrepreneurship and Management Journal*, 13(4): 1221–1237.

Schawbel, D. 2012. How colleges are becoming entrepreneurial. *TechCrunch*. https://social.techcrunch.com/2012/07/08/how-colleges-are-becoming-entrepreneurial/.

Shankar, R. K., & Shepherd, D. A. 2018. Accelerating strategic fit or venture emergence: Different paths adopted by corporate accelerators. *Journal of Business Venturing*, 34(5): 105886.

Stinchcombe, A. 1965. Social structure and organizations. In J. March (Ed.), *Handbook of Organizations*, 142–193. Chicago, IL: Rand McNally.

Stross, R. 2013. *The Launch Pad: Inside Y Combinator*. New York: Penguin.

Sutter, C., Bruton, G. D., & Chen, J. 2019. Entrepreneurship as a solution to extreme poverty: A review and future research directions. *Journal of Business Venturing*, 34(1): 197–214.

Tocher, N., Oswald, S. L., & Hall, D. J. 2015. Proposing social resources as the fundamental catalyst toward opportunity creation. *Strategic Entrepreneurship Journal*, 9(2): 119–135.

Tötterman, H., & Sten, J. 2005. Start-ups: Business incubation and social capital. *International Small Business Journal*, 23(5): 487–511.

Uy, M. A., Foo, M. D., & Ilies, R. 2015. Perceived progress variability and entrepreneurial effort intensity: The moderating role of venture goal commitment. *Journal of Business Venturing*, 30(3): 375–389.

Uy, M. A., Sun, S., & Foo, M. D. 2017. Affect spin, entrepreneurs' well-being, and venture goal progress: The moderating role of goal orientation. *Journal of Business Venturing*, 32(4): 443–460.

Velocity Accelerator. n.d. https://innovationdepot.org/velocity/.

Yusubova, A., & Clarysse, B. 2016. Success factors of business accelerators in three European cities: Paris, London, Berlin. In P. H. Phan, S. A. Mian, & W. Lamine (Eds), *Technology Entrepreneurship and Business Incubation: Theory Practice Lessons Learned*, 35–56. London: Imperial College Press.

APPENDIX: FUTURE RESEARCH QUESTIONS

Exploratory/baseline review questions for clarifying the knowledge base and improving research, teaching, and practice:

- What is the most effective role(s) of an incubator program?
- What is the most effective role(s) of an accelerator program?
- What is (or what should be) the difference between incubators and accelerators?

Value creation/capture-related questions for clarifying the knowledge base and improving research, teaching, and practice:

- Is (how is) value created through incubators/accelerators? Who benefits from capturing value?
- How effective are incubators and accelerators? For the new venture team? For the investor? For the incubator/accelerator program?
- What types of ventures are more likely to participate in an incubator/accelerator?
- What types of ventures (and at what stages) do/don't benefit from incubators/ accelerators?

6. Holistic view of strategic entrepreneurship's results: estimating the implications for performance mean and variability

Oleksiy Osiyevskyy, Kanhaiya Kumar Sinha, Galina V. Shirokova, and Mehrsa Ehsani

Strategic entrepreneurship implies identifying and taking advantage of value-creating opportunities with a strategic perspective of building and sustaining a firm's competitive advantage (e.g., Hitt et al., 2001; Ireland et al., 2003; Shane & Venkataraman, 2000). Successful strategic entrepreneurship brings benefits through the creation and appropriation of entrepreneurial rents, which are inextricably linked with the uncertainty of the results (Rumelt, 1987). The consequence of the condition of uncertainty implies that when entrepreneurs (be it new venture founders or leaders of corporate intrapreneurship projects) aim to create value through entrepreneurial actions, they also expose their firms to variability in the expected outcome of their efforts.[1] For example, a common feature of most strategic actions that are considered entrepreneurial (such as switching from paid job to founding a venture, radical innovation, or explorative learning) is that their results are highly uncertain, or – statistically speaking – that the distribution of their expected outcomes has high dispersion, as compared to their "non-entrepreneurial" counterparts. The extensive empirical strategic entrepreneurship literature, however, with a few exceptions[2] concentrated on assessing the impact of entrepreneurial strategies on the average (conditional mean) of the resulting performance, without analyzing their simultaneous effect on the dispersion of the resulting outcome distribution.

Ignoring explicit analysis of outcomes variance of entrepreneurial actions is unfortunate, as explaining the variability of firms' performance is no less important than explaining the average performance (Wiklund & Shepherd, 2011). First, at the level of a particular firm, high outcome variability implies high risk, which is highly undesirable, particularly in resource-constrained contexts, such as new venturing (Parida et al., 2016). Not surprisingly, highly variable outcomes of entrepreneurial actions increase the chances of getting to the left-hand tail of the performance distribution, leading to higher mortality rates of firms because of getting below the minimal survivorship threshold (Wiklund & Shepherd, 2011).

At the same time, high variability also increases the chances of getting enormously high actual performance because of a higher rate of positive outliers (Sinha & Osiyevskyy, 2018). As such, variability at a firm level is a sought-after property at higher levels of aggregation (e.g., portfolios of angel investors or venture capitalists, or the national economy), when proper selection mechanisms allow eliminating the negative outliers and supporting the positive outliers. That is, high performance variability at the firm level creates the necessary variation, which – when followed by retention mechanisms at higher levels – allows the overall system development thanks to the selection of the winners (Aldrich & Ruef, 2006).

As such, the current chapter addresses the following broad research question: *What is the impact of strategic entrepreneurship actions on the variability of firm performance?* To answer it, we review the existing studies of the variability outcomes of entrepreneurial actions and develop a baseline hypothesis. Then, we discuss the appropriate method for accurate assessment of simultaneous mean and variance effects of entrepreneurship actions – the multiplicative heteroscedasticity regression methodology (Harvey, 1976), which – although not widely known in management – is broadly used in the economics field (e.g., Cheng, 2008). The method is empirically illustrated for two particular strategic entrepreneurship constructs – entrepreneurial orientation (EO) and exploration.

The primary intended contribution of the current chapter is in drawing the attention of strategic entrepreneurship scholars to the need to analyze performance implications of entrepreneurial actions not only from the perspective of their impact on the level (conditional mean of performance, as it is done in the majority of studies based on conventional regression methodology) but also from the perspective of the impact of entrepreneurial actions on the variance of the resulting performance distribution. The chapter also discusses the exemplar entrepreneurship papers that demonstrate the rigorous approaches for theorizing and testing the outcome variability. We finish by outlining the implications of the study's insights for the further theoretical and empirical development of the strategic entrepreneurship field.

BASELINE HYPOTHESIS: THE IMPACT OF ENTREPRENEURIAL ACTIONS ON VARIABILITY IN FIRM PERFORMANCE

Strategic entrepreneurship, or the pursuit of identifying and exploiting the marketplace opportunities with a strategic purpose (Hitt et al., 2001), implies overcoming major uncertainty caused by the discovery of true, *ex post* value of a new firm's resource combinations or patterns of marketplace demand (Rumelt, 1987) in the dynamic competitive landscape. As such, the results of entrepreneurial actions cannot be predicted and properly planned *ex ante*, leading to a lack of reliability (that is, high variability) of the resulting performance distribution. To illustrate this point, let us now consider particular examples of actions (exploration) or orientations (EO) that are conventionally attributed to strategic entrepreneurship.

Organizational exploratory learning (or simply *exploration*) is a major component of strategic entrepreneurial actions (Ireland & Webb, 2009; Shirokova et al., 2013). Exploration implies an active, deliberate search for novel opportunities for developing valuable new competencies or entering new lucrative markets. In the original study, March (1991) famously defined exploration as "search, variation, risk-taking, experimentation, play, flexibility, discovery, and innovation," as opposed to exploitation that implies "refinement, choice, production, efficiency, selection, implementation and execution" (p. 71). Exploitation focuses on continuing and refining the existing business approach through the utilization of existing knowledge, while exploration aims at discovering and creating entirely new knowledge. The insights of a high number of existing studies usually converge on the view that in stable time exploration strategy results in incurring non-trivial costs, e.g., for testing new markets or research and development, as well as occasional losses from negative feedback from new and potential customers (Mudambi & Swift, 2014). Also, exploration results in opportunity costs due to diverting the resources from exploitation (i.e., leveraging current capabilities) to the slow and costly processes of learning and developing the new capabilities (Alvarez, 2018). Admittedly, exploration occasionally results in positive performance thanks to the infrequent discovery of new valuable opportunities; yet, these benefits are highly uncertain and impossible to assess in advance (Lavie et al., 2010). As such, the pursuit of exploration strategy tends to enhance the variability in firm performance (Uotila, 2017).

A crucial enabler of strategic entrepreneurship within established and new firms is the EO (Kantur, 2016). It is the organizational frame of mind, culture, strategy-making practices, and processes that place innovative venturing (be it new products, new services, new markets, or new business models) at the cornerstone of short- and long-term business development (Dess & Lumpkin, 2005; Osiyevskyy et al., 2020a). The study by Wiklund and Shepherd (2011) challenges the conventional view of most prior studies adopting an "EO-as-advantage" perspective (i.e., focusing on the impact of EO on performance average), suggesting complementing and extending it by embracing the "EO-as-experimentation" perspective, which concentrates on the construct's variance-enhancing property.

Based on the insights from the exploration learning literature (in line with the discussion of exploration in the current chapter), the authors provide rigorous theoretical justification for the argument that EO leads to a high level of variability in the firm's performance, then provide empirical evidence for this hypothesis. Indeed, the pursuit of EO-enabled activities presumes a risky departure from established ways of doing business and the necessity to develop new competencies. Of course, engaging in risky venturing does not always produce successful outcomes, but rather enhances the chances of getting extreme results. Therefore, larger EO-enabled gambles are likely to increase the performance variance, creating necessary conditions for more "home runs" and "major losses" (Wiklund & Shepherd, 2011).

As such, the general view of strategic entrepreneurship and analysis of its particular exemplary actions (exploration) and enablers (EO) suggest that identification and pursuit of value-creation opportunities with a strategic purpose have a non-trivial, positive impact on the variability of the resulting performance distribution. This leads to our baseline hypothesis (illustrated in Figure 6.1):

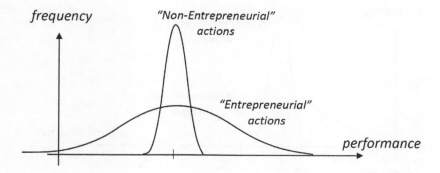

Note: Frequency (*y* axis) denotes the expected occurrences of particular performance figures in the *ex-post* performance distribution.

Figure 6.1   Baseline hypothesis: the impact of strategic entrepreneurship on the performance distribution

Baseline Hypothesis   Strategic entrepreneurial actions (e.g., exploration) and their enablers (e.g., entrepreneurial orientation) have a positive impact on the variability of a firm's performance distribution.

Notably, we do not postulate *a priori* any hypotheses about the effect of strategic entrepreneurship on the level (i.e., mean) of firm performance, in that this impact is highly dependent on the particular context and time frame, and has been extensively studied in the existing literature. As such, firms in both distributions in Figure 6.1 have the same mean, for illustrative purposes only.

In the following section, we will discuss alternative approaches to empirical, quantitative testing[3] of the variance-based hypotheses, presenting the exemplar papers for each one.

METHODOLOGY: ASSESSING THE IMPACT OF PREDICTORS ON VARIABILITY OF THE OUTCOME

Indirect Approach: Analyzing the Failure Rate

The first method for empirical testing of hypothesized variance effects is an indirect one, analyzing their impact on firm survivorship or mortality. As argued previously, the high variability of performance distribution implies high chances of getting to the zone of left-hand-side outliers, beyond the minimal performance needed to maintain the firm's operations. As such, if the design of the study explicitly

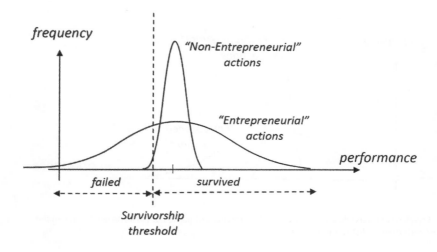

Note: Frequency (*y* axis) denotes the expected occurrences of particular performance figures in the *ex-post* performance distribution.

Figure 6.2   Indirect approach to testing the variability hypotheses: a failure rate analysis

accounts for firm survival or failure, the high variability of entrepreneurial actions will be reflected in lower chances of surviving of entrepreneurial firms, as opposed to their non-entrepreneurial counterparts. This situation is presented in Figure 6.2, illustrating that the failed-to-survived proportion for "entrepreneurial firms" is much higher than the failed-to-survived proportion within the "non-entrepreneurial" group. Interestingly, this selection process is simultaneously increasing the average performance of entrepreneurial firms in the survived subsample, creating a usually false impression of the positive impact of strategic entrepreneurship on firm performance, if the survivorship effect is not properly controlled for.

An exemplar study illustrating a rigorous way of theorizing the variance effects of entrepreneurial constructs (namely EO), with subsequent testing of their impact on the survivorship and average performance of survived firms, is Wiklund and Shepherd (2011).

Of course, this approach to probing the variance effects of strategic entrepreneurship constructs has its major limitations. First, inferring the variance effects from firm survival does not allow direct assessment of these effects, or disentangling the impact of predictors on the mean performance from their variability effects. Second, this approach does not allow accounting for other sources of firm mortality, beyond high variability in outcomes. And finally, the performance survivorship threshold is far from homogenous across firms; rather, it is endogenously determined by the firm's and environment's characteristics (e.g., Gimeno et al., 1997).

Direct Approach: Impact on Standard Deviation

The conventionally used approach to estimating performance variability is using the within-firm standard deviation of performance over a couple of periods (e.g., monthly, quarterly, or annually) as a dependent variable in regression estimates (e.g., Parida et al., 2016; Pearce & Patel, 2018; Wales et al., 2013). An exemplar study using this approach is Wales et al. (2013), theorizing and testing the mediating effect of EO on the association between the chief executive officer's narcissism and firm performance variability, measured as the industry-adjusted standard deviation of revenue for each firm over the five-year period. Similarly, using the standard deviation of firm sales over the nine-year period as a measure of the dependent variable, Parida et al. (2016) explore the association between ambidexterity and variability in entrepreneurial firms' performance.

Although much more appropriate for assessing the variance effects, compared to the previously discussed indirect method, this approach has a crucial shortcoming that might lead to biased results. The matter is that the standard deviation measure reflects the average deviation of actual values of the dependent variable from the calculated firm-level mean. Yet, using an unconditional, invariant mean as a basis for calculating deviations does not take into account the dynamics of firm-level performance over time, or the impact of predictors on the performance. This approach might bias the results: For example, if a particular predictor has a strong positive impact on the firm performance, observations high on this variable will also tend to have high values of the dependent variable; alas, they will also have predictably high positive deviations from the calculated unconditional firm-level mean. Similarly, if a firm's performance is steadily increasing over time, the residuals from the firm-level mean will be high in early and late periods, and small in the middle, because of the time trend's effect on the dependent variable. These high deviations should not indicate high variability, but will still get a high score if the latter is measured as the deviation from the unconditional firm-level mean (e.g., Sørensen, 2002).

In other words, using the performance standard deviation as a dependent variable is appropriate only if the firm-level mean is a good approximation for the performance of a particular firm, i.e., when the latter is stable across the time and not affected by the predictors. If these conditions are not met, the obtained results might be misleading.

Multiplicative Heteroscedasticity Estimation

A more flexible and general approach for empirical assessment of variance effects differs from the previous one in one essential aspect: Instead of using the unconditional, fixed mean as a basis for calculating the residuals, it uses the predicted values of the dependent variable for each observation. In other words, the residuals (which reflect the variance in the outcome) are estimated as a difference between actual and predicted values of the dependent variable. This approach, the multiplicative heteroscedasticity regression methodology (Harvey, 1976; Greene, 1997), explicitly allows for correct simultaneous estimation of the impact of predictors on both level (conditional mean/first moment) and variability (conditional dispersion/second moment) of the outcome variable distribution. Multiplicative heteroscedasticity regression estimations are widely used in economic studies (e.g., Cheng, 2008), yet are still relatively rare in management and entrepreneurship research, with the notable exemplary studies of Sorenson and Sørensen (2001; strategic management), Fleming (2001; innovation), Sørensen (2002; organizational behavior), and Hunter (2003; management information systems). In entrepreneurship, the method was employed by Chrisman and Patel (2012), Shirokova et al. (2020), and Osiyevskyy et al. (2020b).

The idea behind the multiplicative heteroscedasticity regression is performing the estimation of two equations (Greene, 1997; Harvey, 1976): the linear mean equation (1) and the log-linear variability equation (2):

$$Perf_i = X_i B + \varepsilon_i \tag{1}$$

$$\varepsilon_i = e^{Z_i \Gamma} u_i \tag{2}$$

In equation (1), $Perf_i$ denotes the dependent variable (for example, performance) of firm i, X_i is a vector of predictors (firm and environmental characteristics), B is the vector of regression weights, and ε_i is the error term. Equation (1) is suitable for the conventional OLS regression estimation, or more advanced specifications, e.g., using panel analysis data models (Chrisman & Patel, 2012). In line with the standard interpretation of regression models, the estimated parameters (β_j from vector B) of equation (1) reflect the impact of individual predictors on the expected value (conditional mean) of the dependent variable, $Perf_i$.

In addition to estimating the impact of predictors on the expected value of the outcome variable, we also need to estimate the variability of the resulting variable or its deviation from the conditional mean. For this, the error term ε_i from equation (1), representing the residual between the actual and predicted values of $Perf_i$ variable for each observation, is used as a dependent variable in the second regression. In equation (2), ε_i gets represented as a function of a set of independent variables (vector Z_i and a random term u_i. In this regression specification, Γ is a vector of parameter estimates for the effects of predictors Z_i on the variance in the dependent variable from equation (1). For example, a positive significant value of a particular parameter (γ_j in Γ) suggests that the corresponding predictor increases the variabil-

Table 6.1   *Choice of methodology in the study of outcome variability*

Research context and aim	Analyzing the failure rate	Measuring standard deviation	Multiplicative heteroscedasticity estimation
The main focus of the study is survival, while the performance variability is used for theoretical development only	X		
Investigating the effect of predictors on within-firm variability in a longitudinal study, when the predictors have no or little effect on mean performance		X	
Segregating and quantifying the effect of each predictor on variability of outcome between firms			X
Estimating the models when predictors of variability also predict the mean			X
Model building, sensitivity/scenario analysis in performance variability			X

ity in the dependent variable; in other words, the observations with high levels on this predictor tend to have larger residuals ε_i in equation (1).

Equation (2) can be empirically estimated by regressing the logarithm of squared residuals (actual values of dependent variable, $Perf_i$, minus the values predicted in equation (1) for each observation) on the vector of predictors Z_i. Although this is not statistically required, the conventional practice is to use the same set of predictors for the mean and variance models, i.e., $X_i = Z_i$ (Sorenson & Sørensen, 2001).

Technically, there are two ways to estimate equations (1) and (2): a two-step approach, and a simultaneous, maximum-likelihood-based approach (Harvey, 1976). The two-step approach implies regression estimation of equation (1), then calculating log-squared residuals and using them as a dependent variable for the regression estimation of equation (2). Alternatively, these equations can be simultaneously estimated as a system, using, for example, the maximum likelihood (ML) estimator for multiplicative heteroscedasticity models.[4] The latter method is more efficient, yet, as is the case with ML-based techniques, is more sensitive to the incorrect specification of the functional forms of equations (1) and (2), as well as to non-normality of the error distribution.

Table 6.1 presents a suggestion on the possible choices researchers can make when selecting a methodology to study outcome variability.

In the following section, we provide an empirical illustration of the multiplicative heteroscedasticity regression estimation of the variance effects of two previously discussed strategic entrepreneurship constructs, exploration and EO.

EMPIRICAL ILLUSTRATION: THE IMPACT OF EXPLORATION AND ENTREPRENEURIAL ORIENTATION ON FIRM PERFORMANCE VARIABILITY

Context and Sample

Empirically, the current illustrative study focuses on the performance of small and medium enterprises (SMEs) in the emerging market economy, the Russian Federation, during 2015–2016. The data for the study were assembled from two sources: (1) the survey of Russian SMEs conducted in late 2015 and early 2016, and (2) Russian firm-level financial data from the SPARK Interfax database. The matching of the firms was performed on the basis of the company's Main State Registration Number (OGRN).

The firm survey data were derived from a large data collection project (Beliaeva et al., 2020; Laskovaia, 2019; Osiyevskyy et al., 2020b; Shirokova et al., 2019, 2020), aiming at assessing various strategic firm qualities utilizing a comprehensive national random sample of SMEs. Within this project, initially, 10,359 randomly chosen companies from the Unified State Register of Legal Entities database were verified against the SPARK Interfax database, which regularly records updated demographic and financial data for all legally registered Russian firms. After the elimination of large and micro enterprises (with more than 500 and fewer than three employees, respectively), government organizations, firms from the agriculture sector, firms without financial information for the 2014–2015 period, and firms without contact information, 2583 companies remained and were invited to take part in the survey. After disseminating the questionnaire to founders and chief executive officers of the focal companies through an online tool – allowing the interviewer to monitor the progress of each respondent and provide assistance if necessary – a total of 656 filled questionnaires were collected, with a response rate of 25.4 percent. For the current study, the firm-level survey data were matched with financial data from SPARK Interfax database for the after-survey period. The final sample of 521 observations was obtained after excluding 135 companies with missing financial information for 2016.

Measures

Dependent variables
Firm performance was operationalized by using the objective measure of the firm's net income in 2016 (and in 2017 as a robustness check about longer-term impact), which is reported in thousands of rubles and is calculated as the financial results of a firm's activity (positive or negative) after payment of taxes and other required fees. *Firm performance variability* was operationalized following the multiplicative heteroscedasticity regression methodology, as the level of residual variance (degree of deviation of actual dependent variable values from the predicted mean for each observation).

Independent variables

All predictors and control variables were measured in 2015 (secondary financial data) or in early 2016 (survey data). To test the variance-based implications of strategic entrepreneurial actions in line with the baseline hypothesis, as predictors in our study we selected the constructs of exploration (an important component of SE) and EO (a crucial enabler of SE).

The *exploration* and *exploitation* variables were evaluated using the 12-item survey scale of Lubatkin et al. (2006). The common title of the question block requested: "In the period from 2013 to 2015, our firm can be described as one that: (1 – strongly disagree; 7 – strongly agree)." For the *exploration* construct (sample item "looks for novel technological ideas by thinking 'outside the box'"), Cronbach Alpha was 0.90; for *exploitation* (sample item "commits to improve quality and lower cost") Cronbach Alpha was 0.82.

The *EO* was assessed as a unidimensional construct, using the nine-item survey scale of Covin and Slevin (1989) and Lumpkin and Dess (2001) (Alpha = 0.90).

As a theoretical enabler of strategic entrepreneurship (particularly exploration), the EO variable in our context was highly correlated with exploration ($r = 0.713$, $p < 0.001$). The correlation of EO with exploitation was noticeably lower ($r = 0.384$, $p < 0.001$). Finally, the exploration and exploitation variables turn out significantly interrelated ($r = 0.561$, $p < 0.001$), revealing that these are not mutually exclusive approaches.

Control variables

First, in the study, we controlled for *firm size* and *firm age*. The former was captured by incorporating three factors, namely the natural logarithms of firms' total assets in 2015, total sales in 2015, and the number of employees at the time of the survey. *International sales*, as a measure of firms' maturity and exposure to international sanctions, that were severe in the Russian economy at the time of the study, was also accounted for by including a binary variable (1 for any amount of exports and 0 for none).

Second, the fixed effects of *industry* and *region* were controlled for in the study, presuming that the mentioned factors might be essential determinants of both predictors and the outcomes of the study, determining the resource availability, resiliency, legal structure, and other possible firm characteristics. In addition, *environmental dynamism* (five items from Miller & Friesen, 1982; Alpha = 0.81, sample item "The rate at which products/services are getting obsolete in the industry is very high") was controlled for, to capture the firm's assessment of its industry characteristics, inasmuch as *industry* and *region* might not be completely efficient for assessing the external environment of a particular firm.

Finally, the *formalization* variable was assessed using the four-item measure of Cardinal (2001) (Alpha = 0.85, sample item "We have rules and procedures stating how to perform normal daily activities").

Results

The multiplicative heteroscedasticity regression results are presented in Table 6.2 (for exploration predictor) and Table 6.3 (for EO predictor), with two models in each (for the 2016 and 2017 years of measuring the outcome). The models were assessed using the ML estimator.

Each of the models M1–M4 presents two results: the mean regression (equation (1) assessing the impacts β_j of predictors on the conditional mean of the dependent variable), and variance regression (equation (2) assessing the impacts γ_j of predictors on the variability of residuals about the conditional mean).

The results of M1 suggest that in the short term, the exploration activities have a negative impact on performance, while simultaneously enhancing the variability of the resulting distribution ($\beta = -24.534$, $p = 0.043$; $\gamma = 0.198$, $p = 0.001$). Notably, the exploitation variable demonstrates the pposite effect, providing significant improvements and stabilizing the short-term performance ($\beta = 57.549$, $p = 0.024$; $\gamma = -0.308$, $p < 0.001$). Graphically, these interrelationships between exploration, exploitation, and firm performance distribution in the short term are represented in Figure 6.3.

In the longer term (2017 net income measure, M2 in Table 6.2), the mean effects of exploration and exploitation disappear, while the variance effects remain (exploration enhances variability, while exploitation reduces it: $\gamma = 0.354$, $p < 0.001$ and $\gamma = -0.264$, $p < 0.001$, respectively). The variance-enhancing property of exploration activities corroborates this study's baseline hypothesis about the positive impact of strategic entrepreneurship on firm performance variability.

For EO, the results of M3 (see Table 6.3) suggest that in the short term, EO does not affect the mean performance, yet boosts the variability of performance ($\beta = -14.526$, $p = 0.358$; $\gamma = 0.215$, $p < 0.001$). These effects remain significant in the longer term (2017 net income results, M4 in Table 6.3: $\beta = 15.913$, $p = 0.535$; $\gamma = 0.327$, $p < 0.001$), thus corroborating our baseline hypothesis. The configuration of means and variance effects in Figure 6.1 (i.e., no mean effect yet significant positive variance effect) accurately describes the detected performance implications of EO on firms.

DISCUSSION

Summary

In summary, the main contribution of the current chapter is in demonstrating the theoretical need and practical approaches for analyzing the performance implications of entrepreneurial actions more broadly, incorporating mean and variance effects. Drawing on the existing strategic entrepreneurship studies, we argue for the baseline hypothesis that entrepreneurial actions have significant, non-trivial impact on the variability of firm performance, which has major strategic implications in terms of risks, probability of obtaining outliers, and firm survivorship. Then, using the appro-

Table 6.2   *Multiplicative heteroscedasticity regression model for exploration and exploitation*

Dependent variable	M1: Net income in 2016		M2: Net income in 2017	
	Mean regression (β_j)	Variance regression (γ_j)	Mean regression (β_j)	Variance regression (γ_j)
Exploration	−24.534*	0.198***	25.902	0.354***
	(12.114)	(0.061)	(27.468)	(0.063)
	[0.043]	[0.001]	[0.346]	[0.000]
Exploitation	57.549*	−0.308***	−39.195	−0.264***
	(25.560)	(0.073)	(31.386)	(0.076)
	[0.024]	[0.000]	[0.212]	[0.000]
Total assets in 2015, ln	−9.613	1.372***	−2.447	0.928***
	(20.053)	(0.055)	(30.448)	(0.056)
	[0.632]	[0.000]	[0.936]	[0.000]
Sales in 2015, ln	69.925***	0.218***	57.505**	0.585***
	(17.348)	(0.058)	(21.849)	(0.059)
	[0.000]	[0.000]	[0.008]	[0.000]
Firm age, ln	−23.802	−0.361***	−159.695**	−0.608***
	(36.048)	(0.095)	(58.706)	(0.097)
	[0.509]	[0.000]	[0.007]	[0.000]
Number of employees, ln	212.950***	0.354***	56.160	0.083
	(36.550)	(0.076)	(51.929)	(0.077)
	[0.000]	[0.000]	[0.279]	[0.281]
Environmental dynamism	−29.232	0.016	−56.161	−0.181**
	(21.408)	(0.063)	(36.821)	(0.065)
	[0.172]	[0.801]	[0.127]	[0.005]
Formalization	33.004**	0.489***	18.207	0.194***
	(11.959)	(0.043)	(20.479)	(0.045)
	[0.006]	[0.000]	[0.374]	[0.000]
International sales dummy	72.686	−1.316***	−183.924	−0.375
	(173.684)	(0.254)	(332.254)	(0.263)
	[0.676]	[0.000]	[0.580]	[0.153]
Region fixed effects	IN	IN	IN	IN
Industry fixed effects	IN	IN	IN	IN
Intercept	−1254.491***	−1.511*	215.663	2.929***
	(288.589)	(0.725)	(507.851)	(0.717)
	[0.000]	[0.037]	[0.671]	[0.000]
Model χ^2 (df)	2190.08 (40)		2001.49 (40)	
Pseudo R^2	0.310		0.107	
N	521		482	

Note: Standard errors reported in parentheses, exact p-values (two-tailed) reported in brackets. $+p < 0.1$; $* p < 0.05$; $** p < 0.01$; $*** p < 0.001$. Variance-weighted least squares R^2 statistics shown.

priate method for accurate assessment of simultaneous mean and variance effects of entrepreneurship actions, the multiplicative heteroscedasticity regression, we demonstrate the soundness of this prediction for two particular entrepreneurship con-

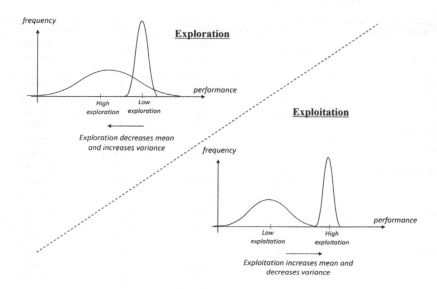

Note: Frequency (*y* axis) denotes the expected occurrences of particular performance figures in the *ex-post* performance distribution.

Figure 6.3   *Detected mean and variance effects of exploration and exploitation on the short-term firm performance: an illustration*

structs – EO (an antecedent of strategic entrepreneurship) and exploration (a crucial component of strategic entrepreneurship).

We develop four models, M1–M4, to assess the impacts of exploration, exploitation, and EO on mean and variance in net income in 2016 and 2017. In the short term, our results demonstrate that exploration and exploitation activities have opposite effects on performance level and variability. While exploration activities have a negative impact on performance and a positive impact on variability, exploitation improves performance while also stabilizing it. In terms of long-term performance, although there is no significant impact of exploration and exploitation on the mean, these variables have significant impacts on the variance: exploration boosts variability, while exploitation reduces it. The study's baseline hypothesis about the positive impact of strategic entrepreneurship on firm performance variability is aligned with the variance-enhancing property of exploration activities. With respect to EO, our results demonstrate that, in the short term, although the mean performance is not affected by EO, the variability of performance is increased by EO. These effects remain significant in the longer term in 2017 net income, confirming our baseline hypothesis.

Table 6.3   *Multiplicative heteroscedasticity regression model for entrepreneurial orientation*

Dependent variable	M3: Net income in 2016		M4: Net income in 2017	
	Mean regression (β_j)	Variance regression (γ_j)	Mean regression (β_j)	Variance regression (γ_j)
Entrepreneurial orientation	−14.526	0.215***	15.913	0.327***
	(15.790)	(0.051)	(25.660)	(0.054)
	[0.358]	[0.000]	[0.535]	[0.000]
Total assets in 2015, ln	−0.292	1.347***	7.045	0.955***
	(19.647)	(0.055)	(31.160)	(0.056)
	[0.988]	[0.000]	[0.821]	[0.000]
Sales in 2015, ln	71.019***	0.256***	39.699+	0.606***
	(19.439)	(0.058)	(22.585)	(0.059)
	[0.000]	[0.000]	[0.079]	[0.000]
Firm age, ln	−9.849	−0.357***	−156.640**	−0.597***
	(34.679)	(0.095)	(58.148)	(0.097)
	[0.776]	[0.000]	[0.007]	[0.000]
Number of employees, ln	159.633***	0.355***	63.198	0.019
	(36.574)	(0.076)	(52.347)	(0.077)
	[0.000]	[0.000]	[0.227]	[0.801]
Environmental dynamism	−44.136*	−0.019	−42.080	−0.232***
	(20.518)	(0.059)	(33.078)	(0.060)
	[0.031]	[0.748]	[0.203]	[0.000]
Formalization	39.089***	0.469***	9.771	0.174***
	(12.001)	(0.042)	(19.292)	(0.043)
	[0.001]	[0.000]	[0.613]	[0.000]
International sales dummy	157.149	−1.484***	−157.781	−0.641*
	(160.918)	(0.254)	(305.690)	(0.262)
	[0.329]	[0.000]	[0.606]	[0.014]
Region fixed effects	IN	IN	IN	IN
Industry fixed effects	IN	IN	IN	IN
Intercept	−1128.577***	−3.199***	100.849	1.417*
	(263.182)	(0.678)	(406.311)	(0.669)
	[0.000]	[0.000]	[0.804]	[0.034]
Model χ^2 (df)	2183.30 (38)		2002.06 (38)	
Pseudo R^2	0.259		0.096	
N	521		482	

Note: Standard errors reported in parentheses, exact p-values (two-tailed) reported in brackets. $+ p < 0.1$; $* p < 0.05$; $** p < 0.01$; $*** p < 0.001$. Variance-weighted least squares R^2 statistics shown.

It is important to note that Figures 6.1, 6.2, and 6.3 are only indicative of the distribution of the variability of the outcome, which may not necessarily be normal. The resulting distribution may have a skew in either direction. The proposed multiplicative heteroscedasticity methodology assesses the impact of predictors on the first and second moments of the resulting distribution (i.e., mean and variance), but not the higher-order moments (namely, skewness and kurtosis). As such, it should be considered the first step in assessing the performance outcomes of entrepreneurial actions, moving beyond a conventional regression's impact on conditional mean only.

Implications

We hope the insights of the current study will stimulate further theoretical and empirical development of the strategic entrepreneurship field, by drawing the attention of the entrepreneurship discipline to the importance and practical ways of analyzing the performance outcomes of entrepreneurial actions not only from the perspective of their effect on the average (expected, conditional mean) of firm performance but also from the perspective of their effect on the variance of the resulting distribution. Understanding both the mean and variability of performance is relevant from both practical and scholarly perspectives (Wiklund & Shepherd, 2011). The essence of the argument is that if the benefits of entrepreneurial actions (i.e., their impact on performance level) come at the cost of disproportionately higher variability, and hence risk, the assessment of these actions can be made from a more informed perspective (Shirokova et al., 2020). We foresee three potentially fruitful research opportunities that are enabled by embracing a variance-based view of strategic entrepreneurship.

First, we believe that assessing the role of performance variability in *explaining the firm survivorship or failure* could be promising research. The importance of finding antecedents of variability in performance (including strategic entrepreneurship actions), therefore, lies in its direct impact on the failure chances of firms (Sørensen, 2002). Embracing a variance-based view of strategic entrepreneurship allows a detailed study of the mediating role of performance variance in the association between entrepreneurial actions and firm mortality. As discussed before, high variability of performance distribution implies high chances of getting to the zone beyond the minimal performance needed to maintain the firm's operations (see illustration in Figure 6.2). As such, variance-enhancing entrepreneurial actions are likely to increase the risks of firm closure, while simultaneously possibly increasing the average performance of survived firms. We suggest that explicit theorizing as well as empirical testing of variability effects of strategic entrepreneurship, complementing the investigations of their mean effects, can push the envelope of the firm mortality studies, allowing to reveal the exact mechanisms leading to firm closure. From this perspective, some firms (particularly SMEs) are likely to prefer lower performance if this serves achieving more reliable performance expectations.

Second, we think the pursuit of *recognizing outliers* is another avenue of research that can be propitious. Variance-based theorizing allows a better understanding of characteristics and behaviors of outlier firms, which are much more likely to be found among the high-performance variance group. As such, the study of variance-enhancing entrepreneurial actions can shed light on the essential features of high growth and scalable new ventures. Of course, high variability in outcomes does not guarantee success for a particular venture, but it is arguably a necessary condition for becoming an outlier. Similarly, firms that are engaged only in variance-reducing actions are highly unlikely to get to the "unicorns"/"gazelles"/"blockbuster" categories, trading this opportunity for predictable, reliable performance. As such, understanding the antecedents of performance variability allows separating the high-growth-potential new ventures from the rest, although obviously cannot predict *ex ante* the success of a particular venture. From a practical perspective, this means that multiplicative heteroscedasticity models cannot predict if a particular firm will become an outlier; yet, they can show which firms are not going to become outliers (i.e., the ones with low levels of predicted variability in outcomes).

Importantly, as discussed before, the multiplicative heteroscedasticity methodology assumes the symmetric impact of predictors on the performance distribution (i.e., that the variance of the distribution changes without the change in skewness and kurtosis). This analysis should serve the first step in assessing the performance outcomes of entrepreneurial actions, moving beyond a conventional regression's impact on conditional mean only. The next steps, if needed, can include the assessment of the impact of entrepreneurial actions on the left- and right-hand-side outliers, using quantile regressions or logistic regression estimations of getting to the top or bottom 1 percent (Singh & Fleming, 2010). Alas, the latter methodology usually requires large datasets, which are not always accessible to researchers. In such cases, the proposed multiplicative heteroscedasticity approach can still yield valuable, although coarse-grained insights.

Third, similarly to the conventionally studied mean effects, as emphasized in this chapter, *variance effects of entrepreneurial actions are context-dependent*. In other words, a strategy that leads to an increase in the variance of performance distribution in one context can stabilize the performance in the other. For example, the study of Osiyevskyy et al. (2020b) reveals that the firm-level crisis context acts as a positive contingency for the impact of exploration on firm performance level and variability, and as a negative contingency for exploitation's level and variability effects. Similarly, Shirokova et al. (2020) reveal that in the context of emerging market firms affected by adverse economic conditions, causation brings marginal performance improvements while also making it highly unreliable (variable), whereas effectuation leads to performance improvements coupled with higher reliability. All these results suggest that mean and variance effects of entrepreneurial actions during "business as usual" situations dramatically differ from their effects in cases of crisis or adversity.

As such, a fertile avenue for future research implies investigating the country-, industry-, and firm-level moderators of variance effects. These investigations might reveal, for example, how to limit the risks of entrepreneurial strategies (e.g., through finding negative moderators of variability effects).

ACKNOWLEDGMENTS

This research has been conducted with financial support from the Russian Science Foundation [project No. 19-18-00081].

NOTES

1.   Whether stemming from measurable risk or unmeasurable *ex-ante* uncertainty (Alvarez & Barney, 2007), all entrepreneurial actions are characterized by the naturally increased variance in the *ex-post* distribution of their outcomes. Measuring the impact of entrepreneurial actions on the variance of resulting performance distribution is the main goal of the current methodological chapter. It should be noted that the distinction between entrepreneurial risk and uncertainty (or the underlying discovery or creation views on entrepreneurial opportunities) lies beyond the scope of the current study, in that both of them support our basic premise about highly variable outcomes of entrepreneurial actions.
2.   While variability studies are prevalent in economics (e.g., Cheng, 2008), a few examples can be found in strategic entrepreneurship (Pearce & Patel, 2018; Wales et al., 2013; Wiklund & Shepherd, 2011).
3.   The variability of performance and its determinants can also been studied qualitatively: e.g., Merrilees and Frazer (2006) have used the case study method to analyze performance variability among franchisees. The qualitative analyses are beyond the scope of the current chapter.
4.   The implementation of multiplicative heteroscedasticity regression models is available on STATA as an add-on package *regh* (Weesie, 1998), or as a built-in command *hetregress*.

REFERENCES

Aldrich, H. E., & Ruef, M. (2006). *Organizations evolving* (2nd edn). London: Sage.
Alvarez, F. (2018). Decomposing risk in an exploitation–exploration problem with endogenous termination time. *Annals of Operations Research, 261*(1–2), 45–77.
Alvarez, S. A., & Barney, J. B. (2007). Discovery and creation: Alternative theories of entrepreneurial action. *Strategic Entrepreneurship Journal, 1*(1–2), 11–26.
Beliaeva, T., Shirokova, G., Wales, W., & Gafforova, E. (2020). Benefiting from economic crisis? Strategic orientation effects, trade-offs, and configurations with resource availability on SME performance. *International Entrepreneurship and Management Journal, 16*(1), 165–194.
Cardinal, L. B. (2001). Technological innovation in the pharmaceutical industry: The use of organizational control in managing research and development. *Organization Science, 12*(1), 19–36.
Cheng, S. (2008). Board size and the variability of corporate performance. *Journal of Financial Economics, 87*, 157–176.
Chrisman, J. J., & Patel, P. C. (2012). Variations in R&D investments of family and nonfamily firms: Behavioral agency and myopic loss aversion perspectives. *Academy of Management Journal*, April 30.
Covin, J. G., & Slevin, D. P. (1989). Strategic management of small firms in hostile and benign environments. *Strategic Management Journal, 10*(1), 75–87.
Dess, G. G., & Lumpkin, G. T. (2005). The role of entrepreneurial orientation in stimulating effective corporate entrepreneurship. *Academy of Management Executive*, February 1.
Fleming, L. (2001). Recombinant uncertainty in technological search. *Management Science, 47*(1), 117–132.
Gimeno, J., Folta, T. B., Cooper, A. C., & Woo, C. Y. (1997). Survival of the fittest? Entrepreneurial human capital and the persistence of underperforming firms. *Administrative Science Quarterly*, 750–783.
Greene, W. H. (1997). *Econometric Analysis* (3rd edn). Upper Saddle River, NJ:Prentice Hall.

Harvey, A. C. (1976). Estimating regression models with multiplicative heteroscedasticity. *Econometrica: Journal of the Econometric Society*, 461–465.

Hitt, M. A., Ireland, R. D., Camp, S. M., & Sexton, D. L. (2001). Strategic entrepreneurship: Entrepreneurial strategies for wealth creation. *Strategic Management Journal*, *22*(6–7), 479–491.

Hunter, S. D. (2003). Information technology, organizational learning and the market value of the firm. *Journal of Information Technology Theory and Application*, *5*(1), 3.

Ireland, R. D., & Webb, J. W. (2009). Crossing the great divide of strategic entrepreneurship: Transitioning between exploration and exploitation. *Business Horizons*, *52*(5), 469–479.

Ireland, R. D., Hitt, M. A., & Sirmon, D. G. (2003). A model of strategic entrepreneurship: The construct and its dimensions. *Journal of Management*, *29*(6), 963–989.

Kantur, D. (2016). Strategic entrepreneurship: Mediating the entrepreneurial orientation–performance link. *Management Decision*, *54*(1), 24–43.

Laskovaia, A., Marino, L., Shirokova, G., & Wales, W. (2019). Expect the unexpected: Examining the shaping role of entrepreneurial orientation on causal and effectual decision-making logic during economic crisis. *Entrepreneurship and Regional Development*, *31*(5–6), 456–475.

Lavie, D., Stettner, U., & Tushman, M. L. (2010). Exploration and exploitation within and across organizations. *Academy of Management Annals*, *4*(1), 109–155.

Lumpkin, G. T., & Dess, G. G. (2001). Linking two dimensions of entrepreneurial orientation to firm performance: The moderating role of environment and industry life cycle. *Journal of Business Venturing*, *16*(5), 429–451.

March, J. G. (1991). Exploration and exploitation in organizational learning. *Organization Science*, *2*(1), 71–87.

Merrilees, B., & Frazer, L. (2006). Entrepreneurial franchisees have hidden superior marketing systems. *Qualitative Market Research: An International Journal*, *9*(1), 73–85.

Miller, D., & Friesen, P. H. (1982). Innovation in conservative and entrepreneurial firms: Two models of strategic momentum. *Strategic Management Journal*, *3*(1), 1–25.

Mudambi, R., & Swift, T. (2014). Knowing when to leap: Transitioning between exploitative and explorative R&D. *Strategic Management Journal*, *35*(1), 126–145.

Osiyevskyy, O., Radnejad, A. B., & MahdaviMazdeh, H. (2020a). An entrepreneurial management system for established companies. *Strategy and Leadership*, *48*(2), 24–31.

Osiyevskyy, O., Shirokova, G., & Ritala, P. (2020b). Exploration and exploitation in crisis environment: Implications for level and variability of firm performance. *Journal of Business Research*, 114, 227–239.

Parida, V., Lahti, T., & Wincent, J. (2016). Exploration and exploitation and firm performance variability: A study of ambidexterity in entrepreneurial firms. *International Entrepreneurship and Management Journal*, *12*(4), 1147–1164.

Pearce, J. A., & Patel, P. C. (2018). Board of director efficacy and firm performance variability. *Long Range Planning*, *51*(6), 911–926.

Rumelt, R. (1987). Theory, strategy and entrepreneurship. In D. J. Teece (Ed.), *The Competitive Strategic Challenge: Strategies for Industrial Innovation and Renewal* (pp. 137–158). Cambridge, MA: Ballinger.

Shane, S., & Venkataraman, S. (2000). The promise of entrepreneurship as a field of research. *Academy of Management Review*, *25*(1), 217–226.

Shirokova, G., Ivvonen, L., & Gafforova, E. (2019). Strategic entrepreneurship in Russia during economic crisis. *Foresight and STI Governance*, *13*(3), 62–76.

Shirokova, G., Osiyevskyy, O., Laskovaia, A., & MahdaviMazdeh, H. (2020). Navigating the emerging market context: Performance implications of effectuation and causation for small and medium enterprises during adverse economic conditions in Russia. *Strategic Entrepreneurship Journal*, 14, 470–500.

Shirokova, G., Vega, G., & Sokolova, L. (2013). Performance of Russian SMEs: Exploration, exploitation and strategic entrepreneurship. *Critical Perspectives on International Business*, *9*(1), 173–203.

Singh, J., & Fleming, L. (2010). Lone inventors as sources of breakthroughs: Myth or reality? *Management Science*, *56*(1), 41–56.

Sinha, K. K., & Osiyevskyy, O. (2018). The impact of founding team's human capital on mean and variability of new venture growth. *Academy of Management Proceedings*, 1, https://doi .org/10.5465/AMBPP.2018.43.

Sørensen, J. B. (2002). The strength of corporate culture and the reliability of firm performance. *Administrative Science Quarterly*, *47*(1), 70–91.

Sorenson, O., & Sørensen, J. B. (2001). Finding the right mix: Franchising, organizational learning, and chain performance. *Strategic Management Journal*, *22*(6–7), 713–724.

Uotila, J. (2017). Exploration, exploitation, and variability: Competition for primacy revisited. *Strategic Organization*, *15*(4), 461–480.

Wales, W. J., Patel, P. C., & Lumpkin, G. T. (2013). In pursuit of greatness: CEO narcissism, entrepreneurial orientation, and firm performance variance. *Journal of Management Studies*, *50*(6), 1041–1069.

Weesie, J. (1998). Regression analysis with multiplicative heteroscedasticity. *Stata Technical Bulletin*, 42, 28–32.

Wiklund, J., & Shepherd, D. A. (2011). Where to from here? EO-as-experimentation, failure, and distribution of outcomes. *Entrepreneurship Theory and Practice*, *35*(5), 925–946.

7. Historical cognition and strategic entrepreneurship

Diego M. Coraiola, Fernanda Yumi Tsujiguchi, and Roy Suddaby

INTRODUCTION

There is an emerging 'historical turn' in strategy and entrepreneurship research (Argyres et al., 2020; Wadhwani, Kirsch, Welter, Gartner, & Jones, in press). Scholars are realizing that history as a variable and the use of historical methodological approaches can contribute to further our understanding of strategic and entrepreneurial action. Particularly insightful is the understanding that history can be a source of competitive heterogeneity and foster entrepreneurial action (Suddaby, Foster, & Trank, 2010). History can be used strategically to develop new businesses and markets (Lamertz, Foster, Coraiola, & Kroezen, 2016), revise organizational identity (Schultz & Hernes, 2013), and promote corporate innovation (Erdogan, Rondi, & De Massis, 2019). In spite of the direct implications of history for both entrepreneurial and strategic behaviour, we lack an overarching theoretical framework clarifying the role of history in strategic entrepreneurship.

As the research domain focused on the intersection of entrepreneurial and strategic action (Ireland, Hitt, & Sirmon, 2003), strategic entrepreneurship inherited from its parent disciplines a traditional understanding of history that conflates history and the past (Coraiola, Foster, & Suddaby, 2015). History is seen as an 'objective fact or a fixed and immutable contextual variable' (Suddaby et al., 2010, p. 149) that minimizes managerial agency and poses limits to the possibilities for strategic and entrepreneurial action. Contrary to this view of history as a burden from the past, recent research emphasizes how the past can become a resource used strategically through the creation of historical narratives (Foster, Coraiola, Suddaby, Kroezen, & Chandler, 2017) and the engagement with a variety of historical artifacts (Ravasi, Rindova, & Stigliani, 2019). The objective and narrative views of history offer conflicting predictions about the role of the past in strategic entrepreneurship. With the intent of shedding some light upon the issue, in this chapter we focus on two interrelated questions. The first is *how should we theorize history in strategic entrepreneurship?* The second is *what is the role of history in strategic entrepreneurship?*

Objective approaches have theorized the inertial and path-dependence effects of historically acquired resources and competencies (Alvarez & Barney, 2007; Barney, 1991) as well as the advantages derived from the application of knowledge acquired in the past to new contexts and situations (Argote & Ingram, 2000; Politis, 2005). More recently, scholars developed a more dynamic approach grounded on the understanding of history as narrative. This perspective argues that history can be conceived as a form of rhetoric used to generate competitive advantage (Suddaby et al., 2010) and foster transgenerational entrepreneurship (Jaskiewicz, Combs, & Rau, 2015). Objective and narrative approaches agree that history matters for strategic entrepreneurship. However, they provide no consensual definition of history and offer contradictory views about its influence on strategic entrepreneurship.

Our goal in this chapter is to develop the groundwork to reconcile these two approaches. We develop an integrative approach to history and analyse its implications for research on strategic entrepreneurship. We aim to bridge the divide by advancing a cognitive approach to history grounded on the notion of *historical consciousness* (Suddaby, 2016; Suddaby, Coraiola, Harvey, & Foster, 2020), which we define as a perception and an attitude towards the past that imposes order and meaning to the temporality of historical experience. We argue that an *objective view of history* is but one of the ways in which the past can be seen and used to inform strategic entrepreneurship. Another way to understand history is to look at different meanings attributed to events in the past. This *interpretive view of history* involves making sense of the past through the construction of historical narratives. We advance the existing knowledge by adding that history also comprises the past as an imagined reality. An *imaginative view of history* encompasses the elaboration of alternative pasts and presents that connect to desired and expected futures by thinking in the future-perfect tense. The focus here is on the multiple ways in which reimagining history may inform alternative paths in the future.

Our approach offers a way to resolve the tensions between objective and interpretive approaches and has the potential to expand our understanding on the contribution of history to strategic entrepreneurship. We argue that objective history is particularly important at the beginning of entrepreneurial activity. Previous experience and acquired skills and resources are important assets that can be used to create new opportunities. Similarly, the ability to see history as factual data and project it into the future supports the discovery of regularities and contributes to the identification of new opportunities in the market. As entrepreneurs move from the development of new opportunities to the creation of new ventures, the challenge becomes acquiring legitimate distinctiveness. We assert that an interpretive view of the past is particularly suited to this task. By engaging creatively with the past, entrepreneurs develop meaningful historical narratives that provide a legitimating and distinctive past to their ventures. Once an organization is in place, a new set of demands emerge. Specifically, it has to manage the maintenance of environmental fitness as the venture grows and ages over time. We contend that in this situation the cognitive capability of future present thinking is appropriate for the organization to engage in both incremental and discontinuous renewal. Looking at the future as if it has already happened allows the organization to reimagine its past and recraft its present strategies for the future.

Our chapter is structured as follows. We first analyse current understandings of history in the field of strategic entrepreneurship. We describe the dominant objective view of history and the emerging interpretive approach and highlight some of the contradictions between them. Second, we introduce an alternative approach that looks at history as a form of cognition. We redefine history as a perception of the past as objective, interpretive, and imaginative. Third, we analyse some of the implications of each view of the past to strategic entrepreneurship and we infer some propositions to guide future research. We then conclude with a call for more empirical research on the role of history in strategic entrepreneurship.

STRATEGIC ENTREPRENEURSHIP AND HISTORY

Strategic entrepreneurship is the result of two complementary disciplines: strategic management and entrepreneurship (Ireland et al., 2003). As such, it brings together entrepreneurial action with a strategic perspective (Hitt, Ireland, Camp, & Sexton, 2001). It implies in the development of new opportunities and markets as well as in the implementation of strategies to create wealth and generate sustainable competitive advantage (Ireland et al., 2003). At the centre of strategic entrepreneurship lies the ability of entrepreneurs to access heterogeneous resources that cannot be easily copied and reproduced and that provide long-term advantages in relation to the competition (Amit & Schoemaker, 1993; Barney, 1991).

As a hybrid approach, strategic entrepreneurship also incorporates the biases inherent in its parent disciplines. From entrepreneurship scholars, it inherited the view of entrepreneurs as future-looking individuals and firms that proactively come up with innovations to create value (Lumpkin & Dess, 1996). From strategy came the understanding that unless the value created by entrepreneurs is attached to sustainable competitive advantages, other players might end up outcompeting them (Barney, 1991). This view is grounded on the assumption that resources and capabilities evolve in a path-dependent fashion. The resulting hybridism suggests that the development of new markets and business models come from looking at the future and anticipating needs, since the accumulative effects of history determine leadership in existing industries. We argue that this view undervalues the importance of history for strategic entrepreneurship and leaves the past an untapped source of resources for entrepreneurial action.

The Dominance of Objective History

The objective understanding of history is associated with a practical realist view of the past (Coraiola et al., 2015) that made its way from the literature on strategy and entrepreneurship into the research on strategic entrepreneurship. From the work of Michael Porter in competitive advantage it inherited a view of history as imprinting (Stinchcombe, 1965; Marquis & Tilcsik, 2013) and a source of organizational inertia (Ruef, 1997). Porter defines history as an acquired set of limited resources from the past that allow some companies to develop past-specific advantages and establish barriers to entry to new entrants (Porter, 1998). Organizations assume aspects from the foundation environment which persist over time as values, process, and routines imprinted in the past hinder future changes in the organization.

The Resource-Based View (RBV) of the firm also influenced the understanding of history in strategy. Early on, Penrose (1959) suggested that firm growth takes place through purposefully developed actions but is shaped by path-dependent processes. As the research on technological path dependence developed (e.g. Arthur, 1989; David, 1985), the idea that events and decisions taken in the past set boundaries for action in the present and future entered the field of strategy and strategic entrepreneurship (Raadschelders, 1998). History matters within RBV to the extent that each firm's singular path provides unique access to VRIO (Valuable, Rare, Inimitable, and Organization) resources that may lead to competitive advantage (Barney, 1991). The difficulties to reproduce resources and competencies that are time dependent turn them into important competitive assets.

History as imprinting and path dependence is also largely shared among entrepreneurship scholars. It corresponds to the two dominant views of history in the field of entrepreneurship identified by Wadhwani and Jones (2014). History as structure is akin to the imprinting approach in which temporal and spatial boundaries circumscribe the forces that influence entrepreneurial behaviour. This perspective sees history as an external variable to the work of entrepreneurs. History sets boundaries that both shape and limit the possibilities for entrepreneurial activity. It defines the availability of opportunities and the appropriate actions to take advantage of them. Entrepreneurs are usually unaware of these historical forces, which can only be fully understood in the aggregate and when analysed retrospectively.

History as a sequence of decisions and events (Wadhwani & Jones, 2014) correspond to the path-dependence perspective in strategy. Both assume the existence of imperceptible patterns and relationships that drive social and economic dynamics. In fact, Schumpeter (1947) assumed the interaction of historical process and creative responses in the evolution of economic order. As entrepreneurs create new opportunity paths, they foreclose the future of other possible paths. Historical sequencing encompasses the effects of past actions and events on the circumstances in which the present and the future are built. Entrepreneurship is thus contingent on a set of actions that took place in the past and cast a shadow in the present. Past entrepreneurial action provides the context and the conditions for the emergence of future opportunities for change.

These dominant, objective views of history in strategy and entrepreneurship share common features that were inherited by strategic entrepreneurship scholarship. First, they assume that the past is an important source of resources that might advantage some players instead of others. Second, they consider that the influence of the past operates under invisible forces that govern the behaviour of economic actors through structural configurations and self-reinforcing mechanisms. Third, they espouse an implicit philosophy of history that is seldom clarified and conflates the concepts of history and the past, treating the representation of the past as the reality of what once was. Fourth, their theory of history emphasizes inertia and social stability, and conflicts with a more dynamic understanding of strategic entrepreneurship.

The Emergence of Narrative History

Recent studies have questioned the inherited objective understanding of history in strategy and entrepreneurship (Suddaby et al., 2010; Wadhwani & Jones, 2014). Influenced by the historical turn in management and organization studies (Clark & Rowlinson, 2004), scholars are reconsidering the value of history for the research on strategic entrepreneurship (Argyres et al., 2020; Wadhwani et al., in press). Among the most prominent developments is the emergence of an interpretive view of the past that redefines history as a narrative resource (Foster et al., 2017). Proponents of this approach argue that a view of history as the past is too limiting to account for the role of history in strategic and entrepreneurial action. Instead, they contend that history should be seen as a narrative account of the past that can be a source of competitive advantage when used to manage relationships with stakeholders (Suddaby et al., 2010).

In contrast to the objectivist conflation of history and the past, a narrative view assumes that history and the past cannot be reduced into one another. First, it assumes that while the past comprises everything that happened before the present time, history is always an interpretation of the past (Carr, 1961). Remnants from the past have no logic and do not speak for themselves, so connecting them into a meaningful arrangement and using them to make sense of the past depends on an act of interpretation. Second, it contends that history encompasses an unavoidable narrative component. History is created through the act of emplotting the past into a narrative (White, 1973). In contrast to the past, history is thus a creative act; a literary genre. It has an author, it bears the prejudices of the time it was written, and it possess rhetorical and stylistic features that characterize it and distinguish it from other genres. This is the case, for example, of the ubiquitous corporate anniversary books that describe the history of the entrepreneur and the evolution of the business in a linear and tautological narrative (Delahahye, Booth, Clark, Procter, & Rowlinson, 2009).

These assumptions lie at the core of the 'uses of the past' approach (Wadhwani, Suddaby, Mordhorst, & Popp, 2018). This novel theoretical perspective focuses on the ways in which social actors repurpose the past to achieve specific goals in the present. The past is defined 'as a source of social symbolic resources available for a wide variety of creative uses' (Wadhwani et al., 2018, p. 1664), while history and memory are understood as different ways of representing the past (Decker, Hassard, & Rowlinson, in press). The past is never accessible as it once was and the events and meanings of what happened in the past are open for interpretation and contestation by various stakeholders (Mena, Rintamäki, Fleming, & Spicer, 2016). The past is constructed in the present through a variety of historical practices that lend the past its pastness and elaborate on the cause–effect relationships between past, present, and future (Kaplan & Orlikowski, 2013).

Rhetorical history, defined as the use of rhetoric and narratives to manage the past and create competitive advantage (Suddaby et al., 2010), is one of the main mechanisms organizations use to mobilize the past for strategic and entrepreneurial purposes. Historical narratives are used to promote continuity and change with the past and to achieve other strategic goals such as providing legitimacy to new ventures and creating a company's entrepreneurial culture (Foster et al., 2017). In addition, rhetorical history has been shown to be relevant to the creation and differentiation of new businesses (Illia & Zamparini, 2016; Lamertz et al., 2016), the implementation of strategic reorganizations (Maclean, Harvey, Sillince, & Golant, 2014; Schultz & Hernes, 2013), and the development of innovations (Erdogan et al., 2019; Ravasi et al., 2019). Rhetorical history thus provides a path for a more dynamic understanding of the role of the past in strategic entrepreneurship. Sinha, Jaskiewicz, Gibb, and Combs' (2020) research on the Gallagher Group provides a sound illustration by uncovering the ways in which the company used rhetorical history to rearrange priorities and alter imprinted strategic guideposts in order to readapt to a changing environment.

This narrative approach challenges well-established assumptions of an objective view of history and creates a divide in the field. For instance, objective and interpretive views diverge on whether history is a positive or negative source of competitive advantage. While some argue that history is an important resource for strategic action (Suddaby et al., 2010), some consider that relying on past successes may lead the organization to inertial paths (Miller, 1990). They also diverge on whether managers have agency over the past or are in fact subject to its influence (Coraiola, Suddaby, & Foster, 2017). The objective view of history highlights forces that influence the way industries and organizations behave beyond their ability of recognizing those patterns, while the interpretive view suggests that they are the ones who create those patterns by attributing logic and meaning to past events. Finally, they diverge regarding the ability of managers to change the past or mobilize it for their own purposes (Suddaby & Foster, 2017; Ybema, 2014). The objective view highlights the influence of history as an exogenous factor while the interpretive view defends that the past can be shaped and bent by managers through storytelling. Fundamental divergences between those approaches suggest that any simple combination of them in a single study is somewhat misleading. For this reason, we move away from attempts to patch over objective understandings of history with narrative theory and advance a new, cognitive approach that we believe can reconcile objective and narrative views of history.

RECONCILING HISTORY AND THE PAST THROUGH COGNITIVE HISTORY

We argue that a cognitive approach to history has the potential to reconcile the divide between an objective view focused on the past as data and evidence and an interpretive view of history centred around narratives about the past. We contend that the past affects the development of strategic entrepreneurship through the historical consciousness of managers and entrepreneurs. We define historical consciousness after Suddaby et al. (2020) as the cognitive capacity to manage the objective, interpretive, and imaginative elements of history to achieve entrepreneurial and strategic

Table 7.1   Approaches to history in strategic entrepreneurship

Approach to history	Objective	Narrative	Cognitive
Definition of history	Fact	Text	Perception
Core construct(s)	Imprinting	Rhetorical history	Historical consciousness
	Path dependence	Historical narratives	Sensemaking and sensegiving
Strategic potential	Acquired resource	Constructed resource	Developed capacity
Entrepreneurial potential	Redeploying past assets	Resignifying past events	Reconnecting past, present, and future

goals. That is, we assume that managers and entrepreneurs exert temporal agency by engaging with history cognitively. We posit that their assumptions about history and their understanding of the past shape their actions in the present and their plans about the future. A comparison between our cognitive approach and the existing objective and narrative views of history is provided in Table 7.1.

A cognitive approach emphasizes the role of subjectivity when dealing with the past. It suggests that individuals and groups may have different temporal orientations, may conceive the past differently, and may have a distinct set of abilities to deal with issues connecting the past, present, and future. Strategic entrepreneurship scholars consider history as a source of competitive advantage (Barney, 1991; Penrose, 1959). However, history tends be seen as laying outside of the realm of human action. Once the present is gone, it becomes history; it is set in stone and cannot be changed. Heterogeneity is understood as a matter of destiny and reinforcing feedback cycles that operate in a path-dependent fashion (e.g. Vergne & Durand, 2011). A narrative approach to history suggests that storytelling can be another source of heterogeneity. Although the past cannot be changed, the stories we tell and the meanings we attach to the past usually can (Gioia, Corley, & Fabbri, 2002). Our cognitive approach to history moves beyond objective and narrative sources of heterogeneity by locating them in the way human cognition makes sense about the past, present, and future. In so doing, we also elaborate on the potential of imaginative history for strategic entrepreneurship.

We depart from the assumption that history is not the past. History is actually more than the past. To think about the past is a creative act of construction that involves the present and the future (Le Goff, 1992). The present is situated between a past we assume we know and a future we envision and expect will likely happen. Consequently, the managerial engagement with history also reconstructs the present and the future as meaningful realities. Making sense of the present involves constructing an understanding of the past and the future as events that already happened. Since sensemaking takes place retrospectively (Weick, 1979), the future can only be known as future-perfect thinking (Gioia et al., 2002). As managers and entrepreneurs engage in temporal sensemaking in strategy making (Kaplan & Orlikowski, 2013; Wiebe, 2010), strategic entrepreneurship is talked into existence (Taylor &

Van Every, 2000) as new connections between past, present, and future are crafted through acts of remembering, imagination, and communication.

From a cognitive perspective, historical time is integral to social actors' sensemaking and sensegiving efforts (Suddaby et al, 2020). History involves a personal experience of time in which the definition of the entrepreneurial self is organized based on references to past, present, and future selves. In this sense, 'the perceived past becomes an integral part of the agency of actors in the social and economic world' (Wadhwani & Jones, 2014, p. 209). The same applies to corporate strategy, as can be seen from the research on corporate identity. Collective identity stories are essential to the creation of new ventures (Wry, Lounsbury, & Glynn, 2011). In addition, identity statements evolve as organizations age (Sasaki, Kotlar, Ravasi, & Vaara, 2019). As circumstances change and the leadership revises core identity claims, there is a fundamental interaction between past identity claims, current perceptions of identity, and what is expected for the future in the historical narratives about the organization (Lyle, Walsh, & Coraiola, in press).

Taken together, we argue that objective, interpretive, and imaginative ways of thinking about history constitute important competencies for the development of strategic entrepreneurship. As a cognitive capacity, objective history involves the transformation of raw data into historical evidence through a process of organization and analysis that looks at history as if it were the past. This is illustrated by Furr, Cavarretta, and Garg's (2012) study that demonstrates how chief executive officers' backgrounds influence their cognitive flexibility and ability to frame change. Similarly, from a cognitive perspective, history as interpretation is seen as the capacity to move beyond historical evidence to elaborate a coherent narrative about the past that can be shared with stakeholders. Research by Hatch and Schultz (2017) on Carlsberg demonstrates how different groups within the organization may look at historical artifacts differently, reinterpreting and repurposing them for product innovation through different narratives of the past.

History also has an imaginative component. In addition to interlinked sets of events and decisions that define consequential trajectories and the associated narratives that render those connections comprehensible and meaningful, imagination construes the future as a concrete and manageable alternative reality against which the past and present of the organization may be projected and contrasted. The relevance of imaginative history for strategic entrepreneurship can be seen through the effects of anticipated futures on the way the entrepreneurial past is perceived and narrated in multigenerational firms (Barbera, Stamm, & DeWitt, 2018). Future present historical thinking can also direct and motivate strategic entrepreneurship actions within industries. As Bátiz-Lazo, Haigh, and Stearns' (2014) research on the United States financial industry highlights, the development of a shared future among players that they were moving towards a 'cashless society' turned into a self-fulfilling prophecy for the industry. Their socially constructed expectations about the disappearance of cash drove and legitimated much of their efforts for establishing strategic alliances and innovation initiatives, creating in the future a strategic context that reflected their anticipation of it in the past.

Our cognitive approach to history incorporates insights from existing approaches with the benefit of reconciling their contradictory predictions. We argue that the contribution of history for strategic entrepreneurship does not lie in the past as a source of material and symbolic resources alone, but depends on the capacity of managers to perceive and redefine the past in ways that are more advantageous to support corporate entrepreneurship and strategic renewal. This includes being able to identify regularities in historical data and develop a persuasive story to convince and mobilize important stakeholders to strategic and entrepreneurial action. In this sense, more than the ability of bashing into glories inherited from the past and framing the past in support to present strategic decisions, is the capacity of managers and entrepreneurs to envision continuities and discontinuities between past, present, and future that lead to novel capabilities and sustainable competitive advantage. We detail some of the implications of our approach for strategic entrepreneurship in the next section.

IMPLICATIONS OF COGNITIVE HISTORY TO STRATEGIC ENTREPRENEURSHIP

In the remainder of this chapter, we explore the implications of a cognitive approach to history to the research in strategic entrepreneurship. We depart from Johnson and Van de Ven's (2002) perspectives on entrepreneurial strategy. The authors develop a framework connecting entrepreneurial action to the creation of competitive advantage. They distinguish four approaches to entrepreneurial strategy based on different theoretical perspectives from organizational strategy. The first is based on population ecology and distinguishes opportunity recognition as a core strategic activity developed by entrepreneurial firms. The second is grounded on institutional theory and the focus is on the entrepreneurial strategies to achieve legitimacy. The third is evolutionary and the goal of the entrepreneurial strategies is to achieve adaptation and fitness. The fourth is the perspective of industrial communities, which suggests that entrepreneurial strategies are applied to four component areas of industrial infrastructure and that multiple firms construct the environment in which they operate. Since an elaboration of the implications of cognitive history to the collective action of multiple firms is beyond the scope of this chapter, we explore in the following sections how our approach contributes to expanding the agenda on the first three forms of strategic entrepreneurship action, i.e. generating opportunities, acquiring legitimacy, and maintaining fitness.

Objective History and Entrepreneurial Opportunities

Entrepreneurial opportunities lie at the core of research on entrepreneurship (Shane & Venkataraman, 2000). History, in the form of prior experience and information, has long been recognized as an important antecedent to opportunity discovery (Shane, 2000). The dispersed and unbalanced distribution of information is associated with both social and personal history factors that lead to 'knowledge corridors'

(Venkataraman, 1997). Similarly, cognition in the form of acquired modes of reasoning and biases also has an important historical component. Past experience, for instance, is an important antecedent of entrepreneurial bias (Zhang & Cueto, 2015). Specific forms of historical reasoning are also known to play a role in the identification of opportunities. For example, research suggests that counterfactual thinking may impact positively or negatively on the development of entrepreneurial action depending on the dispositional attributes of individual entrepreneurs (Arora, Haynie, & Laurence, 2013; Baron, 2000). However, history as a dimension of prior experience distinct from the past still remains undertheorized (Godley & Hamilton, 2020). Specifically, the idea that entrepreneurs perceive and use history in various ways is still underdeveloped within theories of opportunity recognition.

Extant literature has largely treated information and cognitive skills as two independent factors with distinct influence on an entrepreneur's ability to recognize new opportunities. The focus has been on the past as finite and quantifiable information and its role in the development of specific ways of thinking. Past experience is seen as immutable and the cognitive abilities entrepreneurs develop are independent of the information they acquired. Contrary to this view, our cognitive approach to history posits that our cognitive engagement with the past defines the kind of information that is accessible and acceptable to us at a specific point in time (see also Alvarez & Barney, 2007). In addition, we suggest that our ways of thinking about the past condition the possibilities of acting in the world available to us. In other words, we contend that the way we construct the reality of the past and the opportunities for acting in the present and the future are intertwined (see also Kaplan & Orlikowski, 2013). Developing new opportunities is more than having access to privileged information or being able to calculate through a set of alternatives (Baumol, 1993). It also comprises the ability to establish means–end connections in historical data (Shane & Venkataraman, 2000). This ability depends on the capacity of a company to view history as an objective reality and engender new connections about the past, present, and future.

Proposition 1   The more managers and entrepreneurs see history as an objective reality, the higher their capacity to devise new opportunities based on factual knowledge and experience from the past.

We contend that the objectivity of the past and its usefulness for opportunity development are intrinsically attached to the way managers and entrepreneurs look at history. In this regard, we suggest that the more they see history as an objective reality, the higher should be their capacity to devise new opportunities based on factual knowledge and experience from the past. In addition, we argue that their capacity to enact the past as an objective reality is influenced by their level of experience and expertise within a specific field. This is illustrated by Baron and Ensley (2006) who find that more experienced entrepreneurs have more well-developed representations of opportunities than novice entrepreneurs and are thus better able to identify similar patterns in new configurations of events. Objective history and the capacity to connect past and future trends are thus important factors in developing new entrepreneurial opportunities.

Interpretive History and Venture Creation

The creation of new ventures is a challenging process. On the one hand, it requires the mobilization of a great variety of resources (Stevenson & Jarillo, 1990). On the other hand, it demands a positioning strategy that differentiates the new company from others existing in the market (e.g. Boone, Wezel, & van Witteloostuijn, 2013). History is a relevant factor in both these problems of supply and demand. First, the liability of newness (Stinchcombe, 1965) can be defined as a set of difficulties new organizations face because they lack a history of interactions with established players in an industry. The lack of embeddedness of new firms is reflected in low levels of trust and legitimacy and creates additional challenges for resource acquisition. Second, new ventures struggle to balance the requirements for legitimacy and uniqueness (Navis & Glynn, 2011). Differently stated, the demands for optimal distinctiveness (Brewer, 1991) emerge out of the lack of a clear historical identity in the minds of customers vis-à-vis other more established companies. History is thus central to new ventures' ability in creating a distinctive identity, achieving legitimacy, and constructing sustainable competitive advantage (Lyle et al., in press). Notwithstanding, we still lack theory around the role of history in business venturing.

Apart from the objective effects of age and familiarity, scholars have argued that historical narratives are important resources to create identity and achieve legitimacy (Foster et al., 2017). Storytelling is a powerful strategy firms use to create a distinctive identity and gain legitimacy (Lounsbury & Glynn, 2001). New ventures use narratives to signal compliance with the rules of the game and acquire legitimacy (Wry et al., 2011). They also use narratives to craft a distinctive identity among competitors in an existing category (Navis & Glynn, 2011). As such, prior research suggests that narratives are an important tool to overcome the liability of newness as well as achieve optimal distinctiveness. For instance, Gartner (2007) underscores the influence of an entrepreneur's story on the acquisition of resources by young firms. In addition, Martens, Jennings, and Jennings (2007) argue that entrepreneurial storytelling contributes to the acquisition of resources by conveying a unique identity, justifying the financial investments in the company, and associating the corporate purpose with broader social goals. Besides minimizing uncertainty and risk, entrepreneurial narratives also motivate resource providers to invest in the company.

We argue that the past is an important source for the development of entrepreneurial narratives. Bountiful pasts serve as a treasure trove to entrepreneurial storytelling and help foster transgenerational entrepreneurship (Jaskiewicz et al., 2015). However, we contend that the challenges posed by the lack of an objective history or the constraints imposed by it (Fern, Cardinal, & O'Neill, 2012) can be mitigated by an interpretive engagement with the past. That is, in the absence of a positive objective history, entrepreneurial companies may reinterpret their past and/or the past of their venture in a positive light. The more managers and entrepreneurs see history as an interpretive reality, the more likely they are to engage in the production of historical narratives to support the creation of new ventures. That is, entrepreneurs that lack 'external objective evidence' (Aldrich & Fiol, 1994, p. 651) can craft interpretive stories about the past to enhance the credibility and meaningfulness of their new ventures in the eyes of various audiences. The way some craft breweries appropriated a variety of remnants from ancestral breweries and used them in support of their collective identity claims is telling (Lamertz et al., 2016). So are the efforts of Ontario wineries to balance global conformity and local distinctiveness by reinter-preting the past of local wine production and using historical narratives connecting them to European fine wine production (Voronov, De Clercq, & Hinings, 2013). These arguments lead us to our next proposition.

Proposition 2   The more managers and entrepreneurs see history as an interpre-tive reality, the more they engage in the production of historical narratives to support the creation of new ventures.

Godley and Hamilton's (2020) comparative research on the evolution of the poultry industry in the United Kingdom and the United States provides a case in point. They argue that the structural development of the industry has followed similar paths in the two countries and that this objective history is insufficient to explain why the British favoured strategic alliances while the Americans did not. They attribute their distinct behaviour to the shared interpretations about the historical path of the industry in each country. Their findings thus suggest that interpretive history may facilitate or hinder business venturing depending on the shared narratives of the past within an industry.

We anticipate that the ability of managers and entrepreneurs to use the past to support the creation of new ventures should vary based on their narrative skills and storytelling abilities. As Illia and Zamparini's (2016) case study of hotel owners in Segovia shows, their ability in developing legitimate distinctiveness depended on their capacity to appropriate and preserve local historical narratives through histori-cal bricolage. Even though they all drew from a similar pool of historical resources, they distinguished themselves from one another by recrafting the commons stories in particular ways. Interpretive history thus contributes to strategic entrepreneurship by legitimating the creation of new ventures, facilitating the acquisition of resources, and providing a source for categorical distinctiveness.

Imaginative History and Strategic Renewal

Strategic renewal is a third important domain of strategic entrepreneurship (Johnson & Van de Ven, 2002). In contrast with opportunity generation and the development of successful ventures, strategic renewal can be defined as the maintenance of the entrepreneurial spirit across time. It involves the ability of a company to develop new combinations of resources that creates new wealth (Guth & Ginsberg, 1990) by refreshing and replacing organizational attributes (Agarwal & Helfat, 2009). This can be done in one of two ways (Kuratko & Audretsch, 2009). First, a firm may change itself in relation to what it was before. Companies can reformulate the foundational ideas based on which they were constructed. Second, a firm may deviate in relation to industry conventions and standards. That is, it might develop new processes and products that are distinct from other competitors. In both cases, new combinations of resources seem to emerge from an intentional detachment from the past. However, as multiple failed attempts at corporate reengineering suggest (Hammer & Champy, 1993), erasing the past to start with a clean slate is usually a very expensive and inefficient approach to strategic renewal.

We argue, instead, that resource reconfigurations emerge from an interaction between past, present, and future. The past seen as an objective fact has a limited influence that constrains the organizational capacity for change. There is an implicit understanding that history as brute data implies in 'deterministic fatalism' (Suddaby & Foster, 2017), impeding the human ability to modify how the past is interpreted. Indeed, a path-dependence approach to the past leaves little room for managerial agency and processes of strategic renewal (Garud, Kumaraswamy, & Karnøe, 2010). Similarly, the sedimentation of historical interpretations over time might entrap organizational members in a myopic view of the past as a single trajectory punctuated by a handful of meaningful enduring events and understandings that impede change (Suddaby & Foster, 2017). Organizations may be fixated on the elements that made them successful in the past and fail to move forward, setting up their own demise (Miller, 1990). A cognitive approach to history suggests that the past may be embraced in more creative and innovative ways.

An imaginative view of history comprises the organizational capacity to envision the future as if it had already happened (Suddaby et al., 2020). It involves a process of crafting a vision about the future through *pluperfect* reasoning (Weick, 1979) and revisiting narratives and data about the past to provide a coherent path and justification for transformative action. Organizational renewal can be thought of as the process of reimagining the organizational past while constructing new avenues in the future that maintain organizational fitness. One possibility involves organizations engaging in processes of strategy restoration (Miller, Gomes, & Lehman, 2019). Instead of envisioning new strategies by rejecting the past and looking only into the future, organizations may revisit discontinued strategies and bring them back adapted to the needs of the present. While the past as an objective reality and its effects cannot be changed, the meanings attributed to the past as well as to the futures projected for the organization can be revised by reimagining the connections between past, present, and future as if they were already settled. As such, imaginative history has serious implications to discontinuous and incremental renewal (Agarwal & Helfat, 2009) and corporate innovation (De Massis, Frattini, Kotlar, Petruzzelli, & Wright, 2016), as we argue in the following proposition.

Proposition 3   The more managers and entrepreneurs see history as an imaginative reality, the more likely they are to craft new futures in order to engage in strategic renewal.

Lego's strategic renewal is a good example of a discontinuity-with-continuity approach to organizational renewal (Schultz & Hernes, 2013). A new strategic direction within the company became possible only once the organization had redefined and rearticulated its identity based on a renewed attention and understanding to specific artifacts and narratives from the past. Lego's case suggests that some organizations might be more effective than others in managing heritage and leveraging it for competitive advantage (see also Ravasi et al., 2019). This can also be seen in cases of incremental renewal in which change takes place through multiple generations. Erdogan et al. (2019) uncovered a tradition-innovation paradox within family firms. They have argued that temporal symbiosis, or the use of retrospective and prospective approaches to manage firms' resources, is an appropriate strategy to maintain a firm's tradition and generate innovation. However, from a history-as-cognition standpoint, this paradox is just apparent. The feeling of divide between past and future, tradition and innovation, depends on the way history is perceived by the family. Historical imagination, in this case, can be an important mechanism to devise alternative ways to connect the traditional past of the organization with its innovative future. Future-perfect reasoning and reimagination of the past are thus important mechanisms for strategic renewal.

Developing a Cognitive History Framework for Strategic Entrepreneurship

The association of three dimensions of historical cognition with three modes of strategic entrepreneurship allows us to outline some possibilities for future theorizing. Specifically, this arrangement lends itself to the association of different types of historical consciousness to different phases of business development. Integrating the three propositions outlined before into a tentative framework, we expect an inverted relationship between the objectivity of history and the development of entrepreneurial activity. In other words, we argue that the more malleable entrepreneurs see the past then the more likely they are to manage history in connection with their entrepreneurial actions. Objective history seems to be more important in the beginning of entrepreneurial activity since it leverages acquired experience and factual thinking about pattern configuration and supports the development of new opportunities.

As an entrepreneurial venture develops a more bountiful past, entrepreneurs tend to focus more on the narrative construction of how the past should be interpreted and remembered as well as on the lessons that the past bring to the present. The development of interpretive history thus seems to be secondary to the generation of opportunities. For a new start-up, the most pressing demands are the acquisition of resources and legitimacy. In the absence of an objective history that can be used as a proxy for performance and trust, entrepreneurs tend to rely on other, richer historical sources such as the founder's previous experience and the family tradition to craft narratives that can provide them the resources and legitimacy necessary to develop their ventures.

As interpretations of the past become common sense and solidify, they tend to acquire a factual character as taken-for-granted truths (Berger & Luckmann, 1967).

Over time, the meanings attached to the past become less problematic and open, and a shared understanding of the trajectory of the organization becomes sedimented. Once these agreed-upon trajectories emerge, corporate entrepreneurship and change may become less likely and this may bring negative consequences for the future of the business. Entrepreneurial firms thus need to engage with history in novel, imaginative ways in order to devise new futures. Imaginative history then becomes an important mechanism for the development of processes of organizational renewal.

In spite of the suggested correspondence between forms of historical consciousness and the development of a business, we do not expect a simple and linear correlation between them. We recognize that history is a compound perception of the past that combines objective, interpretive, and imaginative elements. In addition, we acknowledge that firms vary in their reflexive capacity to understand and manage history as well as in their ability to mobilize the past for strategic and entrepreneurial purposes. Future research should be able to clarify the ways in which historical cognition is used for strategic entrepreneurship. In addition, future studies should distinguish whether particular renderings of the past have more traction than others. Moreover, empirical research could uncover when organizations switch between different perceptions of the past and how their efforts to concatenate alternative histories impact on strategic entrepreneurship.

CONCLUSION

Our chapter offers a renewed view of history to the research on strategic entrepreneurship. We argued that the dominant view of history conflates history and the past. From this perspective, history is a hindrance to strategic and entrepreneurial action and a potential source of lock-in. A narrative approach to history recently emerged as an alternative to imprinting and path-dependence approaches. This view dissociates history from the past and argues that history is a widely believed fictional recount of the past. We argue that the divide between these approaches is unnecessary and unproductive and we offer a cognitive approach to history as an attempt to bridge this divide.

History as cognition involves a perception of the past as an objective, interpretive, and imaginative reality. An objective view of history highlights regularities and distinguishes cause–effect relations between past and present events and decisions. An interpretive view assumes that the past may be imbued with different meanings and comprises the creation of narratives that organize and reinterpret the meanings of past events and decisions. An imaginative view of history is grounded on the actualization of the future as if it had already happened and the restructuring of past happenings that led into it. We argue that these three ways of looking at the past have important implications to the study of strategic entrepreneurship and our understanding of entrepreneurial opportunities, business venturing, and strategic renewal.

We propose a framework in which different understandings of history are more appropriate for different stages of business development. For instance, an objective view may facilitate the creation of new opportunities. Narrative history may support the acquisition of resources and legitimacy to keep a new venture afloat. And corporate renewal may be grounded on companies' ability to envision a variety of alternative paths in the future and use that to motivate change or continuity in corporate strategy. This does not mean that historical consciousness should be seen exclusively in a linear way. Different perceptions of the past may be used in different contexts and may be combined depending on the ability of different managers and entrepreneurs. A cognitive approach to history thus reconciles objective and interpretive understandings and calls for more clarification on the agentic uses of history for strategic entrepreneurship.

REFERENCES

Agarwal, R., & Helfat, C. E. (2009). Strategic renewal of organizations. *Organization Science*, *20*(2), 281–293.

Aldrich, H. E., & Fiol, C. M. (1994). Fools rush in? The institutional context of industry creation. *Academy of Management Review*, *19*(4), 645–670.

Alvarez, S. A., & Barney, J. B. (2007). Discovery and creation: Alternative theories of entrepreneurial action. *Strategic Entrepreneurship Journal*, *1*(1–2), 11–26.

Amit, R., & Schoemaker, P. J. H. (1993). Strategic assets and organizational rent. *Strategic Management Journal*, *14*(1), 33–46.

Argote, L., & Ingram, P. (2000). Knowledge transfer: A basis for competitive advantage in firms. *Organizational Behavior and Human Decision Processes*, *82*(1), 150–169.

Argyres, N. S., De Massis, A., Foss, N. J., Frattini, F., Jones, G., & Silverman, B. S. (2020). History-informed strategy research: The promise of history and historical research methods in advancing strategy scholarship. *Strategic Management Journal*, *41*(3), 343–368.

Arora, P., Haynie, J. M., & Laurence, G. A. (2013). Counterfactual thinking and entrepreneurial self-efficacy: The moderating role of self-esteem and dispositional affect. *Entrepreneurship Theory and Practice*, *37*(2), 359–385.

Arthur, W. B. (1989). Competing technologies, increasing returns, and lock-in by historical events. *The Economic Journal*, *99*(394), 116–131.

Barbera, F., Stamm, I., & DeWitt, R. (2018). The development of an entrepreneurial legacy: Exploring the role of anticipated futures in transgenerational entrepreneurship. *Family Business Review*, *31*(3), 352–378.

Barney, J. (1991). Firm resources and sustained competitive advantage. *Journal of Management*, *17*(1), 99–120.

Baron, R. A. (2000). Counterfactual thinking and venture formation: The potential effects of thinking about 'what might have been'. *Journal of Business Venturing*, *15*, 79–91.

Baron, R. A., & Ensley, M. D. (2006). Opportunity recognition as the detection of meaningful patterns: Evidence from comparisons of novice and experienced entrepreneurs. *Management Science*, *52*(9), 1331–1344.

Bátiz-Lazo, B., Haigh, T., & Stearns, D. L. (2014). How the future shaped the past: The case of the cashless society. *Enterprise and Society*, *15*(1), 103–131.

Baumol, W. J. (1993). Formal entrepreneurship theory in economics: Existence and bounds. *Journal of Business Venturing*, *8*(3), 197–210.

Berger, P. L., & Luckmann, T. (1967). *The Social Construction of Reality: A Treatise in the Sociology of Knowledge*. London: Penguin Books.

Boone, C., Wezel, F. C., & van Witteloostuijn, A. (2013). Joining the pack or going solo? A dynamic theory of new firm positioning. *Journal of Business Venturing*, *28*(4), 511–527.

Brewer, M. B. (1991). The social self: On being the same and different at the same time. *Personality and Social Psychology Bulletin, 17*, 475–482.

Carr, E. H. (1961). *What Is History?* London: Macmillan.

Clark, P., & Rowlinson, M. (2004). The treatment of history in organisation studies: Towards an 'historic turn'? *Business History, 46*(3), 331–352.

Coraiola, D. M., Foster, W. M., & Suddaby, R. (2015). Varieties of history in organization studies. In P. G. McLaren, A. J. Mills, & T. G. Weatherbee (Eds), *The Routledge Companion to Management and Organizational History* (pp. 206–221). New York: Routledge.

Coraiola, D. M., Suddaby, R., & Foster, W. M. (2017). Mnemonic capabilities: Collective memory as a dynamic capability. *Revista de Administração de Empresas, 57*(3), 258–263.

David, P. A. (1985). Clio and the Economics of QWERTY. *American Economic Review, 75*(2), 332–337.

De Massis, A., Frattini, F., Kotlar, J., Petruzzelli, A. M., & Wright, M. (2016). Innovation through tradition: Lessons from innovative family businesses and directions for future research. *Academy of Management Perspectives, 30*(1), 93–116.

Decker, S., Hassard, J., & Rowlinson, M. (in press). Rethinking history and memory in organization studies: The case for historiographical reflexivity. *Human Relations*.

Delahaye, A., Booth, C., Clark, P., Procter, S., & Rowlinson, M. (2009). The genre of corporate history. *Journal of Organizational Change Management, 22*(1), 27–48.

Erdogan, I., Rondi, E., & De Massis, A. (2019). Managing the tradition and innovation paradox in family firms: A family imprinting perspective. *Entrepreneurship Theory and Practice, 44*(1), 20–54.

Fern, M. J., Cardinal, L. B., & O'Neill, H. M. (2012). The genesis of strategy in new ventures: Escaping the constraints of founder and team knowledge. *Strategic Management Journal, 33*(4), 427–447.

Foster, W. M., Coraiola, D. M., Suddaby, R., Kroezen, J., & Chandler, D. (2017). The strategic use of historical narratives: A theoretical framework. *Business History, 59*(8), 1176–1200.

Furr, N. R., Cavarretta, F., & Garg, S. (2012). Who changes course? The role of domain knowledge and novel framing in making technology changes. *Strategic Entrepreneurship Journal, 6*(3), 236–256.

Gartner, W. B. (2007). Entrepreneurial narrative and a science of the imagination. *Journal of Business Venturing, 22*(5), 613–627.

Garud, R., Kumaraswamy, A., & Karnøe, P. (2010). Path dependence or path creation? *Journal of Management Studies, 47*(4), 760–774.

Gioia, D. A., Corley, K. G., & Fabbri, T. (2002). Revising the past (while thinking in the future perfect tense). *Journal of Organizational Change Management, 15*(6), 622–634.

Godley, A. C., & Hamilton, S. (2020). Different expectations: A comparative history of structure, experience, and strategic alliances in the US and UK poultry sectors, 1920–1990. *Strategic Entrepreneurship Journal, 14*(1), 89–104.

Guth, W. D., & Ginsberg, A. (1990). Guest editors' introduction: Corporate entrepreneurship. *Strategic Management Journal*, 5–15.

Hammer, M., & Champy, J. (1993). *Reengineering the Corporation*. New York: Harper Business.

Hatch, M. J., & Schultz, M. (2017). Toward a theory of using history authentically: Historicizing in the Carlsberg Group. *Administrative Science Quarterly, 62*(4), 657–697.

Hitt, M. A., Ireland, R. D., Camp, M., & Sexton, D. L. (2001). Guest editors' introduction to the special issue Strategic Entrepreneurship: Entrepreneurial strategies for wealth creation. *Strategic Management Journal, 22*, 479–491.

Illia, L., & Zamparini, A. (2016). Legitimate distinctiveness, historical bricolage, and the fortune of the commons. *Journal of Management Inquiry, 25*(4), 397–414.

Ireland, R. D., Hitt, M. A., & Sirmon, D. G. (2003). A model of strategic entrepreneurship: The construct and its dimensions. *Journal of Management, 29*(6), 963–989.

Jaskiewicz, P., Combs, J. G., & Rau, S. B. (2015). Entrepreneurial legacy: Toward a theory of how some family firms nurture transgenerational entrepreneurship. *Journal of Business Venturing, 30*(1), 29–49.

Johnson, S., & Van de Ven, A. (2002). A framework for entrepreneurial strategy. In M. A. Hitt, R. D. Ireland, S. M. Camp, & D. L. Sexton (Eds), *Strategic Entrepreneurship: Creating a New Mindset* (pp. 66–86). Oxford: Blackwell.

Kaplan, S., & Orlikowski, W. J. (2013). Temporal work in strategy making. *Organization Science, 24*(4), 965–995.

Kuratko, D. F., & Audretsch, D. B. (2009). Strategic entrepreneurship: Exploring different perspectives of an emerging concept. *Entrepreneurship Theory and Practice, 33*(1), 1–17.

Lamertz, K., Foster, W. M., Coraiola, D. M., & Kroezen, J. (2016). New identities from remnants of the past: An examination of the history of beer brewing in Ontario and the recent emergence of craft breweries. *Business History, 58*(5), 796–828.

Le Goff, J. (1992). *History and Memory.* New York: Columbia University Press.

Lounsbury, M., & Glynn, M. A. (2001). Cultural entrepreneurship: Stories, legitimacy, and the acquisition of resources. *Strategic Management Journal, 22*(6/7), 545–564.

Lumpkin, G. T., & Dess, G. G. (1996). Clarifying the entrepreneurial orientation construct and linking it to performance. *Academy of Management Review, 21*(1), 135–172.

Lyle, M., Walsh, I., & Coraiola, D. M. (in press). What is NORML? Sedimented Meanings in Ambiguous Organizational Identities. *Organization Studies.*

Maclean, M., Harvey, C., Sillince, J. A. A., & Golant, B. D. (2014). Living up to the past? Ideological sensemaking in organizational transition. *Organization, 21*(4), 543–567.

Marquis, C., & Tilcsik, A. (2013). Imprinting: Toward a multilevel theory. *Academy of Management Annals, 7*(1), 195–245.

Martens, M. L., Jennings, J. E., & Jennings, P. D. (2007). Do the stories they tell get them the money they need? The role of entrepreneurial narratives in resource acquisition. *Academy of Management Journal, 50*(5), 1107–1132.

Mena, S., Rintamäki, J., Fleming, P., & Spicer, A. (2016). On the forgetting of corporate irresponsibility. *Academy of Management Review, 41*(4), 720–738.

Miller, D. (1990). *The Icarus Paradox: How Exceptional Companies Bring about Their Own Downfall.* New York: Harper Business.

Miller, K. D., Gomes, E., & Lehman, D. W. (2019). Strategy restoration. *Long Range Planning, 52*(5), 101855.

Navis, C., & Glynn, M. A. (2011). Legitimate distinctiveness and the entrepreneurial identity: Influence on investor judgments of new venture plausibility. *Academy of Management Review, 36*(3), 479–499.

Penrose, E. (1959). *The Theory of the Growth of the Firm.* Oxford: Blackwell.

Politis, D. (2005). The process of entrepreneurial learning: A conceptual framework. *Entrepreneurship Theory and Practice, 29*(4), 399–424.

Porter, M. E. (1998). Cluster and the new economics of competition. *Harvard Business Review, 76*(6), 77–90.

Raadschelders, J. C. N. (1998). Evolution, institutional analysis, and path dependency: An administrative-history perspective on fashionable approach and concepts. *International Review of Administrative Sciences, 64*(4), 565–582.

Ravasi, D., Rindova, V., & Stigliani, I. (2019). The stuff of legend: History, memory, and the temporality of organizational identity construction. *Academy of Management Journal, 62*(5), 1523–1555.

Ruef, M. (1997). Assessing organizational fitness on a dynamic landscape: An empirical test of the relative inertia thesis. *Strategic Management Journal, 18*(11), 837–853.

Sasaki, I., Kotlar, J., Ravasi, D., & Vaara, E. (2019). Dealing with revered past: Historical identity statements and strategic change in Japanese family firms. *Strategic Management Journal, 41*(3), 1–34.

Schultz, M., & Hernes, T. (2013). A temporal perspective on organizational identity. *Organization Science, 24*(1), 1–21.

Schumpeter, J. A. (1947). *Capitalism, Socialism and Democracy*. Whitefish, MT: Kessinger Publishing.

Shane, S. (2000). Prior knowledge and the discovery of entrepreneurial opportunities. *Organization Science, 11*(4), 448–446.

Shane, S., & Venkataraman, S. (2000). The promise of entrepreneurship as a field of research. *Academy of Management Review, 25*(1), 217–226.

Sinha, P. N., Jaskiewicz, P., Gibb, J., & Combs, J. G. (2020). Managing history: How New Zealand's Gallagher Group used rhetorical narratives to reprioritize and modify imprinted strategic guideposts. *Strategic Management Journal, 41*, 557–589.

Stevenson, H. H., & Jarillo, J. C. (1990). A paradigm of entrepreneurship: Entrepreneurial management. *Strategic Management Journal, 11*, 17–27.

Stinchcombe, A. (1965). Social structure and organizations. In J. March (Ed.), *Handbook of Organizations* (pp. 142–193). Chicago, IL: Rand-McNally.

Suddaby, R. (2016). Toward a historical consciousness: Following the historic turn in management thought. *M@n@gement, 19*(1), 46–60.

Suddaby, R., Coraiola, D., Harvey, C., & Foster, W. (2020). History and the micro-foundations of dynamic capabilities. *Strategic Management Journal, 41*(3), 530–556.

Suddaby, R., & Foster, W. M. (2017). History and organizational change. *Journal of Management, 43*(1), 19–38.

Suddaby, R., Foster, W. M., & Trank, C. Q. (2010). Rhetorical history as a source of competitive advantage. In J. A. C. Baum & J. Lampel (Eds), *Advances in Strategic Management: The Globalization of Strategy Research* (pp. 147–173). Bingley: Emerald.

Taylor, J. R., & Van Every, E. J. (2000). *The Emergent Organization: Communication as Its Site and Surface*. Mahwah, NJ: Lawrence Erlbaum.

Venkataraman, S. (1997). The distinctive domain of entrepreneurship research: An editor's perspective. In J. Katz & R. Brockhaus (Eds), *Advances in Entrepreneurship, Firm Emergence, and Growth*, Vol. 3 (pp. 119–138). Greenwich, NY: JAI Press.

Vergne, J. P., & Durand, R. (2011). The path of most persistence: An evolutionary perspective on path dependence and dynamic capabilities. *Organization Studies, 32*(3), 365–382.

Voronov, M., De Clercq, D., & Hinings, C. R. (2013). Conformity and distinctiveness in a global institutional framework: The legitimation of Ontario fine wine. *Journal of Management Studies, 50*(4), 607–645.

Wadhwani, R. D., & Jones, G. (2014). Schumpeter's plea: Historical reasoning in entrepreneurship theory and research. In M. Bucheli & R. D. Wadhwani (Eds), *Organizations in Time: History, Theory, Methods*. Oxford: Oxford University Press.

Wadhwani, R. D., Kirsch, D., Welter, F., Gartner, W., & Jones, G. (in press). Context, time, and change: Historical approaches to entrepreneurship research. *Strategic Entrepreneurship Journal*.

Wadhwani, R. D., Suddaby, R., Mordhorst, M. & Popp, A. (2018). History as organizing: The uses of the past in organization studies. *Organization Studies, 39*(12), 1–41.

Weick, K. (1979). *The Social Psychology of Organizing*. Reading, MA: Addison-Wesley.

White, H. V. (1973). *Metahistory: The Historical Imagination in Nineteenth-Century Europe*. Baltimore, MD: Johns Hopkins University Press.

Wiebe, E. (2010). Temporal sensemaking: Managers' use of time to frame organizational change. In S. Maitlis & T. Hernes (Eds), *Process, Sensemaking, and Organizing*. Oxford: Oxford University Press.

Wry, T., Lounsbury, M., & Glynn, M. A. (2011). Legitimating nascent collective identities: Coordinating cultural entrepreneurship. *Organization Science, 22*(2), 449–463.

Ybema, S. (2014). The invention of transitions: History as a symbolic site for discursive struggles over organizational change. *Organization, 21*(4), 495–513.

Zhang, S. X., & Cueto, J. (2015). The study of bias in entrepreneurship. *Entrepreneurship Theory and Practice*, *41*(3), 419–454.

8. Making strategic entrepreneurship visible: an ethnomethodology primer

Betsy Campbell

In recent years there has been a drive to develop theories of entrepreneurship that can provide more meaningful guidance to scholars and practitioners (Alvarez, Audretsch, & Link, 2016). Along these lines, scholars of strategic entrepreneurship (SE) have embraced three main concerns: (1) the interdependencies between entrepreneurial doing (action) and thinking (cognition); (2) the emergent and ongoing nature of strategizing in entrepreneurial work; and (3) an expansion of the set of methods used to study processes over time (Ott, Eisenhardt, & Bingham, 2017). While it is the third concern that mainly prompts this chapter, all three themes can be addressed through an ethnomethodological approach to SE.

Much of the existing research on SE has relied on a relatively small suite of methodological approaches. Traditional qualitative methods such as ethnographies, interviews, and case studies often are used to explore strategy formation (Langley, 1999). However, this work is often descriptive rather than analytical. Computational simulations are also used (Baumann & Siggelkow, 2013; Gavetti, Levinthal, & Rivkin, 2005) to enable experiments with longitudinal and non-linear processes. However, this work, like some of the entrepreneurial orientation work before it (Lumpkin & Dess, 1996), is divorced from the authentic efforts of actual entrepreneurs in action.

The limited amount of research that probes the dynamic processes of SE through empirically based analysis may be related to the methodological challenges associated with studying actual work in context over time. Such studies require methodologies that can make the processes and practices of SE accessible to analysts. Ethnomethodology (Garfinkel, 1967) is one approach that makes the dynamic socio-material and interactional aspects of situated work available for analysis.

An ethnomethodological approach reveals the ways in which entrepreneurs interactionally accomplish their shared tasks, their organizations, and their identities (Campbell, 2019, 2021). Ethnomethodology can offer a richer understanding of SE by revealing a more nuanced understanding of the emergent practices and processes inherent in entrepreneurial work. Consequently, studies that draw on ethnomethodological traditions can underpin more accurate theories of entrepreneurial work. They can also influence practitioners and educators by offering models for processes in the field and learning goals for contexts of entrepreneurship education such as accelerators.

This chapter offers an overview of ethnomethodology for scholars interested in SE. The chapter begins by reviewing traditional methodological approaches to SE before it explains the foundational concepts of ethnomethodological inquiries. It then highlights several ethnomethodological traditions, including conversation analysis (CA), embodied CA, membership category analysis (MCA), and workplace interaction. It then describes the process of doing an ethnomethodological study and guides readers through an example. Next, the chapter explores some of the benefits of and misunderstandings about ethnomethodology. The chapter concludes by encouraging readers to sample several publications that feature ethnomethodological studies and by underscoring the potential contributions that ethnomethodology can make to SE.

EVOLVING METHODOLOGICAL APPROACHES IN STRATEGIC ENTREPRENEURSHIP

SE research relies on a constellation of methods to examine both the opportunity-seeking and advantage-seeking aspects entrepreneurial endeavors. The choice of a methodological approach for any given study is connected to the theories that drive SE research. While many theories are seen as relevant to SE, they often have compartmentalized SE within a single level of analysis such as the individual, the firm, or the environment (Mazzei, Ketchen, & Shook, 2017). Consequently, the methodologies have been attuned to these theoretical foundations, and many SE studies have relied on descriptive qualitative or detached quantitative methodological approaches (Ott et al., 2017).

Recently, more context-sensitive views of SE research have come to the forefront along with a growing interest in the emergent nature of entrepreneurial work (Mazzei, 2018; Fletcher, 2006). The word "entreprenuering" has been suggested as a way to capture this complex and dynamic nature of entrepreneurial work (Steyaert, 2007). Studies of entrepreneuring are aligned with practice theories and require methodologies that can transcend a particular person or firm, for example, and attend to interdependencies across people, places, and time.

To study the practices and processes of SE, scholars must grapple with dynamic and complex dimensions of entrepreneuring (Anderson & Starnawska, 2008). Ethnomethodology allows scholars to analyze (not merely describe) entrepreneuring as it emerges in context (Johannisson, 2020). Ethnomethodology transcends the limitations of interviews, questionnaires, and other forms of data collection that either impose an analyst's perspective on the data or rely on the entrepreneurs' recollection and framing. By taking an ethnomethodological approach, SE scholars can address critical questions of where, when, and how – features of SE that have been missing from the literature (Luke, Kearins, & Verreynne, 2011).

WHAT IS ETHNOMETHODOLOGY?

Ethnomethodology has its roots in the 1950s and 1960s when several sociologists became interested in the ways that ordinary people create and navigate all forms of social life for themselves. These scholars – including Harold Garfinkel, Erving

Goffman, Gail Jefferson, Harvey Sacks, and Emanuel Schegloff – began investigating the ways that real people accomplish things in real settings; even just "doing being" ordinary (Sacks, 1984b). These efforts to understand the ethnomethods of ordinary people in mundane settings considered social action as a mutually intelligible flow of situated practices (Button, 1991). By attending to the situated procedural aspects of social activities, ethnomethodology introduced a revolutionary reframing of social science; all of the background details (typically taken for granted) became the main focus of research. For example, the constitutive structures of verbal interaction are overlooked in traditional sociology, but ethnomethodology examines how these mundane structures are oriented to and used by speakers to establish identities, moral boundaries, and organizational norms.

In other words, ethnomethodology inverts the goals of classical sociology. Instead of attempting to explain social actions in terms of the analysts, ethnomethodology analyzes the social mechanisms by which ordinary people (re)create social life for themselves. It reveals how people make intelligible, for and by themselves, all of the aspects of a social context. Where classical sociologists might see a fact – for example an identity of an individual such as a founder, or an organization such as a venture, or a wider context such as an entrepreneurial ecosystem – ethnomethodologists see interactional accomplishments that are achieved moment by moment by the people involved (Bogen & Lynch, 1996).

The concept of a member is central to this kind of investigation. Membership in ethnomethodological terms is connected to the observable practices of participating and belonging. Members use "a natural language" of words and actions which is recognized by other members as the way that people do things in that context (Garfinkel & Sacks, 1970). If someone strays from these ways of saying and doing, other members either seek to clarify and repair the breach or dismiss the offender as a non-member. Because these ways of saying and doing are accessible to members through the interaction, they also are observable to analysts. Of course analysts need to bring a member's sensitivity to the context – a kind of "unique adequacy" – to understand a particular interaction as a member would (Garfinkel & Wieder, 1992).

By prioritizing the perspective of the members over the analyst, ethnomethodological studies avoid the temptations of scholarly over-reach. Why should scholars be allowed to "stipulate the terms of reference to which the world is to be understood – when there has already been a set of terms by reference to which the world was understood – by those endogenously involved in its very coming to pass" (Schegloff, 1997: 167). An ethnomethodological perspective rejects a "bucket approach" whereby individuals such as entrepreneurs are seen as nothing more than "cultural dopes" (Garfinkel, 1967) who fulfil prescribed roles that have been defined by extrinsic forces. Entrepreneurs, or any other social actors, play active roles in the (re)creation of identities, organizations, and other contexts, and they have established ways of accomplishing these complex mutual actions for themselves. The goal of ethnomethodology is to focus on the ways that social actors (re)produce and recognize for themselves the context of their work (Maynard & Clayman, 1991). The task of analysts is to uncover just how people accomplish all of the complexities of social life through ordinary means (Garfinkel, 2002).

To be clear: uncovering just how people accomplish social life for and by themselves does not mean a tighter focus on smaller slices of practice. Ethnomethodology rejects "micro" (or "macro" for that matter) explanations for social action (Hilbert, 1990). Instead: scholars gain insights into the ways that people "construct a mutually intelligible world" by attending to members' situated actions and interactions and the sequence of those actions and interactions (Rawls, 2006: 7). From an ethnomethodological perspective, mutual intelligibility is not something that people possess (e.g., shared cognition); it is something that people enact on a moment-by-moment basis. The ways that people display their shared understanding for each other is the observable data that are analyzed by researchers. Simply put: Ethnomethodology provides ways of observing, documenting, and analyzing the methods that people use to create, maintain, and repair mutual intelligibility.

In order to be mutually intelligible, members' interactions have a design and structure that are reflexive, indexical, and accountable (Rawls, 2008). These aspects of ordering action and interaction provide a practical means for creating, continuing, and evolving social identities and institutions and engender the contexts that beget cultures (Schegloff, 2006). How people in real time determine what is going on by doing or saying this or that, in just that way, at just this moment in this specific interaction is a core interest of ethnomethodology (Schegloff, 2006).

In ethnomethodology, reflexivity is not a reflective experience of the analyst as it might be understood in other circumstances. Instead reflexivity means that the next thing said or done by a member reflects back on previous things encountered by members and has the potential to show those things in a new light to members. Objects, utterances, actions, and identities become clear in a sequence over time to members. The situated nature of understanding is a key concept; it is why a student's raised hand in a classroom sends a clear signal, but the same gesture presented by a founder giving a pitch or a product demonstration would be puzzling.

Indexicality is the context-determined meaning that members intend and recognize. The pronouns "I" and "we," for example, have meanings that continually change and can be understood only in an indexical way by members as a conversation unfolds (Sacks, 1992). Indexicality reveals that all interaction is bound to context, and members continually work to contextualize words, gestures, and other interactional efforts. Ethnomethodology focuses on situated action and on the practical reasoning that enables members to (inter)act meaningfully in an indexical way.

Accountability refers to the ways that members display their actions so that their meaning is immediately clear to other members, or at least the actions are explicable if clarification is sought. Founders in an accelerator who stand beside their product innovation during the demo day, for example, show that they are giving demonstrations by the way they position their bodies vis-à-vis their innovation and the audience. They also are able to answer questions such as "Are you giving demonstrations?" or "Could you show me what your product does?" In other words, the meaning and recognition of an activity as an intelligible action is an essential aspect of that action.

By applying an ethnomethodological approach to the study of SE, scholars can identify members' ways of making entrepreneurial actions and interactions intelligible. Of course, analysts need ways to examine how members understand and display the situated and sequential unfolding of these actions and interactions. Ethnomethodology's centrally organizing notion of sequence has influenced several methodological traditions, such as CA, embodied CA, MCA, and workplace interaction (Heritage, 1984; Mondada, 2020; Nevile, 2004; Sacks, 1992). These traditions enable scholars to bring the background to the foreground; to treat practical activities and contexts as topics of empirical investigation.

WHAT ARE ETHNOMETHODOLOGICAL APPROACHES?

Not long after the articulation of the importance of understanding ethnomethods, Sacks and others began developing a systematic science to study conversation as the means by which members made plain their situated ways of doing and being (Garfinkel, 1967). Because verbal interactions have "order at every point," members use them to co-construct and interpret real-world contexts (Sacks, 1984a: 22; Schegloff, 1991). Scholars realized that studies of conversation can reveal the interactional mechanisms by which members understand and continually (re)create social life. With that insight, CA, or ethnomethodological interaction analysis (Psathas, 1990), got its start.

Conversation Analysis

Early CA studies focused on conversational mechanics such as turn-taking and adjacency pairs. Analysts explored the commonsense rules that enable people to know when a speaker's turn is completed and who talks next, for example (Sacks, Schegloff, & Jefferson, 1974). They also considered the conversational mechanisms that enable speakers to open and close topics and encounters (Schegloff & Sacks, 1973). These studies into the fundamental machinery (Sacks, 1984a) of verbal interaction were able to show that conversation is both context creating and context renewing (Garfinkel, 1967). Speakers use utterances that create contexts in that their words cannot be understood except by their use in a given time and place. Similarly, utterances renew contexts in that they promote an enduring environment for future words and actions. Conversational moves are contributed and experienced "for another first time" by speakers within an enduring architecture of interactional rules (Garfinkel, 1967: 9).

Embodied Conversation Analysis

While conversation includes verbal moves, it is not exclusively verbal. Speakers also use gestures in order to communicate effectively. Embodied CA studies explore how bodies are positioned and gazes are used as part of interactions. Early studies focused on gestures and gazes as they were used to enable turn-taking and sequence organization. More recently, studies have considered body-material arrangements and have featured verbal utterances in conjunction with objects, motions, sensory experiences, and spatial configurations (Heath & Luff, 2000; Mondada, 2018a; Nevile, Haddington, Heinemann, & Rauniomaa, 2014). For example, Mondada (2018a) has done several studies that highlight how expression, gesture, gaze, and non-verbal sound make cheese tasting an interactional sequence that contributes to the sales process in specialty food shops.

Membership Category Analysis

As CA reveals the interactional means by which people co-create and maintain all aspects of social life, CA also uncovers the ways by which speakers establish "who [they] are to one another" (Drew, 2005: 74). MCA builds on this foundation of CA; it identifies the ways that members refer to others and how this shapes moral aspects of the social world (Schegloff, 2007). Critical analysis of the ways that members use categories in their ordinary interaction uncovers how members define that category and the acceptable actions for people in that category (Sacks, 1995). Thus, MCA makes moral aspects of identities, relationships, and culture visible as a turn-generated phenomenon (Stokoe, 2012). As an example, Sacks offered a short story: "The baby cried. The mommy picked it up" (Schegloff, 2007; Sacks, 1974). Because this account makes sense to most readers, it suggests that we are members of a culture in which people who belong to the category of "baby" cry, and people who belong to the category of "mommy" are attentive to crying babies. The fact that today many of us would be unsurprised to see people in the category of "daddy" also attending to crying babies says something about contemporary culture and the acceptable identities of women and men that might not have been as expected decades ago.

Workplace Interaction Studies

The acceptable range of identities and order of activities in workplaces is another context of ongoing change. Ethnomethodological studies of work – workplace interaction (Luff, Hindmarsh, & Heath, 2000) – present a theory of work based on an interactional accomplishment of mutual understanding that requires members' orientation to shared situational expectancies and displays of attentiveness, competence, and trust. They focus on the production and coordination of workplace activities in real-time interaction (Heath & Luff, 2000) by analyzing both face-to-face (inter) action and technologically mediated interaction. Garfinkel argues that any workplace interaction contains the shared (re)production of the social organization of work (Rawls, 2008). Details such as leadership or strategy within a workplace can be found by investigating the interactional order as it is understood and enacted by and for members of that workplace. In other words, workplace interaction studies show how – just exactly how – critical features of work are made recognizable and acceptable to members through situated and sequential methods that can be seen turn by turn in their interactions. Because many workplaces are technologically rich settings, workplace interaction studies leverage not only CA but also embodied CA. Similarly, because workplaces involve many groups of people inside and outside of the organization, workplace interaction studies also make use of MCA, especially in highly structured institutions such as the legal court system (Atkinson & Drew, 1979).

Outside of SE, ethnomethodological approaches are sometimes used in multimethod studies. For example, CA is sometimes used in combination with ethnography or interviews to provide analytical insights about the entrepreneurial context (Nicolini, 2009). Quantitative methods also can accompany ethnomethodology; some studies outside of SE have used quantitative CA as a way to demonstrate interactional changes over time or socio-demographic variables of interaction that lead to different outcomes (Clayman & Heritage 2002; Heritage & Stivers, 1999; Stivers, 2015).

Each of the aforementioned ethnomethodological traditions has practical implications for analysts. The practices of doing ethnomethodological studies are as simple and as difficult as starting from a place of unmotivated noticing (Psathas, 1995). Attending to the actions and interactions of members without imposing the knowledge of an analyst may be the foremost thing to know about conducting ethnomethodological studies.

HOW TO DO ETHNOMETHODOLOGICALLY INFORMED STUDIES OF STRATEGIC ENTREPRENEURSHIP

Since all ethnomethodological traditions build on CA, the guidelines of CA also apply to embodied CA, MCA, and workplace interaction studies. The guiding principles include (Psathas, 1995: 2–3):

- Order is produced by members in context; it is situated and occasioned by members; it is repeatable and recurring.
- Analysts do not impose an order based on pre-formulated ideas about the roles or actions that should exist; discovering, describing, and analyzing the produced orderliness are the tasks of the analyst.
- The tasks of discovering, describing, and analyzing the structures, machinery, organized practices, formal procedures, and ways in which members produce order takes precedence over issues about how frequently or how often interactional phenomena occur.
- The structures of social action, once identified in members' interactions, can be articulated by the analyst in structural, organizational, logical, and topically countless, consistent, and abstract terms.

Clearly, CA and all ethnomethodologically informed practices differ substantially from discourse analysis and other approaches that attend to matters of language. One key difference worth emphasizing is that ethnomethodological studies are data driven; they do not start with pre-determined categories of interest to the analyst. Ethnomethodological studies do not guess about the thoughts, feelings, or intensions of members. Instead, they focus on the observable data that are available to members for members. A second core difference is that ethnomethodological studies are concerned with the sequential development of interaction; on seeing what happens and what happens next for and by the members as they construct and enact social practices (Drew & Heritage, 1992; ten Have, 2007). They are focused not on the topics of conversation but on the ordered and sequential structure of interaction.

As the organizing properties of interactions are recognizable to members on a turn-by-turn basis, they also are observable to analysts. However, conversation is fleeting, and analysts need to attend to the details of interaction in ways that cannot be captured by observation or field notes alone. Consequently, ethnomethodological studies require audio or video recordings. Traditionally these recordings have been done by analysts wielding recording devices in the room with members. However, newer technologies are making it possible for analysts to empower members to record themselves and share the data over the cloud (Campbell, 2019, 2021). These same technologies also enable members to self-publish naturally occurring interactions (e.g., YouTube, Vimeo, and other repositories of self-made video and audio content).

In whatever ways the recordings are produced and obtained (with the necessary permissions), the recorded data must be transcribed. The transcription process begins with a review that is "unmotivated" by existing theories or categories (Psathas, 1995). This opening step enables the analyst to notice aspects of the interactions as they occur and frees him/her to consider the situated and emergent nature of the interaction (Pomerantz & Fehr, 1997; ten Have, 2007). This step also enables the analyst to discover if any sections of the recordings are unusable because of ambient noise or other problems that obscure the details of the conversation. Lastly, the purpose of this exploratory phase is to allow the analyst to organically notice sections of interaction that are worthy of sustained analytical attention.

Because ethnomethodological studies stay close to the data, the transcriptions must include significant levels of detail. Special symbol systems have been developed to capture the observable details of verbal conversation and embodied action (Jefferson, 1984, 2004; Mondada, 2018a; see Tables 8.1 and 8.2). Members use these details to understand each other in context, and analysts use the notations that represent these details to show how members interactionally accomplish their work. While more detail is generally a good thing, each analyst needs to determine how much detail is necessary. This may be especially true in ethnomethodological studies of SE; readers of management literature might be unfamiliar with ethnomethodological notation systems.

Creating a good transcription takes time and requires an iterative approach. Tips that help include:

● Listen to and/or watch the recording and make a rough transcription that attributes specific utterances to individual members.

Table 8.1   Jeffersonian notation prioritizes audible details of interactions

Symbol	Name	Indication
[text]	Brackets	Start and end points of overlapping speech
=	Equal sign	Break and then continuation of a single utterance
(# of seconds)	Timed pause	Number within parentheses indicates seconds consumed by a pause in speech
(.)	Micropause	Brief pause, usually less than 0.2 seconds
. or ↓	Period or down arrow	Falling pitch or intonation
? or ↑	Question mark or up arrow	Rising pitch or intonation
,	Comma	Temporary rise or fall in intonation
-	Hyphen	Abrupt halt or interruption in utterance
>text<	Greater than/less than	Speech within the marks was delivered more rapidly than usual for the speaker
<text>	Less than/greater than	Speech within the marks was delivered more slowly than usual for the speaker
°	Degree symbol	Whispered, reduced volume, or quieter speech
ALL CAPS	Capitalized text	Shouted or increased volume of speech
underline	Underlined text	Emphasized or stressed speech
:::	Colon(s)	Prolongation of a sound
(hhh)	Hhh	Audible exhalation
˙ or (.hhh)	High dot or period with hhh in parentheses	Audible inhalation
(text)	Parentheses	Speech which is garbled, unclear, or in doubt
((*italic text*))	Double parentheses plus italics	Annotation of non-verbal activity

Source: Jefferson (1984, 2004).

Table 8.2   Mondada multimodal marking system notes embodied actions that are essential for interactional intelligibility

Symbol	Name	Indication
* text * + text + □ text □	Pair of asterisks or other symbols surrounding text	Embodied movements described between a set of identical symbols that appear with corresponding speech (one symbol per participant)
*--->	Asterisk, dashes, and greater than	Beginning of an action that continues across utterances
--->*	Dashes, greater than, and asterisk	End of an action that continues across utterances
>>	Double greater than	Action described begins before the utterance's beginning
--->>	Dashes and double greater than	Action described continues after the utterance's end
....	Periods	Preparation of a physical action
------	Dashes	Apex of a physical action is reached and maintained
,,,,,	Commas	Retraction of a physical action
Ric	Letters ric	Participant doing embodied action who is not the speaker
fig #	Letters fig and number	Moment represented by screen shot (inserted after the textual representation)

Source: Mondada (2018b)

- Return to the data and prioritize the inclusion of background elements such as audible breaths, clicks, laughs, and other sonic markers (mm, um, aa, etc.).
- Listen or watch again and attend to verbal overlaps and pauses. Note precisely where each overlapping utterance begins and how long each pause lasts.
- Listen or watch again and attend to the quality of voice used by each member. Intonation, pitch, and speed all can inform the meanings intended and understood in context.
- Listen or watch again and attend to physical actions such as gestures, gazes, and body positions.
- Lastly, number each utterance and/or identify each speaker (while maintaining anonymous status for the participants) line by line.

It is important to state that technology cannot replace the transcription process. However, as the tools for transcription evolve, some analysts are experimenting with automated transcription services (e.g., Otter.ai or Zoom closed captions) for the initial rough rendering of text from the recordings. No automated transcription service currently exists that can match the accuracy of an ethnomethodological transcript; nor are they attuned to the special notation systems. They excel at generating a rapid, if flawed, transcript which can save an analyst time. The analyst can put this inaccurate and incomplete text rendering into the traditional iterative transcription process, make corrections, and add the essential details (e.g., the pauses, false starts, and other audible features as well as markers of embodied communication). The vital goal is to craft a final transcript that represents the interactions as they happened for and by the members in context as captured on the recording.

As the transcription nears completion, the analyst looks for important features for members in the sequence of utterances. Knowing what to look for can be summed up by the question "why that now" (Schegloff & Sacks, 1973: 299). Members continually work to understand what each other intends to accomplish by offering a particular utterance and why that particular utterance has been offered in exactly that way to accomplish it. By reflecting on "why that now," analysts can get to the interactional means by which members are enacting their work moment by moment for themselves.

Below is a short example from a recent study that might serve as a helpful illustration. The following excerpt captures a brief exchange between two co-founders, Perry and Gerry, as they are hatching a plan to raise funds for their early-stage venture. The recording of this naturally occurring conversation was transcribed using a modified version of Jeffersonian Notation.

This ordinary exchange demonstrates how analysts can do transcription for ethnomethodological studies. It also shows how entrepreneurs orient to and accomplish their shared work through their interactions. Their utterances are accountable, reflexive, and indexical. And turn by turn, the co-founders reveal their understanding of acceptable entrepreneurial processes, responsibilities, and relationships through the order and structure of their interactions.

Table 8.3   *Excerpt from a naturally occurring workplace conversation*
between co-founders

Line	Speaker	Utterance
1	Perry	So yeah so we were supposed to get them (.) a revised deck that took into account all the feedback (.) Instead we've spent all our time working on the website and patent
2	Gerry	Well let's send them an email ((laugh)) and postpone it because we've got travel and uh-
3	Perry	Yeah
4	Gerry	and putting the rest of today on a (.) deck feels to m:ee-
5	Perry	Well °we wouldn't even have enough time today°
6	Gerry	yeah exactly >we wouldn't have enough time today< yeah agreed↓ (6) But you know↓ we can say > ˌlook at the website,< ((laugh))
7	Perry	Exactly (.) a thing they <u>can</u> do to help us give us feedback on the website (.) So I'll I'll toss that out as a consolation prize

The utterances in the excerpt are uncomplicated (see Table 8.3). Perry names a situation: they had promised to deliver a fundraising PowerPoint deck to a mentor for additional feedback, but the deck is not done. Gerry suggests that they postpone the meeting and offers several reasons to justify this course of action. Perry notes yet another reason why they cannot produce a deck in time for the meeting. Gerry agrees and proposes an alternative way for the mentor to be helpful. Perry embraces the suggestion and frames it as a "consolation prize" for the mentor. While a content analysis might stop there, an ethnomethodological study has much more to reveal.

The order and structure of the utterances reveal aspects about the nature of doing entrepreneurial work and being a member of an entrepreneurial team. Turn by turn these co-founders demonstrate that entrepreneurial work involves intra-team solidarity, a responsibility to follow through on external obligations, and the need to maintain the best external relations possible. These aspects of doing entrepreneurial work and being an entrepreneur are evident, not by what they talk about but by how they talk. For example, Perry hears the laugh in Gerry's utterance "send them an email ((laugh)) and postpone" (line 2) as an expression of uncertainty about the appropriateness of the suggestion to postpone; as a way for Gerry to save "face" (Goffman, 1967) in case his suggestion is too bold. Perry affirms Gerry's suggestion in his immediate response, and in doing so, he absolves Gerry of the concerns he may have had about suggesting that course of action. When Gerry next suggests that they tell the mentors to "look at the website" (line 6), he again laughs, which signals that he understands the suggestion might seem disrespectful of the mentors. Perry, however, again confirms the acceptability of Gerry's suggestion by nearly repeating it (line 7) (Schegloff, 1996). Perry also adds a bit of irreverence by framing the suggestion to look at the website "as a consolation prize" and deepens his alliance with Gerry.

Those laughs along with the tones and speed of the alternative suggestions signal an awareness that it would be better to have had the revised deck ready to share with the mentors. On a similar note, Perry's emphasis on "can" (line 7) suggests that he understands that the mentors were generous and sincere in their offer to look at the deck. While they cannot benefit at the moment from the mentor's expertise in that way, they can invite the mentor to support them with reactions to the website and stay in a conversation with the mentor in that way. Nevertheless, while they acknowledge there are limits to how they can treat the mentor, the founders have the socially acceptable agency to postpone meetings with mentors if done in a heedful manner.

The process by which this analysis is done relies on the "next turn proof" (Arminen, 2005; Hutchby & Wooffitt, 1998). Each recorded turn of conversation reveals the speaker's orientation to the previous turn and presents the speaker's expectations for the next turn. So, the implications of Gerry's laugh in line 6 are revealed by Perry's reaction in line 7. Perry's turn is designed not so much as an answer but as an assessment. He nearly echoes and builds on Gerry's utterance before bringing the topic to its end point. To clarify: the next-turn proof highlights the reflexive connections between adjacent turns of conversation for analysts. However, speakers are using the same methods in real time; a speaker uses his/her turn in the conversation as a demonstration of his/her understanding of the previous turn and the construction of his/her utterance will prompt the following turn. In other words, each speaker's understanding – of their role, task, organization, and more – is revealed during the actual interaction. These ethnomethods and what they reveal are the focus of scholarly attention.

As Garfinkel asserted: "the methods essential to work (and organization) will be found in details of attention and mutually oriented methods of work, and ordered properties of mutual action" (Rawls, 2008: 702). This example of an ethnomethodological treatment of several turns of co-founder conversation showcases what he meant. Ethnomethodology enables analysts to consider the members' perspective in SE and see how concepts such as roles, functions, and processes are accomplished by members for and by themselves in context. The exchange between Perry and Gerry, for example, shows how these co-founders are oriented toward their role as entrepreneurs and team mates, the value of mentoring relationships in the entrepreneurial process, and the need to adapt and make choices in imperfect circumstances. This example shows how ethnomethodological traditions enable the analysis of language and social practices as "integrated elements of coherent courses of action" (Goodwin & Heritage, 1990: 301).

WHY DO ETHNOMETHODOLOGICALLY INFORMED STUDIES OF STRATEGIC ENTREPRENEURSHIP?

Ethnomethodology is geared to study the local accountability of any kind of practice, including SE. Attending to the mundane aspects of SE does not mean that other aspects of SE do not matter. Instead, by following the ethnomethods in detail, ethnomethodology can reveal how the core practices of SE are embedded in ordinary competencies, and how these practices uniquely contribute to the particular and ongoing culture of a given venture and the wider entrepreneurial ecosystem.

Because ethnomethodology brings the methods used by members – the entrepreneurs or other stakeholders involved in the enactment of entrepreneurial work – to the foreground, ethnomethodologically informed studies can make two interrelated contributions to SE. First, they can show how stances of strategy and opportunity are ongoing and interdependent. Members display their practices through various audible and visible behaviors that either advance or suspend (or redirect) a task. Second, they can show how sequence and order are used by members as a resource in the enactment of strategic entrepreneurial work. Members' shared expectations about the appropriate sequencing of their interactions contribute to mutual intelligibility. Moreover, shared systems of interactional sequence help members to prompt and recognize transitions, especially through salient forms of interaction such as questions and repair.

By rejecting the idea of the "cultural dope," ethnomethodology provides ways to explore the roles of interactions in the formulation of entrepreneurial strategy and the enactment of entrepreneurial work. This suggests ways that scholars might challenge or complement existing quantitative studies that miss the complexity of entrepreneurship in practice or qualitative studies that offer more description than analysis.

An ethnomethodological approach is aligned with the literature's increasingly contextualized understanding of SE (Wright & Hitt, 2017). Scholars are connecting entrepreneurship with spatial, social, cultural, and temporal contexts (Dimov, 2011; Lounsbury & Glynn, 2019; Wadhwani, Kirsch, Welter, Gartner, & Jones, 2020; Wood, Bakker, & Fisher, 2020; Zahra, Wright, & Abdelgawad, 2014). Additional studies are needed that attend to the temporal and spatial aspects of contextual change (Wright, 2011). Ethnomethodology can address this need – albeit in ways that may be surprising. Temporal changes do not only take place across historical eras; they occur turn by turn in the mundane workplace interactions of entrepreneurs. Similarly, spatial changes do not only occur over great distances; they occur moment by moment in the arc of a gesture or the use of a technical aid. Context is continually (re)created by entrepreneurs' interactional practices; entrepreneurs "do" context through the situated ways of saying and doing entrepreneurship (Baker & Welter, 2018; Mondada, 1998).

Ethnomethodological traditions, data sources, and methods of interpretation present an opportunity to advance SE research. Ethnomethodology prioritizes valuable and underused data sources, offers a variety of methods for investigating matters of context (including matters of time, space, and embodiment), and offers unique forms of theorizing. For example, ethnomethodological approaches can reframe traditional SE questions by focusing attention on epistemological variations rather than ontological differences. While traditional studies might probe the nature of opportunities (Alvarez & Barney, 2007; Klein, 2008), an ethnomethodologically informed study using MCA could explore how entrepreneurs categorize opportunities for themselves. Similarly, an ethnomethodologically informed study using CA, embodied CA, or workplace interaction studies could reveal how the notion of an opportunity (or an advantage) is developed, negotiated, and accepted by entrepreneurs in the order and structure of their routine interactions.

Ethnomethodological approaches extend the reach of other methodologies. No traditional qualitative or quantitative study can reveal all there is to say about a complex activity such as entrepreneurship. There is always some element of "just what" that is missing from the data set or description – and therefore missing in the theoretical or practical contributions of the studies. Ethnomethodology provides a central means by which SE scholars can attend to the haecceity – the just what or just this – of entrepreneurial work (Garfinkel, 1991, 2002).

COMMON MISPERCEPTIONS ABOUT ETHNOMETHODOLOGY

While it is accurate to note that ethnomethodological approaches pay careful attention to mundane aspects of entrepreneurial interaction, it is mistaken to assume that ethnomethodology is micro-oriented. Ethnomethodology transcends any micro-macro labeling (Hilbert, 1990). It emphasizes empirical social practices that generate any and all micro- and macro-structures as they are produced by and for members.

Another misunderstanding about ethnomethodology is that the details of its findings are idiosyncratic and only relevant to the particular case investigated. The mechanisms that enable mutual intelligibility between any set of co-founders are "generically informative" (Arminen, 2005; Sacks et al., 1974). Ethnomethodologically informed studies reveal the constitutive features of interactionthat enable intersubjective understanding across various contexts. By avoiding decontextualized generalizations, it can focus on how entrepreneurs display and use forms of knowing to interactionally accomplish their work for and by themselves. Thus, ethnomethodology, with its analysis of the procedures members use to reflexively constitute social activities and settings, is useful in understanding both local and general cultural contexts (Goodwin & Goodwin, 1992).

Lastly, given the similarities of their names, ethnomethodology and ethnography also might be the source of some confusion. While there are a variety of differences between them, the core distinction is that conventional ethnography treats features of social life (e.g., race or gender), in an unexplicated way, whereas ethnomethodology treats them as situated social accomplishments (Garfinkel, 1967; Pollner & Emerson, 2001).

SUGGESTED READINGS

Ethnomethodological approaches have a decades-long history of development and use in organizational contexts. Nevertheless, they are only beginning to play a role in the entrepreneurship literature as part of the turn to practice in entrepreneurship (Nicolini, 2009; Steyaert, 2007). While this chapter can serve as a springboard into ethnomethodology, it cannot summarize all that has been done or all of the ways that ethnomethodology can contribute to SE. To reach beyond the limitations of this primer, scholars of SE may wish to sample other readings about ethnomethodology, beginning with seminal works by Garfinkel, Psathas, Sacks, and Schegloff. While

Table 8.4 *Suggested ethnomethodological publications*

Category	Reference
General introductory works	Garfinkel, H. 1967. *Studies in ethnomethodology*. Hoboken, NJ: Prentice Hall.
	Schegloff, E. 1997. Whose text? Whose context?, *Discourse and Society*, 8(2): 165–187.
Entrepreneurship-oriented works	Campbell, B. 2019. *Practice theory in action: Empirical studies of interaction in innovation and entrepreneurship*. London: Routledge.
	Campbell, B. 2021. Entrepreneurial uncertainty in context: An ethnomethodological perspective. *International Journal of Entrepreneurial Behaviour and Research*, 27(3): 648–667.
	Campbell, B. In press. Using conversation to reveal talk in practice and as practice. In Thompson, N., Byrne. O., Teague, B., & Jenkins, A. (Eds), *Research handbook of entrepreneurship as practice*. Cheltenham, UK and Northampton, MA, USA: Edward Elgar Publishing.
	Chalmers, D. & Shaw, E. 2017. The endogenous construction of entrepreneurial contexts: A practice-based perspective. *International Small Business Journal*, 35(1), 19–39.
	Hughes, J., Sharrock, W., & Anderson, R. 1989. *Working for profit: The social organization of calculation in an entrepreneurial firm*. Aldershot: Avebury.
Organization-oriented works	Arminen, I. 2005. *Institutional interaction: Studies of talk at work*. Burlington, VT: Ashgate.
	Drew, P., & Heritage, J. (Eds). 1992. *Talk at work: Interaction in institutional settings*. Cambridge: Cambridge University Press.
	Heritage, J. 1984. *Garfinkel and ethnomethodology*. Cambridge: Polity Press.
	Llewellyn, N., & Spence, L. 2009. Practice as a members' phenomenon. *Organization Studies*, 30(12), 1419–1439.
	Lynch, M. 1997. *Scientific practice and ordinary action: Ethnomethodology and social studies of science*. Cambridge: Cambridge University Press.
	Mondada, L., Banninger, J., Bouaouina, S., Gauthier, G., Hanggi, P., Koda, M., Svensson, H., & Tekin, B. 2020. Doing paying during the Covid-19 pandemic. *Discourse Studies*, 22(6), 720–752.
	Rawls, A. 2008. Harold Garfinkel, ethnomethodology and workplace studies. *Organization Studies*, 29(5), 701–732.
	Rouncefield, M., & Tolmie, P. (Eds). 2016. *Ethnomethodology at work*. London: Routledge.
	Sidnell, J., & Stivers, T. (Eds). 2012. *The handbook of conversation analysis*. Chichester: Wiley-Blackwell.
	Stokoe, E., & Attenborough, F. 2014. Ethnomethodological methods for identity and culture. In Dervin, F., & Risager, K. (Eds), *Researching identity and interculturality* (pp. 89–108). London: Routledge.
	Suchman, L., Trigg, R., & Blomberg, J. 2002. Working artefacts: Ethnomethods of the prototype. *British Journal of Sociology*, 53(2), 163–179.

only a few ethnomethodologically informed studies of entrepreneurship have been done, the traditions of ethnomethodology have been used for years to understand other types of organizations (see Table 8.4).

CONCLUDING REMARKS

Ethnomethodology can add new details to the traditional SE constructs. It can also offer entirely new ways of understanding entrepreneurship that can spark new theories for scholars and generate new value for practitioners. Ethnomethodological approaches – including CA, embodied CA, MCA, and workplace interaction studies – reveal how advantages and opportunities can be understood in terms of interactional structures; how advantages and opportunities and all contextual elements of entrepreneurial work are interactional accomplishments.

By focusing on members' methods, ethnomethodology opens up new ways of analyzing the social means by which entrepreneurs continually (re)create entrepreneurial work for and by themselves. It makes visible to analysts the interactional means by which entrepreneurs continually recognize, create, and maintain identities (founder, funder, etc.), tasks (pitching, hiring, etc.), and contexts (venture, ecosystem, etc.) as part of doing entrepreneurial work.

Ethnomethodology can make a multifold contribution to SE studies. It presents systematic ways of investigating members' interaction as a dynamic and emergent aspect of SE. It enables scholars to analyze, not just describe, how entrepreneurial features of identity, task, and context are accomplished by and for entrepreneurs themselves. It also makes plain the ordinary means by which any and every entrepreneur "talks into being" their ventures and the entrepreneurial ecosystem despite pervasive uncertainties and ongoing challenges (Campbell, 2021). By making SE visible, the traditions of ethnomethodology can respecify the major themes of the entrepreneurship literature as situated displays of intelligible practice.

In summary, ethnomethodology offers a particular way of doing sociology that highlights the observation of entrepreneurial work as it unfolds for real members in real situations. The key word here might be observation, which is meant to convey that the entrepreneurial activities are observable both to scholars and to the entrepreneurs themselves. By observing the ordinary work of entrepreneurs in action, scholars can begin to appreciate how all entrepreneurial work is an interactional accomplishment. The trick is to identify the ways that entrepreneurs themselves display and recognize what is taking place as they do their authentic work. The work of the analyst, then, is twofold: to discover how entrepreneurial activities are done such that they are immediately recognizable to members and to explicate just how SE is done. In other words: our task as scholars is to make visible the taken-for-granted background elements of SE.

REFERENCES

Alvarez, S., Audretsch, D., & Link, A. 2016. Advancing our understanding of theory in entrepreneurship. *Strategic Entrepreneurship Journal*, 10(1): 3–4.
Alvarez, S., & Barney, J. 2007. Discovery and creation: Alternative theories of entrepreneurial action. *Strategic Entrepreneurship Journal*, 1(1–2): 11–26.

Anderson, A., & Starnawska, M. 2008. Research practices in entrepreneurship problems of definition, description and meaning, *International Journal of Entrepreneurship and Innovation*, 9(4): 221–230.

Arminen, I. 2005. *Institutional interaction: Studies of talk at work*. Burlington, VT: Ashgate.

Atkinson, J., & Drew, P. 1979. *Order in court: The organisation of verbal interaction in judicial settings*. Atlantic Highlands, NJ: Humanities Press.

Baker, T., & Welter, F. 2018. Contextual entrepreneurship: An interdisciplinary perspective. *Foundations and Trends in Entrepreneurship*, 14(4): 357–426.

Baumann, O., & Siggelkow, N. 2013. Dealing with complexity: Integrated vs. chunky search processes. *Organization Science*, 24(1): 116–132.

Bogen, D., & Lynch, M. 1996. *The spectacle of history: Speech, text, and memory at the Iran-contra hearings*. Durham, NC: Duke University Press.

Button, G. (Ed.). 1991. *Ethnomethodology and the human sciences*. Cambridge: Cambridge University Press.

Campbell, B. 2019. *Practice theory in action: Empirical studies of interaction in innovation and entrepreneurship*. London: Routledge.

Campbell, B. 2021. Entrepreneurial uncertainty in context: An ethnomethodological perspective. *International Journal of Entrepreneurial Behavior and Research*, 27(3): 648–667.

Campbell, B. In press. Using conversation to reveal talk in practice and as practice. In Thompson, N., Byrne. O., Teague, B., & Jenkins, A. (Eds), *Research handbook of entrepreneurship as practice*. London: Edward Elgar.

Chalmers, D., & Shaw, E. 2017. The endogenous construction of entrepreneurial contexts: A practice-based perspective. *International Small Business Journal*, 35(1): 19–39.

Clayman, S., & Heritage, J. 2002. Questioning presidents: journalistic deference and adversarialness in the press conferences of Eisenhower and Reagan. *Journal of Communication*, 52(4): 749–775.

Dimov, D. 2011. Grappling with the unbearable elusiveness of entrepreneurial opportunities. *Entrepreneurship Theory and Practice*, 35(1): 57–81.

Drew, P. 2005. Conversation analysis. In Fitch, K., & Sanders, R. (Eds), *Handbook of language and social interaction*. Mahwah, NJ: Psychology Press.

Drew, P., & Heritage, J. (Eds). 1992. *Talk at work: Interaction in institutional settings*. Cambridge: Cambridge University Press.

Fletcher, D. 2006. Entrepreneurial processes and the social construction of opportunity. *Entrepreneurship and Regional Development*, 18(5): 421.

Garfinkel, H. 1967. *Studies in ethnomethodology*. Hoboken, NJ: Prentice Hall.

Garfinkel, H. 1991. Respecification: Evidence for locally produced, naturally accountable phenomena of order, logic, reason, meaning, method, etc. in and as of the essential quiddity of immortal ordinary society. In Button, G. (Ed.), *Ethnomethodology and the human sciences* (pp. 103–109). Cambridge: Cambridge University Press.

Garfinkel, H. 2002. *Ethnomethodology's program: Working out Durkheim's aphorism*. Lanham, MD: Rowman and Littlefield.

Garfinkel, H., & Sacks, H. 1970. On formal structures of practical actions. In McKinney, J., & Tiryakian, E. (Eds), *Theoretical sociology: Perspectives and developments* (pp. 337–366). New York: Appleton-Century-Crofts.

Garfinkel, H., & Wieder, D. 1992. Two incommensurable, asymmetrically alternate technologies of social analysis. In Watson, G., & Seiler, R. (Eds), *Text in context: Contributions to ethnomethodology* (pp. 175–206). Beverley Hills, CA: Sage.

Gavetti, G., Levinthal, D., & Rivkin, J. 2005. Strategy making in novel and complex worlds: The power of analogy. *Strategic Management Journal*, 26(8): 691–712.

Goffman, E. 1967. *Interaction Ritual*. Garden City, NY: Doubleday.

Goodwin, C., & Goodwin, M. 1992. Assessments and the construction of context. In Duranti, A., & Goodwin, C. (Eds), *Rethinking context: Language as an interactive phenomenon* (pp. 147–190). Cambridge: Cambridge University Press.

Goodwin, C., & Heritage, J. 1990. Conversation analysis. *Annual Review of Anthropology*, 19(1): 283–307.

Heath, C., & Luff, P. 2000. *Technology in action*. Cambridge: Cambridge University Press.

Heritage, J. 1984. *Garfinkel and ethnomethodology*. Cambridge: Polity Press.

Heritage, J., & Stivers, T. 1999. Online commentary in acute medical visits: A method of shaping patient expectations. *Social Science and Medicine*, 49(11): 1501–1517.

Hilbert, R. 1990. Ethnomethodology and the micro-macro order. *American Sociological Review*, 55(6): 794–808.

Hughes, J., Sharrock, W., & Anderson, R. 1989. *Working for profit: The social organization of calculation in an entrepreneurial firm*. Aldershot: Avebury.

Hutchby, I., & Wooffitt, R. 1998. *Conversation analysis: Principles, practices and applications*. Cambridge: Polity Press.

Jefferson, G. 1984. Transcript notation. In Heritage, J. (Ed.), *Structures of social interaction* (pp. 346–69). New York: Cambridge University Press.

Jefferson, G. 2004. Glossary of transcript symbols with an introduction. In Lerner, G. (Ed.), *Conversation analysis: Studies from the first generation* (pp. 13–31). Philadelphia, PA: John Benjamins.

Johannisson, B. 2020. Searching for the roots of entrepreneuring as practice: Introducing the enactive approach, in Gartner, W., & Teague, B. (Eds), *Research handbook for entrepreneurial behavior, process, and practice* (pp. 138–167). Cheltenham, UK and Northampton, MA, USA: Edward Elgar Publishing.

Klein, P. 2008. Opportunity discovery, entrepreneurial action, and economic organization. *Strategic Entrepreneurship Journal*, 2(3): 175–190.

Langley, A. 1999. Strategies for theorizing from process data. *Academy of Management Review*, 24(4): 691–710.

Llewellyn, N., & Spence, L. 2009. Practice as a members' phenomenon. *Organization Studies*, 30(12), 1419–1439.

Lounsbury, M., & Glynn, M. 2019. *Cultural entrepreneurship*. Cambridge: Cambridge University Press.

Luff, P., Hindmarsh, J., & Heath, C. 2000. *Workplace studies: Recovering work practice and informing system design*. Cambridge: Cambridge University Press.

Luke, B., Kearins, K., & Verreynne, M.-L. 2011. Developing a conceptual framework of strategic entrepreneurship. *International Journal of Entrepreneurial Behavior and Research*, 17(3): 314–337.

Lumpkin, G., & Dess, G. 1996. Clarifying the entrepreneurial orientation construct and linking it to performance. *Academy of Management Review*, 21(1): 135-172.

Lynch, M. 1997. *Scientific practice and ordinary action: Ethnomethodology and social studies of science*. Cambridge: Cambridge University Press.

Maynard, D., & Clayman, S. 1991. The diversity of ethnomethodology. *Annual Review of Sociology*, 17(1): 385–418.

Mazzei, M. 2018. Strategic entrepreneurship: Content, process, context, and outcomes. *International Entrepreneurship and Management Journal*, 14(3): 657–670.

Mazzei, M., Ketchen, D., Jr., & Shook, C. 2017. Understanding strategic entrepreneurship: A "theoretical toolbox" approach. *International Entrepreneurship and Management Journal*, 13(2): 631–663.

Mondada, L. 1998. Therapy interactions: Specific genre or "blown up" version of ordinary conversational practices? *Pragmatics*, 8(2): 155–166.

Mondada, L. 2018a. The multimodal interactional organization of tasting: Practices of tasting cheese in gourmet shops. *Discourse Studies*, 20(6): 743–769.

Mondada, L. 2018b. Multiple temporalities of language and body in interaction: Challenges for transcribing multimodality. *Research on Language and Social Interaction*, 51(1): 85–106.

Mondada, L. 2020. Membership categorization and the sequential multimodal organization of action. In Smith, R., Fitzgerald, R., & Housley, W. (Eds) *On Sacks: Methodology, materials, and inspirations*. London: Routledge.

Mondada, L., Banninger, J., Bouaouina, S., Gauthier, G., Hanggi, P., Koda, M., Svensson, H., & Tekin, B. 2020. Doing paying during the Covid-19 pandemic. *Discourse Studies*, 22(6), 720–752.

Nevile, M. 2004. *Beyond the black box: Talk-in-interaction in the airline cockpit*. Aldershot: Ashgate Publishing.

Nevile, M., Haddington, P., Heinemann, T., & Rauniomaa, M. (Eds). 2014. *Interacting with objects: Language, materiality, and social activity*. Philadelphia, PA: John Benjamins.

Nicolini, D. 2009. Zooming in and out: Studying practices by switching theoretical lenses and trailing connections. *Organization studies*, 30(12): 1391–1418.

Ott, T., Eisenhardt, K., & Bingham, C. 2017. Strategy formation in entrepreneurial settings: Past insights and future directions. *Strategic Entrepreneurship Journal*, 11(3): 306–325.

Pollner, M., & Emerson, R. 2001. Ethnomethodology and ethnography. In Atkinson, P., Coffey, A., Delamont, S., Lofland, J., & Lofland, L. (Eds), *Handbook of ethnography* (pp. 118–135). London: Sage.

Pomerantz, A., & Fehr, B. 1997. Conversation analysis: An approach to the study of social action as sense making practices. In van Dijk, T. (Ed.), *Discourse as social interaction: Discourse studies 2 – a multidisciplinary introduction* (pp. 64–91). London: Sage.

Psathas, G. (Ed.). 1990. *Interaction competence*, Vol. 1. Boston, MA: University Press of America.

Psathas, G. 1995. *Conversation analysis: The study of talk in interaction*. Beverley Hills, CA: Sage.

Rawls, A. 2006. Respecifying the study of social order: Garfinkel's transition from theoretical conceptualization to practices in details. In Garfinkel, H. (Ed.), *Seeing sociologically: The routine grounds of social action* (pp. 1–97). Boulder, CO: Paradigm Publishers.

Rawls, A. 2008. Harold Garfinkel, ethnomethodology and workplace studies. *Organization Studies*, 29(5): 701–732.

Rouncefield, M., & Tolmie, P. (Eds). 2016. *Ethnomethodology at work*. London: Routledge.

Sacks, H. 1974. On the analyzability of stories by children. In Turner, R. (Ed.), *Ethnomethodology: Selected readings* (pp. 216–232). Harmondsworth: Penguin.

Sacks, H. 1984a. Notes on methodology. In Atkinsen, J., & Heritage, J. (Eds), *Structures of social action: Studies in conversation analysis* (pp. 21–27). Cambridge: Cambridge University Press.

Sacks, H. 1984b. On doing "being ordinary." In Atkinsen, J., & Heritage, J. (Eds), *Structures of social action: Studies in conversational analysis* (pp. 413–429). Cambridge: Cambridge University Press.

Sacks, H. 1992. *Lectures on conversation*, Vol. 1. Oxford: Blackwell.

Sacks, H. 1995. *Lectures on conversation*, Vol. 2. Oxford: Blackwell.

Sacks, H., Schegloff, E., & Jefferson, G. 1974. A simplest systematics for the organization of turn-taking for conversation. *Language*, 50(4): 696–735.

Schegloff, E. 1991. Reflections on talk and social structure. In Boden, D., & Zimmerman, D. (Eds), *Talk and social structure: Studies in ethnomethodology and conversation analysis* (pp. 44–70). Cambridge: Polity Press.

Schegloff, E. 1996. Confirming allusions: Toward an empirical account of action. *American Journal of Sociology*, 102(1): 161–216.

Schegloff, E. 1997. Whose text? Whose context?, *Discourse and Society*, 8(2): 165–187.

Schegloff, E. 2006. Interaction: The infrastructure for social institutions, the natural ecological niche for language, and the arena in which culture is enacted. In Enfield, N., & Levinson,

S. (Eds), *Roots of human sociality: Culture, cognition and interaction* (pp. 70–96). Oxford: Berg.

Schegloff, E. 2007. *Sequence organization in interaction: A primer in conversation analysis*, Vol. 1. Cambridge: Cambridge University Press.

Schegloff, E., & Sacks, H. 1973. Opening up closings. *Semiotica*, 8(4): 289–327.

Sidnell, J., & Stivers, T. (Eds). 2012. *The handbook of conversation analysis*. Chichester: Wiley-Blackwell.

Steyaert, C. 2007. "Entrepreneuring" as a conceptual attractor? A review of process theories in 20 years of entrepreneurship studies. *Entrepreneurship and Regional Development*, 19(6): 453.

Stivers, T. 2015. Coding social interaction: A heretical approach in conversation analysis? *Research on Language and Social Interaction*, 48(1): 1–19.

Stokoe, E. 2012. Moving forward with membership categorization analysis: Methods for systematic analysis. *Discourse Studies*, 14(3): 277–303.

Stokoe, E., & Attenborough, F. 2014. Ethnomethodological methods for identity and culture. In Dervin, F., & Risager, K. (Eds), *Researching identity and interculturality* (pp. 89–108). London: Routledge.

Suchman, L., Trigg, R., & Blomberg, J. 2002. Working artefacts: Ethnomethods of the prototype. *British Journal of Sociology*, 53(2), 163–179.

ten Have, P. 2007. *Doing conversation analysis: A practical guide*. London: Sage.

Wadhwani, R., Kirsch, D., Welter, F., Gartner, W., & Jones, G. 2020. Context, time, and change: Historical approaches to entrepreneurship research. *Strategic Entrepreneurship Journal*, 14(1): 3–19.

Wood, M., Bakker, R., & Fisher, G. 2020. Back to the future: A time-calibrated theory of entrepreneurial action. *Academy of Management Review*.

Wright, M. 2011. Entrepreneurial mobility. In Bergh, D., & Ketchen, D. (Eds), *Research methodology in strategy and management*, Vol. 6 (pp. 137–159). Bingley: Emerald.

Wright, M., & Hitt, M. 2017. Strategic entrepreneurship and SEJ: Development and current progress. *Strategic Entrepreneurship Journal*, 11(3): 200–210.

Zahra, S., Wright, M., & Abdelgawad, S. 2014. Contextualization and the advancement of entrepreneurship research. *International Small Business Journal*, 32(5): 479–500.

9. The eye as a window to the soul: entering the strategic entrepreneurial mind

Jef Naidoo, Ron Dulek, Elliott Miller Graves, and Yeong Hyun Hong

If, as Proverb 30:17 states, "The eye is the window to the soul," then eye tracking may prove to be an enlightening research path to help further reveal how and why entrepreneurs behave and act as they do from a strategic perspective. In that spirit, the goal of this chapter is to review how eye-tracking methods are currently being employed in a broad range of research settings, including business research, and to evaluate its potential for providing valuable insights in the area of strategic entrepreneurship. More specifically, this chapter will initially examine eye movement behavior as a compelling physiological measure for studies in behavioral research. It will then highlight the fundamental aspects of eye tracking – from a methodological and a technological perspective – and its influence on research in a broad range of disciplines. Following this discussion, the chapter will show how entrepreneurial research, with its emphasis on cognitive and physiological studies, is already moving in the path of eye tracking. Then, to begin an examination of ways that eye tracking could be beneficial to strategic entrepreneurship research, the study will conduct a review of eye-tracking research within the domain of business literature. The purpose of this latter review is to capture the present state of knowledge about the use of eye-tracking methods and to look for ways that it can prove beneficial to strategic entrepreneurship research. The chapter will conclude by identifying areas of opportunities for future research and applications within the scholarly domain of strategic entrepreneurship. Overall, this study will contribute to the body of literature in strategic entrepreneurship by providing an increased understanding of eye-tracking research and by showing how this tool could prove beneficial in advancing knowledge within the field of strategic entrepreneurship.

TOWARD PHYSIOLOGICAL MEASURES

Researchers employ physiological measures as a supplemental and more accurate way to understand human behavior (Carrasco, 2011; Peterson, Reina, Waldman, & Becker, 2015). The empirical observation of behavior associated with the regular functioning of systems and subsystems in the human body provides valuable physiological measures that can offer compelling insights into perception and conduct (Allen, 2017). These approaches overcome the frequently cited limitations of self-report methods (Paulhus & Vazire, 2007), including predispositions and latent biases such as consistency bias (Sadler & Woody, 2003), response bias (Tran et al., 2007), image management and social desirability bias (Ellison, Heino, & Gibbs, 2006; Lavrakas, 2008), introspective bias (Peterson et al., 2015), and confabulation of events and memory bias (Coan, 1997). To this end, multi-method data sources beyond traditional self-reported measures are increasingly being urged (DiClemente, Swartzendruber, & Brown, 2013; Bailenson et al., 2004).

Physiological measurements help mitigate certain limitations endemic to conventional methods of data collection (Tran et al., 2007). Examples of physiological measures include, but are not limited to, heart rate variability, galvanic skin response or electrodermal activity, respiratory rate variability, brain activity, and facial muscle activity (Bell et al., 2018). In essence, proponents of physiological measures contend, much like proponents of lie detector tests, that bodily measurements provide more accurate and less biased data than does that which comes from self-reports.

EYE-TRACKING INSIGHTS

Eye tracking is obviously an important and highly promising domain within this physiological segment. Ashby, Johnson, Krajbich, and Wedel (2016) contend that eye activity measurements reveal "insights into the cognitive processes underlying a wide variety of human behaviors" (p. 96). Genco, Pohlmann, and Steidl (2013) observe that researchers leverage a rich array of well-established eye activity metrics that help them understand the complexities of visual attention and conscious and unconscious cognitive reactions.

Defined simply, eye tracking refers to the observation and recording of eye activity. The resulting data provide investigators with a continuous, real-time measure of how an individual is visually and mentally processing any stimuli toward which their gaze is directed (Bell et al., 2018). The underlying patterns of cognitive processes that are engaged during eye activity help researchers understand the complex interplay between vision and decision-making/preference (e.g., Bird, Lauwereyns, & Crawford, 2012), perception (e.g., Mastrantuono, Saldaña, & Rodríguez-Ortiz, 2017), problem solving (e.g., Yoon & Narayanan, 2004), motivation (e.g., Issa & Morgan-Short, 2015), and judgment (e.g., Wang, 2018).

FUNDAMENTALS OF EYE-TRACKING TECHNOLOGY

Eye-tracking technologies essentially quantify the dynamics of visual behavior. Technological advances in recent years, as well as rapid improvements in ease of use, accuracy, unobtrusiveness, and cost of devices, have greatly lowered the barriers for the employment of eye tracking as a data collection tool (Wedel, 2015; Duchowski, 2017).

Eye-tracking devices are able to measure the salient variables of interest in eye movement behavior, namely, the pupil size, position, and movement of the eye, and the blink rate to identify specific areas of interest of the respondent at a given time (Sánchez, Martín-Pascual, Gruart, & Delgado-García, 2017). While first-generation devices were cumbersome and warranted arduous experimental setups, present-day devices – which have evolved in both design and portability – are easier to work with and provide an extremely organic experience for respondents (Venkat, 2016). Three main types of eye trackers are currently available: (1) screen-based devices, which are individual trackers that can be attached to a laptop, desktop, or monitor; (2) wearable devices such as glasses and virtual reality headsets; and (3) webcam devices that are built into a phone or computer.

EYE ACTIVITY MEASURES

Three prominent metrics, namely, fluctuation in pupil size, gaze pattern, and blink rate, hold specific interest for researchers with respect to measurement of eye activity (Spector, 1990). These will be discussed in turn.

Pupil Size

Dilation and constriction in pupil size is a function of both cognitive and luminance-related factors (Knapen et al., 2016). In essence, pupil size changes when the individual encounters low-light and bright-light conditions, processes emotional signals, engages in decision-making, and expends mental effort during non-emotional perceptual tasks (Spector, 1990; Oliva & Anikin, 2018). Pupillary dilation thus correlates with arousal (Fong, 2012), excitement (Tullis & Albert, 2008), problem solving and task difficulty (Kahneman & Beatty, 1966), language processing and comprehension (Lee, Ojha, Kang, & Lee, 2015), memory recall (Kucewicz et al., 2018), and emotion (Bradley, Miccoli, Escrig, & Lang, 2008). Because of the profound insight it offers into the mechanisms underlying a broad array of cognitive and affective processes, pupil size is one of the most widely leveraged response measures in psychophysiology research (Kret & Sjak-Shie, 2018).

Gaze Pattern/Gaze Behavior

Gaze patterns help researchers understand how the eye responds to visual stimuli. Two prominent gaze-based metrics inform most eye activity studies – fixations and saccades.

Fixations are discrete samples of static points that represent the time spent looking at a specific location (Borys & Plechawska-Wójcik, 2017). Fixation points and durations help researchers to identify areas and objects that stimulate observer interest and those that generate confusion (Burridge, 2014). Prolonged fixation duration, for example, is associated with increased cognitive workload and effort (Ries, Touryan, Ahrens, & Connolly, 2016), which helps researchers understand how problem solving and learning occurs (e.g., Grant & Spivey, 2003; Rehder & Hoffman, 2005; Lai et al., 2013).

Saccades are rapid movements of the eyes that redirect the fovea from one object to another, allowing an individual to shift between points of fixation. They range in magnitude from the small eye movements made while reading a book, for example, to the much larger eye movements made while watching a football game (Purves, 2001). Measurement and analysis of saccadic eye movements help us understand how successfully an individual is visually processing information and interacting with the environment (Goettker, Braun, Schütz, & Gegenfurtner, 2018). Saccadic eye movement also provides insights into the speed of visual processing (Kirchner & Thorpe, 2006), cognitive behavior control (Hutton, 2008), and perceptual performance (Zhao, Gersh, Schnitzer, Dosher, & Kowler, 2012).

Blink Rate

Defined as the number of blinks per second or minute, this metric has proven to be a reliable measure of mental workload (Muczyński & Gucma, 2013). The temporal pattern of blinks changes in response to an individual's internal cognitive state (Nakano & Miyazaki, 2019). Blinks reflect either "initial stimulus processing or preparation for engagement of cognitive resources" (Siegle, Ichikawa, & Steinhauer, 2008, p. 680). To this end, it provides insight into the processes underlying learning and goal-directed behavior (Eckstein, Guerra-Carrillo, Singley, & Bunge, 2017), cognitive performance (Paprocki & Lenskiy, 2017), attention control (Tharp & Pickering, 2011), points of transition in information processing (Martins & Carvalho, 2015), arousal (Tanaka, 1999), and interest (Nakano & Miyazaki, 2019).

Table 9.1 summarizes the descriptions and salient aspects of these primary metrics that are employed in eye-tracking research.

MECHANICS AND DATA GENERATION

How It Works

Most modern eye trackers employ the pupil-corneal reflection (P-CR) technique, which uses near infrared light along with a high-definition camera (or other optical sensor) to track gaze direction (Mantiuk & Bazyluk, 2013). The light is directed toward the pupil, which is the opening in the iris of the eye. This initiates visible reflections in the cornea, which is the outermost optical element of the eye (Venkat, 2016). The direction of these reflections is recorded by the camera and relayed to the software, which then employs sophisticated algorithms to calculate the position of the eye and determine exactly where it is focused (Tobii Pro, n.d.). These coordinates are recorded multiple times each second and a dataset is generated. This dataset allows researchers to examine, among other things, an ordered list of fixations, the

Table 9.1   *Summary of frequently used eye movement measures*

Response measure	Description and salient features	Helps us measure
Pupil size	Refers to the size of the iris or opening of the eye	Level of arousal
	Fluctuates when an individual:	Level of excitement
	• is exposed to low-light and bright-light conditions	Problem solving and task difficulty
		Language processing and comprehension
	• processes emotional signals	
	• engages in decision-making	Memory recall
	• expends mental effort during non-emotional perceptual tasks	Emotional state
Fixation (gaze behavior)	Refers to the time spent focusing on a specific location	Degree of cognitive workload and effort
	May be prolonged or short	Areas and objects that stimulate observer interest
		Areas and objects that generate confusion
Saccade (gaze behavior)	Refers to the amplitude or distance between two fixation points. Also known as gaze path or scan path	Speed and success of visual processing
		Cognitive behavior control
	May range in magnitude from small to large	Perceptual performance
Blink rate	Refers to the number of blinks per second or minute	Underlying learning and goal-directed behavior
	May exhibit long or short patterns	Cognitive performance
		Attention control
		Points of transition in information processing
		Level of arousal and interest

time taken to arrive at a specific fixation point, the duration of a given fixation, and the number of fixations per visual element (Dawson, 2014).

Data Visualizations

The software may also generate heat map and gaze plot visualizations of cumulative gaze data. A heat map is generated from the aggregated fixation counts over each element for the entire duration of the interaction (Pohl, Schmitt, & Diehl, 2009). It provides an overview of the intensity and density of the fixation/saccade, as well as the overall distribution of visual attention (Rakoczi & Pohl, 2012). "Hot spots" are a function of higher aggregated fixation count; "cold spots" are a function of lower aggregated fixation count. Intermediate spots are also represented. "Hotspots" essentially point to areas of high interest or most visual activity, while cold spots point to areas of minimal or no visual interest. An example of a heat map visualization is shown in Figure 9.1.

Gaze plots visualize the order of fixation, general gaze traceability (or scan path), the beginning and end of each fixation, and transitions between areas of interest

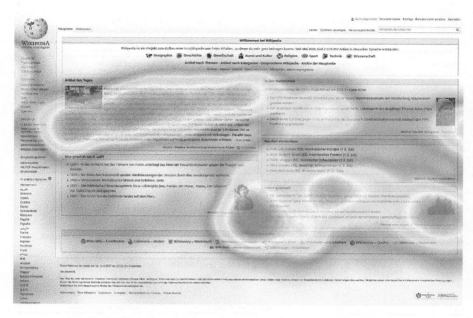

Figure 9.1   Heat map of visual activity

(Rakoczi & Pohl, 2012). A gaze plot visualization is comprised of circles and connectors. The circles represent gaze fixation and duration. The size of the circle is correlated with the length of the fixation duration; in other words, the longer the fixation, the larger the circle. The order of fixation from one area of interest to the next is represented by a number within the circle. An example of a gaze plot visualization is shown in Figure 9.2.

Heat map and gaze plot visualizations offer great utility. A prominent example can be seen in interface engineering and user experience design. By highlighting areas of an interface that are of most interest to a user, visual elements can be optimally placed to enhance user experience and capture maximum engagement.

RESEARCH APPLICATIONS: AN OVERVIEW

Eye-tracking methods have been successfully leveraged in a broad variety of research contexts to analyze visual attention as reflected in eye movement patterns. These methods have helped provide nuanced understandings of the impact of visual interpretation in diverse settings. The following discussion focuses on a few selected areas of application.

In psychology, this method has been employed to study what internal motivations guide our attentional window (Carrasco, 2011); reading and information processing (Rayner, 1998; Jarodska & Brand-Gruwel, 2017); eye movement control during scene

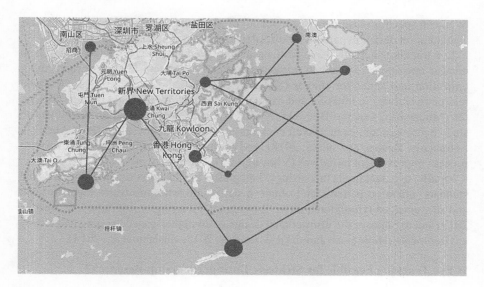

Figure 9.2   Gaze plot of visual activity

perception (Schütz, Braun, & Gegenfurtner, 2011; Castelhano, Mack, & Henderson, 2009); visual search techniques (Drew, Boettcher, & Wolfe, 2017; Gomes & Riggs, 2017); natural tasks (Mele & Federici, 2012; Duchowski, 2002); and other cognitive processes (Kret & Sjak-Shie, 2018; Just & Carpenter, 1976).

Marketing and consumer behavior research are additional areas where eye-tracking approaches have proven beneficial. Studies include investigations into consumer decisions and behavior prediction (Goyal, Miyapuram, & Lahiri, 2015); visual behavior in mobile shopping environments (Hwang & Lee, 2017); retail and retail marketing (Huddleston, Behe, Driesener, & Minahan, 2018); consumer attention in social commerce (Menon, Sigurdsson, Larsen, Fagerstrøm, & Foxall, 1973); visual marketing (Wedel & Pieters, 2008); neuromarketing (Ćosić, 2015); brand aware-ness (Pretorius & Calitz, 2011); and print advertising (Puškarević, Nedeljković, Dimovski, & Možina, 2016).

In the medical domain, eye tracking has transformed both clinical practice and medical education (Brunye, Drew, Weaver, & Elmore, 2019). Applications include research into how visual search and recognition tasks are performed in medical imaging (Lévêque, Bosmans, Cockmartin, & Liu, 2018); visual expertise in medical decisioning (Fox & Faulkner-Jones, 2017); usability testing of medical devices (Koester, Brøsted, Jakobsen, Malmros, & Andreasen, 2017); study of eating disor-ders (Kerr-Gaffney, Harrison, & Tchanturia, 2018); study of cognitive mechanisms that underlie complex high-level judgments (Faad, 2017); enhanced usability of molecular diagnostics reports in cancer precision medicine (Sharma et al., 2018). Eye tracking has also been employed in neurological research, including the study of autism spectrum disorders (Yale School of Medicine, 2009), Alzheimer's disease, and attention deficit hyperactivity disorder (Doležal & Fabian, 2015).

Eye-tracking methods have also been employed in human factors research in nuclear operations to facilitate measurement and evaluation in control room modernization and simulator studies (Kovesdi, Spielman, LeBlanc, & Rice, 2018); in marine operations to measure and evaluate bridge environment and officers' behavior (Muczyński, Gucma, Bilewski, & Zalewskia, 2013); in aviation operations to study neuroergonomics of aircraft cockpits and enhance flight safety (Peysakhovich, Lefrançois, Dehais, & Causse, 2018); and in the manufacturing sector to facilitate process improvement initiatives (Vijayan, Mork, & Hansen, 2018).

Finally, eye tracking is increasingly being used in education science to understand students' attention patterns and obtain insights into what motivates them to learn and stay engaged (Hooijdonk, 2016; Rosengrant, Hearrington, Alvarado, & Keeble, 2012) and to improve the instructional design of computer-based learning and testing environments (Holmqvist, Jarodzka, & Gruber, 2017; Busjahn et al., 2014).

Is Eye Tracking Feasible for Strategic Entrepreneurship Research?

The underlying question of this chapter is whether eye-tracking techniques can create feasible research questions and practical, pragmatic answers in the field of strategic entrepreneurship. In other words, does this technique provide viable tools for researchers and practitioners alike to gain fresh insights and new perspectives about the dynamic field of strategic entrepreneurship? A brief review of the literature leads us to answer not just "yes" to these questions, but to provide an addendum to that "yes": the field of strategic entrepreneurship is already making an almost organic progression in the direction of eye-tracking technology. This progression can be traced back to the turn of the millennia, which began with a heightened focus on the cognitive connections between strategy and entrepreneurship.

Hitt, Ireland, Camp, and Sexton (2001) observe that strategic focus implies actions, decisions, and commitments designed to achieve competitive advantage and above-average returns. Put another way, strategy involves *thinking about* and making decisions that lead to a competitive advantage. Covin and Miles (1999) link competitive advantage to entrepreneurship through mental processes such as organizational rejuvenation, strategic renewal, and domain redefinition. Finally, Kuratko and Audretsch (2009) explain that both strategic management and entrepreneurship are dynamic processes concerned with firm performance. However, whereas strategic management seeks this advantage in an environmental context, entrepreneurship does so through choices about product and process and creative insights that lead to market innovations.

A significant body of research in entrepreneurship and strategic entrepreneurship focused largely on cognition, with a special emphasis on biases and heuristics (Baron, 2004; Busenitz, 1999; Mitchell et al., 2004, 2007), simultaneously emerged at the turn of the century. This research proved beneficial in that it led to academic analyses and even conferences such as the Second Conference on Entrepreneurial

Cognition (fall 2005) that sought to answer one key question: How do entrepreneurs think? To answer that question, researchers realized that it was necessary to move beyond the emphasis on biases and heuristics, which Mitchell, Randolph-Seng, and Mitchell (2011) labeled *boxologies*, and begin to examine a parallel movement toward sense making. This research was similarly cognitive, but placed more emphasis on language-based methodologies (Weick, Sutcliffe, & Obsfeld, 2005; Cornelissen & Clarke, 2010; Cornelissen, Clarke, & Cienki, 2012). More recently, this cognitive, sense-making approach has progressed into the area of sense giving (Hoyt, Noke, Mosey, & Marlow, 2019), with an emphasis on how social exchanges enable entrepreneurs to refine and modify ideas (Leyden, Link, & Siegal, 2014; Vaghely & Julien, 2010).

This exploration of the connection between entrepreneurs, sense making, and language has yielded beneficial results. Thanks to these efforts the field has a better understanding of how an entrepreneur's interpretation of meaning constrains and informs actions (Mills, 2003) and influences understanding of the entrepreneur's actions (Gioia & Chittipeddi, 1991; Matheias, Williams, & Smith, 2015). Even more importantly, from a language perspective, we now see how fundamental communication tools such as narrative (Holt & Macpherson, 2010), metaphor (Nicholson & Anderson, 2005), and gestures (Cornelissen & Clarke, 2010) shape and frame the entrepreneurial experience.

Finally, a third parallel path has also accompanied this cognitive approach. This approach looks for connections between an entrepreneur's brain and body. Smith and Semin (2004) contend that the body shapes the mind while White, Thornhill, and Hampson (2007) explore a connection between testosterone levels and new venture development. Following in this path, Nicolaou, Shane, Cherkas, Hunkin, and Spector (2007) examine the connection between genetics and entrepreneurial engagement. Finally, and more recently, Nicolau, Patel, and Wolfe (2017) find a moderate connection between prenatal testosterone levels and a tendency to engage in self-employment.

This emphasis on cognition, and particularly the direct link between an entrepreneur's brain and body, makes the research tool of eye tracking the almost inevitable next step in strategic entrepreneurial research. For the eyes show, as we have demonstrated earlier, both where the body is looking and, by implication, what the brain is considering.

Prior to looking for areas in strategic entrepreneurial research where eye tracking may prove beneficial, we chose to first conduct an in-depth examination of areas in business-focused research where this approach has already been used.

RESEARCH APPLICATIONS OF EYE TRACKING IN BUSINESS DOMAINS: A SYSTEMATIC REVIEW OF THE LITERATURE

To ascertain which business domains employ eye-tracking methods in empirical studies, and to gain an understanding of how these methods are operationalized, we conducted a systematic review of the business literature. Meißner and Oll's (2017) exploration of the use of eye tracking in organizational research provided the framework for our study. More specifically, Meißner and Oll proposed an integrative taxonomy for eye-tracking research and used it to investigate the methodological potential of eye tracking and its scope of application in organizational research. We applied their taxonomy to investigate the potential and scope of eye-tracking methods in business research in general.

Consistent with the systematic review framework, we established a research question along with a review protocol for attempting to answer those questions. The research question and a description of the protocol follow.

Research Question

In seeking to extend the earlier work by Meißner and Oll (2017), we adopt their taxonomy to guide our study and serve as our analytical framework. Our ultimate goal was to ascertain if common practices were emerging across the interdisciplinary spectrum of business research paradigms when eye-tracking experiments were employed as part of the research protocol. We explore this through the following research question: What common patterns of association emerge with regard to the techniques used to influence the direction of attention to stimuli, the indices used to measure the respective change in attention, and the psychophysiological constructs operationalized?

REVIEW PROTOCOL

Our review protocol embodied the following components: (1) the strategic selection of peer-reviewed academic journals for inclusion in the examination, (2) the review of selection criteria regulating which studies were incorporated in, or omitted from, the systematic review, (3) the development of a strategy for extracting and uniquely identifying the data, (4) the creation of coding practices and standards to ensure that the evaluation criteria were applied consistently, validly, and reliably by each evaluator, and (5) the establishment of a strategy for synthesizing and analyzing the output.

Corpus Selection and Data Extraction

To obtain a comprehensive overview of how eye tracking is being employed as a tool in business research, we selected a purposive sample of all manuscripts published in the University of Texas at Dallas Naveen Jindal School of Management's list of the 24 leading business journals. This list hosts an inventory ranging from *The Accounting Review* to *Strategic Management Journal*. The decision to limit the evaluation to papers published in the journals identified on this list was predicated on the fact that, in addition to being prestigious and well regarded both nationally and globally, this list includes journals that are considered as leading in the field of business studies (Vogel, Hattke, & Petersen, 2017).

We used a list of search terms relating to eye-tracking methods (i.e., "ET," "eye tracking," "eye movement," "eye fixations," "saccades," "blink rate," and "pupil dilation") to retrieve our data corpus. No additional inclusion criteria were applied, which led to the retrieval of a corpus of 35 articles. We did, however, apply one exclusion criterion once the corpus was extracted. Because our goal was to appraise and synthesize evidence from empirical studies that employed eye-tracking methods as part of their experimental procedure, we excluded studies that failed to satisfy this requirement. Consequently, the following three articles were excluded from the study:

Dimoka, A., Davis, F., Gupta, A., Pavlou, P., Banker, R., Dennis, A., ... Weber, B. (2012). On the use of neurophysiological tools in IS research: Developing a research agenda for NeuroIS. *MIS Quarterly, 36*(3), 679–702.
Hui, S., Fader, P., & Bradlow, E. (2009). Path data in marketing: An integrative framework and prospectus for model building. *Marketing Science, 28*(2), 320–335.
Krüger, T., Mata, A., & Ihmels, M. (2014). The presenter's paradox revisited: An evaluation mode account. *Journal of Consumer Research, 41*(4), 1127–1136.

Thus, the final data corpus comprised of 32 articles that were subjected to a systematic review (see Table 9.2).

Corpus Evaluation

We employed a robust taxonomic paradigm based on a previous study conducted by Meißner and Oll (2017) to structure and assemble our analysis of the existing body of research relating to how eye-tracking methods are being utilized in business research. The authors of the study propose an integrative taxonomy for cross-disciplinary eye-tracking research derived from empirical, theoretical, and evolutionary perspectives (see Figure 9.3). This integrative protocol helps to provide a more holistic and nuanced view of the data corpus explored in this study.

Taxonomy, broadly defined, is a scientific classification mechanism (Usman, Britto, Börstler, & Mendes, 2017) that fundamentally assists in providing a baseline for comparing studies (Curkovic & Sroufe, 2016). Meißner and Oll's (2017) taxonomy espouses four salient dimensions: areas of application, drivers of attention, eye-tracking measures, and psychological constructs. The "areas of application" dimension seeks to highlight the specific domain that the study outcomes will apply or provide benefit to. The "drivers of attention" dimension speaks to the stimuli that instigate attentional bias, and if and how the researcher manipulates these stimuli. The next dimension (eye-tracking measures) focuses on the aspects of eye movement

Table 9.2   *Data corpus for systematic literature review*

Journal	Author(s)	Year	Title
Journal of Marketing	Rik Pieters & Michel Wedel	2004	Attention capture and transfer in advertising: Brand, pictorial, and text-size effects
Journal of Marketing	S. Adam Brasel & James Gips	2008	Breaking through fast-forwarding: Brand information and visual attention
Journal of Marketing	Pierre Chandon, J. Wesley Hutchinson, Eric T. Bradlow, & Scott H. Young	2009	Does in-store marketing work? Effects of the number and position of shelf facings on brand attention and evaluation at the point of purchase
Journal of Marketing Research	Thales Teixeira, Michel Wedel, & Rik Peters	2012	Emotion-induced engagement in internet video advertisements.
Journal of Marketing Research	Anocha Aribarg, Rik Pieters, & Michel Wedel	2010	Raising the BAR: Bias adjustment of recognition tests in advertising
American Marketing Association	Jie Zhang, Michel Wedel, & Rik Pieters	2009	Sales effects of attention to feature advertisements: A Bayesian meditation analysis
Journal of Marketing	Sungtak Hong, Kanishka Misra, & Naufel J. Vilcassim	2016	The perils of category management: The effect of product assortment on multicategory purchase incidence
Journal of Marketing	Rik Pieters, Michel Wedel, & Rajeev Batra	2010	The stopping power of advertising: Measures and effects of visual complexity
Journal of Marketing Research	Luca Cian, Aradhna Krishna, & Ryan S. Elder	2014	This logo moves me: Dynamic imagery from static images
Journal of Marketing Research	Rik Pieters, Edward Rosbergen, & Michel Wedel	1999	Visual attention to repeated print advertising: A test of scanpath theory
Marketing Science	Thales Teixeira, Michel Wedel, & Rik Peters	2010	Moment-to-moment optimal branding in TV commercials: Preventing avoidance by pulsing
Marketing Science	Michel Wedel & Rik Pieters	2000	Eye fixations on advertisements and memory for brands: A model and findings
Management Science	Rik Pieters, Michel Wedel, & Jie Zhang	2007	Optimal feature advertising design under competitive clutter
Marketing Science	Rik Pieters, Luk Warlop, & Michel Wiedel	2002	breaking through the clutter: Benefits of advertisement originality and familiarity for brand attention and memory
MIS Quarterly	Anthony Vance, Jeffrey Jenkins, Bonnie Brinton Anderson, Daniel Bjornn, & Brock Kirwan	2018	Tuning out security warnings: A longitudinal examination of habituation through fMRI, eye tracking, and field experiments
MIS Quarterly	Dianne Cyr, Milena Head, Hector Larios, & Bing Pan	2009	Exploring human images in website design: A multi-method approach
Management Science	Savannah Wei Shi, Michel Wedel, & Rik Pieters	2013	Information acquisition during online decision-making: A model-based exploration using eye-tracking data
Journal of Marketing Research	Vinod Venkatraman, Angelika Dimoka, & Paul A. Pavlou, Khoi Vo, William Hampton, Bryan Bollinger, Hal E. Hershfield, Masakazu Ishihara, & Russell S. Winer	2015	Predicting advertising success beyond traditional measures: New insights from neurophysiological methods and market response modeling
Journal of Consumer Research	Luca Cian, Aradhna Krishna, & Ryan S. Elder	2015	A sign of things to come: Behavioral change through dynamic iconography

Journal	Author(s)	Year	Title
Journal of Marketing Research	Liu (Cathy) Yang, Olivier Toubia, & Martijn G. de Jong	2018	Attention, information processing, and choice in incentive-aligned choice experiments
Journal of Marketing Research	Xioyan Deng, Barbara E. Kahn, H. Roa Unnava, & Hyojin Lee	2016	A "wide" variety: Effects of horizontal versus vertical display on assortment processing, perceived variety, and choice
Journal of Marketing Research	Liu (Cathy) Yang, Olivier Toubia, & Martijn G. de Jong	2015	A bounded rationality model of information search and choice in preference measurement
Journal of Marketing Research	Martin Miebner, Andres Musalem, & Joel Huber	2016	Eye tracking reveals processes that enable conjoint choices to become increasingly efficient with practice
Journal of Marketing	Dhruv Grewal, Carl-Philip Ahlbom, Lauren Beitelspacher, Stephanicee M. Noble, & Jens Nordfalt	2018	In-store mobile phone use and customer shopping behavior: Evidence from the field
Journal of Marketing Research	Hans Baumgartner, Bert Weijters, & Rik Pieters	2019	Misresponse to survey questions: A conceptual framework and empirical test of the effects of reversals, negations, and polar opposite core concepts
Marketing Science	Peter Stuttgen, Peter Boatwright, & Robert T. Monroe	2012	A satisficing choice model
Marketing Science	Olivier Toubia, Martijn G. de Jong, Daniel Stieger, & Johann Fuller	2012	Measuring consumer preferences using conjoint poker
Journal of Consumer Research	A. Selin Atalay, H. Onur Bodur, & Dina Rasolofoarison	2012	Shining in the center: Central gaze cascade effect on product choice
Journal of Consumer Research	Claudia Townsend & Barbara E. Kahn	2014	The "visual preference heuristic": The influence of visual versus verbal depiction on assortment processing, perceived variety, and choice overload
Journal of Consumer Research	Rik Pieters & Michel Wedel	2007	Goal control of attention to advertising: The Yarbus implication
Journal of Marketing Research	Henrik Hagtvedt & S. Adam Brasel	2016	Cross-modal communication: Sound frequency influences consumer responses to color lightness.
Journal of Accounting Research	Yasheng Chen, Johnny Jermias, & Tota Panggabean	2015	The role of visual attention in the managerial judgment of balanced-scorecard performance evaluation: Insights from using an eye-tracking device

behavior that were measured. The final dimension (psychological constructs) spotlights what, if any, physiological effects were investigated.

Coding

Despite the use of an established taxonomy with well-defined key terms, coding is inherently subjective in nature. A typical method to test inter-coder reliability in content analysis methodology is to have two coders analyze the same subset of

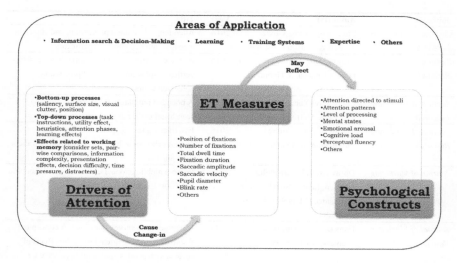

Source: Adapted from Meißner & Oll (2017).

Figure 9.3   *Integrative taxonomy for eye-tracking research*

a sample (Potter & Levine-Donnerstein, 1999). Therefore, parallel independent assessments were conducted by two reviewers to minimize the risk of errors of judgment. We defined and agreed upon a consensus strategy to address the occurrence of potential disagreements between reviewers.

Following a review and discussion of the classification rules, each reviewer coded a sample of three papers that were randomly selected from the extracted corpus. This constituted approximately 10 percent of the sample, which is consistent with conventional practice (Potter & Levine-Donnerstein, 1999). The results of the coding were discussed among the research team and specific areas of ambiguity and concern were addressed (Neuendorf, 2016). After establishing that both participants understood the definitions of the coding categories and were able to apply the definitions reliably and consistently, each coder evaluated the remaining 28 publications, resulting in a 100 percent overlap in the coding sample. At the conclusion of the coding exercise the research team compared the individual assessments submitted by each reviewer. The small corpus size made it possible for the researchers to conduct a side-by-side comparison of each entry. The few discrepancies that emerged were resolved through consensus, obviating the need for the computation of reliability coefficients.

Data Analysis

Following the evaluation of the corpus, the results were collated, summarized, and analyzed. Because Meißner and Oll's (2017) taxonomy serves as the analytical framework for our study, we summarize our findings within the context of the classification categories they propose.

We first summarize the percentage of observations in a few salient categories to provide an overall description of our data. Next we employ cluster analysis, a data reduction method for exploratory analysis, to investigate what, if any, degrees of association existed among the different data variables, and to determine if any new structures, patterns, or combination of patterns emerged for this specific corpus. In essence, we utilized this method to separate the corpus into groups that could be recognized and characterized by common themes and trends.

We performed our analysis with IBM SPSS (version 18) statistical software using the two-step clustering method. Two-step cluster analysis was selected because it held three major advantages over other clustering methods. First, both categorical and continuous variables can be handled (Norusis, 2008). Second, it automatically yields the optimal number of clusters and subcluster membership for each case and, thus, subjective judgments are alleviated (Norusis, 2011; Holman, 2013). Third, both distance change (e.g., Euclidean distance) and Bayesian Inference Criterion are utilized in its automatic clustering process, resulting in more credible results than when either of the two is used individually (SPSS Corporation, 2001).

With regards to the specific clustering procedure, we performed two analyses with different input variables. In the first instance we explored whether any patterns of association emerged among and across the various disciplines with regard to the type of devices used for measuring eye-tracking behavior and the process used to influence the direction of attention to stimuli (i.e., goal driven or stimulus driven). In the second instance we explored whether any patterns of association emerged with regard to the process used to influence the direction of attention to stimuli, the type of eye-tracking measures used to measure the respective change in attention directed to stimuli, and specific psychophysiological constructs that were operationalized. Each analysis yielded two interpretable clusters.

RESULTS

Descriptive Statistics

In Tables 9.3–9.6, we provide a descriptive summary of our dataset. The summary first highlights the make-up of the corpus in terms of subject area of interest and of journals in which these studies are published. Marketing/advertising and consumer behavior are dominant topics of study (see Table 9.3) and, not surprisingly, marketing journals are apparently the most frequently selected venue for these studies (see Table 9.4).

In Tables 9.5–9.7 we summarize the frequency of use of specific elements from the taxonomy that informed this analysis. Table 9.5 suggests that fixation metrics are the most frequently employed eye-tracking measure. We know that fixation metrics help the researcher to determine the degree of cognitive workload and effort expended,

Table 9.3   Distribution of publications by subject area

Subject	Percentage of corpus
Accounting	2.70
Marketing/advertising	40.54
Human–computer interaction	8.11
Cognitive behavior	5.41
Consumer behavior	37.83
Management	5.41

Table 9.4   Distribution of publications by journal

Journal	Percentage of corpus
American Marketing Association	2.86
Journal of Consumer Research	17.14
Journal of Marketing	17.14
Journal of Marketing Research	31.44
Management Science	5.71
Marketing Science	17.14
MIS Quarterly	8.57

Table 9.5   Frequency of use of specific eye-tracking measures

Eye-tracking measure	Frequency
Position of fixation	24 (75.0%)
Number of fixation	19 (59.4%)
Duration of fixation	20 (62.5%)
Pupil diameter	2 (6.3%)
Saccadic amplitude	2 (6.3%)
Saccadic velocity	2 (6.3%)
Saccadic distance	6 (18.8%)

Note: Since some publications used several eye-tracking measures together, the sum of frequencies of each measure exceeds the corpus size ($n = 32$).

which areas or objects stimulate observer interest, and which areas or objects gen-erate confusion. The tie-in to advertising and consumer behavior is evident here. Professionals in that discipline have to ensure that their marketing messages are easily and swiftly comprehended.

Table 9.6 shows a moderate preference for bottom-up processes that employ visual characteristics of the stimulus rather than goals of the participant to instigate attentional bias during experiments. A likely reason for this finding is that visual characteristics (e.g., clutter, surface size, position) are often easier to manipulate in an experimental environment.

Table 9.7 suggests that the direction of attention to stimuli is the most commonly operationalized psychological construct. This finding means that the majority of the studies in our corpus focused on measuring how attention is directed to different

Table 9.6   *Frequency of use of specific drivers of attention*

Drivers of attention	Frequency
Top-down	19 (59.4%)
Bottom-up	22 (68.8%)
Working memory	16 (50.0%)

Note: Since some publications used several drivers of attention together, the sum of frequencies of each measure exceeds the corpus size ($n = 32$).

Table 9.7   *Frequency of operationalization of specific psychological constructs*

Psychological constructs	Frequency
Attention to stimuli	29 (90.6%)
Attention pattern	6 (18.8%)
Cognitive load	5 (15.6%)
Emotional load	7 (21.9%)
Level of processing	13 (40.6%)
Mental states	4 (12.5%)
Perpetual fluency	5 (15.6%)

Note: Since some publications used several eye-tracking measures together, the sum of frequencies of each measure exceeds the corpus size ($n = 32$).

areas of interest. According to Meißner and Oll (2017), "the question of how much attention participants direct to one piece of information compared to other pieces is often interpreted as an indicator of relevance" (p. 7).

Cluster Analysis

Through cluster analysis methods, groups of manuscripts from the corpus showing similarity in certain research approaches were identified.

Analysis 1

The first analysis consisted of five inputs. These inputs were journal type, experimental setting, and drivers of attention (separated into top-down processes, bottom-up processes, and effective use of working memory). The two-step cluster analysis yielded two clusters. Cluster 1 comprised 22 publications (68.75 percent of the dataset) and cluster 2 comprised 10 publications (31.25 percent of the dataset). The results are summarized in Table 9.8 and Figure 9.4.

Cluster 1 comprised publications in the marketing domain that focused on investigating which working memory effects influence the direction of attention to stimuli. The effects identified included direction of attention, information complexity, presentation effects, decision difficulty, time pressure, and distractors.

Cluster 2 comprised publications in the non-marketing domain that focused on investigating which top-down processes influence the direction of attention to

Table 9.8   *Means and standard deviations of the measures separated by*
                  cluster groups in Analysis 1

	Cluster 1		Cluster 2		F
	M	SD	M	SD	
N	22		10		
Index	1.45	.74	2.70	1.25	12.52**
Journal name	2.36	1.47	5.30	1.64	25.70**
Experimental setting	1.95	1.50	1.40	1.26	1.03
Drivers of attention (top)	.40	.50	1.00	0	13.54**
Drivers of attention (bottom)	.68	.48	.70	.48	.01
Drivers of attention (working memory)	.64	.49	.20	.42	5.87*

Note: Index was coded as 1 = marketing, advertising, consumer research; 2 = consumer behavior and psychology; 3 = human–computer interaction; 4 = neuroscience; 5 = accounting; 6 = management. Journal name was coded as 1 = *Journal of Marketing*; 2 = *Journal of Marketing Research*; 3 = *American Marketing Association*; 4 = *Marketing Science*; 5 = *Journal of Consumer Research*; 6 = *MIS Quarterly*; 7 = *Management Science*; and 8 = *Journal of Accounting Research*. Experimental setting was coded as 1 = desktop-based eye-tracking; 2 = screen-based eye-tracking; 3 = outsourced; 4 = grocery store; 5 = not available. Three drivers of attention measures were coded as 1 if the specific method was used or investigated in each publication and 0 if the specific method was neither used nor investigated. $* p < .05$, $** p < .01$.

stimuli. The processes identified included task instructions, utility effects, attention phases, and learning effects.

Analysis 2

The second analysis consisted of 17 inputs. These inputs were drivers of attention (separated into top-down processes, bottom-up processes, and effective use of working memory), psychological constructs (such as attention patterns, level of processing, mental states, emotional arousal, cognitive load, and perceptual fluency), and eye-tracking measures (such as blink rate, number of fixations, and pupil diameter). The two-step cluster analysis yielded two clusters. Cluster 1 comprised 18 publications (56.25 percent of dataset) and cluster 2 comprised 14 publications (43.75 percent dataset). The results are summarized in Table 9.9 and Figure 9.5.

Cluster 1 comprised publications that focused on leveraging bottom-up processes (such as surface size, visual clutter, and position) to influence the direction of attention to stimuli (a psychophysiological measure) and evaluated the effect by measuring the duration of fixation (an eye-tracking measure).

Cluster 2 comprised publications that focused on investigating variations in emotional arousal (a psychophysiological measure) by measuring the position of fixations (eye-tracking measure) and number of fixations (eye-tracking measure).

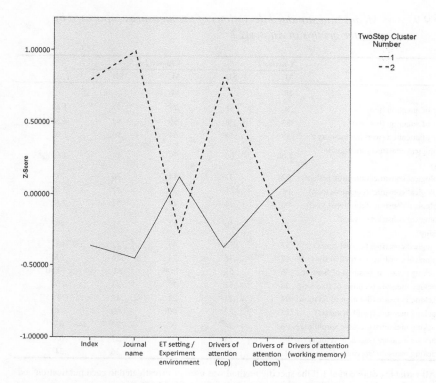

Figure 9.4   *Standardized mean scores of the assessed constructs across two cluster groups*

BLENDING EYE-TRACKING TECHNOLOGY INTO STRATEGIC ENTREPRENEURSHIP RESEARCH

The analysis of journal-based publications on eye tracking shows a concentration of work in one field – marketing. That focus makes sense from a perspective of consumer analysis. Being able to see into the mind of the consumer is a veritable gold mine for consumer research (Arnould & Thompson, 2005). But this study shows that other domains, including strategic entrepreneurship, are now beginning to scratch the surface of this productive field and will, we believe, find seams of gold as well.

With specific regard to strategic entrepreneurship this study identifies a number of variables to explore, but two in particular deserve mention: (1) drivers of attention, especially with an emphasis on attentional bias; and (2) psychological constructs, with an emphasis on stimuli and emotional arousal. Both have proven beneficial to the marketing field and may prove similarly so to strategic entrepreneurship. We discuss each in turn.

Table 9.9   *Means and standard deviations of the measures separated by cluster groups in Analysis 2*

	Cluster 1		Cluster 2		F
	M	SD	M	SD	
N	18		14		
Drivers of attention (top)	.50	.51	.71	.47	1.48
Drivers of attention (bottom)	.83	.38	.50	.52	4.38*
Drivers of attention (working memory)	.39	.50	.64	.50	2.03
Psychological construct (attention to stimuli)	1.00	.00	.79	.43	4.60*
Psychological construct (attention pattern)	.22	.43	.14	.36	.31
Psychological construct (cognitive load)	.06	.24	.29	.47	3.29
Psychological construct (emotional load)	.06	.24	.43	.51	7.52*
Psychological construct (level of processing)	.39	.50	.43	.51	.48
Psychological construct (mental states)	.17	.38	.07	.27	.63
Psychological construct (perpetual fluency)	.17	.38	.14	.36	.03
Eye-tracking measure (position of fixation)	.56	.51	1.00	.00	10.50**
Eye-tracking measure (number of fixation)	.44	.51	.79	.43	4.05
Eye-tracking measure (duration of fixation)	.94	.24	.21	.43	38.15**
Eye-tracking measure (pupil diameter)	.11	.32	.00	.00	1.64
Eye-tracking measure (saccadic amplitude)	.06	.24	.07	.27	.03
Eye-tracking measure (saccadic velocity)	.06	.24	.07	.27	.03
Eye-tracking measure (saccadic distance)	.22	.43	.14	.36	.31

Note: All variables were coded 1 if the specific method was used or investigated in each publication and 0 if the specific method was neither used nor investigated. * $p < .05$, ** $p < .01$.

Drivers of Attention

Eye-tracking studies focused on attentional bias should provide valuable insights into the areas that venture capitalists and other funding sources fixate on when examining proposals (Hall & Hofer, 1993; Riquelme & Rickards, 1992), listening to pitches (Zimmerman & Zeitz, 2002; Pollack, Rutherford, & Nagy, 2012), and examining cash flow analyses (Bertoni, Colombo, & Croce, 2010). Studies that examine listeners' and readers' pupil size, fixation, saccade, and blink rate could produce a plethora of new insights as to how entrepreneurs and their investors cognitively process information in each of these dimensions. We additionally suspect that entrepreneurial research examining the relationship between drivers of attention and opportunity recognition (Dyer, Gregersen, & Christensen, 2008) could prove particularly fruitful.

A second area within strategic entrepreneurship in which attentional bias may prove promising is entrepreneurial intention (Zhao, Seibert, & Hills, 2005; Krueger, Reilly, & Carsrud, 2000; Santos, Caetano, Mitchell, Landstrom, & Fayolle, 2017; Krueger, 2017), with special emphasis on entrepreneurial masking (Benson, Brau, Cicon, & Ferris, 2015) and strategic deception (Wanasika & Adler, 2011; Pittz & Adler, 2014). From an intention perspective, eye-tracking studies may provide useful

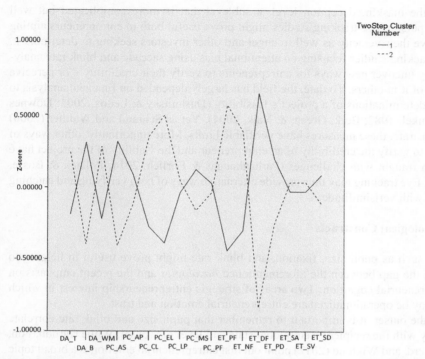

Note: DA_T: drivers of attention (top); DA_B: drivers of attention (bottom); DA_WM: drivers of attention (working memory); PC_AS: psychological construct (attention to stimuli); PC_AP: psychological construct (attention pattern); PC_CL: psychological construct (cognitive load); PC_EL: psychological construct (emotional load); PC_LP: psychological construct (level of processing); PC_MS: psychological construct (mental states); PC_PF: psychological construct (perpetual fluency); ET_PF: eye-tracking measure (position of fixation); ET_NF: eye-tracking measure (number of fixation); ET_DF: eye-tracking measure (duration of fixation); ET_PD: eye-tracking measure (pupil diameter); ET_SA: eye-tracking measure (saccadic amplitude); ET_SV: eye-tracking measure (saccadic velocity); ET_SD: eye-tracking measure (saccadic distance).

Figure 9.5   *Standardized mean scores of the assessed constructs across two cluster groups*

insights about the importance of placement of information in presentations and business plans, both at the macro-level of the presentation and at the micro-level of an individual page or PowerPoint slide. Such studies could assist those constructing these materials to strategically place key information in the most effective location possible and display it in the most effective manner possible (Withers, Ireland, Miller, Harrison, & Boss, 2018). Simultaneously, these studies might help people learn when to foreground and when to bury material that is minimally important or perhaps has negative connotations to funding sources (Dulek & Campbell, 2015; Smith, Jamil, Johari, & Ahmad, 2006; Smith & Anderson, 2004).

At the masking/deception level, a sublevel that is more complicated but well worth pursuit, eye-tracking studies might prove useful both to entrepreneurs aiming to prove their veracity as well to angel and other investors seeking to determine it. Eye-tracking studies focusing on attentional bias using saccade and blink rate analysis may uncover new ways for entrepreneurs to verify their credibility – or perceive a lack of it in others. To date, the field has largely depended on financial analysis to make determinations of a project's feasibility (Dushnitsky & Lenox, 2005; Downes & Heinkel, 1982; Berk, Green, & Naik, 2004). Yet as Schrand and Walther (2000) demonstrate, these measures have verifiable limits. More importantly, other ways of trying to verify the credibility of an entrepreneur and the viability of the project have proven fraught with challenges (Parhankangas & Ehrlich, 2014; Pollack & Bosse, 2014). Eye tracking may thus provide alternative ways of both verifying and catching issues with verisimilitude.

Psychological Constructs

Tools such as pupil size, fixation, and blink rate might prove useful in helping to bridge the gap between the aforementioned *boxologies* and the recent emphasis on entrepreneurial cognition. Two areas of strategic entrepreneurship interest in which this may be operationalized are entrepreneurial emotion and trust.

At the outset, it is important to remember that pupil size and blink rate correlate closely with the recipient's emotional state and level of arousal. While Cardon, Foo, Shepherd, and Wiklund (2012) point out that entrepreneurial emotion is a broad topic that ranges from excitement and anticipation to displeasure and grief, it is similarly an important topic that needs to be examined objectively within the field of strategic entrepreneurship. Current research in areas such as emotional support (Klyver, Schenkel, & Nielsen, 2020), entrepreneurial job satisfaction (Nikolaev, Shir, & Wiklund, 2020), anxiety in the entrepreneurial process (Thompson, van Gelderen, & Keppler, 2020), regulation of entrepreneurial emotion (De Cock, Denoo, & Clarysse, 2020), and the need for entrepreneurs to control their emotions during times of challenge and failure (Fang He, Sirén, Singh, Solomon, & von Krogh, 2018) show both the immediate interest in the topic as well as the need to explore the topic through an eye-tracking perspective.

Fixation, an eye-tracking measure that helps to evaluate cognitive workload and interest, may prove to be most valuable in exploring the vital area of entrepreneurial trust. Again, as with entrepreneurial emotion, the area of entrepreneurial trust is complex. It involves the probability that a different party will behave as expected (Gambetta, 2000) and can be categorized into segments such as personal trust, risk, and institutional trust (Williamson, 1993). From an entrepreneurial perspective, researchers have focused attention on the influence that trust has in new ventures (Zahra, Yavuz, & Ucbasaran, 2006), trust networks (Anderson & Jack, 2002), trust and the perception of legitimacy (Aldrich, 2000), and the interdependence of trust with context (Welter, 2012). Yet, despite these multiple avenues of approach, trust is an important area for strategic entrepreneur researchers to examine and eye tracking may prove to be a helpful vehicle for doing so.

Recent research by Levine (2019) points toward an innate human capacity to default to trust. In other words, when given a choice, we choose to trust the other individual. That tendency has enormous implications for entrepreneurial research since, as Levine additionally notes, deception is much easier to accomplish than previously thought. Gladwell (2019) further supports this challenge by observing that the well-established belief that people can accurately read non-verbal signals and determine a person's trustworthiness is often untrue. Gladwell (2019) attributes this inclination to a desire to trust. Zak (2017) additionally supports these observations by citing studies that show how our bodies produce a feel-good chemical, oxytocin, when we trust someone else. Hence, our bodies so want to trust that our minds are easily deceived. Goel and Karri (2006) find a similar tendency in entrepreneurial areas and label it as "overtrust."

Laboratory experiments, scenarios, and even case studies that investigate traits such as those identified in cluster 2 may provide important insights that bridge the gap between the entrepreneur's need to establish trust and the need that angel investors, venture capitalists, and other funding sources have to discover truth while controlling their tendencies to default to trust. Thus eye-tracking methods help each party in the entrepreneurial equation to function more effectively, efficiently, and ethically. We conclude with a specific experimental scenario that demonstrates how eye-tracking methods might be effectively leveraged in strategic entrepreneurship research.

Operationalizing Eye-Tracking Methods in Strategic Entrepreneurship Research

As highlighted previously, eye-tracking metrics are useful for measuring visual attention, cognitive load, and implicit preferences. These metrics allow researchers to obtain very detailed insights into attention, cognitive reactions, and decision-making (Genco et al., 2013). To illustrate how this would be useful in a strategic entrepreneurship research study, let's consider the following scenario.

A researcher seeks to understand how venture capitalists form their judgments and make the decisions they do after viewing an electronic/digital pitch deck. One of the study goals might potentially be to identify the best mix of variables in a digital pitch deck to optimize the engagement funnel and increase performance. This investigation presents a good fit for the integration of eye-tracking methods as part of the experimental protocol. According to Rowe and Burridge (2012), "In a digital environment, the messages we display, the context in which we display them and how we exploit peripheral vision are the skills most needed to close the sale."

In this experimental context, the independent or stimulus variable will be the digital pitch deck. The dependent variable or the effect measured would be the venture capitalist's visual attention. To measure the effect, data that the researcher may wish to collect are given below.

Metric 1: Fixation
Fixations refer to the period of time when the focus of the participant's gaze is relatively stagnant on an area, absorbing information about what they are viewing. Components of the fixation metric include time to first fixation, fixation duration, and fixation count. The researcher may employ fixation metrics to understand which information in the pitch deck grabbed the attention of the participant first, how interested the participant was in a particular aspect of the pitch deck, or if a specific item was difficult to process or comprehend (Tobii, n.d.).

Metric 2: Dwell time
Dwell time (also known as the "visit" metric) refers to the period of time when a participant first focuses on a specific area of the pitch deck until they look away from that area. Components of dwell time include visit duration, visit count, and total visit duration. These data can be very informative when examining participant interest or their ease of understanding of the information in the pitch deck. As an example, spending a shorter duration on a specific area may signal quicker comprehension of information, and a longer duration may signal confusion or difficulty in comprehension. Examples of variables that could influence visit metrics include the complexity of the information and use of visual elements (Tobii, n.d.).

Metric 3: Change in pupil diameter
By measuring and analyzing change in pupil diameter of the participants, the researcher can obtain insight into possible emotional reaction cues such as level of physical arousal and cognitive load as the participant navigates the digital pitch.

Collecting and analyzing the data identified above will help the researcher understand: (1) what aspects of the pitch deck resonate most with venture capitalists, (2) what areas of the pitch deck are potentially confusing or difficult to comprehend, and (3) what elements of the pitch deck need to be emphasized to capitalize on the venture capitalist's interest and encourage performance.

CONCLUSION

This study sought to identify eye tracking as a viable area of research within the field of strategic entrepreneurship. It accomplished this end by first demonstrating that eye tracking is already an established domain within physiological research. The emphasis on pupil size, gaze pattern, blink rate, and associated subcategories establishes the widespread presence of eye tracking within this domain. The study then proceeded to show how eye-tracking data are visualized through gaze plots and heat maps. Each of these manifestations provides valuable perspectives for viewing and interpreting eye-tracking data. Having established eye tracking as a valuable research perspective, the study then sought to examine the state of eye-tracking research within the domain of business research. The study leveraged an established taxonomy to evaluate the present state of eye-tracking research within business using 24 leading business journals as the corpus for the evaluation. The results of the study showed that thus far the preponderance of eye-tracking research appears in marketing-oriented journals, with some emerging presence in other business fields such as management information systems. A cluster analysis revealed that studies tend to congregate around two approaches. The first approach focuses on leveraging bottom-up processes to influence the direction of attention to stimuli, while evaluating the effect by measuring the duration of fixation, an eye-tracking measure. The second approach focuses on investigating variations in emotional arousal by measuring the position of fixations and number of fixations. Ultimately, we conclude that eye tracking is both a viable field of interest for strategic entrepreneurship and a highly promising area of investigation that could yield interesting and beneficial results for the field of strategic entrepreneurship.

ACKNOWLEDGMENTS

The authors would like to thank Daniel McCool and Sam Raburn for their contributions to this research.

REFERENCES

Aldrich, H. (2000). Entrepreneurial strategies in new organizational populations. In Swedberg, R. (ed.), *Entrepreneurship: The Social Science View* (pp. 211–228). Oxford: Oxford University Press.

Allen, M. (2017). Physiological measurement. *Sage Encyclopedia of Communication Research Methods*, 1–4.

Anderson, A. R., & Jack, S. L. (2002). The articulation of social capital in entrepreneurial networks: A glue or a lubricant? *Entrepreneurship and Regional Development*, 14(3), 193–210.

Arnould, E. J. & Thompson, C. J. (2005). Consumer culture theory (CCT): Twenty years of research. *Journal of Consumer Research*, 31(4), 868–882.

Ashby, N. J. S., Johnson, J. G., Krajbich, I., & Wedel, M. (2016). Applications and innovations of eye-movement research in judgment and decision making. *Journal of Behavioral Decision Making*, 29(2–3), 96–102.

Bailenson, J. N., Aharoni, E., Beall, A. C., Guadagno, R. E., Dimov, A., & Blascovich, J. (2004). Comparing behavioral and self-report measures of embodied agents' social presence in immersive virtual environments. *Proceedings of the International Society for Presence Research Annual Conference*.

Baron, R. (2004). The cognitive perspective: A valuable tool for answering entrepreneurship's basic "why" questions. *Journal of Business Venturing*, 19, 221–239.

Bell, L., Vogt, J., Willemse, C., Routledge, T., Butler, L., & Sakaki, M. (2018). Beyond self-report: A review of physiological and neuroscientific methods to investigate consumer behavior. *Frontiers in Psychology*, 9, 1655.

Benson, D. F., Brau, J. C., Cicon, J., & Ferris, S. P. (2015). Strategically camouflaged corporate governance in IPOs: Entrepreneurial masking and impression management. *Journal of Business Venturing*, 30(6), 839–864.

Berk, J. B., Green R. C., & Naik, V. (2004). Valuation and return dynamics of new ventures. *Review of Financial Studies*, 17(1), 1–35.

Bertoni, F., Colombo, M. G., & Croce, A. (2010). The effect of venture capital financing on the sensitivity to cash flow of firms' investments. *European Financial Management*, 16, 528–551.

Bird, G. D., Lauwereyns, J., & Crawford, M. T. (2012). The role of eye movements in decision making and the prospect of exposure effects. *Vision Research*, 60, 16–21.

Borys, M., & Plechawska-Wójcik, M. (2017). Eye tracking metrics in perception and visual attention research. *European Journal of Medical Technologies*, 3(16), 11–23.

Bradley, M. M., Miccoli, L., Escrig, M. A., & Lang, P. J. (2008). The pupil as a measure of emotional arousal and autonomic activation. *Psychophysiology*, 45(4), 602–607.

Brunyé, T., Drew, T., Weaver, D., & Elmore, J. (2019). A review of eye tracking for understanding and improving diagnostic interpretation. *Cognitive Research: Principles and Implications*, 4(1), 1–16.

Burridge, L. (2014). Review of *Social Media*. In Bergstrom, J. R., & Schall, A. J. (eds), *Eye Tracking in User Experience Design* (pp. 217–253). Waltham, MA: Morgan Kaufmann.

Busenitz, L. W. (1999). Entrepreneurial risk and strategic decision making. *Journal of Applied Behavioral Science*, 35, 325–340.

Busjahn, T., Schulte, C., Sharif, B., Begel, A., Hansen, M., Bednarik, R., & Antropova, M. (2014). Eye tracking in computing education. Paper presented at International Computing Education Research, 3–10. doi:10.1145/2632320.2632344.

Cardon, M. S., Foo, M. D., Shepherd, D., & Wiklund, J. (2012). Exploring the heart: Entrepreneurial emotion is a hot topic. *Entrepreneurship Theory and Practice*, 36(1), 1–10.

Carrasco, M. (2011). Visual attention: The past 25 years. *Vision Research*, 51(13), 1484–1525.

Castelhano, M. S., Mack, M. L., & Henderson, J. M. (2009). Viewing task influences eye movement control during active scene perception. *Journal of Vision*, 9(3), 1–6.

Coan, J. A. (1997). Lost in a shopping mall: An experience with controversial research. *Ethics and Behavior*, 7(3), 271–284.

Cornelissen, J. P., & Clarke, J. S. (2010). Imagining and rationalizing opportunities: Inductive reasoning and the creation and justification of new ventures. *Academy of Management Review*, 35(4), 539–557.

Cornelissen, J. P., Clarke J. S., & Cienki, A. (2012). Sensemaking in entrepreneurial contexts: The use of metaphors in speech and gesture to gain and sustain support for novel business ventures. *International Small Business Journal*, 30(3), 213–241.

Ćosić, D. (2015). Neuromarketing in market research: Eye tracking application. *Proceedings of the Entrenova – Enterprise Research Innovation Conference*, 295–302.

Covin, J. G., & Miles, M. P. (1999). Corporate entrepreneurship and the pursuit of competitive advantage. *Entrepreneurship Theory and Practice*, 23(3), 47–63.

Curkovic, S., & Sroufe, R. (2016). A literature review and taxonomy of environmentally responsible manufacturing. *American Journal of Industrial and Business Management*, 6(3), 323–346.

Dawson, N. (2014). Eye tracking: What is it for and when to use it. https://usabilitygeek.com/what-is-eye tracking-when-to-use-it/.

De Cock, R., Denoo, L., & Clarysse, B. (2020). Surviving the emotional rollercoaster called entrepreneurship: The role of emotion regulation. *Journal of Business Venturing*, 35(2), 105936.

DiClemente, R. J., Swartzendruber, A. L., & Brown, J. L. (2013). Improving the validity of self-reported sexual behavior: No easy answers. *Sexually Transmitted Diseases*, 40(2), 111–112.

Doležal, J., & Fabian, V. (2015). 41 applications of eye tracking in neuroscience. *Clinical Neurophysiology*, 126(3), e44.

Downes, D. H., & Heinkel, R. (1982). Signaling and the valuation of unseasoned new issues. *Journal of Finance*, 37(1), 1–10.

Drew, T., Boettcher, S. E. P., & Wolfe, J. M. (2017). One visual search, many memory searches: An eye tracking investigation of hybrid search. *Journal of Vision*, 17(11), 5.

Duchowski, A. T. (2002). A breadth-first survey of eye tracking applications. *Behavior Research Methods, Instruments, and Computers*, 34(4), 455–470.

Duchowski, A. T. (2017). *Eye Tracking Methodology: Theory and Practice* (3rd edn). Cham: Springer International.

Dulek, R. E., & Campbell, K. S. (2015). On the dark side of strategic communication. *International Journal of Business Communication*, 52(1), 122–142.

Dushnitsky, G., & Lenox, M. J. (2005). When do firms undertake R&D by investing in new ventures? *Strategic Management Journal*, 26(10), 947–965.

Dyer, J. H., Gregersen, H. B., & Christensen, C. (2008). Entrepreneur behaviors, opportunity recognition, and the origins of innovative ventures. *Strategic Entrepreneurship Journal*, 2(4), 317–338.

Eckstein, M., Guerra-Carrillo, B., Singley, A., & Bunge, S. (2017). Beyond eye gaze: What else can eyetracking reveal about cognition and cognitive development? *Developmental Cognitive Neuroscience*, 25, 69–91.

Ellison, N., Heino, R., & Gibbs, J. (2006). Managing impressions online: Self-presentation processes in the online dating environment. *Journal of Computer-Mediated Communication*, 11(2), 415–441.

Faad, M. B. (2017). Eye-tracking uncovers cognitive mechanisms underlying high level human judgments. Medical Research.com, October 19. https://medicalresearch.com/author -interviews/eye-tracking-uncovers-cognitive-mechanisms-underlying-high-level-human -judgements/37580/.

Fang He, V., Sirén, C., Singh, S., Solomon, G., & von Krogh, G. (2018). Keep calm and carry on: Emotion regulation in entrepreneurs' learning from failure. *Entrepreneurship Theory and Practice*, 42(4), 605–630.

Fong, J. (2012). The meaning of pupil dilation. www.the-scientist.com/daily-news/the -meaning-of-pupil-dilation-40076.

Fox, S., & Faulkner-Jones, B. (2017). Eye tracking in the study of visual expertise: *Methodology and Approaches in Medicine: Frontline Learning Research*, 5(3), 43–54.

Gambetta, D. (2000). Can we trust trust? *Trust: Making and Breaking Cooperative Relations*, 13, 213–237.

Genco, S. J., Pohlmann, A. P., & Steidl, P. (2013). What eye tracking can and can't tell you about attention. www.nmsba.com/buying- neuromarketing/neuromarketing-techniques/ what-eye tracking-can-and-cant-tell-you-about-attention.

Gioia D. A., & Chittipeddi, K. (1991). Sensemaking and sensegiving in strategic change initiation. *Strategic Management Journal*, 12(6), 433–448.

Gladwell, M. T. (2019). *Talking to Strangers: What We Should Know about the People We Don't Know*. New York: Little, Brown and Company.

Goel, S., & Karri, R. (2006). Entrepreneurs, effectual logic, and over-trust. *Entrepreneurship Theory and Practice*, 30(4), 477–493.

Goettker, A., Braun, D. I., Schütz, A. C., & Gegenfurtner, K. R. (2018). Execution of saccadic eye movements affects speed perception. *Proceedings of the National Academy of Sciences of the United States of America*, 115(9), 2240–2245.

Gomes, K. M., & Riggs, S. L. (2017). Analyzing visual search techniques using eye tracking for a computerized provider order entry (CPOE) task. *Proceedings of the Human Factors and Ergonomics Society Annual Meeting*, 61(1), 691–695.

Goyal, S., Miyapuram, K. P., & Lahiri, U. (2015). Predicting consumers' behavior using eye tracking data. Paper presented at the 2015 Second International Conference on Soft Computing and Machine Intelligence, 126–129. doi:10.1109/ISCMI.2015.26.

Grant, E. R., & Spivey, M. J. (2003). Eye movements and problem solving: Guiding attention guides thought. *Psychological Science*, 14(5), 462–466.

Hall, J., & Hofer, C. W. (1993). Venture capitalists' decision criteria in new venture evaluation. *Journal of Business Venturing*, 8(1), 25–42.

Hitt, M., Ireland, R. D., Camp, S. M., & Sexton, D. (2001). Strategic entrepreneurship: Entrepreneurial strategies for wealth creation. *Strategic Management Journal*, 22(6–7), 479–491.

Holman, D. (2013). Job types and job quality in Europe. *Human Relationships*, 66, 475–502.

Holmqvist, K., Jarodzka, H., & Gruber, H. (2017). Eye tracking in educational science: Theoretical frameworks and research agendas. *Journal of Eye Movement Research*, 10(1), 1–18.

Holt, R., & Macpherson, A. (2010). Sensemaking, rhetoric and the socially competent entrepreneur. *International Small Business Journal*, 28(1), 20–42.

Hooijdonk, R. v. (2016). The magic of biometric eye tracking in education and rehabilitation. Emerging education technologies. www.emergingedtech.com/2016 /06/the-magic-of-biometric-eye tracking-in-education/.

Hoyt, C., Noke, H., Mosey, S., & Marlow, S. (2019). From venture idea to venture formation: The role of sensemaking, sensegiving and sense receiving. *International Small Business Journal*, 37(3), 268–288.

Huddleston, P. T., Behe, B. K., Driesener, C., & Minahan, S. (2018). Inside-outside: Using eye tracking to investigate search-choice processes in the retail environment. *Journal of Retailing and Consumer Services*, 43(C), 85–93.

Hutton, S. B. (2008). Cognitive control of saccadic eye movements. *Brain and Cognition*, 68(3), 327–340.

Hwang, Y. M., & Lee, K. C. (2017). Using eye tracking to explore consumers' visual behavior according to their shopping motivation in mobile environments. *Cyberpsychology, Behavior and Social Networking*, 20(7), 442–447.

Issa, B., & Morgan-Short, K. (2015). An eye tracking study on the role of attention and its relationship with motivation. *EUROSLA Yearbook: Annual Conference of the European Second Language Association*, 15, 114–142.

Jarodzka, H., & Brand-Gruwel, S. (2017). Tracking the reading eye: Towards a model of real world reading. *Journal of Computer Assisted Learning*, 33(3), 193–201.

Just, M. A., & Carpenter, P. A. (1976). The role of eye-fixation research in cognitive psychology. *Behavior Research Methods and Instrumentation*, 8(2), 139–143.

Kahneman, D., & Beatty, J. (1966). Pupil diameter and load on memory. *Science*, 154(3756), 1583–1585.

Kerr-Gaffney, J., Harrison, A., & Tchanturia, K. (2018). Eye tracking research in eating disorders: A systematic review. *International Journal of Eating Disorders*, 52(1), 3–27.

Kirchner, H., & Thorpe, S. J. (2006). Ultra-rapid object detection with saccadic eye movements: Visual processing speed revisited. *Vision Research*, 46(11), 1762–1776.

Klyver, K., Schenkel, M. T., & Nielsen, M. S. (2020). Can't always get what I want: Cultural expectations of emotional support in entrepreneurship. *International Small Business Journal*. 0266242620915675.

Knapen, T., Willem de Gee, J., Brascamp, J., Nuiten, S., Hoppenbrouwers, S., & Theeuwes, J. (2016). Cognitive and ocular factors jointly determine pupil responses under equiluminance. *PLoS One*, 11(5).

Koester, T., Brøsted, J. E., Jakobsen, J. J., Malmros, H. P., & Andreasen, N. K. (2017). The use of eye tracking in usability testing of medical devices. *Proceedings of the International Symposium on Human Factors and Ergonomics in Health Care*, 6(1), 192–199.

Kovesdi, C., Spielman, Z., LeBlanc, K., & Rice, B. (2018). Application of eye tracking for measurement and evaluation in human factors studies in control room modernization. *Nuclear Technology*, 202(2–3), 220–229.

Kret, M., & Sjak-Shie, E. (2018). Preprocessing pupil size data: Guidelines and code. *Behavior Research Methods*, 51(3).

Krueger, N. F. (2017). Entrepreneurial intentions are dead: Long live entrepreneurial intentions. In M. Brännback & A. L. Carsrud (eds), *Revisiting the Entrepreneurial Mind* (pp. 13–34). Cham: Springer.

Krueger, Jr., N. F., Reilly, M. D., & Carsrud, A. L. (2000). Competing models of entrepreneurial intentions. *Journal of Business Venturing*, 15(5–6), 411–432.

Kucewicz, M. T., Dolezal, J., Kremen, V., Berry, B. M., Miller, L. R., Magee, A. L., … Worrell, G. A. (2018). Pupil size reflects successful encoding and recall of memory in humans. *Scientific Reports*, 8(1), 4949–4957.

Kuratko, D. F., & Audretsch, D. B. (2009). Strategic entrepreneurship: Exploring different perspectives of an emerging concept. *Entrepreneurship Theory and Practice*, 33(1), 1–17.

Lai, M., Lombardo, M. V., Suckling, J., Ruigrok, A. N. V., Chakrabarti, B., Ecker, C., . . . Baron-Cohen, S. (2013). Biological sex affects the neurobiology of autism. *Brain: A Journal of Neurology*, 136(Pt 9), 2799–2815.

Lavrakas, P. J. (2008). Social desirability. *Encyclopedia of Survey Research Methods*. doi: 10.4135/9 781412963947.

Lee, G., Ojha, A., Kang, J., & Lee, M. (2015). Modulation of resource allocation by intelligent individuals in linguistic, mathematical and visuo-spatial tasks. *International Journal of Psychophysiology: Official Journal of the International Organization of Psychophysiology*, 97(1).

Lévêque, L., Bosmans, H., Cockmartin, L., & Liu, H. (2018). State of the art: Eye tracking studies in medical imaging. *IEEE Access*, 6, 37023–37034.

Levine, T. R. (2019). *Duped: Truth-Default Theory and the Social Science of Lying and Deception*. Tuscaloosa, AL: University of Alabama Press.

Leyden, D. P., Link, A. N., & Siegel D. S. (2014). A theoretical analysis of the role of social networks in entrepreneurship. *Research Policy*, 43(7), 1157–1163.

Mantiuk, R. K., & Bazyluk, B. (2013). Gaze-driven object tracking for real time rendering. *Computer Graphics Forum*, 32(2.2), 163–173.

Martins, R., & Carvalho, J. (2015). Eye blinking as an indicator of fatigue and mental load: A systematic review. In P. M. Arezes, J. Santos Baptista, M. P. Barroso et al. (eds), *Occupational Safety and Hygiene* III (pp. 243–248). Boca Raton, FL: CRC Press.

Mastrantuono, E., Saldaña, D., & Rodríguez-Ortiz, I. R. (2017). An eye tracking study on the perception and comprehension of unimodal and bimodal linguistic inputs by deaf adolescents. *Frontiers in Psychology*, 8, 1044.

Matheias, B. D., Williams, D. W., & Smith, A. (2015). Entrepreneurial inceptions: The role of imprinting in entrepreneurial action. *Journal of Business Venturing*, 30(1), 11–28.

Meißner, M., & Oll, J. (2017). The promise of eye tracking methodology in organizational research: A taxonomy, review, and future avenues. *Organizational Research Methods*, 22(2), 590–617.

Mele, M. L., & Federici, S. (2012). Gaze and eye tracking solutions for psychological research. *Cognitive Processing*, 13(1), 261–265.

Menon, R. G. V., Sigurdsson, V., Larsen, N. M., Fagerstrøm, A., & Foxall, G. R. (1973). Consumer attention to price in social commerce: Eye tracking patterns in retail clothing. *Journal of Business Research*, 69(11), 5008–5013.

Mills J. H. (2003). *Making Sense of Organizational Change*. London: Routledge.

Mitchell, R. K., Busenitz, L., Bird, B., Gagliio, C. M., McMullen, J. S., Morse, E. A., & Smith, J. B. (2007). The central question in entrepreneurial cognition research 2007. *Entrepreneurship Theory and Practice*, 31(1), 1–27.

Mitchell, R. K., Busenitz, L., Lant, T., McDougall, P. P., Morse, E. A., & Smith, B. (2004). The distinctive and inclusive domain of entrepreneurial cognition research. *Entrepreneurship Theory and Practice*, 28(6), 505–518.

Mitchell, R. K., Randolph-Seng, B., & Mitchell, J. R. (2011). Socially situated cognition: Imagining new opportunities for entrepreneurship research (dialogue). *Academy of Management Review*, 36(4), 774–776.

Muczyński, B., & Gucma, M. (2013). Application of eye-tracking techniques in human factor research in marine operations: Challenges and methodology. *Scientific Journals Maritime University of Szczecin*, 36(108), 116–120.

Muczyński, B., Gucma, M., Bilewski, M., & Zalewski, P. M. (2013). Using eye tracking data for evaluation and improvement of training process on ship's navigational bridge simulator. *Scientific Journals*, 33(105), 75–78.

Nakano, T., & Miyazaki, Y. (2019). Blink synchronization is an indicator of interest while viewing videos. *International Journal of Psychophysiology*, 135, 1–11.

Neuendorf, K. A. (2016). *The Content Analysis Guidebook* (2nd edn). Thousand Oaks, CA: Sage.

Nicholson, L., & Anderson, A. R. (2005). News and nuances of the entrepreneurial myth and metaphor: Linguistic games in entrepreneurial sense-making and sense-giving. *Entrepreneurship Theory and Practice*, 29(2), 153–172.

Nicolaou, N., Patel, P. C., & Wolfe, M. T. (2017). Testosterone and tendency to engage in self-employment. *Management Science*, 64(4), 1825–1841.

Nicolaou, N., Shane, S., Cherkas, L., Hunkin, J., & Spector, T. D. (2007). Is the tendency to engage in entrepreneurship genetic? *Management Science*, 54(1), 167–179.

Nikolaev, B., Shir, N., & Wiklund, J. (2020). Dispositional positive and negative affect and self-employment transitions: The mediating role of job satisfaction. *Entrepreneurship Theory and Practice*, 44(3), 451–474.

Norusis, M. J. (2008). *SPSS 16.0 Guide to Data Analysis*. Englewood Cliffs, NJ: Prentice Hall.

Norusis, M. J. (2011). Eye tracking uncovers cognitive mechanisms underlying high-level human judgments. *IBM SPSS Statistics 19 Statistical Procedures Companion*.

Oliva, M., & Anikin, A. (2018). Pupil dilation reflects the time course of emotion recognition in human vocalizations. *Nature*, 8.

Paprocki, R., & Lenskiy, A. (2017). What does eye-blink rate variability dynamics tell us about cognitive performance? *Frontiers in Human Neuroscience*, 11, 620.

Parhankangas, A., & Ehrlich, M. (2014). How entrepreneurs seduce business angels: An impression management approach. *Journal of Business Venturing*, 29(4), 543–564.

Paulhus, D., & Vazire, S. (2007). The self-report method. In R. W. Robins, R. C. Fraley, & R. F. Krueger (eds), *Handbook of Research Methods in Personality Psychology* (pp. 224–239). New York: Guilford.

Peterson, S., Reina, C., Waldman, D., & Becker, W. (2015). Using physiological methods to study emotions in organizations. *New Ways of Studying Emotions in Organizations*, 11, 1–27.

Peysakhovich, V., Lefrançois, O., Dehais, F., & Causse, M. (2018). The neuroergonomics of aircraft cockpits: The four stages of eye tracking integration to enhance flight safety. *Aviation Safety*, 4(8).

Pittz, T. G., & Adler, T. R. (2014). Entrepreneurial piracy through strategic deception: The "make, buy, or steal" decision. *International Journal of Entrepreneurship and Small Business*, 22(4), 466–481.

Pohl, M., Schmitt, M., & Diehl, S. (2009). Comparing the readability of graph layouts using eyetracking and task-oriented analysis. Eurographics Association.

Pollack, J. M., & Bosse, D. A. (2014). When do investors forgive entrepreneurs for lying? *Journal of Business Venturing*, 29(6), 741–754.

Pollack, J. M., Rutherford, M. W., & Nagy, B. G. (2012). Preparedness and cognitive legitimacy as antecedents of new venture funding in televised business pitches. *Entrepreneurship Theory and Practice*, 36(5), 915–939.

Potter, W. J., & Levine-Donnerstein, D. (1999). Rethinking validity and reliability in content analysis. *Journal of Applied Communication Research*, 27, 258–284.

Pretorius, M., & Calitz, A. (2011). The contribution of eye tracking to brand awareness studies. Paper presented at the Fifth International Business Conference.

Purves, D. (2001). *Neuroscience*, 2nd edn. Sunderland, MA: Sinauer Associates.

Puškarević, I., Nedeljković, U., Dimovski, V., & Možina, K. (2016). An eye tracking study of attention to print advertisements: Effects of typeface figuration. *Journal of Eye Movement Research*, 9(5), 1–18.

Rakoczi, G., & Pohl, M. (2012). Visualisation and analysis of multiuser gaze data: Eye tracking usability studies in the special context of E-learning. Paper presented at the 12th IEEE International Conference on Advanced Learning Technologies, July, 738–739. doi:10.1109/ICALT.2012.15.

Rayner, K. (1998). Eye movements in reading and information processing. *Psychological Bulletin*, 124(3), 372–422.

Rehder, B., & Hoffman, A. B. (2005). Thirty-something categorization results explained: Selective attention, eye tracking, and models of category learning. *Journal of Experimental Psychology: Learning, Memory, and Cognition*, 31(5), 811–829.

Ries, A. J., Touryan, J., Ahrens, B., & Connolly, P. (2016). The impact of task demands on fixation-related brain potentials during guided search. *PLoS One*, 11(6), e0157260.

Riquelme, H., & Rickards, T. (1992). Hybrid conjoint analysis: An estimation probe in new venture decisions. *Journal of Business Venturing*, 7(6), 505–518.

Rosengrant, D., Hearrington, D., Alvarado, K., & Keeble, D. (2012). Following student gaze patterns in physical science lectures. *AIP Conference Proceedings*, 1413, 323–326.

Rowe, A., & Burridge, L. (2012). Ten inbox secrets: What eye tracking reveals about designing better emails. *Journal of Direct, Data and Digital Marketing Practice*, 14, 46–65.

Sadler, P., & Woody, E. (2003). Is who you are who you're talking to? Interpersonal style and complementarity in mixed-sex interactions. *Journal of Personality and Social Psychology*, 84(1), 80–96.

Sánchez, C., Martín-Pascual, M. Á, Gruart, A., & Delgado-García, J. M. (2017). Eyeblink rate watching classical Hollywood and post-classical MTV editing styles, in media and non-media professionals. *Scientific Reports*, 7(1), 43267.

Santos, S. C., Caetano, A., Mitchell, C. Landstrom, H., & Fayolle, A. (2017). *The Emergence of Entrepreneurial Behavior: Intention, Education and Orientation*. Cheltenham, UK and Northampton, MA, USA: Edward Elgar Publishing.

Schrand, C. M., & Walther, B. R. (2000). Strategic benchmarks in earnings announcements: The selective disclosure of prior-period earnings components. *Accounting Review*, 75(2), 151–177.

Schütz, A. C., Braun, D. I., & Gegenfurtner, K. R. (2011). Eye movements and perception: A selective review. *Journal of Vision*, 11(5), 9.

Sharma, V., Fong, A., Beckman, R. A., Rao, S., Boca, S. M., McGarvey, P. B., Ratwani, R. M., & Madhavan, S. (2018). Eye tracking study to enhance usability of molecular diagnostics reports in cancer precision medicine. CO Precision Oncology. doi: 10.1200/PO.17.00296.

Siegle, G. J., Ichikawa, N., & Steinhauer, S. (2008). Blink before and after you think: Blinks occur prior to and following cognitive load indexed by pupillary responses. *Psychophysiology*, 45(5), 679–687.

Smith, M., Jamil, A., Johari, Y. C., & Ahmad, S. A. (2006). The chairman's statement in Malaysian companies. *Asian Review of Accounting*, 14 (1–2), 49–65.

Smith, R., & Anderson, A. R. (2004). *The Devil is in the e-Tale: Form and Structure in the Entrepreneurial Narrative*. Cheltenham, UK and Northampton, MA, USA: Edward Elgar Publishing.

Smith, R., & Semin G. U. (2004). Socially situation cognition: Cognition in its social context. *Advances in Experimental Social Psychology*, 36, 53–117.

Spector, R. (1990). The pupils. In H. K. Walker & J. W. Hurst (eds), *Clinical Methods: The History, Physical, and Laboratory Examinations*. Boston, MA: Buttersworth.

SPSS Corporation (2001). *The SPSS TwoStep cluster component: Technical report*. Chicago, IL: SPSS.

Tanaka, Y. (1999). Arousal level and blink activity. *Shinrigaku Kenkyu: The Japanese Journal of Psychology*, 70(1), 1–8.

Tharp, I. J., & Pickering, A. D. (2011). Individual differences in cognitive-flexibility: The influence of spontaneous eyeblink rate, trait psychoticism and working memory on attentional set-shifting. *Brain and Cognition*, 75(2), 119–125.

Thompson, N. A., van Gelderen, M., & Keppler, L. (2020). No need to worry? Anxiety and coping in the entrepreneurship process. *Frontiers in Psychology*, 11, 398.

Tobii (n.d.). www.tobii.com.

Tobii Pro (n.d.). www.tobiipro.com.

Tran, T. Q., Boring, R. L., Dudenhoeffer, D. D., Hallbert, B. P., Keller, M. D., & Anderson, T. M. (2007). Advantages and disadvantages of physiological assessment for next generation control room design. *2007 IEEE 8th Human Factors and Power Plants and HPRCT 13th Annual Meeting*, 259–263.

Tullis, T., & Albert, W. (2008). *Measuring the User Experience: Collecting, Analyzing, and Presenting Usability Metrics*. San Francisco, CA: Morgan Kaufmann.

Usman, M., Britto, R., Börstler, J., & Mendes, E. (2017). Taxonomies in software engineering: A systematic mapping study and a revised taxonomy development method. *Information and Software Technology*, 85, 43–59.

Vaghely I. P., & Julien, P. A. (2010). Are opportunities recognized or constructed? An information perspective on entrepreneurial opportunity identification. *Journal of Business Venturing*, 25(1), 73–86.

Venkat, A. (2016). Eye tracking 101: How does it work? https://assistivetechnologyblog.com/2016/08/eye tracking-101-how-does-it-work.html.

Vijayan, K., Mork, J., & Hansen, E. (2018). Eye tracker as a tool for engineering education. *Universal Journal of Educational Research*, 6(11), 2647–2655.

Vogel, R., Hattke, F., & Petersen, J. (2017). Journal rankings in management and business studies: What rules do we play by? *Research Policy*, 46(10), 1707–1722.

Wanasika, I., & Adler, T. R. (2011). Deception as strategy: Context and dynamics. *Journal of Managerial Issues*, 23, 364.

Wang, S. (2018). Face size biases emotion judgment through eye movement. *Scientific Reports*, 8(1), 317.

Wedel, M. (2015). Attention research in marketing: A review of eye-tracking studies. In Fawcett, J. M., Risko, E. F., & Kingstone, A. (eds), *The Handbook of Attention* (pp. 569–588). Boston, MA: MIT Press.

Wedel, M., & Pieters, R. (2008). Eye tracking for visual marketing. *Foundations and Trends in Marketing*, 1(4), 231–320.

Weick, K. D., Sutcliffe, K. M., & Obsfeld, D. (2005). Organizing and the process of sensemaking. *Organization Science*, 16(4), 327–451.

Welter, F. (2012). All you need is trust? A critical review of the trust and entrepreneurship literature. *International Small Business Journal*, 30(3), 193–212.

White, R. E., Thornhill, S., & Hampson, E. (2007). A biosocial model of entrepreneurship: The combined effects of nurture and nature. *Journal of Organizational Behavior*, 28(4), 451–466.

Williamson, O. E. (1993). Calculativeness, trust, and economic organization. *Journal of Law and Economics*, 36(1, Part 2), 453–486.

Withers, M. C., Ireland, R. D., Miller, D., Harrison, J. S., & Boss, D. S. (2018). Competitive Landscape shifts: The influence of strategic entrepreneurship on shifts in market commonality. *Academy of Management Review*, 43(3), 349–370.

Yale School of Medicine (2009). In Yale autism research, the eyes have it. https://medicine .yale.edu /news/medicineatyale/in-yale-autism-research-the-eyes-have-it/.

Yoon, D., & Narayanan, N. (2004). Mental imagery in problem solving: An eye tracking study. *ACM ETRA Symposium*. https://citeseerx.ist.psu.edu/viewdoc/download?doi=10.1.1 .9.9982&rep=rep1&type=pdf.

Zahra, S. A., Yavuz, R. I., & Ucbasaran, D. (2006). How much do you trust me? The dark side of relational trust in new business creation in established companies. *Entrepreneurship Theory and Practice*, 30(4), 541–559.

Zak, P. J. (2017). The neuroscience of trust. *Harvard Business Review*, 95(1), 84–90.

Zhao, M., Gersch, T. M., Schnitzer, B. S., Dosher, B. A., & Kowler, E. (2012). Eye movements and attention: The role of pre-saccadic shifts of attention in perception, memory and the control of saccades. *Vision Research*, 74, 40–60.

Zhao, H., Seibert, S. E., & Hills, G. E. (2005). The mediating role of self-efficacy in the development of entrepreneurial intentions. *Journal of Applied Psychology*, 90(6), 1265.

Zimmerman, M. A., & Zeitz, G. J. (2002). Beyond survival: Achieving new venture growth by building legitimacy. *Academy of Management Review*, 27(3), 414–443.

10. New frontiers? Approaches to computerized text analysis in strategic entrepreneurship research

Anna M. Pastwa and William J. Wales

INTRODUCTION

The foci of studies within strategic entrepreneurship (SE) are broad and rich. Explorations of SE build upon research from diverse disciplines such as economics, finance, psychology, and sociology, as well as other subdisciplines within management (Anderson, Wennberg, & Mcmullen, 2019; Hitt, Ireland, Sirmon, & Trahms, 2011). Yet, research about SE phenomena presents a particular difficulty, mainly because of the complexity of the process through which SE unfolds, as well as the ongoing change of its expression (Davidsson, 2016). In accordance, a broad range of methods and approaches have been employed to investigate SE. Following the norms of social science, to acquire fine-grained information SE researchers have typically relied on small-scale primary data collection through surveys, and to a lesser extent interviews and case studies. These data have then typically been combined with techniques such as factor analysis of indicator variables to extract latent traits or to develop other SE-related measures for further analysis (Short, Broberg, Cogliser, & Brigham, 2010). A notable constraint of these methods, next to limited scalability, is the availability and willingness of informants to participate in the research. In particular, senior decision makers or practicing entrepreneurs, who are often challenging to access and severely time constrained, are typically sought after as expert informants. Further limitations relate to the accurate recall of past events by the respondents, their dispositions, or social desirability of responses.

However, copious volumes of textual documents are being generated daily by organizations, their members at various levels, as well as third-party accounts about these actors. This textual information presents a wealth of untapped resources which may shed light on a range of organizational factors, including individual and group behaviors, key inter and intra-organizational dynamics, managerial policy choices, and other aspects of great interest within SE research. For instance, identifying linguistic markers of SE in large collections of textual data could not only reveal unique insights into the organizations' competitive approaches but also provide temporal insights which are often lacking within the frequent cross-sectional constraints of primary research. This chapter focuses therefore on providing a guide to handling important and often overlooked alternative sources of data for SE researchers, namely texts, which help overcome some of the prominent limitations of key informant research. We focus on both providing an overview of textual data sources as well as the methods available for cleaning and extracting information from them to help advance the investigation of SE-related phenomena. These techniques include more familiar approaches for construct operationalization like dictionary word counts, and emerging new algorithmic text processing, such as topic modeling and neural networks-based word embeddings.

Applications of methods for the content analysis of textual collections have a long tradition (Berelson, 1952). Scholars recognize the opportunities that voluminous textual data offer to answer both new research questions as well as revisit old ones (Haans, 2019). Yet, manual content analysis of texts, as in grounded theorizing (Denzin & Lincoln, 2011), is restricted by human capacity to process large volumes of documents. Such an approach is both time and resource intensive. Data collection and analysis in this modality have therefore frequently resulted in small samples covering brief time periods (e.g., Salmivaara & Kibler, 2019) – limitations often shared with manual primary data collection in general. Moreover, such an approach places the burden of recognizing relationships within and across documents on the researcher. Consequently, while text analysis can certainly be performed manually by humans (e.g., Gupta, Dutta, & Chen, 2014; Noble, Sinha, & Kumar, 2002), the focus of our study is upon providing a deeper understanding of computerized textual analysis within SE research.

Sustained advances within computational capacities for document storage, data extraction, handling, and analysis have made textual analysis more feasible at larger scales for scholars. These advancements draw upon novel discoveries within computer science, which also belong to a broader family of artificial intelligence-based approaches. Numerous terminologies to describe them include text mining, computer-aided text analysis, computational content analysis, or natural language processing (NLP). At their heart lies a clear focus on automated, computerized processing and analysis of text as an expression of natural language (Chowdhury, 2003). Automated text processing allows researchers to leverage large datasets over long periods of time, discover patterns and trends in vast amounts of data, and do so faster than manual content analysis methods would permit. The abundance of textual data along with accessible computational resources present opportunities to apply emerging dedicated techniques as evidenced by their systematic inclusion within popular statistical programs such as R or Stata (Schwarz, 2018). A deeper understanding of SE-relevant phenomena and constructs based upon textual data is therefore quite timely given the increasing sophistication of automated analysis in terms of software, methodologies, and techniques.

In the remaining part of this chapter, we first outline the categories of textual data sources in SE for operationalizing key constructs and discovering new insights into conceptual interrelationships. We provide guidance concerning textual source selection criteria, as well as how to prepare textual data for quantitative analyses. Subsequently, we review several of the popular automated text analysis methods. We then move to providing an overview and assessment of the applicability of selected techniques of text analysis for SE. Finally, we showcase the overlooked utility of topic modeling with Latent Dirichlet Allocation (LDA) within SE research based upon several thousand chief executive officer (CEO) letters to the shareholders (LTS) of their publicly listed companies over time. LDA is a powerful technique, which has been widely applied across scientific domains for data mining and pattern discovery. It is a notably promising method for textual analysis that may generate deeper, bottom up-driven insights into central questions within SE research. We focus on topic modeling with LDA for two reasons in particular. First, in contrast to word count-based dictionary methods, which require substantial prior effort to develop them, topic models automatically summarize whole document collections into topics of words that occur in similar contexts. Second, as LDA helps to uncover hidden semantic structures of the textual collection at once, its output is less likely to be driven by researchers' assumptions about it and thereby reduces the risk of confirmation bias (Mahmoodi, Leckelt, van Zalk, Geukes, & Back, 2017). Additionally, we provide an illustrative example of how more advanced NLP techniques such as LDA can considerably enhance longitudinal, comparative studies within SE, and how they help compliment extant approaches.

USING TEXT AS DATA IN STRATEGIC ENTREPRENEURSHIP: APPROACHES, ACHIEVEMENTS, AND POSSIBILITIES

A central assumption of content analysis when studying the meaning and structure underpinning collections of text is that language reflects one's understanding of their surroundings, and thereby reflects their cognitive processes (Holsti, 1968). For that reason interest into using texts to study organizational phenomena, including attitudinal, behavioral, or ideological concepts, has attained considerable and growing attention within business research (Short et al., 2010). It has been recently amplified and sharpened by what Hannigan et al. (2019) describe as a linguistic "turn" within management research. That is, in recent years we have witnessed an unprecedented increase in the volumes and diversity of accessible digital textual data as well as the means available to analyze them to generate new insights.

At this point it is necessary to acknowledge an important distinction between structured data and unstructured text. Structured data are represented by numeric or categorical values that gain their meaning through a fully specified model or other representation that relates them to physical reality (Losiewicz, Oard, & Kostoff, 2000). In contrast, text is conveyed in natural language, a format that can express more than one meaning (e.g., "I made her duck"), surrounded by challenges of ambiguity, uncertainty, and incompleteness. Therefore, a critical first step for SE researchers is to carefully assess and select textual sources relevant for their investigation. The next step, once the texts have been acquired, is the transformation of sequences of characters to structured numerical data that can be processed and analyzed by machines to uncover meaning. In the following section we offer guidance on how to approach text source selection, what types of textual data sources are available for SE research, and finally, how to transform text to numerical data and prepare them for analyses.

Guidance on Source Selection

Selection of textual data requires an understanding of the goals and objectives of the study, domain knowledge, and awareness of the available sources. In navigating this process, researchers may consider a number of criteria (Losiewicz et al., 2000), including study design, coverage, availability, format, and cost of acquisition.

Study design
Generally, as a first step, scholars need to reflect a priori on their research questions and whether textual data will help them in verifying any hypotheses. This pertains to an important assessment as to whether there is an alignment among the study design, data collection, and relevance of the types of insights possible to uncover from the analysis of texts.

Coverage
For the analysis to be useful, the collection must consist of texts that provide the needed information and a high signal-to-noise ratio. In this respect, ensuring sufficient coverage also relates to establishing sampling validity (Shelley & Krippendorff, 1984). The extent of topical coverage is typically a critical criterion for source selection. Other aspects that may be important in certain research design settings are temporal coverage (i.e., for longitudinal studies) and geographic coverage (i.e., for international comparative studies).

Availability
Next, the desired collection needs to be available. The rapid proliferation of the Internet has made it possible to access collections that were previously unavailable or would have been impractical to acquire. At the same time, the intense ongoing digitization of human communication has facilitated unprecedented access to textual materials. Several public and commercial collections are available, such as those provided by the Securities and Exchange Commission (SEC) EDGAR Archives, Lexis/Nexis, or Bloomberg. Access to legacy documents that were formerly obtainable only in hard copy has also been facilitated through technological improvements in optical character recognition (OCR). The cost of retrospective conversion to an appropriate digital format has plummeted as OCR does not require manual transcribing, a task frequently cost prohibitive in many applications.

Format
The availability of full texts has become common as large numbers of documents are generated, captured, and broadly distributed in electronic form. Yet, these full texts may come in various formats, such as pdf, picture, html, and txt, which require extraction into a common unified plain text format. In addition, some full text collec-

tions may include structural markup, which can be useful in information extraction of smaller textual units of interest such as paragraphs, tables, or lists. For instance, researchers might desire to analyze only the business description section of 10-K reports, which is included under Item 1.

Cost

Although digitization has offered access to a wealth of freely available information, there are two types of cost that researchers need to consider when selecting sources for their research. First is the cost of acquisition, which requires not only technical skills to automatically assemble large collections (i.e., through web scraping), but also necessitates sufficient storage and computational capacity to process the entire collection. Second, commercial interests often own the copyright to specialized text collections already available in electronic form. Other organizations only allow for a desktop access through site licensing arrangements, a practice which is becoming increasingly common whether through term-length subscription or per access pricing models (i.e., LexisNexis or Bloomberg).

Sources of Texts for Strategic Entrepreneurship Research

Next, our goal is to raise awareness among SE scholars concerning the remarkable diversity of available text sources. Some attractive collections, such as private communications of company employees and internal documents, especially those relating to strategic aspects and trajectories, may be difficult to obtain. Yet, the proliferation of publicly accessible disclosures and filings still offers a wide variety of potential means to explore important organizational and SE-related phenomena. We present a non-exclusive list and brief descriptions of such textual data sources related to a variety of different sampling units, which have shown a potential to gauge relevant information in past SE research.

To guide the presentation, we have divided textual sources into major groups along two dimensions. Most notably, texts can originate from the primary sources of research interest themselves, i.e., CEO LTS, or can stem from secondary accounts describing the actors or phenomena of interest, i.e., news or research papers. Moreover, in terms of primary sources we distinguish natively textual data that were generated and published electronically from multimedia sources that can be transformed to text from other formats, i.e., audio or video transcripts. Table 10.1 presents this simple classification of textual sources along with representative examples exploring SE-related phenomena.

Natively textual data from primary sources

The primary sources available for SE research are diverse and numerous. Along these lines, annual disclosures known as 10-K reports contain insights and information about an organization's competitive approach and financial performance. All publicly traded firms in the United States are required to file 10-Ks with the SEC. These types of annual reports contain, in particular, management discussion and analysis

Table 10.1   *Example sources of textual data and representative studies*

Source type and format	Examples of sources and studies
Primary sources in natively textual format	• Annual 10-K reports (McKenny, Short, Ketchen, Payne, & Moss, 2018b)
	• CEO letters to shareholders (Short, Payne, Brigham, Lumpkin, & Broberg, 2009)
	• Letters to government agencies (Pandey, Pandey, & Miller, 2017)
	• Press releases (Luger, Raisch, & Schimmer, 2018)
	• IPO prospectuses (Liu, Tang, Yang, & Arthurs, 2019)
	• Patents (Kaplan & Vakili, 2015; Rhee, Ocasio, & Zajac, 2018)
	• Venture business plans (Wales, Cox, Lortie, & Sproul, 2019)
	• Company website content (Haans, 2019; Zachary, McKenny, Short, & Payne, 2011)
	• Crowdfunding campaign descriptions (Moss, Renko, Block, & Meyskens, 2018)
	• Social media and microblogs, e.g., Twitter (Obschonka, Fisch, & Boyd, 2017)
	• Open-ended survey responses (Jackson & Trochim, 2002)
Primary sources in multimedia format	• Earnings calls (Jancenelle, Storrud-Barnes, & Javagli, 2017)
	• Press conferences (Wolfe & Shepherd, 2015)
	• CEO speeches (Choudhury, Wang, Carlson, & Khanna, 2019; Heracleous & Klaering, 2017)
	• Interviews (Ljungkvist, Boers, & Samuelsson, 2019)
Secondary accounts in natively textual format	• News articles (Basque & Langley, 2018; Belderbos, Grabowska, Kelhctermans, & Ugur, 2017)
	• Narrative content on third-party websites (Corritore, Goldberg, & Srivastava, 2020)
	• Third-party social media and microblogs (Ma, Sun, & Kekre, 2015)
	• Research papers (Persaud & Chandra Bayon, 2019)

sections valuable for gleaning information regarding firm traits, as expressed by management (Boling, Pieper, & Covin, 2016; McKenny, Short, Ketchen, Payne, & Moss, 2018b). Other required sections include business description, risk factors, selected financial data, financial statements, and supplementary data. Notably, 10-K reports are public information and can be retrieved through a number of sources, including the SEC's EDGAR database.

CEO LTS belong to a larger genre of corporate reporting. LTS, which usually accompany annual reports, are introductory narrative sections informing investors and other stakeholders about the long-term viability of companies (Engelen, Neumann, & Schmidt, 2016; Grühn, Strese, Flatten, Jaeger, & Brettel, 2017; Gupta, Mortal, & Yang, 2016). In contrast to fairly long and complicated 10-Ks, LTS are short, typically two to three pages long, and not audited. These corporate disclosures are considered to convey key information about the company's past, present, and future competitive approach. LTS are not mandatory disclosures, hence not all listed companies release them. These data usually need to be hand collected from annual company reports, company websites, SEC filings, or other archival sources.

Initial public offering (IPO) prospectuses provide a business summary and firm's strategic overview at a company's IPO. These documents are required by law to be as accurate, forthcoming, and diligently prepared as possible in the United States (Marino, Castaldi, & Dollinger, 1989). Thereby, similar to other formal organizational communications such as 10-Ks or LTS, prospectuses can be indicative of the firm's SE posture (Mousa, Wales, & Harper, 2015). IPO prospectuses can be downloaded from the SEC's EDGAR Archives.

Business plans are documents intended to convince investors about the fundability of their venture and offer signals pertaining to a firm's SE competitive approach. Business plans provide a common means available to investors to assess the strategic orientation of very young, often nascent ventures, which are seeking funding in the pursuit of growth (Wales, Cox, Lortie, & Sproul, 2019). Plans are typically proprietary documents. Yet, submissions can often be obtained from business plan competitions.

Company websites contain information directed to stakeholders, i.e., mission statements, which encompass and communicate a firm's identity and help delineate an organization's overall purpose (Palmer & Short, 2008). These narratives can be used in guiding resource allocation decisions (Ireland & Hitt, 1992). Therefore, they can be indicative of firms' SE postures (Moss, Short, Payne, & Lumpkin, 2011).

Moreover, SE-focused textual narratives can be found on crowdfunding campaign websites, i.e., Kickstarter or Indiegogo, presenting project descriptions of entrepreneurs seeking microloans (Allison, McKenny, & Short, 2013; Josefy, Dean, Albert, & Fitza, 2017).

Social media also presents a rich disclosure channel. There is a growing interest in the analysis of corporate communications occurring on microblog platforms such as Twitter or Facebook (Teoh, 2018). Previous research has indicated that digital footprints may, for instance, reliably reflect individuals' personalities (e.g., Kosinski, Stillwell, & Graepel, 2013). Intriguingly, the personality features of individuals derived through their language on Twitter may be indicative of entrepreneurial traits (Obschonka, Fisch, & Boyd, 2017).

Multimedia sources transformed to text
Other media such as audio and visual present another source of information useful for SE research. Audio data can be distilled down to textual data using speech-to-text technology, potentially complemented with specific audio features (Kaminski & Hopp, 2019).

Earnings conference calls and press conferences are mediums to communicate with stakeholders about future and/or current earnings. During these calls firms present their current and future strategy (Kimbrough, 2005), as well as other information upon which stockholders are expected to make investment decisions (Larcker & Zakolyukina, 2012). SE-focused dialogue may trigger stock price movements (Jancenelle, Storrud-Barnes, & Javalgi, 2017).

Transcripts of press conferences by key informants, which stakeholders may view and react to, are another useful source of textual data and strategic information.

For instance, Wolfe and Shepherd (2015) analyze the transcripts of postgame press conferences with football coaches following their team's first loss of the season to examine its effect on subsequent performance.

Natively textual data from secondary accounts

Secondary accounts are also useful areas for SE researchers to explore. In this vein, third-party websites may provide textual information of interest. For instance, reviews by company employees on jobsite portals such as Glassdoor.com are a rich resource for obtaining private or qualitative information pertaining to working conditions, available incentives, relationships with management, degree of autonomy, etc. Glassdoor's online portal can also serve as a means of analyzing employees' perceptions of the business outlook of their firm (Hales, Moon, & Swenson, 2018). Similarly, recruitment websites of franchising firms (Zachary, McKenny, Short, & Payne, 2011) or promotional entries in online directories (Watson, Dada, Wright, & Perrigot, 2019) can provide additional useful resources for textual analyses of firms' corporate culture, innovation, and SE.

News articles offer another comprehensive source of public information about firms' business activities, such as mergers and acquisitions, international activity, or strategic change (Bednar, Boivie, & Prince, 2013). Firm news, however, is heterogeneous in form and subject, and therefore it is important to ensure that the texts selected for analysis are informative on the study purpose (Belderbos, Grabowska, Kelchtermans, & Ugur, 2017).

Scholarly publications also present an opportunity for the discovery of patterns and trends within research fields such as SE. In particular, textual analyses can reveal how scholarly domains and topical areas of research have developed over time, what themes and concepts have been emerging and declining, and how conceptual discussions have evolved over a period of time. Such information can subsequently shed light, for instance, on the nomological network of emerging phenomena (Li & Larsen, 2011) or intertheory relationships.

In sum, whether primary or secondary in origin, once a source of potential textual data has been identified it must be collected before being prepared for analysis. Depending on its type and specificity, this process might be performed manually by domain experts or it may be fully automated. Researchers often employ an archival approach by collecting existing textual data when automation is not possible, such as in the case of CEO LTS. Otherwise, techniques like web scraping serve to automatically gather Internet-based texts, such as social media data (e.g., Twitter, Facebook). Each document in an assembled text collection then represents a single observation. Collectively, the documents are often referred to as a "corpus" within textual processing communities. The next step, once documents are acquired, is to transform them into useful structured data that can be analyzed. We describe the elements of this process in more detail in the next section.

Data Preparation for Analysis

The creation of an analyzable dataset from a collection of unstructured textual data requires researchers to initially take a sequence of preparatory steps, commonly referred to as preprocessing. These operations include a series of important decisions about how to clean and normalize the raw text data within an exploratory, iterative process. The goal of these procedures is to remove as much potential noise as possible and maximize the underlying signals of desired attributes when transforming the textual data into a structured format. We recommend that researchers describe their preprocessing steps and text-cleaning decisions within their research methods discussion, in particular, whether any of these decisions or steps could impact conclusions drawn based on the subsequent extracted textual information.

First, *tokenization* in its simplest form involves splitting strings of characters to individual words, otherwise called tokens. White spaces, numbers, or punctuation are removed. Raw documents in other formats, such as HTML, or the ones covering more informal communication, such as Twitter microblogs, may require application of further, more advanced character removal steps since they typically contain non-standard elements such as HTML tags or emoticons. *Lowercasing*, in turn, prevents words like "New" and "new" being considered as distinct by the chosen algorithm in the analysis. These two steps are typically sufficient to apply dictionary and word count methods.

More advanced techniques may benefit from further data cleaning. In this vein, researchers can consider an evaluation and removal of *stop words* such as "and," "the," and "then." These are words which occur very frequently in documents but are considered not to carry any meaning, and therefore are of little value in, for instance, topic modeling. Removing these tokens additionally has the benefit of faster processing by text algorithms in the subsequent analysis. A further option to consider is *stemming* the words, reducing them to their roots by cutting off the end of words. For instance, "organize," "organization," and "organizing" would be changed to "organ." However, researchers should be mindful that such an operation can change the meaning of the original word. Therefore, it is usually recommended to apply this step with care. Another approach to reduce word variability is *lemmatization*, which aims to remove inflectional endings and replaces the word with its dictionary form (the lemma). For instance, "am," "are," and "is" would be replaced with "be."

Further preprocessing can include *word filtering* based on term frequency, such as minimum frequency filtering for words appearing in very few documents, as well as a maximum frequency filtering for words appearing in many to most documents. Excluding sparse and very frequent terms aims to reduce noise and helps to speed up computations.

The steps so far consider a *unigram* approach, where a term or token corresponds to a single word. Researchers can also consider implementing *bigrams*, *tri-grams*, or higher-order *n-grams* to further enhance how subtleties of communication are captured within the data. Many terms within textual collections are indeed natural bigrams, for example: "income statement." Including multiword terms can improve upon unigram-based models.

Other preprocessing operations may include extraction of information in a form of tags to words or phrases. These features might be useful to annotate certain text elements or to structure texts in the collection. For example, named entity recognition allows researchers to distinguish documents containing names of certain persons (i.e., entrepreneurs or CEOs), organizations, or locations. Part-of-speech tagging aids scholars interested in linguistic expressions with tagging words or phrase classes based upon their grammatical function (e.g., nouns, verbs, adjectives, or adverbs).

The treated documents can be subsequently used to create a document-term matrix (DTM). This tabular form associates each row with a document and each column with a word in the corpus. Its entries reflect word counts in documents. It should be noted that a typical DTM is sparse, that is, most of its values are zero. This is because not all of the unique words in the collection vocabulary occur in every document. Further extension might include application of weighting schemas (Salton & Buckley, 1988). One such popular method is termed frequency-inverse document frequency, which aims to reflect word importance within documents while accounting for word frequency across the whole collection. Finally, this numeric representation of collected documents, either weighted or unweighted, can be used to build text analytic models based upon it.

UNCOVERING MEANING FROM TEXT DATA: TOOLS AND METHODS

A growing array of approaches to text analysis offer a set of novel tools to SE researchers interested in measuring contextual, linguistic, psychological, or semantic concepts and constructs for theory building and testing. In this vein, SE-related phenomena have already been investigated using one or more of these techniques, most often with the goal of predicting firm outcomes. Among them, scholars approached the identification of specific characteristics, such as of individuals or organizations (Obschonka et al., 2017), the sense-making role of figurative language in entrepreneurship (Nicholson & Anderson, 2005), network associations with venture capitalists (Ahlstrom & Bruton, 2006), discourse on women's entrepreneurship (Ahl, 2006), content of organizational strategies (Menon, Choi, & Tabakovic, 2018), and an operationalization of the entrepreneurial orientation (EO) construct (McKenny, Aguinis, Short, & Anglin, 2018a; Short et al., 2010).

Automated content analysis in general can be categorized into two main approaches: (1) simpler count-based, dictionary methods, and (2) more advanced algorithmic vector space representations such as topic models or word embeddings. These techniques can be combined, depending on a given research question and goal. Each of these approaches has its own assumptions, advantages, as well as limitations, which we aim to discuss within the following subsections. Table 10.2 offers an illustrative selection of studies tackling SE phenomena based on different forms of

Table 10.2   *Exemplar strategic entrepreneurship studies utilizing textual analysis*

Textual analysis technique	Source of data	Exemplar studies	Textual insight
Dictionaries and word counts			
Dictionary	10-K annual reports	Boling et al. (2016); McKenny et al. (2018a); Short et al. (2010)	Operationalization of entrepreneurial orientation multidimensional construct
Dictionary	Letters to shareholders of S&P 500 companies	Zachary et al. (2011)	Operationalization of market orientation, competitor orientation, customer orientation, interfunctional coordination, long-term focus, profitability
Dictionary	LexisNexis newswire archive	Belderbos et al. (2017)	Operationalization of global mindset construct
N-gram frequency analysis	Transcripts of videos (video-to-speech-to-text content) of Kickstarter crowdfunding campaigns	Kaminski et al. (2017)	Linguistic particularities of "lead user" entrepreneurs
Dictionary	Press releases on firms' websites	Luger et al. (2018)	Operationalization of ambidexterity
Phrase-level dictionary	Letters to the board of education from New Jersey school districts	Pandey et al. (2017)	Measure of innovativeness
Topic models			
LDA	Patents granted by the United States Patent and Trademark Office	Kaplan & Vakili (2015)	Measure of novel ideas in patents
LDA	Websites of Google Play app store, Google Plus, and Factiva	Guo et al. (2017)	Competitor analysis
LDA	United States Patent and Trademark Office patent abstracts of Motorola	Rhee et al. (2018)	Measure of attentional specialization and coupling
LDA	Websites of firms in the Dutch creative industries	Haans (2019)	Firms' positioning, their similarity, and distinctiveness
Distributed representations			
Word2vec	Annual reports	Bhattacharya et al. (2019)	Measures of entrepreneurial orientation and market orientation
Doc2vec	Textual descriptions, speech and video transcripts of Kickstarter crowdfunding campaigns	Kaminski & Hopp (2019)	Features of successful crowdfunding projects

Textual analysis technique	Source of data	Exemplar studies	Textual insight
Doc2vec	Startup profile texts provided by Crunchbase database and patent abstracts of acquiring companies	Kim et al. (2020)	Technical position characteristics to estimate technological similarity between startups and companies
BERT	Quarterly earnings calls of publicly traded firms	Vicinanza et al. (2020)	Measures of contextual novelty and prescience

textual analysis. These studies apply the various techniques with differing degrees of automation and methodical sophistication across a diversity of data sources we reviewed previously.

Dictionary-Based Methods

Within the study of SE-related phenomena, the most common approach applied within textual analyses has been dictionary based (Short et al., 2010). In this methodology, buckets of terms are designed to represent concepts. More specifically, text is processed into quantitative data based on the frequency of predefined terms, which intend to reflect identified constructs (McKenny et al., 2018a). The goal of this approach is to infer latent random variables in a more objective and scalable way as compared to popular alternative approaches, such as survey-based research designs. Most notably, since computers do not suffer from fatigue, this approach can offer highly accurate word counts across large collections of text. It is the most straightforward and efficient technique provided that a valid and reliable dictionary has been developed. Along these lines, Short et al. (2010) outline recommended procedures for building textual dictionaries and illustrate an example of this process for the EO construct. Therefore, this approach known also as "term counting" assumes that the presence of keywords matters greatly to the overall "tone" of a document and its message, irrespective of the words' ordering in it. In such an analysis, words are in fact considered independent of their context within a given text. Rather, the occurrence of specific predefined dictionary keywords indicates the salience of a construct and all the keywords are considered to equally contribute to its measurement. Term frequencies are usually normalized to account for typical differences in document length.

As a complimentary approach, *phrase-level dictionaries* can offer a more precise extension of word-level dictionaries in certain contexts (Pandey et al., 2017). Identification and analysis of multiword noun or verb phrases serves to augment context sensitivity (Pandey & Pandey, 2019). Such fundamental linguistic components arguably more clearly signify linguistic meaning (Crystal, 2011). While decomposing texts into individual words results in substantial decontextualization, phrase-level decomposition retains more of the intended linguistic connotation.

When considered separately, words like "new," "existing," and "technology" fail to convey distinct meaning as in the multiword expressions "new technology" or "existing technology." Moreover, decontextualization of words such as "risk" is especially problematic given that it is not clear if the word "risk" is being employed to discuss "risk taking" or "risk avoidance." This observation has led to the revision of popular SE-related construct dictionaries (McKenny et al., 2018a).

As such, the dictionary-based methods also present several shortcomings. One stems from the subjectivity of the researcher who is tasked with the selection of dictionary words. It is challenging to provide a comprehensive list of words related to a given concept. Moreover, dictionary methods assume every word is of equal importance and carries the same weight, which raises concerns about whether the construct of interest is being adequately captured. To that end, recent studies have demonstrated that revising unsatisfactory dictionaries and adding more related words can increase the precision with which these concepts are captured (McKenny et al., 2018a). Nonetheless, such revised dictionaries may still experience difficulties with capturing key concepts within certain contexts. At times they may incorrectly indicate the lack of presence of a particular construct of interest, such as within shorter texts which employ no language from the dictionary. In reality, complete absence is unlikely to be the case as latent traits usually exist to *some* degree. Moreover, it is possible that even *minor* dictionary revisions may lead to different conclusions when researching outcome relationships. Overall, when the objective is to extract latent constructs with minimum researcher input, dictionary methods might provide less than satisfactory conclusions (Hansen, Mcmahon, & Prat, 2017).

Advanced Algorithmic Text Analysis

In contrast to count-based dictionaries, vector space models (VSM) offer a more advanced methodological approach for automated textual analysis within future SE research. VSM are based upon vector representations of words in documents which, simply put, correspond to lists of numbers. More precisely, all N distinct words in a given collection form an N-dimensional space and may describe documents through their presence and absence (represented by ones and zeros) or frequencies (count vectorizing), which can be further weighted, e.g., using term frequency-inverse document frequency algorithms, or other properties. VSM are particularly useful for learning the underlying latent features of a document collection without the need for imposing specific categories of interest a priori. Notably, sometimes categories cannot be easily conceptualized upfront and their application might also limit discoveries.

The two main families for learning word vectors are matrix factorization methods (co-occurrence based) and local context window methods (prediction based). Matrix factorization methods aim to decompose the N-dimensional matrix describing the whole text collection into a product of several matrices. Subsequently, these can be used to explore the data through topic modeling or other forms of clustering such as, for instance, principal component analysis. Local context window methods (Mikolov,

Le, & Sutskever, 2013b), called also distributed representations, conversely, instead of learning merely the co-occurrence probabilities, learn their ratios, which helps to capture semantic- or meaning-related word relationships. This word-embedding encoding property of VSM makes it possible to compute word similarities and perform mathematical operations on them. Next, we describe in more detail prominent representative methods for each of these two approaches, namely topic modeling with LDA to demonstrate matrix factorization methods (co-occurrence based) and word embeddings including word2vec to clarify local context window methods (prediction based).

Topic Models (Co-occurrence-Based Vector Space Models)

Topic modeling, which is a co-occurrence count-based method, is becoming increasingly popular to gauge different aspects of texts in an automatic way (Hannigan et al., 2019). The distributional hypothesis of linguistics underlies the main logic behind these algorithms, which stands that words found in similar contexts tend to have similar meanings (Harris, 1954). Topic modeling in its standard form relies on unsupervised machine learning methods, comparable to exploratory, inductive approaches. Topics are lists of words that co-occur in a statistically meaningful way in the textual collection. A document is modeled as a list of topics with weights for each of them. In such setups, instead of using a predefined coding schema by researchers, codes or topics are automatically extracted from the statistical patterns of words in the text (Quinn, Monroe, Colaresi, Crespin, & Radev, 2010; Urquhart, 2012). Based on the words contained in a document, topic models learn latent relations by assuming that each document covers multiple topics. This can help in extracting high-level semantic information. In particular, topic models allow for the exploration and summarization of document collections without specifying any particular information need. They can also be useful when the information needed is known but difficult to search for. This property makes them especially valuable, because potentially hard-to-define and hard-to-codify concepts or dimensions can be inferred based on the model output, e.g., entrepreneurial strategy discussion in CEO letters.

The principal units of data in topic models are words or terms as represented in the DTM. Rows correspond to individual documents in the analyzed collection and columns correspond to terms, such that each entry in a DTM is a count of term occurrence in the document. These unique terms form a vocabulary, indexed by a set of numbers. Typically, these terms are unigram words, however, they can also be N-grams composed of multiple terms. A document is then considered to be composed of a bag of N terms. A collection of M documents forms a corpus. Each document within a corpus is considered as a mixture of K latent topics. The user needs to specify the number of topics a priori. Topics are then represented by distributions over words. For such a collection of documents $D = d_1, ..., d_n$, a collection of K topics $Z = z_1, ..., z_k$ and the number of words $W = w_1, ...,w_m$, probabilistic topic models estimate the probabilities $P(z_k|d_j)$ and $P(w_i|z_k)$. These probabilities denote the distribution of topics in a document and distribution of words per topic, respectively. To illustrate this approach visually, Figure 10.1 presents a basic matrix factorization intuition behind a probabilistic topic modeling process.

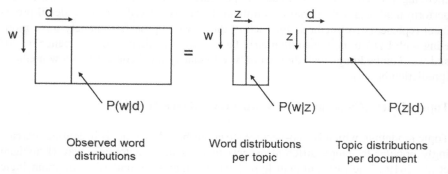

Source: Hofmann (1999).

Figure 10.1   *Topic (z) modelling process intuition as factorization of the observed words (w) in documents (d) into word-per-topic (P(w|z)) and topic-per-document (P(z|d)) distributions*

Most notably, LDA has offered a flexible topic modeling approach, which explains its wide popularity (Blei & Lafferty, 2009; Blei, Ng, & Jordan, 2003). The reasoning behind this hierarchical Bayesian statistical technique is to model documents as mixtures of multiple topics, which are contained in each document with different proportions. LDA is thereby a mixed-membership model with words having the possibility to belong to multiple topics. This assumption of LDA allows for combining a portion of main topical themes that pervade the whole collection of heterogenous documents with those topics more specific to subthemes. The remaining challenge is that the topics are typically not known to the user in advance and therefore the main objective is to learn and interpret them from the data.

Topic models can therefore present a useful alternative or a supporting tool for SE researchers interested in extracting latent constructs from textual data. The top words listed in each topic returned by a topic model form a basis for their interpretation, as opposed to inductive dictionary building. For instance, a topic with the most prominent words such as compensation, salary, pay, and bonus might be labeled "remuneration systems" (Kobayashi, Mol, Berkers, Kismihók, & Den Hartog, 2018). Topic models may not only help in extracting concepts of interest, but also serve as a triangulation method for other content analysis approaches, such as dictionaries (Anderson et al., 2019). Moreover, they might be particularly useful when the language employed by sample participants is not customary to typical dictionaries commonly employed to capture a construct of interest. To illustrate the benefits of an LDA-based approach, in the latter part of this chapter we showcase a step-by-step LDA analysis for an organizational entrepreneurial strategic orientation.

Despite its strengths, there are notable shortcomings of this method that researchers need to be mindful of. In the classic implementation of LDA, the word clusters forming topics are unlabeled and require the user to manually annotate them. This can posit a challenge since it puts a significant cognitive burden on interpretation and this process is rather subjective (Lau, Grieser, Newman, & Baldwin, 2011; Lau, Newman, & Baldwin, 2014). Furthermore, purely unsupervised topic models may return at least some topics which exemplify strong statistical word patterns, e.g., grammatical artifacts, but do not match researcher expectations of what is semantically meaningful.

Distributed Neural Network-Based Representations (Prediction-Based Vector Space Models)

In the prediction-based category, word-embedding approaches, e.g., word2vec (Mikolov, Chen, Corrado, & Dean, 2013a) or GloVe (Pennington, Socher, & Manning, 2014), have become the most well-known neural network representations. Full document text or paragraph vector models known as doc2vec are an extension to a word2vec, where a neural network transforms a list of words into a set of vectors representing them (Le & Mikolov, 2014). These techniques are based on distributed vector representations of words, which are meant to capture syntactic and semantic word relationships more precisely. Words closer to each other in a specific linguistic context manifest a more similar quantitative representation since they are assumed to reflect similar meaning. These approaches are considered to be very efficient and powerful methods. In contrast to a DTM, which is based on a local representation and considers the whole vocabulary, word embeddings are limited to a fixed-size vector with each of its dimensions exhibiting some distinct properties (Mitra & Craswell, 2018). See Figure 10.2 for a visual depiction of these two approaches based on simple examples.

Local representation in Figure 10.2a considers the terms "banana," "mango," and "dog" as strictly distinct items. Distributed vector representation in panel b, however, may indicate that "banana" and "mango" have common features (both are fruits), while "dog" is substantially different (Mitra & Craswell, 2018). Words therefore can

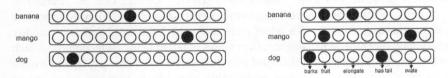

Source: Mitra and Craswell (2018).

Figure 10.2   *Local (a) and distributed (b) vector representations of words in a collection of documents*

be close along one dimension (i.e., tea and coffee are both beverages) but separate along another. Thus, word embedding-based models learn word meanings from the context window that surrounds them, rather than merely based on their co-occurrence within a document. Such models trained on large datasets make it possible to account for syntax, as well as the higher-level meaning structures of words. These attributes allow for defining some type of similarity, e.g., cosine similarity, among the different terms or documents based on their desired properties. Basic mathematical operations on these word vectors are then possible, such as summing or averaging, and have been shown to generate very useful document representations. For instance, "Madrid" − "Spain" + "France" ≈ "Paris" (Mikolov et al., 2013a).

Scholars of SE can productively use these methods, for instance, to support dictionary building by expansion of dictionary keywords with semantically similar words, which are difficult to identify otherwise (Tsai & Wang, 2015). For instance, relevant indicators of SE behavior could be captured, which might be industry specific. Other applications can include constructing new measures based on strategic disclosures and comparing those among firms in the collection, e.g., firms' competitive strategy types (Hu, Qiu, & Liang, 2018). It is worth noting that next to training these models directly on their own text data, researchers can also use generic embeddings pretrained on very big datasets in other domains of application, e.g., news articles or Wikipedia. These word vectors can be subsequently considered for examining documents in different contexts, for example, contents of annual reports. This property has made a case for transfer learning in NLP where pretrained word-embedding models are reused in a host of different domains. This is a beneficial feature because it enables researchers to employ them as a readily available tool, thereby saving the time and other resources that would be required for training such language models from scratch.

Nonetheless, an embedding approach also has notable limitations. Simple distributed vector representations do not fully reflect the context, and therefore may not account for linguistic phenomena such as polysemy (DiMaggio, Nag, & Blei, 2013) – or put more simply, the same words may have different meanings in different contexts in which they appear. For instance, different meanings of a word cloud would be all associated with one vector. A recent objective of NLP developments has been the attempt to overcome this problem through introducing dynamic word embeddings, e.g., Embeddings from Language Models (Peters et al., 2018), Bidirectional Encoder Representations from Transformers (Devlin, Chang, Lee, & Toutanova, 2019), or Generative Pre-trained Transformer 3 (Brown et al., 2020), which consider the semantic representation in a wider context in which the word appears. Another limitation is that embeddings might reflect biases inherent in the collections on which they are trained. For instance, the word *entrepreneur* could be biased toward a male versus female pronoun. Therefore, undesirable associations between words might persist in any system that uses them.

VALIDITY AND RELIABILITY CONSIDERATIONS

An important aspect of every robust research design is to alleviate validity and reliability concerns. Validity relates to the extent to which an indicator of interest accurately represents a focal concept (Cronbach, 1971). Reliability, in turn, particularly in a longitudinal context, requires the text collection to cover the indicator of interest over regular intervals to accurately identify changes. Content analysis scholars, especially those using automatized techniques, have been concerned with the validity and reliability of their various methods. While manual techniques could rely on the use of protocols and multiple human coders for text selection and analysis (Weber, 1990), the scale of the contemporary collections is virtually prohibitive to apply the same approach outside of small "test" samples from the typically immense datasets. In recent years, content analysis has chiefly relied on computer-aided text analysis using software and predefined dictionaries, such as those included in Linguistic Inquiry and Word Count (Tausczik & Pennebaker, 2010) or CAT Scanner (Short, McKenny, & Reid, 2018), primarily to improve scalability and the systematic nature of SE research. Yet, a notable caveat of dictionaries in general is that they preclude polysemy or do not properly handle negations. A wider critique of dictionary-based content analysis is that it provides decontextualized results and reduces complex constructs to overly simplistic indices (Dey, 1995).

Yet, related problems may also occur with respect to more advanced computerized analysis methods. For instance, it is still critically important to assess validity and reliability when interpreting topics that emerge from the automatically processed data. Specifically, with respect to construct validity, it is essential to ensure that the identified topics indeed capture the meaning they appear to represent. Several statistical metrics have been developed for topic models to help in this assessment. The most popular quantitative measure is based on perplexity. It is the inverse of the geometric mean per word likelihood. Smaller perplexity indicates a better model. Other metrics relate more to the quality criteria of convergent and discriminant validity, namely coherence and exclusivity. Semantic coherence assesses the internal coherence of topics and can serve as a validity indicator for the identified topics. It has been found to better align with human judgments of topic quality as compared to the more widely adopted use of perplexity (Mimno, Wallach, Talley, Leenders, & McCallum, 2011). Technically, semantic coherence evaluates the extent of co-occurrence of the most probable words in a given topic across the whole collection of documents. It focuses therefore on the internal qualities of individual topics. Exclusivity, on the other hand, measures how distinctive topics are by comparing the similarity of their word distributions. A topic is considered exclusive if its top words are less likely to be in the top words of other topics. Since both coherence and exclusivity as metrics are functions of the number of topics in a topic model, they can also serve to guide the choice of an "optimal" number of K topics. Furthermore, careful qualitative expert examination needs to be performed with respect to the phenomenon of interest. When inspecting the topic model output, researchers might conclude that some of the extracted topics are essentially outside of the interest of the study (e.g., topics related to the document structure) (Schmiedel, Müller, & vom Brocke, 2018), which may then be excluded from further analyses. This verification of external validity comes at the expense of greater uncertainty about the nature of expert judgment with respect to the model output.

Evaluation of word embeddings also posits notable problems as it lacks standardized extrinsic evaluation methods (Faruqui, Tsvetkov, Rastogi, & Dyer, 2016). The notion of word similarity, which has served as a proxy for intrinsic evaluation, that is, related to a specific goal for which the technique has been applied, primarily because of its ease of use, might have considerable limitations. First, it is rather subjective and is often confused with the notion of relatedness. For example, *cup* and *tea* are related to each other, but they are not similar. Even though separation of similarity and relatedness might be useful, extant research is not clear as to which one word vector models should be capturing. Next, word vectors trained as part of a neural network tasked to solve a particular problem are thereby precisely task specific in nature. In essence, these embeddings capture task-specific and collection-specific word similarity. This raises the question: what kind of word similarity should be captured by the model? These aspects call for further research on embedding-based evaluation methods. In light of these shortcomings, we thus suggest SE researchers to demonstrate the robustness of their word vector models in downstream tasks and present task-specific evaluation. These can include, for instance, demonstrating the relationship with commonly used firm performance metrics, or other known predictors of interest in regression models.

Nevertheless, despite the shortcomings inherent in each of these methods, dictionaries, topic models, and word embeddings can all be potentially useful for uncovering theoretical artifacts, especially in large textual collections, which are impractical to process manually (Hannigan et al., 2019). In Table 10.3, we provide a succinct overview of key advantages and shortcomings for each of these computerized textual analysis methods.

What Types of Insights Can We Uncover Utilizing Automated Text Analyses?

Finally, we wish to point out that SE scholars can integrate textual analysis findings into their research design in several ways. First, it can constitute a stand-alone analysis, i.e., showcasing text mining or a particular algorithm as the primary research approach. Given the comparative novelty of advanced methods there is a vast scope for potential novel applications within SE research. Second, it can be a means to an end through the operationalization of key variable(s) and integration within econometric models. For instance, by combining text mining with complementary qualitative or quantitative statistical analysis researchers can dig deeper into case studies or build panel data models. Third, scholars can use automated text analysis techniques for reviewing academic literatures on SE-related phenomena or review the conceptual progress of SE's subfields over the years.

In the next section, we turn our attention to one such example of demonstrating how topic modeling based upon LDA can be applied within SE research and what

Table 10.3   *Key advantages and shortcomings of prominent textual analysis techniques*

Textual analysis technique	Key advantages	Key limitations
Dictionaries	Faster and more reliable compared to expert coding. A variety of validated dictionaries for SE-related phenomena are available free of charge. Phrase-level dictionaries can account for the linguistic structure of compound words that jointly have a specific meaning.	Rather difficult and time consuming to develop and validate. Neglects the linguistic structure within a document treating it as a "bag of words." May not capture latent traits if keywords are not present in a document.
Topic models (LDA as a prominent representative)	N-gram analysis of word frequencies is unsupervised and does not require prior knowledge about the collection. Useful for inductive, bottom-up, exploratory studies. LDA can be easily extended to accommodate various modeling needs, e.g., topics over time, structural topic models.	Prone to shortcomings of a "bag-of-words" approach and large dimensionality. Difficult to set and tune multiple hyperparameters, including the choice of a number of topics. Unsupervised nature of LDA makes evaluation challenging in terms of topic quality, coherence, and stability. May generate low-quality topics that are difficult to interpret.
Word embeddings (distributed vector representations)	Pretrained models are relatively easy to use for word or document similarity evaluation tasks. Overcomes the problem of dimensionality because words are represented by fixed-length vectors. Context-aware embeddings are able to capture distinct context-dependent word meanings.	Simpler context-independent models such as word2vec do not account for polysemy or homonymy. Training requires a large number of documents for quality word vectors. Pretrained embeddings are corpus dependent. May not handle unknown and rare words too well.

new insights might be generated. We showcase the utility of topic models with LDA based upon CEO LTS from a large sample of public companies. We focus on topic modeling using LDA, a co-occurrence-based VSM approach due to its growing popularity within the literature. Its utility has been demonstrated across scientific disciplines, which could further inspire SE researchers toward innovating in terms of methods and theorizing. An LDA model can readily identify a variety of topics, which in our example aim to statistically capture the themes which CEOs discuss in their LTS, and to allow for the identification of key SE characteristics. In the following section, we also focus on illustrating how topic models can be used to help explain changes in the strategic communication of entrepreneurial companies over time, predict major performance outcomes, and serve as a critical triangulation method for other content analysis approaches.

EXAMPLE USE CASE: LATENT DIRICHLET ALLOCATION TOPIC MODELING OF ORGANIZATIONAL STRATEGIC ORIENTATIONS IN CHIEF EXECUTIVE OFFICERS' LETTERS

LDA can serve as an important tool for inductive discovery and grounded inquiry within SE research. In this vein, Baumer, Mimno, Guha, Quan, and Gay (2017) indicate that there is a close link between the aspects which researchers discover manually by applying grounded theory procedures (Alammar, Intezari, Cardow, & Pauleen, 2018) and the topics discovered by an LDA model. Past grounded theory research employing LTS has identified several common themes within CEO letters. Kohut and Segars (1992) analyzed Fortune 500 LTS and found six recurring themes: environmental factors, growth, operating philosophy, product/market mix, unfavorable financial reference, and favorable financial reference. Conaway and Wardrope (2010) differentiated eight themes: corporate governance, customer relations, environmental (external economic, political, natural forces), financial reporting, infrastructure and expansion, leadership, social responsibility, and vision, mission, and outlook. More recently, Rhee, Ocasio, and Zajac (2018) analyzed LTS of software companies and indicate that industry experts and interviewees at five software firms in the Bay Area agreed that the CEOs covered five different managerial topic areas within their LTS. These topics relate to financial performance, growth and market prospects, research and development, customer service, and relationship with stakeholders other than customers, acquired firms, and collaborators with other firms.

As a reminder, by fitting the LDA model to the LTS text data, we can estimate the topic coverage in each document across desired latent features. The goal is to learn topic proportions for each document and firm-year observation, and then assign it a quantitative score. In our case, we are interested in identifying topics that relate to discussions of strategic aspects of S&P 500 firms. These concepts should reflect, for instance, the pursuit of competitive advantages and growth opportunities through product, market, or process innovations (Kuratko & Audretsch, 2009). Therefore, topics of primary interest should contain words strongly related to these aspects.

It is necessary to emphasize that restricting the analysis to a particular domain-specific textual data source guides the topic models towards a particular structure. For instance, in a multi-industry corpus, each industry exhibits its own characteristic words, jargon, and definitions, which carry meaning specific to them. For instance, the word "operation" means something different in the context of healthcare than it does in software engineering (Schuelke-Leech & Barry, 2016). As such, it is important to note that many artifacts of industry are contextual, and language based. Along these lines, unlike LDA, established dictionaries may often fall short of capturing this nuanced communication characteristic within a particular industry setting.

Data and Preprocessing

The document collection used for our topic modeling analysis is a proprietary dataset of 3455 CEO LTS of companies included in the S&P 500 index in 2004 and followed until 2015. The letters were hand collected from annual company reports, company websites, SEC filings, or other archival sources, and in various formats: pdf, picture, html, and txt. Next, they were extracted into a common unified plain text format and saved separately into txt files with distinct identifiers. Beyond textual data, additional information about the firms was available from external sources, primarily from COMPUSTAT and Datastream financial databases.

We tokenized the text using the Natural Language Toolkit (NLTK) Python library (Loper & Bird, 2002), removing all tokens that were not alphabetic, including punctuation and any digits from them. We then converted all terms to lower case. Next we removed the common English stop words included within the predefined dictionaries of two popular language-processing packages: spaCy (305 words) and NLTK (179 words). Combining both stop word lists offered a stronger foundation for subsequent modeling. We lemmatized nouns to have only singular forms, such that for example, the word "businesses" becomes "business." We excluded the two most common words based on frequency distribution: "year" and "business," which appeared in virtually all documents and could be considered as generic for the CEO letters corpus. We also removed words that occur only once across the collection. Finally, we set the minimum term length to be three letters and exclude all tokens shorter than that. Following this stage, LDA models can be applied to the prepared DTM to reveal latent topics.

LDA Training and Hyperparameter Tuning

Depending on the software used for the analysis, researchers have control over a set of LDA model parameters. Adjusting them based on the quantitative metrics and through close qualitative inspection in an iterative process helps to refine the extracted topics. For instance, in the dedicated Gensim module for LDA modeling in Python (Rehurek & Sojka, 2010), more than ten different parameters can be set by the user depending on the modeling goal.

We tuned a list of key LDA parameters and evaluated their performance in terms of convergence and coherence before making qualitative interpretability inspection. Table 10.4 includes an overview of the parameters of interest and their tuning ranges assessed in the experiments.

First, we inspect the impact of α and β Dirichlet priors, which are related to prior beliefs about topic sparsity/uniformity in the documents and words in topics, respectively. In simple terms, priors denote the probability of an event before the data are provided. The magnitudes of α and β control the variances of the priors. Larger α and

Table 10.4   *Hyperparameters and tuning ranges*

Parameters	Tuning range	Description
α	[0, 1]	Prior of document topic distribution
β	[0, 1]	Prior of topic word distribution
Number of iterations	[1, 1000]	Number of times the model iterates over the entire training data (epoch)
K	[5, 400]	Number of topics

β mean stronger priors. Practically, for a higher α, documents are more likely to be mixtures of most of the topics. A very small α emphasizes a single topic. Similarly, higher values of the β parameter indicate that topics are likely mixtures of most of the words rather than any word specifically. We set both parameters to "auto" for automatically learning their values from the data directly instead of specifying them explicitly, with the goal of ensuring that our analysis provided the most meaningful topics which were sufficiently varied.

Figure 10.3 shows the convergence results in terms of perplexity and coherence with varying numbers of iterations through the entire collection while other parameters are held constant. A small change in these metrics is considered a good indicator of model convergence. We observe that in this example, increasing the number of iterations levels off perplexity and coherence scores fairly quickly. As there is little marginal benefit to setting the maximum number of iterations very high, we set the value of this parameter to 100.

Although the choice of the number of topics (K) and the model performance evaluation is frequently guided with perplexity scores on held-out test data, denoting observations not included previously in model estimation, coherence metrics have been proposed and found to be better correlated with human ratings on the interpretability of topics (Chang, Gerrish, Wang, Boyd-Graber, & Blei, 2009). In Figure 10.4, we show both aspects as a function of different numbers of topics generated across different runs of the exploratory analyses. A higher number of LDA topics generally provides better results at the beginning. However, there is an inflection point to this

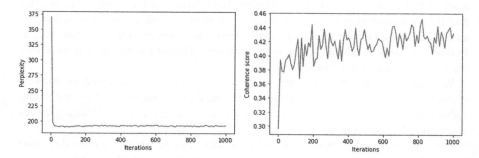

Figure 10.3   *Perplexity (left) and coherence (right) as a function of the number of iterations*

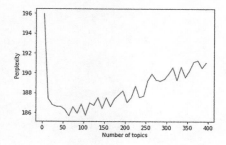 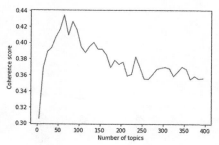

Figure 10.4   Perplexity (left) and coherence (right) as a function of the number of topics

trend, after which increasing the number of topics is observed to be detrimental to model performance. Considering these effects, to maintain a reasonably good trade-off between perplexity and coherence, we decided to keep 55 topics.

Once we evaluated the quantitative properties of our LDA model, we then began a qualitative assessment of the resulting topics output by the model.

Results

To visualize how the extracted topics relate to each other and how they differ, we use the LDAvis system (Sievert & Shirley, 2015). This provides a global view on the clustering of topics, which are represented as circles, by showing intertopic distances and topic prevalence. As shown in Figure 10.5, a number of small topics cluster in close proximity. On closer inspection, these topics generally relate to company names. Other, more distinct topics cover for instance words related to various industry sectors. Overall, in our qualitative evaluation, the spread of the topics appears to indicate satisfactory exclusivity.

Subsequently, we inspected the resultant word lists and word clouds based on estimated word probabilities to identify topics of interest. Good topics can be considered those that capture semantically related word co-occurrences, which can be assigned a short, clear label based on their top terms. After examining the content of all 55 topics, we marked and excluded those that were not meaningful to our research goal, e.g., topics clustering words related to industry sectors or company names. Beyond these extraneous topics, we found that the majority of the remaining topics represent organizational or financial word patterns. Among those we selected interesting topics for further analysis which we considered as relating to strategic aspects and assigned appropriate labels to them. Table 10.5 presents an overview of these five topics, their labels and word clouds, with the most prominent words for each of them.

Figure 10.6 shows how the selected topics pervade the collection over time. While the majority of them rather uniformly cover the analysis period (Topics 2, 21, 23,

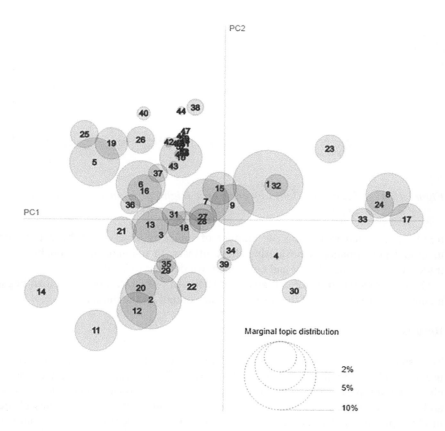

Figure 10.5   Intertopic distance map (via multidimensional scaling) considering the marginal topic distribution employing the first and second principal components (PC1 and PC2)

and 40) with some minor fluctuations, interestingly, Topic 51, which we consider as related to a growth orientation, shows a clear pattern.

Topic 51 can also be considered as closely related to the SE aspect since the most prominent words contained in it next to "growth" are "new," "product," and "market." As Mintzberg (1973: 46) conceptualized, "Growth is the dominant goal of the entrepreneurial organization." That is, this topic appears to tap into a similar conceptual domain as that of EO, which has been commonly assessed using word counts based upon available dictionaries (McKenny et al., 2018a; Short et al., 2010). A visual comparison of their similarity is demonstrated in Figure 10.7.

However, there are subtle yet notable differences in terms of what the scores obtained from topic models and dictionaries represent. In the LDA case, topic score represents a probability distribution, while dictionary-based measures indicate the proportion of dictionary words covered within the documents normalized by their

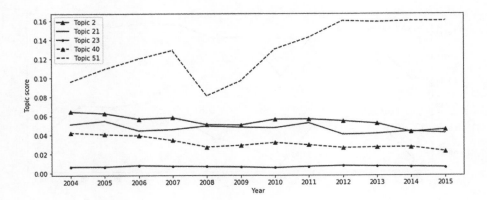

Figure 10.6   Coverage of selected topics in the collection of chief executive officers' letters by years

Table 10.5   Selected Latent Dirichlet Allocation topics and their assigned labels

Topic number	Topic label	Most frequent words
2	Selling orientation	percent net increase million sale increased store market growth continue fiscal customer retail new share
21	Customer orientation	customer new fiscal technology revenue service million solution growth mobile market data product network wireless
23	Stock market orientation	ratingmoody credit financial risk market solution product service revenue new growth global packaging customer
40	Market orientation	industry revenue market share growth sale technology fiscal product system customer new manufacturing semiconductor
51	Growth orientation	product new company strong customer continue growth global market technology performance value sale innovation strategy

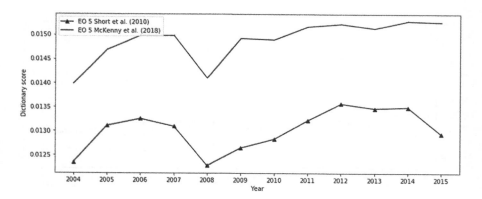

Figure 10.7   *Developments of entrepreneurial orientation dictionary scores
based on frequency word counts*

length. These two techniques can therefore be used to independently assess similar characteristics present in the same collection.

As a final step, we evaluate the usefulness of the retrieved topics to predict firm financial performance, which is one of the most widely studied relationships in SE and management (Short et al., 2010). To this end we relied on two measures. The first is Tobin's Q to assess a firm's stock market value relative to its replacement cost (Perfect & Wiles, 1994). The second measure is sales growth, which is an indicator of the effectiveness with which firms take advantage of current or new product–market opportunities (Shepherd & Wiklund, 2009). We control for firm size with a natural logarithm of sales volume. Regression results shown in Table 10.6 indicate that some of the identified topics significantly predict the performance of the S&P 500 companies in our sample. For comparison, we also present regression results for the revised dictionary-based EO in Table 10.6.

Tobin's Q is negatively associated with Topic 21 related to customer orientation, while sales growth is positively predicted by Topic 23 related to stock market orientation. Topic 51 related to growth is negatively associated with sales growth but positively with Tobin's Q. With respect to EO dimensions we find a similar pattern to Topic 51, which while beyond the scope of our present investigation is nonetheless intriguing given a presumed positive relationship between EO and firm sales growth. Certainly, there are numerous critical boundary conditions at play within EO–performance relationships (Rauch, Wiklund, Lumpkin, & Frese, 2009).

Taken together, we provide initial insight and evidence, and hope to spark further discussion into how topic models can serve as a useful exploratory method for concept extraction and a possible triangulation for popularly employed dictionaries.

Table 10.6   *Regression analyses for Latent Dirichlet Allocation-derived topic measures and dictionary-based entrepreneurial orientation predicting Tobin's Q and sales growth*

LDA-derived latent topics	(1) Tobin's Q	(2) Sales growth	Dictionary-based entrepreneurial orientation	(3) Tobin's Q	(4) Sales growth
Topic 2	0.005	−0.014			
	(0.034)	(0.020)			
Topic 21	−0.009*	−0.003			
	(0.037)	(0.035)			
Topic 23	0.007	0.034*			
	(0.080)	(0.053)			
Topic 40	0.018	−0.005			
	(0.044)	(0.022)			
Topic 51	0.044*	−0.048**	Entrepreneurial	−0.124***	−0.042*
	(0.033)	(0.019)	orientation	(0.734)	(0.565)
Firm size	−0.154***	0.009	Firm size	−0.151***	0.008
	(0.004)	(0.002)		(0.004)	(0.002)
R^2	0.026	0.004		0.039	0.002

Note: $n = 3451$; standardized beta coefficients, standard errors in parentheses; $^+ p < 0.1$; $^* p < 0.05$; $^{**} p < 0.01$; $^{***} p < 0.001$.
Source: McKenny et al. (2018a).

CONCLUDING REMARKS

In this chapter, we focus on providing an overview of textual data sources and methods of extracting information from them, which are of interest to scholars investigating SE. These include more familiar techniques for construct operationalization like dictionary word counts, along with more advanced emerging techniques such as topic models or word embeddings.

The large volume and wide variety of available textual documents produced by firms, their organizational leadership or other individuals or entities, as well as the rapid advancements in computerized text analysis offer ways to substantially expand the breadth, scope, and reliability of SE research. As Prüfer and Prüfer (2020) rightfully remark, the upward shift of the technological frontier simultaneously inspires changes in the very object of entrepreneurship research, allowing for unprecedented possibilities to model individual, social, and economic phenomena more precisely. Researchers have therefore a unique opportunity to leverage rich sources of textual data in new ways to extract novel information and combine these data with key indicators of interest.

We are mindful that some of the reviewed methods cannot be easily taken advantage of due to required programming skills or exposure to big data computational methods. Moreover, Popping (2012) warns that there remains a need for an expert qualitative assessment of automated quantitative data-processing outputs to ensure validity and reliability. Certainly, methods such as LDA topic modeling require specific knowledge for model calibration and a careful assessment of the resulting topical clusters. Hence, while we highlight the benefits and usefulness of automated text analysis, we also underline that challenges remain for researchers to consider when employing more advanced computational text analysis methods to devise new insights. We hope this chapter will serve as encouragement to explore these methods which have the potential to enhance our domain's methodological toolbox and open new horizons for future research endeavors.

REFERENCES

Ahl, H. 2006. Why research on women entrepreneurs needs new directions. *Entrepreneurship: Theory and Practice*, 30(5): 595–621.
Ahlstrom, D., & Bruton, G. D. 2006. Venture capital in emerging economies: Networks and institutional change. *Entrepreneurship: Theory and Practice*, 30(2): 299–320.
Alammar, F. M., Intezari, A., Cardow, A., & Pauleen, D. J. 2018. Grounded theory in practice: Novice researchers' choice between Straussian and Glaserian. *Journal of Management Inquiry*, 28(2): 228–245.
Allison, T. H., McKenny, A. F., & Short, J. C. 2013. The effect of entrepreneurial rhetoric on microlending investment: An examination of the warm-glow effect. *Journal of Business Venturing*, 28(6): 690–707.
Anderson, B. S., Wennberg, K., & Mcmullen, J. S. 2019. Editorial: Enhancing quantitative theory-testing entrepreneurship research. *Journal of Business Venturing*, 34(5): 1–11.
Basque, J., & Langley, A. 2018. Invoking Alphonse: The founder figure as a historical resource for organizational identity work. *Organization Studies*, 39(12): 1685–1708.
Baumer, E. P. S., Mimno, D., Guha, S., Quan, E., & Gay, G. K. 2017. Comparing grounded theory and topic modeling: Extreme divergence or unlikely convergence? *Journal of the Association for Information Science and Technology*, 68: 1397–1410.
Bednar, M. K., Boivie, S., & Prince, N. R. 2013. Burr under the saddle: How media coverage influences strategic change. *Organization Science*, 24(3): 910–925.
Belderbos, R., Grabowska, M., Kelchtermans, S., & Ugur, N. 2017. On the use of computer-aided text analysis in international business research. *Global Strategy Journal*, 7: 312–331.
Berelson, B. 1952. *Content Analysis in Communication Research*. New York: Free Press.
Bhattacharya, A., Misra, S., & Sardashti, H. 2019. Strategic orientation and firm risk. *International Journal of Research in Marketing*, 36(4): 509–527.
Blei, D. M., & Lafferty, J. D. 2009. *Topic models*. Survey Paper.
Blei, D. M., Ng, A. Y., & Jordan, M. I. 2003. Latent Dirichlet Allocation. *Journal of Machine Learning Research*, 3: 993–1022.
Boling, J. R., Pieper, T. M., & Covin, J. G. 2016. CEO Tenure and entrepreneurial orientation within family and nonfamily firms. *Entrepreneurship: Theory and Practice*, 40(4): 891–913.
Brown, T. B., Mann, B., Ryder, N., Subbiah, M., Kaplan, J. et al. 2020. Language models are few-shot learners. *ArXiv*. http://arxiv.org/abs/2005.14165.
Chang, J., Gerrish, S., Wang, C., Boyd-Graber, J. L., & Blei, D. M. 2009. Reading tea leaves: How humans interpret topic models. *Advances in Neural Information Processing Systems*, 22: 288–296.

Choudhury, P., Wang, D., Carlson, N. A., & Khanna, T. 2019. Machine learning approaches to facial and text analysis: Discovering CEO oral communication styles. *Strategic Management Journal*, 40(11): 1705–1732.

Chowdhury, G. 2003. Natural language processing. *Annual Review of Information Science and Technology*, 37: 51–89.

Conaway, R. N., & Wardrope, W. J. 2010. Do their words really matter? Thematic analysis of U.S. and Latin American CEO letters. *Journal of Business Communication*, 47(2): 141–168.

Corritore, M., Goldberg, A., & Srivastava, S. B. 2020. Duality in diversity: How intrapersonal and interpersonal cultural heterogeneity relate to firm performance. *Administrative Science Quarterly*, 65(2): 359–394.

Cronbach, L. J. 1971. Test validation. In R. L. Thorndike (Ed.), *Educational Measurement*. Washington, DC: American Council on Education.

Crystal, D. 2011. *A Dictionary of Linguistics and Phonetics*. Chichester: John Wiley & Sons.

Davidsson, P. 2016. Researching entrepreneurship. *International Studies in Entrepreneurship*, 5. https://doi.org/10.1007/978-3-319-26692-3.

Denzin, N. K., & Lincoln, Y. 2011. Disciplining the practice of qualitative research. In *The SAGE Handbook of Qualitative Research*. Thousand Oaks, CA: SAGE.

Devlin, J., Chang, M. W., Lee, K., & Toutanova, K. 2019. BERT: Pre-training of deep bidirectional transformers for language understanding. *NAACL HLT 2019 – 2019 Conference of the North American Chapter of the Association for Computational Linguistics: Human Language Technologies – Proceedings of the Conference*, 1: 4171–4186.

Dey, I. 1995. Reducing fragmentation in qualitative research. In U. Kelle (Ed.), *Computer-Aided Qualitative Data Analysis: Theory, Methods, and Practice*: 69–79. London: SAGE.

DiMaggio, P., Nag, M., & Blei, D. 2013. Exploiting affinities between topic modeling and the sociological perspective on culture: Application to newspaper coverage of U.S. government arts funding. *Poetics*, 41(6): 570–606.

Engelen, A., Neumann, C., & Schmidt, S. 2016. Should entrepreneurially oriented firms have narcissistic CEOs? *Journal of Management*, 42(3): 698–721.

Faruqui, M., Tsvetkov, Y., Rastogi, P., & Dyer, C. 2016. Problems with evaluation of word embeddings using word similarity tasks. *Proceedings of the 1st Workshop on Evaluating Vector-Space Representations for NLP*: 30–35. Berlin.

Grühn, B., Strese, S., Flatten, T. C., Jaeger, N. A., & Brettel, M. 2017. Temporal change patterns of entrepreneurial orientation: A longitudinal investigation of CEO successions. *Entrepreneurship: Theory and Practice*, 41(4): 591–619.

Guo, L., Sharma, R., Yin, L., Lu, R., & Rong, K. 2017. Automated competitor analysis using big data analytics: Evidence from the fitness mobile app business. *Business Process Management Journal*, 23(3): 735–762.

Gupta, V. K., Dutta, D. K., & Chen, X. 2014. Entrepreneurial orientation capability and firm performance under conditions of organizational learning. *Journal of Managerial Issues*, 26(2): 157–173.

Gupta, V. K., Mortal, S. C., & Yang, T. 2016. Entrepreneurial orientation and firm value: Does managerial discretion play a role? *Review of Managerial Science*, 12(1): 1–26.

Haans, R. F. J. 2019. What's the value of being different when everyone is? The effects of distinctiveness on performance in homogeneous versus heterogeneous categories. *Strategic Management Journal*, 40(1): 3–27.

Hales, J., Moon, J. R., & Swenson, L. A. 2018. A new era of voluntary disclosure? Empirical evidence on how employee postings on social media relate to future corporate disclosures. *Accounting, Organizations and Society*, 68–69: 88–108.

Hannigan, T. R., Haan, R. F. J., Vakili, K., Tchalian, H., Glaser, V. L. et al. 2019. Topic modeling in management research: Rendering new theory from textual data. *Academy of Management Annals*, 13(2): 586–632.

Hansen, S., McMahon, M., & Prat, A. 2017. Transparency and deliberation within the FOMC: A computational linguistics approach. *Quarterly Journal of Economics*, 133(2): 801–870.

Harris, Z. S. 1954. Distributional structure. *Word*, 10(2–3): 146–162.

Heracleous, L., & Klaering, L. A. 2017. The circle of life: Rhetoric of identification in Steve Jobs' Stanford speech. *Journal of Business Research*, 79: 31–40.

Hitt, M. A., Ireland, R., Sirmon, D., & Trahms, C. 2011. Strategic entrepreneurship: Creating value for individuals, organizations, and society. *Academy of Management Perspectives*, 25(2): 57–75.

Hofmann, T. 1999. Probabilistic Latent Semantic Indexing. *Proceedings of the 22nd Annual International ACM SIGIR Conference on Research and Development in Information Retrieval*: 50–57.

Holsti, O. R. 1968. Content analysis. In L. Grdner & E. Aronson (Eds), *The Handbook of Social Psychology*: 596–692. Reading, MA: Addison-Wesley.

Hu, N., Qiu, F., & Liang, P. 2018. Competitive strategy and earning persistence: Evidence from large sample based on natural language processing and deep learning. Available at SSRN 3281448.

Ireland, R. D., & Hitt, M. A. 1992. Mission statements: Importance, challenge, and recommendations for development. *Business Horizons*, 35(3): 34–43.

Jackson, K. M., & Trochim, W. M. K. 2002. Concept mapping as an alternative approach for the analysis of open-ended survey responses. *Organizational Research Methods*, 5(4): 307–336.

Jancenelle, V. E., Storrud-Barnes, S., & Javalgi, R. G. 2017. Corporate entrepreneurship and market performance: A content analysis of earnings conference calls. *Management Research Review*, 40(3): 352–367.

Josefy, M., Dean, T. J., Albert, L. S., & Fitza, M. A. 2017. The role of community in crowdfunding success: Evidence on cultural attributes in funding campaigns to "Save the local theater." *Entrepreneurship: Theory and Practice*, 41(2): 161–182.

Kaminski, J. C., & Hopp, C. 2019. Predicting outcomes in crowdfunding campaigns with textual, visual, and linguistic signals. *Small Business Economics*, 55: 627–649.

Kaminski, J. C., Jiang, Y., Piller, F., & Hopp, C. 2017. Do user entrepreneurs speak different? Applying natural language processing to crowdfunding videos. *Conference on Human Factors in Computing Systems – Proceedings*, Part F1276: 2683–2689.

Kaplan, S., & Vakili, K. 2015. The double-edged sword of recombination in breakthrough innovation. *Strategic Management Journal*, 36(10): 1435–1457.

Kim, H. J., Kim, T. S., & Sohn, S. Y. 2020. Recommendation of startups as technology cooperation candidates from the perspectives of similarity and potential: A deep learning approach. *Decision Support Systems*, 130: 113229.

Kimbrough, M. D. 2005. The effect of conference calls on analyst and market underreaction to earnings announcements. *The Accounting Review*, 80(1): 189–219.

Kobayashi, V. B., Mol, S. T., Berkers, H. A., Kismihók, G., & Den Hartog, D. N. 2018. Text mining in organizational research. *Organizational Research Methods*, 21(3): 733–765.

Kohut, G. F., & Segars, A. H. 1992. The president's letter to stockholders: An examination of corporate communication strategy. *Journal of Business Communication*, 29(1): 7–21.

Kosinski, M., Stillwell, D., & Graepel, T. 2013. Private traits and attributes are predictable from digital records of human behavior. *Proceedings of the National Academy of Sciences of the United States of America*, 110(15): 5802–5805.

Kuratko, D. F., & Audretsch, D. B. 2009. Strategic entrepreneurship: Exploring different perspectives of an emerging concept. *Entrepreneurship: Theory and Practice*, 33(1): 1–17.

Larcker, D. F., & Zakolyukina, A. A. 2012. Detecting deceptive discussions in conference calls. *Journal of Accounting Research*, 50(2): 495–540.

Lau, J. H., Grieser, K., Newman, D., & Baldwin, T. 2011. Automatic labelling of topic models. *ACL-HLT 2011 – Proceedings of the 49th Annual Meeting of the Association for Computational Linguistics: Human Language Technologies.*

Lau, J. H., Newman, D., & Baldwin, T. 2014. Machine reading tea leaves: Automatically evaluating topic coherence and topic model quality. *14th Conference of the European Chapter of the Association for Computational Linguistics 2014.*

Le, Q., & Mikolov, T. 2014. Distributed representations of sentences and documents. *31st International Conference on Machine Learning.*

Li, J., & Larsen, K. R. 2011. Establishing nomological networks for behavioral science: A natural language processing based approach. *Thirty Second International Conference on Information Systems*, 109: 101–109. Shanghai.

Liu, K., Tang, J., Yang, K., & Arthurs, J. 2019. Foreign IPOs in the U.S.: When entrepreneurial orientation meets institutional distance. *Journal of Business Research*, 101: 144–151.

Ljungkvist, T., Boers, B., & Samuelsson, J. 2019. Three stages of entrepreneurial orientation: The founder's role. *International Journal of Entrepreneurial Behaviour and Research*, 26(2): 285–306.

Loper, E., & Bird, S. 2002. NLTK: The natural language toolkit NLTK: The Natural Language Toolkit. *Proceedings of the ACL Workshop on Effective Tools and Methodologies for Teaching Natural Language Processing and Computational Linguistics.*

Losiewicz, P., Oard, D. W., & Kostoff, R. N. 2000. Textual data mining to support science and technology management. *Journal of Intelligent Information Systems*, 15(2): 99–119.

Luger, J., Raisch, S., & Schimmer, M. 2018. Dynamic balancing of exploration and exploitation: The contingent benefits of ambidexterity. *Organization Science*, 29(3): 449–470.

Ma, L., Sun, B., & Kekre, S. 2015. The squeaky wheel gets the grease-an empirical analysis of customer voice and firm intervention on twitter. *Marketing Science*, 34(5): 627–645.

Mahmoodi, J., Leckelt, M., van Zalk, M. W. H., Geukes, K., & Back, M. D. 2017. Big data approaches in social and behavioral science: Four key trade-offs and a call for integration. *Current Opinion in Behavioral Sciences*, 18: 57–62.

Marino, K. E., Castaldi, R. M., & Dollinger, M. J. 1989. Content analysis in entrepreneurship research: The case of initial public offerings. *Entrepreneurship: Theory and Practice*, 14(1): 51–66.

McKenny, A. F., Aguinis, H., Short, J. C., & Anglin, A. H. 2018a. What doesn't get measured does exist. *Journal of Management*, 44(7): 2909–2933.

McKenny, A. F., Short, J. C., Ketchen, D. J., Payne, G. T., & Moss, T. W. 2018b. Strategic entrepreneurial orientation: Configurations, performance, and the effects of industry and time. *Strategic Entrepreneurship Journal*, June: 504–521.

Menon, A., Choi, J., & Tabakovic, H. 2018. What you say your strategy is and why it matters: Natural language processing of unstructured text. *Academy of Management Proceedings.* https://doi.org/10.15713/ins.mmj.3.

Mikolov, T., Chen, K., Corrado, G., & Dean, J. 2013a. Efficient estimation of word representations in vector space. *International Conference on Learning Representations*: 1–12.

Mikolov, T., Le, Q. V., & Sutskever, I. 2013b. Exploiting similarities among languages for machine translation. *ArXiv.* http://arxiv.org/abs/1309.4168.

Mimno, D., Wallach, H. M., Talley, E., Leenders, M., & McCallum, A. 2011. Optimizing semantic coherence in topic models. *Proceedings of the 2011 Conference on Empirical Methods in Natural Language Processing*, 2: 262–272.

Mintzberg, H. 1973. Strategy-making in three modes. *California Management Review*, 16(2): 44–53.

Mitra, B., & Craswell, N. 2018. An introduction to neural information retrieval. *Foundations and Trends in Information Retrieval*, 13(1): 1–129.

Moss, T. W., Renko, M., Block, E., & Meyskens, M. 2018. Funding the story of hybrid ventures: Crowdfunder lending preferences and linguistic hybridity. *Journal of Business Venturing*, 33(5): 643–659.

Moss, T. W., Short, J. C., Payne, G. T., & Lumpkin, G. T. 2011. Dual identities in social ventures: An exploratory study. *Entrepreneurship: Theory and Practice*, 35(4): 805–830.

Mousa, F. T., Wales, W. J., & Harper, S. R. 2015. When less is more: EO's influence upon funds raised by young technology firms at IPO. *Journal of Business Research*, 68(2): 306–313.

Nicholson, L., & Anderson, A. R. 2005. News and nuances of the entrepreneurial myth and metaphor: Linguistic games in entrepreneurial sense-making and sense-giving. *Entrepreneurship: Theory and Practice*, 29(2): 153–172.

Noble, C. H., Sinha, R. K., & Kumar, A. 2002. Market orientation and alternative strategic orientations: A longitudinal assessment of performance implications. *Journal of Marketing*, 66(4): 25–39.

Obschonka, M., Fisch, C., & Boyd, R. 2017. Using digital footprints in entrepreneurship research: A Twitter-based personality analysis of superstar entrepreneurs and managers. *Journal of Business Venturing Insights*, 8: 13–23.

Palmer, T. B., & Short, J. C. 2008. Mission statements in U.S. colleges of business: An empirical examination of their content with linkages to configurations and performance. *Academy of Management Learning and Education*, 7(4): 454–470.

Pandey, S., & Pandey, S. K. 2019. Applying natural language processing capabilities in computerized textual analysis to measure organizational culture. *Organizational Research Methods*, 22(3): 765–797.

Pandey, S., Pandey, S. K., & Miller, L. 2017. Measuring innovativeness of public organizations: Using natural language processing techniques in computer-aided textual analysis. *International Public Management Journal*, 20(1): 78–107.

Pennington, J., Socher, R., & Manning, C. D. 2014. GloVe: Global vectors for word representation. *2014 Conference on Empirical Methods in Natural Language Processing – Proceedings of the Conference*.

Perfect, S. B., & Wiles, K. W. 1994. Alternative constructions of Tobin's Q: An empirical comparison. *Journal of Empirical Finance*, 1(3–4): 313–341.

Persaud, A., & Chandra Bayon, M. 2019. A Review and analysis of the thematic structure of social entrepreneurship research: 1990–2018. *International Review of Entrepreneurship*, 17(4): 495–528.

Peters, M. E., Neumann, M., Iyyer, M., Gardner, M., Clark, C. et al. 2018. Deep contextualized word representations. *ArXiv*. http://arxiv.org/abs/1802.05365.

Popping, R. 2012. Qualitative decisions in quantitative text analysis research. *Sociological Methodology*, 42(1): 88–90.

Prüfer, J., & Prüfer, P. 2020. Data science for entrepreneurship research: Studying demand dynamics for entrepreneurial skills in the Netherlands. *Small Business Economics*, 55(3): 651–672.

Quinn, K. M., Monroe, B. L., Colaresi, M., Crespin, M. H., & Radev, D. R. 2010. How to analyze political attention with minimal assumptions and costs. *American Journal of Political Science*, 54(1): 209–228.

Rauch, A., Wiklund, J., Lumpkin, G. T., & Frese, M. 2009. Entrepreneurial orientation and business performance: An assessment of past research and suggestions for the future. *Entrepreneurship: Theory and Practice*, 33(3): 761–787.

Rehurek, R., & Sojka, P. 2010. Software Framework for topic modelling with large corpora. *Proceedings of the LREC 2010 Workshop on New Challenges for NLP Frameworks*.

Rhee, L., Ocasio, W. C., & Zajac, E. J. 2018. How cognitive congruence drives innovation in interfirm collaborations. *SSRN Electronic Journal*. https://doi.org/10.2139/ssrn.3119825.

Salmivaara, V., & Kibler, E. 2019. "Rhetoric mix" of argumentations: How policy rhetoric conveys meaning of entrepreneurship for sustainable development. *Entrepreneurship: Theory and Practice*, 44(4): 700–732.

Salton, G., & Buckley, C. 1988. Term-weighting approaches in automatic text retrieval. *Information Processing and Management*, 24(5): 513–523.

Schmiedel, T., Müller, O., & vom Brocke, J. 2018. Topic modeling as a strategy of inquiry in organizational research: A tutorial with an application example on organizational culture. *Organizational Research Methods*, 22(4): 941–968.

Schuelke-Leech, B.-A., & Barry, B. L. 2016. Complexity of textual data in entrepreneurship and innovation research. *Complexity in Entrepreneurship, Innovation and Technology Research*: 459–480. Cham: Springer.

Schwarz, C. 2018. Ldagibbs: A command for topic modeling in stata using Latent Dirichlet Allocation. *The Stata Journal: Promoting Communications on Statistics and Stata*, 18(1): 101–117.

Shelley, M., & Krippendorff, K. 1984. Content analysis: An introduction to its methodology. *Journal of the American Statistical Association*, 79(385): 240.

Shepherd, D. A., & Wiklund, J. 2009. Are we comparing apples with apples or apples with oranges? Appropriateness of knowledge accumulation across growth studies. *Entrepreneurship: Theory and Practice*, 33(1): 105–123.

Short, J. C., Broberg, J. C., Cogliser, C. C., & Brigham, K. H. 2010. Construct validation using computer-aided text analysis (CATA). *Organizational Research Methods*, 13(2): 320–347.

Short, J. C., McKenny, A. F., & Reid, S. W. 2018. More than words? Computer-aided text analysis in organizational behavior and psychology research. *Annual Review of Organizational Psychology and Organizational Behavior*, 5: 415–437.

Short, J. C., Payne, G. T., Brigham, K. H., Lumpkin, G. T., & Broberg, J. C. 2009. Family firms and entrepreneurial orientation in publicly traded firms: A comparative analysis of the S&P 500. *Family Business Review*, 22(1): 9–24.

Sievert, C., & Shirley, K. 2015. LDAvis: A method for visualizing and interpreting topics. *Proceedings of the Workshop on Interactive Language Learning, Visualization, and Interfaces*, 63–70.

Tausczik, Y. R., & Pennebaker, J. W. 2010. The psychological meaning of words: LIWC and computerized text analysis methods. *Journal of Language and Social Psychology*, 29(1): 24–54.

Teoh, S. H. 2018. The promise and challenges of new datasets for accounting research. *Accounting, Organizations and Society*, 68–69: 109–117.

Tsai, M.-F., & Wang, C.-J. 2015. Financial keyword expansion via continuous word vector representations. *Proceedings of the 2014 Conference on Empirical Methods in Natural Language Processing*: 1453–1458.

Urquhart, C. 2012. *Grounded Theory for Qualitative Research: A Practical Guide*. Thousand Oaks, CA: SAGE.

Vicinanza, P., Goldberg, A., & Srivastava, S. 2020. Who sees the future? A deep learning language model demonstrates the vision advantage of being small. *SocArXiv*. https://doi.org/10.31235/osf.io/j24pw.

Wales, W. J., Cox, K. C., Lortie, J., & Sproul, C. R. 2019. Blowing smoke? How early-stage investors interpret hopeful discourse within entrepreneurially oriented business plans. *Entrepreneurship Research Journal*, 9(3): 1–16.

Watson, A., Dada, O., Wright, O., & Perrigot, R. 2019. Entrepreneurial orientation rhetoric in franchise organizations: The impact of national culture. *Entrepreneurship: Theory and Practice*, 43(4): 751–772.

Weber, R. 1990. *Basic Content Analysis*. Beverly Hills, CA: SAGE.

Wolfe, M. T., & Shepherd, D. A. 2015. "Bouncing back" from a loss: Entrepreneurial orientation, emotions, and failure narratives. *Entrepreneurship: Theory and Practice*, 39(3): 675–700.

Zachary, M. A., McKenny, A. F., Short, J. C., & Payne, G. T. 2011. Family business and market orientation: Construct validation and comparative analysis. *Family Business Review*, 24(3): 233–251.

11. Endogeneity in strategic entrepreneurship research

Brian S. Anderson

INTRODUCTION

There is an inherent quandary facing strategic entrepreneurship scholarship. The pursuit of new opportunities and building new lines of business is a necessary condition for firm survival (Wright & Hitt, 2017). Organizations simply will not grow, and will eventually die, if they do not engage in some form of entrepreneurial behavior (Ireland, Covin, & Kuratko, 2009; Miller & Friesen, 1982). This reality makes strategic entrepreneurship research and theory of paramount importance to senior decision-makers. Ideally, this research yields predictive insights—the ability for a decision-maker to make an informed prediction about the performance implications of a specific entrepreneurial decision. But to create predictive theory, researchers must build and test causal models (Pearl, 2009). Causal modeling, in turn, requires substantive design and empirical sophistication (Angrist & Pischke, 2008). Thus the quandary—for strategic entrepreneurship research to be useful in practice, it must also be rigorous in its design.

There is nothing novel in calling for increased methodological sophistication (Anderson, Wennberg, & McMullen, 2019; Antonakis, 2017; Bettis, Ethiraj, Gambardella, Helfat, & Mitchell, 2016). Further, modern scholarship increasingly recognizes the false trade-off between rigorous research design and practitioner utility (Anderson et al., 2019). The challenge for strategic entrepreneurship researchers is increasing rigor when the most valuable tool for inferring a causal relationship—the randomized controlled experiment (Pearl, 2009)—is not usable. It is neither ethical nor practical to randomly assign one business to an "entrepreneurial" condition and another to a "non-entrepreneurial" condition. This places many of the research questions we ask as strategic entrepreneurship scholars closer in many ways to the fields of labor economics, sociology, and epidemiology (Angrist & Krueger, 2001; Morgan & Winship, 2014; Pearl, 2018a). To test causal models and build predictive theory, strategic entrepreneurship scholars must think deeply about the threats to causal inference in their models, and to think creatively about potential solutions to those threats.

The purpose of this chapter is to help scholars identify the primary threats to causal inference in strategic entrepreneurship research, which collectively manifests as endogeneity in a statistical model. It is worthwhile to note that even if a study is not meant to infer or test a causal claim, endogeneity may be—and likely is—biasing a model result; a zero-order correlation with an omitted confounder is just as wrong

(Antonakis, Bendahan, Jacquart, & Lalive, 2010). To ground the discussion, I start with two common perspectives in strategic entrepreneurship research—building an explanation for what has happened in the past, and creating a prediction of what will happen in the future (Gelman & Imbens, 2013)—and discuss how specific causal inference concerns enter into research designs meant to test models from both perspectives. I then move to discussing why so-called "ideal" solutions to tackling endogeneity, such as instrumental variable methods and methods that depend on exogenous manipulations, may be infeasible in practice for strategic entrepreneurship scholars. Lastly, I outline a Bayesian methodology that offers researchers flexibility when building causal models and in addressing multiple endogeneity problems in observational research designs.

In tackling the causal modeling question, this chapter makes three contributions. The first contribution is to shift the endogeneity and causal inference foci from a generic social science problem to one centered specifically on strategic entrepreneurship. Within this realm, researchers typically face three related problems. First, firms typically adopt entrepreneurial strategies expressly to improve performance; this selection effect renders strategic choice endogenous to the performance outcome (Rocha, van Praag, Folta, & Carneiro, 2018). Second, strategic entrepreneurship scholars make substantial use of multidimensional latent constructs and proxy variables, both of which contain measurement error not easily delimited into random and systematic sources for modeling purposes (Anderson, Eshima, & Hornsby, 2018). Third, entrepreneurial strategic decisions typically blur the distinction between planning and execution, between planned and emergent strategy, and between exploration and exploitation, making it difficult to isolate the strategic choice from an observed outcome variable (Rocha et al., 2018; Semadeni, Withers, & Certo, 2014). The preceding also manifests in a temporal adjacency problem—the observed strategic choice may be distal to the outcome and with multiple intervening variables accounting for the causal connection.

The second contribution is to outline an alternative approach to modeling that works well for strategic entrepreneurship research questions drawing from observational data. Instrument variable (IV) and associated methods require the researcher to identify a strong exogenous instrument or other source of variation (Angrist & Pischke, 2008). This includes methods such as conditioning on observed covariates, regression discontinuity, difference-in-differences, and propensity score matching. In practice, it is exceptionally difficult to identify an instrument that addresses multiple endogeneity problems and threats to causal inference in strategic entrepreneurship research. In this chapter, then, I discuss how Bayesian modeling provides a useful alternative to IVs—in particular contexts—to address multiple endogeneity concerns and improve model efficacy (Feller & Gelman, 2015).

The final contribution of this chapter is to provide a sample code and best practices for strategic entrepreneurship researchers to draw upon when designing studies meant to build predictive theory. Without question, building a causal model requires more than sophisticated statistical methodologies, and is very much a function of extensive theoretical development and research design (Anderson et al., 2019). That said, providing researchers with alternatives to common econometric approaches that may be ill-suited for strategic entrepreneurship researchers opens new research questions and new opportunities to advance strategic entrepreneurship theory from a descriptive lens to a predictive lens.

CAUSAL QUESTIONS IN STRATEGIC ENTREPRENEURSHIP

The Challenge of Causal Inference

Most empirical work in strategic entrepreneurship involves descriptive analyses and hypotheses of some kind, drawing primarily from observational data. By descriptive, I am referring to questions of association, such as identifying patterns of research and development (R&D) spending among firms that actively patent new technologies. What defines associational work with observational data is the inherent inability to draw causal inference from the research design itself. That is, the researcher did not— or was not able to—collect data in such a way as to satisfy the necessary and sufficient conditions for causal inference (Morgan & Winship, 2014). This is an important distinction—the inability to make a causal claim manifests first as a limitation of the data generation process (Pearl, 2009). Certainly, even when data generation provides temporal distance between the predictor and outcome and controls for alternate explanations, model misspecification or errors in statistical analysis may diminish, if not eliminate, causal inference (Morgan & Winship, 2014). Nonetheless, the process begins with research design and data generation, which itself is predicated on a deep theoretical understanding of the relationship under study (Pearl, 2009).

The challenge for strategic entrepreneurship is that we often cast, or misinterpret, associational research questions and analyses as rising to the level of a causal claim. Consider, for example, a common hypothesis that entrepreneurial orientation (EO) increases sales growth rate (Covin & Slevin, 1989). The researcher may not explicitly state that EO *causes* the sales growth rate increase. Further, the researcher warns readers *not* to infer a causal association. Nonetheless, implicit in the hypothesis— and perhaps in the chapter's discussion section—is that variation in EO precedes variation in sales growth rate; the change in EO leads to a change in sales growth. The hypothesis implies a causal claim that influences future research on EO; that is, researchers embed the assumption of a causal connection between EO and performance in future work. While there may be sound theoretical reasoning behind the assumption that EO causes an increase in sales growth rate, the empirics of the study support no such claim.

The preceding is not meant to diminish the importance of associational research. Quite the contrary, conducting high-quality associational research requires careful attention to sampling, measurement error, and modeling (Gelman, 2011). Further, associational research often yields insights that guide future research (Wennberg & Anderson, 2019). The challenge, however, for strategic entrepreneurship research is to avoid placing unnecessary weight on associational research to yield causal predictions. That is, we do a disservice to managers, policy-makers, and entrepreneurs when we suggest that strategic behaviors, such as adopting a more entrepreneurial posture, *causally* yield a performance increase without a strong empirical basis to make the causal claim. To help avoid this tendency, of which I am also guilty, it is helpful to categorize two broad categories of causal questions in strategic entrepreneurship research, and how they differ from associational questions.

Explanations of What Happened

Sometimes referred to as "causes of effects" or "reverse causal questions" (Gelman, 2011), explanations of why something happened necessarily involve retrospection. The researcher observed some outcome, y, and wants to uncover what caused variation in y. In strategic entrepreneurship research, performance variation is the most straightforward observed outcome. While strategic entrepreneurship shares firm performance with the strategic management discipline as a focal outcome, strategic entrepreneurship research generally asks the extent to which a performance differential is due to pursuing entrepreneurial and innovative behaviors. For example, a researcher observes firms with higher than industry-average sales growth, and asks the extent to which EO caused superior performance.

While a common perspective, it is inordinately difficult to isolate the underlying causes of an observed outcome. Take the high EO firm—was the firm entrepreneurial because of a visionary chief executive officer (CEO) (Engelen, Neumann, & Schmidt, 2013), or because of surplus resources (Wales, Patel, Parida, & Kreiser, 2013), or because of its organizational knowledge (Anderson, Covin, & Slevin, 2009), or because of its external operating environment (Kreiser, Marino, Dickson, & Weaver, 2010)? The answer may be one of the preceding, none of the preceding, or a complex interaction among what we can observe and what we cannot. Unfortunately, most statistical tools and causal inference frameworks provide little utility in answering reverse causal questions; there are simply too many factors to account for and too complicated a model to properly specify to yield an unbiased answer (Gelman, 2011). Nonetheless, reserve causal questions remain a foundation of the scientific process, in that researchers generally observe a phenomenon of interest and seek an explanation for what they observed.

Central, then, to the feasibility of answering reverse causal questions and explaining why something happened requires constraining the scope of the research question and the temporal separation between the outcome and a potential cause. As illustrated previously, the question of why we observe high EO firms necessarily requires us to consider potentially dozens (if not hundreds) of individual variables, some of which may take a non-linear form and vary over time and magnitude, and the ensuing complexity of multiple, multivariate interactions. Modeling these variables is an impossible task for any single study. However, constraining the scope and temporal boundary of the question improves the prospect of isolating potential causal factors. In an extreme example of specificity, the researcher may ask whether a commercialized patent within the past two years increased EO among small (100–250 employee) firms in the kitchen appliance manufacturing sector, each of which range between five and ten years old, with between $10 million and $25 million in total assets, and with founder CEOs who each have prior startup experience. While specific, answering this question is not likely to generate the theoretical contribution often expected among major entrepreneurship research journals!

Fundamentally, drawing causal inference in a reserve causal question requires directly observing or holding constant all possible factors that *could* have caused variation in the outcome beyond the variable or variables the researcher specifies. The difficulty in meeting this bar motivates a somewhat extreme perspective that there is *no study* capable of isolating a cause of an effect from observational data (Angrist & Pischke, 2008). While I do not take such a position, it is worthwhile to note that truly answering reverse causal questions is an aspirational goal; the best IV methods, or as I will demonstrate later in the chapter, well specified prior in Bayesian inference, provide at reasonable best an approximate answer.

Statements of Prediction

Statements of prediction, also termed "effects of causes" or "forward causal questions" reflect a traditional experimental paradigm (Gelman, 2011). Forward causal questions start with a predictor, or treatment, x, create variance in that predictor, and then observe an outcome, y. Most causal inference frameworks including the Rubin counterfactual model (Rubin, 2005), the Shadish, Cook, and Campbell (2002) causal inference criteria, and the graphical approach pioneered by Pearl (2009) generally discuss causal inference from a predictive lens. A pharmaceutical experiment provides an example—what is the difference on a health outcome among patients who took a medication versus patients who took a placebo? From this example, we find the familiar formula of the effect of treatment x for patient i on outcome y as the difference $y_i(x = 1) - y_i (x = 0)$ (Morgan & Winship, 2014). Given a research design meeting a strict series of assumptions, we can extend the formula's results to an estimated average causal effect of x on y within a given population (Morgan & Winship, 2014).

Underpinning the usefulness of the experimental design is the randomization assumption. Under perfect randomization, the researcher assumes that any alternate explanation influencing or confounding the relationship between x and y reduces to zero in a large enough sample and the absence of any selection effect on the part of the study participants (Morgan & Winship, 2014). Specifically, the researcher must control the experimental conditions such that a participant has no ability to influence his or her ability to be in a treatment group or control group, and that differences among study participants occur only at random (Angrist & Pischke, 2008). While conceptually straightforward, a traditional experimental design lies outside the possibility for most strategic entrepreneurship questions. At a simplistic level, to estimate the causal effect of EO on sales growth rate the researcher must manipulate, at random, a large sample of firms' EO. Some firms would take a "high EO pill" and some firms a "low EO pill," and a given firm would not know what condition it is in, and the firm would have no ability to adjust its EO during the study window. It is difficult to imagine a CEO agreeing to the protocol!

We do find research designs attempting to mimic the randomization of a laboratory in a field setting—the natural experiment being one common, although elusive in practice, option (Morgan & Winship, 2014). Policy capture, conjoint experiments, and simulation-type experimental designs provide the randomization and control of a laboratory setting, but at the expense of generalizability and connection to practice. These studies may provide insights into senior executive decision-making and judgment, but they remain artificial representations of actual firms pursuing actual entrepreneurial decisions (Lohrke, Holloway, & Woolley, 2009). As such, they inform causal inference in strategic entrepreneurship, but for most research questions of interest to the field, remain limited in application.

That said, answering forward causal questions provides the connection to predictive theory that many strategic entrepreneurship researchers seek. For example, the ability to tell managers that adjusting R&D spend by some amount yields a certain increase in the probability of a new patent is actionable, useful business intelligence. Further, predictive theory effectively culls the theoretical landscape of explanations of causal effects that do not exist in practice (Ghoshal, 2005). As such, predictive models yielding robust causal estimates provide benefits for theory and for practice. Unfortunately, building these models necessitates creating some type of manipulation and randomization, or some mechanism to "stand in for" manipulation and randomization, *before* observing an outcome of interest. This reality makes these research designs elusive for strategic entrepreneurship research.

Interplay between Understanding the Past and Predicting the Future

While a study's research design would provide an answer consistent with one perspective or the other, the theoretical development often draws on both types of causal questions. Consider again the EO–performance relationship. Does a firm perform better as a result of its entrepreneurial behaviors (Anderson & Eshima, 2013); or does its prior performance cause the firm to pursue future entrepreneurial behaviors (Eshima & Anderson, 2017)? The answer is likely to be both, with multiple intervening mechanisms unfolding over time and interacting with countless contextual factors that change the nature and shape of the EO–performance connection (Covin & Wales, 2019). That we cannot easily tease out which comes first—a classic chicken and egg dilemma—diminishes our ability to make a causal claim, but does not diminish the value of high-quality EO research. While much strategic entrepreneurship research yields associational claims, these associations provide the foundation for further, more rigorous, associational work that aims toward the ultimate objective of predictive modeling.

The challenge for strategic entrepreneurship researchers is to adopt research designs that improve our ability to answer reverse causal questions, and ideally, forward causal questions. The aim is not perfection, nor is it reasonable for any one study to provide an ideal way in which to evaluate a causal claim. Rather, the aim is to approach a research question with an eye toward eliminating implausible predictors while beginning to isolate potential causal factors that warrant additional scrutiny. This systematic approach shifts the conversation from the contribution of a single study to the contribution of a research stream, such that over time and across multiple replications, a body of research emerges that while not proving an unequivocal causal association gives researchers, managers, and policy-makers confidence in a causal prediction. However, improving our ability to conduct useful research that maximizes inference requires strategic entrepreneurship scholars to address several specific challenges inherent to our field.

ENDOGENEITY AS AN INHERENT PROBLEM

The two causal questions discussed previously described a general omitted variable problem; there is some factor, z, that provides either an alternate explanation or confounds the observed effect (Antonakis et al., 2010). The omitted variable problem bedevils all social science research, and solutions abound to deal with its influence (Angrist & Pischke, 2008). What I would like to address here are three specific factors common to strategic entrepreneurship research that are also a source of endogeneity. Individually, these factors manifest in analogous ways in psychology, sociology, economics, epidemiology, and related fields, and so are not unique. What is challenging for strategic entrepreneurship research is that in addition to the general omitted variable problem, the three factors below appear in virtually all studies in our field and at the same time.

Strategic Choice

Just as a researcher cannot exogenously manipulate a firm's strategic action, the decisions made by the firm's managers represent, to some degree, meaningful decisions about where and how the firm competes. Assuming some degree of economic rationality, these decisions represent management's view of the firm and its markets, and the way in which the firm positions itself to be successful (Rocha et al., 2018). Informing these decisions are forward-looking opinions and retrospective analyses; how managers interpret what has happened and what they perceive may happen in the future influences strategic choice (Rocha et al., 2018). This is not a novel conceptualization of strategic decision-making—it is commonsensical and an accurate depiction of strategy making in practice. The challenge for the researcher, however, is that the strategic choice itself as a discrete variable is not independent of the organizational factors occurring before it, nor the expectation of the organizational outcomes stemming from it.

The lack of independence between an entrepreneurial strategic choice and, for example, organizational culture as antecedent or organizational performance as consequence, creates an endogeneity condition in a statistical model (Semadeni et al., 2014). It would not be possible to capture all possible antecedent relationships informing a strategic choice, nor would it be practical to separate the performance expectation of an entrepreneurial behavior from the performance outcome. As such, for most strategic entrepreneurship constructs involving some type of behavior, action, investment, or related choice, these constructs will *always* be endogenous to a performance outcome (Shaver, 1998). Similarly, in models with strategic entrepreneurship constructs as outcome variables, predictors are also likely to be endogenous. For example, the firm manipulates, at least in part, its level of slack resources to enable or constrain innovation activities. Thus, strategic choice as an endogeneity problem is a trait of strategic entrepreneurship research, and not an exceptional case.

Selection Effects

The preceding discussion represents one form of selection effects—self-selection into the treatment condition (Clougherty, Duso, & Muck, 2016). An analogous problem in psychology would be a study participant making the decision as to which condition—treatment or control—to join in an experiment, with the concern being that there may be an unobserved factor leading the participant to choose his or her condition. In strategic entrepreneurship research, we deal with self-selection and we deal with multiple forms of equally pernicious sample selection effects. The first sample selection problem is the problem of the unobservable firm. We are generally only able to observe the firms that self-selected into some type of strategic entrepreneurial behavior or activity; we do not observe those firms who considered pursuing an entrepreneurial strategic behavior but then did not do so for some reason; nor are we often able to observe the entire range of strategic behaviors adopted by the firm over its history.

The unobservable firm problem is substantial for many popular constructs in our field. Take domain redefinition, for example, which involves a firm making minor to substantial changes in its business model as it develops (Covin & Miles, 1999). To model the effect of a domain redefinition on performance, we must first observe a firm that undertakes such a change. Leaving aside the problem of measuring domain redefinition accurately, what we would not observe are similar firms with similar business models that did not change, potentially biasing upward any estimated effect of domain redefinition on a performance outcome.

A closely related unobservable firm problem is the prevalence of strategic entrepreneurship constructs that rarely occur. Consider strategic renewal, a firm's ability to change the basis of its competition (Covin & Miles, 1999). Strategic renewal involves the fundamental reshaping of much of the firm's business—what emerges after the process is a firm that engages with its market in a very different way. Microsoft provides an illustrative example. At founding, Microsoft's dominant business involved software sold predominantly on individual computers. Later, its predominant business changed to client server products for the enterprise market, and today Microsoft is changing again to a predominantly cloud-based software-as-a-service model. While subjective, it is reasonable to argue that Microsoft pursued strategic renewal only three times during the company's 40-year history. The unobservable challenge is the difficulty in building a causal model of a high-impact, but low-frequency event, where there is little between-firm variance (Certo, Withers, & Semadeni, 2017), and there is ambiguity about the construct itself and when and how to measure that construct.

The second sample selection problem is the well-known survival bias problem (Clougherty et al., 2016); we do not observe firms that pursued an entrepreneurial strategy but that failed or otherwise ceased being observable. Survivor bias creates two endogeneity problems. The first problem is to upwardly bias the observed estimate of the effect of the strategic choice on a performance outcome. For example, despite EO associating with a higher probability of failure (Wiklund & Shepherd, 2011), an analysis estimating the relationship between EO and performance absent firms that failed would overestimate the effect, because both the level of EO and the level of performance is likely to be higher among surviving firms (Wiklund & Shepherd, 2011). The second problem with survivor bias is a false positive error. Because we do not observe the value of a focal variable among failed firms, we may incorrectly conclude that the focal variable caused the performance outcome. For example, if there is an equivalent probability of a firm failing or being successful for an equivalent level of EO, then there is some other factor—or interaction of factors—causing the performance variation.

Measurement Error

A particularly problematic endogeneity problem for strategic entrepreneurship research involves measurement error. Our field makes heavy use of latent constructs and proxy variables (Boyd, Bergh, Ireland, & Ketchen, 2013). Further, strategic entrepreneurship researchers often utilize multidimensional or multilevel constructs (Wright & Hitt, 2017). Measurement error is inherent to both types of variables, and as such warrants specific attention. Antonakis et al. (2010) provide a detailed explanation for how measurement error manifests as endogeneity, and I refer interested readers there for a discussion. Here, I am focusing on the conceptual problem with measurement error as it relates to building a causal model.

In thinking through measurement error's impact on causal inference, we must draw a distinction between whether the focal construct is the outcome or the predictor. In the case of the former, measurement error does not directly influence model efficacy (Cohen, Cohen, West, & Aiken, 2003). Measurement error in an outcome variable manifests as unexplained variance; a portion of the variance in the outcome unaccounted for by the model (Bollen, 1989). In the case of simple linear regression, measurement error in the outcome lowers model R^2, but does not affect our ability to recover a consistent parameter estimate. However, if the predictor contains measurement error, this represents a substantive challenge to causal inference.

While Antonakis et al. (2010) provide a mathematical basis for measurement error as an endogeneity problem, we can use a conceptual example to illustrate the same point. Imagine investigating the causal effect of a risk-tolerant culture on a firm's patent activity. As a latent construct, there is an inherent difference between how we conceptualize a risk-tolerant culture and the firm's actual, underlying culture (Jarvis, MacKenzie, & Podsakoff, 2003). This is true for all latent—unobservable— constructs; because we cannot directly observe and measure the construct, we must assume a degree of incongruence between the conceptual space defined by the researcher and the actual phenomenon we intended to study. As such, before we decide how to measure risk-tolerant culture, we already introduced unobservable error—what we eventually measure will not be exactly what we intend to measure, even if we have highly reliable indicators (Podsakoff, MacKenzie, & Podsakoff, 2016). While programs such as latent variable structural equation modeling can model some type of residual measurement error directly, we cannot model unobservable measurement error that exists at a conceptual level (Bollen, 1989). This type of measurement error thus represents a threat to causal inference—was the observed effect because of a true underlying connection between the latent construct and outcome, or was it an artifact of a faulty conceptualization?

A similar problem extends to the use of proxy variables researchers employ in place of directly observable indicators (Boyd et al., 2013). A common example is R&D expenses, which proxies for a host of strategic entrepreneurship phenomena. A causal hypothesis that increasing innovativeness increases firm sales growth rate, but modeled with R&D expenses as a proxy for innovativeness, does not actually test our hypothesis. The model simply estimates an effect (with error) of R&D on sales growth rate, and we cannot make any causal claim for innovativeness on performance.

The myriad ways in which endogeneity enters empirical strategic entrepreneurship research suggests that any given model is more likely to be wrong in some way—the material question being just how wrong, and whether we can draw any useful insights from the model despite its limitations. I do not mean to dissuade researchers, nor to condemn strategic entrepreneurship research. Rather, my point is that it is difficult to design strategic entrepreneurship studies that maximize causal inference, and they require careful attention to the variety of causal inference threats and the bias they create. It also means, as I will discuss in the next section, that in practice there are no "silver bullets" that solve all causal inference problems in a single study.

LIMITATIONS OF COMMON ENDOGENEITY REMEDIES

Regression discontinuity, difference-in-differences, synthetic control methods, and natural experiments provide viable methods to address endogeneity and improve causal inference with observational data (Morgan & Winship, 2014). But, these methods also depend on a strong assumption—that the observable variables standing in for random assignment to the treatment condition capture the entirety of the observed and unobserved variance outside of the focal relationship of interest (Angrist & Pischke, 2008). That is, conditioning on these observable variable(s) allows the researcher to account for all sources of unobservable heterogeneity in assignment to a treatment condition (Angrist & Pischke, 2008). The treatment condition verbiage ties these methodologies to research designs meant to mimic a laboratory condition. For example, Abadie, Diamond, and Hainmueller (2010) employed a synthetic control method to investigate the effect of anti-smoking legislation on cigarette consumption. The treatment in this case is the binary case of a state adopting anti-smoking legislation versus a control condition being a state that did not.

The above designs provide robust inference under specific assumptions, but struggle when the causal variable under study does not easily resemble a binary treatment condition. Consider the previous example of a risk-tolerant culture. While possible to conceive of this construct as dichotomous—a firm either has it or it does not—it makes more sense to conceive of a culture variable along a continuum ranging from low to high. In this case, under a classic experimental design, each discrete "level" of the continuum becomes its own treatment condition, for example, 2 mg of a drug versus 3 mg versus 4 mg and so forth. As such, the notion of a treatment effect of culture has limited usefulness. In this case, researchers often turn to the workhorse of econometrics, the IV.

Instrument Variable Approaches

For detailed expositions of IVs, assumptions, and mathematical proofs, I refer readers to excellent existing work (Angrist & Pischke, 2008; Morgan & Winship, 2014). The management literature also provides excellent analyses of IV methods and applicability to business research (Antonakis et al., 2010; Semadeni et al., 2014). Rather than expand on these comprehensive resources, I will discuss IVs in mostly conceptual terms, borrowing from Pearl's (2009) non-parametric approach. The key point is not to understand the mathematics behind IVs, but rather the theoretical assumptions underpinning their usefulness—and their limitations—for strategic entrepreneurship researchers.

Before discussing IVs, it is helpful to briefly revisit how endogeneity will bias model estimates. In a statistical model, endogeneity biases a model when a portion of a predictor's variance covaries with the estimator's disturbance term. Figure 11.1 provides a graphical depiction of how endogeneity enters a model (Anderson, 2018). Panel 1 depicts a simple causal model, with one predictor, x, and one outcome, y. What is absent is what is noticeable about Panel 1. There are no other predictors depicted, and the specification of Cov = 0 between x and the disturbance term for y equals 0. In this case, while there is likely unexplained variance in y not explained by x, this variance does nor correlate with x, so we say that x is exogenous with respect to y. In Panel 2, we depict a different model with another predictor, z, that also covaries with x. This is our "true" model, in the sense that both x and z meaningfully relate to y, and to each other. The latter point is critical to our endogeneity problem—for endogeneity to enter a model, z must covary with x, if it does not, omitting z from the model simply results in unexplained variance in y (Angrist & Pischke, 2008).

Panel 3 in Figure 11.1 depicts endogeneity in action, by showing a dotted line between z and y. If we omit z from our model, because of z's covariance with x,

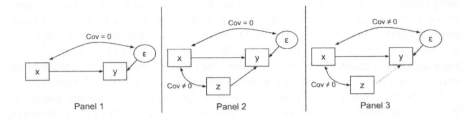

Figure 11.1   How endogeneity enters a model

a portion of the variance in the disturbance term ε necessarily covaries with x (Antonakis et al., 2010). Notably, endogeneity has nothing to do with sample size or statistical power, nor anything to do with standard errors or consistency of statistical inference (Semadeni et al., 2014). Omitting z from a model, should z represent unmodeled strategic choice, selection effects, measurement error, or some other threat to causal inference the statistical estimator—be it least squares, maximum likelihood, Bayesian, or other—renders a biased estimate of the effect of x on y.

Figure 11.2 provides a graphical depiction of how an IV addresses endogeneity. I depict the true model in Panel 1, with both x and z predicting y, and a non-zero covariance between x and z. In Panel 2, we omit z, but include our instrument, I as a predictor of x. IVs work by inducing change in x that exists independent from variance in z. The resulting variance in x does not covary with z, i exogenously varied x with respect to z.

Graphically, it is easy to see the paths between I to x to y as a causal chain, with x representing the mechanism through which variance in the instrument induces variance in the outcome (Pearl, 2018b). Notably, this is a *fully mediated* model, in the sense that x is the sole mechanism through which I relates to y —this is the logic behind the oft-repeated admonition that an instrument should relate strongly to x, but should not relate in any way to y except through its causal effect on x (Antonakis et

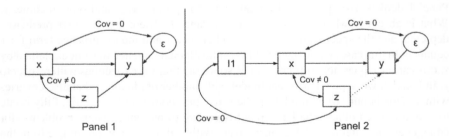

Figure 11.2   The instrument variable estimation process

al., 2010). This assumption also implies that I must not have any relationship with z; if I covaries with z, then variance in x stemming from I would necessarily incorporate unobserved variance z, and endogeneity remains. Thus we have the two key assumptions underlying all IV methodologies—instruments must strongly predict x, and instruments must have no relationship at all (i.e., Cov = 0) with the unknown and unmodeled confounding factors, z. It is these two assumptions that make IV methodologies exceptionally challenging for strategic entrepreneurship researchers.

Finding the "Ideal" Instrument

Consider EO for example, which has multiple conceptual definitions and measurement models (Covin & Wales, 2019). Depending on the choice of EO conceptualization, a researcher may construe EO as representing a set of behaviors that capture observable manifestations of a firm's entrepreneurial activities (Covin & Slevin, 1991), or a managing philosophy or gestalt representing a firm's strategic orientation towards acting entrepreneurially (Lumpkin & Dess, 1996), or a combination of strategic behaviors and managerial attitudes (Anderson et al., 2015), or another perspective altogether (Covin & Wales, 2012). There is not one clear, or superior choice when modeling a causal effect of EO on a performance outcome. The issue for researchers, as with many constructs in strategic entrepreneurship research, is that solving the identification problem and identifying a valid instrument depends heavily on how the researcher defines the conceptual space of the potentially endogenous construct, and how the researcher measures that construct.

Returning to the EO example, imagine a researcher choosing the Miller (1983)/ Covin and Slevin (1991) EO conceptualization of a multidimensional construct represented as the shared variance between a firm's innovativeness, proactiveness, and risk-taking. Importantly, the researcher makes the same ontological assumptions whether he or she models EO as a first-order reflective construct or a first-order reflective/second-order reflective construct (Anderson, Kreiser, Kuratko, Hornsby, & Eshima, 2015). Because EO arises from the shared variance of three underlying dimensions, the researcher makes the assumption that any antecedent variable must relate, in the same way and in the same magnitude, to the three underlying dimensions (Anderson et al., 2015). As an instrument, this antecedent variable must rise above an associational relationship to one of causally influencing innovativeness, proactiveness, and risk-taking in the same way, at the same time, and of the same strength to be valid.

Of course, this instrument must fulfill the requirement to be exogenous to the ultimate outcome variable. Considering the common EO–performance relationship, a valid instrument must be strong enough to causally influence EO's underlying dimensions, while also relating only to firm performance through its causal impact on EO. Considering the breadth of EO's conceptual space, as with many other constructs in strategic entrepreneurship, it is an exceptional task to find an instrument strong enough to causally change EO, while also meeting the strict exclusion requirements. Further, given that weakly predictive instruments or instruments that are weakly exogenous often renders parameter estimates more biased than that caused by the original endogeneity problem, IVs have a high bar for validity, and for usefulness, in strategic entrepreneurship research.

Addressing Multiple Endogeneity Problems

The diversity and simultaneity of endogeneity problems poses a further complicating factor for IVs in strategic entrepreneurship research. As discussed previously, a given strategic entrepreneurship empirical study likely faces problems of selection effects, strategic choice, and measurement error. The "and" in the preceding is the critical consideration—recovering a causally valid estimate requires dealing effectively with all three problems, in addition to the general omitted variable of concern. To be clear, no statistical method alone facilitates drawing causal conclusions in observational research (Angrist & Pischke, 2008; Morgan & Winship, 2014). Effective use of statistical tools, together with a deep theoretical understanding of the research question, a research design optimized to maximize causal inference, and careful attention to measurement and measurement error may enable a researcher to make—although not prove—a causal claim (Gelman, 2011).

Theoretically, a strong, causal predictor, strongly exogenous to the equation's disturbance term (e.g., $Cov = 0$), effectively deals with all sources of endogeneity biasing a model (Angrist & Pischke, 2008). If the researcher finds such an instrument, and *proves* its predictive ability and its proper exclusion, the researcher can confidently claim a causal model (Morgan & Winship, 2014). The challenge is not the theory, nor the mathematics; the challenge is the practicality. In the case of a single instrument, there is no statistical way to evaluate whether the researcher properly excluded the variable, that is, to evaluate whether the instrument does not covary with the equation disturbance term (Antonakis et al., 2010). At best, the researcher justifies the exclusion restriction on theoretical grounds, supported by appropriate analyses that provide evidence—although not proof—of instrument validity (Angrist & Pischke, 2008). With the presence of two instruments per endogenous variable, statistical tools become available, although these tools require validity of both instruments for efficacy (Wooldridge, 2010). The challenge then for strategic entrepreneurship researchers is to identify not just one but two instruments, each being causally related to the focal predictor, and each being associated with the outcome only through their effect on the focal predictor to provide statistical evidence in favor of making a causal claim.

It is useful then for strategic entrepreneurship scholars to draw the distinction between the possible and the probable. It is possible to identify multiple valid instruments for various strategic entrepreneurship constructs. However, it is also not very probable. In an ideal scientific setting a researcher starts with a workflow beginning with deep theoretical understanding of a research question to designing a study, collecting and modeling data, and ultimately drawing appropriate conclusions (Anderson et al., 2019). In reality, the research process involves multiple fits and starts, with learning and refinement generated as part of a dialogue between the researcher and the data (Wennberg & Anderson, 2019). It is simply not very probable that a researcher would be able to identify multiple valid instruments early in the research design process, particularly when dealing with constructs of large conceptual domains that typify strategic entrepreneurship.

Addressing strategic entrepreneurship's multiple endogeneity requires not just careful attention to research design and measurement, but making use of emerging tools that do not necessarily rely on the strict assumptions underlying IV methods (Greenland, 2017; Westfall & Yarkoni, 2016). I am not debating the mathematical certainty of a perfect valid instrument in recovering a causal estimate. Rather, I am suggesting that it is not realistic to find multiple perfect instruments in practice. As such, to advance predictive strategic entrepreneurship theory, I am suggesting that researchers turn to new approaches that, while not without limitation, provide a useful remedy to multiple endogeneity problems in a strategic entrepreneurship study. The standard is not perfection; the standard is quantitative improvement that meaningfully advances the goal of causal modeling in strategic entrepreneurship research.

One such approach, as I turn to next, involves the use of Bayesian inference. While not a panacea, Bayesian inference and related methodologies provide several advantages over frequentist statistics, including addressing many of the limitations of IV approaches to recover causal parameter estimates. With Bayesian inference, we make use of prior information on the relationship under study in the modeling process to yield a model result that is, ideally, a better approximation of the data generation process and, under certain assumptions, a causal parameter estimate. To be clear, I am not arguing that Bayesian methodologies inherently yield a causal claim. However, given an appropriate research design, Bayesian inference offers the potential to deal with multiple endogeneity problems in a single specified model and may yield a less biased, and hence more accurate, answer to a causal question.

INTEGRATING BAYESIAN METHODOLOGIES

A Gentle Introduction to Bayesian Inference

We may represent Bayesian inference with a simple equation:

$Posterior \propto Prior \times Likelihood.$

We read the equation as the posterior estimate being in proportion to the prior, multiplied by the likelihood function. There are ample, and excellent, discussions of Bayesian statistics generally, and in management research specifically, and I refer readers to these resources for an introduction to Bayesian inference: Gelman et al., 2013; Kruschke, 2010; Kruschke, Aguinis, & Joo, 2012; Kruschke & Liddell, 2018. I will also avoid a mathematical discussion of Bayesian modeling, because for our purposes, we require only a conceptual understanding of Bayesian inference and its applicability to improve causal modeling (Feller & Gelman, 2015).

Bayesian inference is useful because it allows a researcher to combine what we know, or think we know, about a research question with data available to evaluate this question. In the null hypothesis testing framework, a researcher—whether knowingly or not—starts each study under the assumption of a true null hypothesis (Kruschke & Liddell, 2018). To illustrate, imagine planning a new study on the relationship between EO and firm performance. Ample prior literature, and multiple meta-analyses, suggest a positive, non-zero relationship between EO and performance (Covin & Wales, 2019). Yet, should we adopt null hypothesis testing and its corresponding reliance on *p*-values, we would ignore all prior literature—and likely our own better judgment—and assume no meaningful effect of EO on performance, but also that the *true* relationship is in fact zero (Cov[EO, Performance] = 0) (Gelman et al., 2013). Under the null hypothesis testing paradigm, we begin each study under the veil of ignorance.

In contrast, Bayesian inference frees us to muse, based on prior research, logic, experience, and even intuition, on the true relationship between EO and performance. Further, we can leverage that information, called the *prior*, to update our beliefs about EO and performance, called the *posterior*, by combining the prior with data at hand, called the *likelihood*. Bayesian inference is not a panacea, nor is it without substantive limitations (Kruschke, 2010). As we will see, however, the usefulness of the prior, under certain conditions, provides a degree of freedom in dealing with the multiple endogeneity concerns found in strategic entrepreneurship research.

The Critical Role of the Prior

Returning to the equation for Bayesian inference, it is easy to see that the ability of the prior to influence the posterior estimate depends on the strength of the prior relative to the data at hand (the likelihood). At its core, Bayesian inference is a simple multiplication problem. A weak (small) prior and limited data yields a weak (though not necessarily wrong) posterior estimate; a strong prior and expansive data yields a robust (though not necessarily correct) posterior estimate (Gelman et al., 2013). Interestingly, however, we can get robust posterior estimates with both a weak prior/ expansive data combination, and with a strong prior/limited data combination—as in all multiplication problems, a product of two factors will be large so long as at least one of the factors is large.

Within Bayesian inference, we find three generic categories of priors (Kruschke & Liddell, 2018). On one extreme is an uninformative prior, where we believe that the prior relationship could take on all possible values with equal probability. In our EO–performance example, an uninformative prior would assume that there would be an equivalent probability of EO's effect on performance to be zero, –10, 100, or even 1 billion, and every possible value in between. An uninformative prior does not imply that the researcher does not know what the "true" relationship is, rather the prior suggests that the true relationship can have any possible value with equal probability (Gelman et al., 2013). While we may not realize it, when we use null hypothesis testing and draw inference with *p*-values, we are actually making use of an uninformative prior (Kruschke et al., 2012).

Moving beyond uninformative priors are weakly informative priors. Empirical Bayes, naive Bayes, and other types of Bayesian inference make heavy use of weakly informative priors as a method of regularization and parameterization (Kruschke, 2014). Effectively, the researcher encodes some prior information about the parameter of interest, but mostly to help the estimator solve the complex mathematics necessary to derive a posterior estimate. In "big data" problems, machine learning settings, and other research settings involving a substantial amount of data, weakly informed priors do not much influence the posterior, but provide useful stabilization (Yarkoni & Westfall, 2017).

Moving beyond weakly informative priors are informative priors. Informative priors encode substantial information about a relationship, and depending on the strength of our beliefs, remain resistant to change in the face of even large amounts of data (Kruschke & Liddell, 2018). An example is helpful here. It is possible that when flipping a fair coin, the coin physically lands vertically, on its narrow edge. The result of this flip is neither heads nor tails. But while possible, the likelihood of this happening, even if we flipped the coin millions of times, is so remote that we do not even account for the possibility, and say that there is a 50 percent chance that a fair coin lands on heads (or tails). Further, if we flipped the coin millions of times, and happened to observe the coin landing vertically, it likely happened so few times that we would safely assume the occurrence of the vertical landing happens as a trivial fluke. That is, even in the face of a very large amount of data, we are not likely to waiver from our belief in a 50/50 chance in the outcome of a coin flip.

Strong, informative priors require strong assumptions. A frequent, and reasonable, criticism of Bayesian inference is the reliance on priors, and the assumptions necessary to justify using more informative priors (Kruschke et al., 2012). Mathematically, weakly informed priors in even modestly sized data often yield parameter estimates very close to frequentist (e.g., least squares)/uninformative prior estimates (Gelman et al., 2013). To influence a posterior estimate, then, in datasets of the size typically found in strategic entrepreneurship research, we require demonstrably informative priors, which require commensurate justification. It is not simply enough to say that we believe, for example, EO to have a positive impact on performance. We must go deeper to understand both conceptually and empirically what we believe to be true about the underlying relationship between a predictor and outcome. In the case of using an informative prior to address endogeneity, it also requires us to reason and to quantify how different sources of endogeneity will impact a relationship, and how those factors may interact to bias a model estimate.

How an Informative Prior Addresses Multiple Endogeneity Problems

This chapter contends that it is highly probable that a given observational strategic entrepreneurship study contains the three sources of endogeneity mentioned previously—strategic choice, selection effects, and measurement error. The challenge when using an informative prior to address these problems is understanding the magnitude, direction, and compounding effect of all three. Addressing this challenge necessarily involves making a guess and quantifying the size of the bias each problem has on the parameter of interest.

The simplest way to approach quantification is to start with a realistic estimate for the "true" effect under study, and to use a standardized metric (e.g., z score, correlation coefficient, standard deviation, and so forth) for comparability. Prior literature is the most useful resource here, along with judgment and critically considering the likelihood of the effect. For example, meta-analyses of the EO–performance relationship suggest that EO and performance share roughly 5 percent of their variance ($r \cong .2$) (Rauch, Wiklund, Lumpkin, & Frese, 2009; Rosenbusch, Rauch, & Bausch, 2013). Importantly, the constituent studies in these meta-analyses do not address endogeneity problems, except for measurement error in a small number of cases. As such, it is reasonable to assume some degree of bias in the existing literature, and this would be the case for most strategic entrepreneurship research (Anderson et al., 2019). Unlike with the null hypothesis testing framework, however, we may start from the assumption of a non-zero relationship in the focal relationship (Kruschke, 2010).

Directionality of the endogeneity problem is, fortunately, somewhat straightforward for dealing with strategic choice and with selection effects. I stress here that this is an assumption, but a conservative approach would be to argue that both strategic choice and selection effects are likely to upwardly bias an expected parameter. In the case of strategic choice, firms generally undertake strategic moves with the *a priori* expectation that such a decision will improve its competitive position, and thereby its performance (Rocha et al., 2018). Even in the case where a specific strategic choice results in a performance decline, presumably, the firm undertakes a new choice to address the shortcoming. As such, over time, it is reasonable to expect strategic choice to exhibit a positive bias on most strategic entrepreneurship relationships with performance as an outcome variable (Rocha et al., 2018). Similarly, we may safely assume selection effects in the strategic entrepreneurship literature positively bias most focal relationships. The underlying issue, as discussed previously, is that researchers generally observe only surviving firms (Wiklund & Shepherd, 2011).

Measurement error presents more complications, in terms of directionality and magnitude, because in a multivariate context, measurement error attenuates or accentuates parameter estimates depending on the covariances among the predictor variables (Bollen, 1989; Cohen et al., 2003). In the univariate case, measurement error attenuates the parameter, resulting in a negative bias (Cohen et al., 2003), but rarely would we expect a univariate model in an observational strategic entrepreneurship study. As such, the researcher will need to use his or her best judgment in deciding about the nature of the bias. A conservative assumption would be accentuation, in the sense that measurement error would make an expected positive relationship more positive, and an expected negative relationship more negative (Loken & Gelman, 2017).

Collectively, then, assuming all three endogeneity problems bias a parameter in the same direction, we can further assume that the problems pool into a single omitted variable problem, exhibiting a cumulative upward bias on the model (Angrist & Pischke, 2008; Rocha et al., 2018). This assumption, consistent with general identification strategy using an IV methodology (Pearl, 2009), allows us to consider a single informative prior as a mechanism to address the likelihood of parameter accentuation. The logic is similar to LASSO or Regularized Least Squares methodologies in machine learning applications (Hainmueller & Hazlett, 2014), where the researcher adopts a general approach towards regularization, by employing a methodology to force the model parameter downwards. As I show in the illustration, while quantifying the magnitude of the bias remains challenging, the method represents a general, and approachable, way to address multiple endogeneity concerns that does not rely on an exogenous source of variation.

Limitations of the Methodology

I do not mean to suggest that using an informative prior to address endogeneity in a Bayesian analytical framework solves the underlying problem of improving causal inference in strategic entrepreneurship research. Making effective use of a strong prior requires deep conceptual understanding of the phenomenon under study. This is not a method that lends itself to a quick publication cycle, and is likely appropriate in those cases where the researcher has been working in the field and with the research question for some time, and has a familiarity with the literature to evaluate the strengths and weaknesses of existing findings. Further, the method requires understanding, and being able to reasonably quantify, the sources of endogeneity impacting a model. Some of these endogeneity problems may be easier to resolve with alternate means or methods. For example, in the case of measurement error in a latent variable model, a researcher may employ Bayesian structural equation modeling to directly model measurement error at the indicator level, while layering an informative prior to address other endogeneity concerns at the structural level (Smid, McNeish, Miočević, & van de Schoot, 2019).

Further, the method will require multiple simulations and applications to understand its usefulness in more complicated endogeneity problems. For example, it is unclear how to apply the method in a moderation model. It is exceptionally challenging to model interaction effects in the presence of endogenous variables (Antonakis et al., 2010; Wooldridge, 2010). The specific challenge is the instability of the direction and magnitude of bias as multiple sources of endogeneity themselves interact (Bun & Harrison, 2018). Depending on the method employed, mediation models may be easier to tackle, in the sense that if the researcher directly measures each path (e.g., using structural equation modeling), and he or she may construct an informative prior for each possible path, although that requires an understanding of how endogeneity biases the causal path in the model (Rohrer, 2018). Lastly, the growing use of panel data provides its own challenges to causal inference, although combining approaches such as hybrid models with strong priors may be an effective combination for dealing with endogeneity in multilevel models (Feller & Gelman, 2015; McNeish & Kelley, 2018).

Illustration

It is fortunately straightforward to implement an informative prior in cross-sectional data, in limited dependent variable models, in multilevel models, and with latent variable structural equation modeling. That said, while easy to implement, the methodology requires careful attention to model specification, the distribution of the prior, and recognizing that the larger the number of observations, the stronger the prior. I recommend Kruschke (2014) and Gelman et al. (2013) as excellent resources for thinking through specification of Bayesian models, including tutorials of common Bayesian software. For the purposes of this chapter, I will illustrate a simple linear model, common to those found in the strategic entrepreneurship literature. I provide the code for the illustration in the Appendix.

Data generation process

I simulated a cross-sectional, observational dataset with 1,000 observations; similar in structure to a survey-based design with responses by a single-informed respondent. All variables are continuous and normally distributed for simplicity. I included one focal predictor, x, and two control variables to illustrate a multiple regression model. I set the true effect of x on the outcome, y, at 0.25, and the effect of control 1 at 0.1 and control 2 at 0.2. I included z to represent a general omitted variable. In this case, z represents the cumulative effect of endogeneity on the model (e.g., strategic choice + selection effects + measurement error). I set the covariance between z and x and between z and y to 0.4, which suggests a somewhat large endogeneity problem on the model. I simulated all data in R with the simulateData function in the lavaan package, which incorporates a random disturbance term with distribution $N(0,1)$ (Rosseel, 2012).

Importantly, in this illustration I am assuming that there is an underlying effect between x and y—the endogeneity problem in the model should, therefore, accentuate the effect between x and y. As we move to building predictive theory, there is a corresponding necessity to go beyond directional hypotheses to greater specificity in effect sizes (Gelman, 2018). To put it another way, if the purpose of a study is associational only, and the model is well established in the prior literature (i.e., less of a concern of a true omitted causal variable), then endogeneity biasing upward a parameter estimate that is already of sufficient magnitude and in the expected direction may not be particularly concerning. If, however, the intention is to build a predictive model and test a causal hypothesis such that the researcher wants to understand how much of a change in y stems from incremental changes in x, then even modest endogeneity becomes a significant concern (Ketokivi & McIntosh, 2017).

Table 11.1   *Regression models*

Coefficient	True model		Naive model	
	Est.	CI (95%)	Est.	CI (95%)
Intercept	−0.01	−0.08–0.05	−0.00	−0.07–0.06
x	0.25	0.19–0.32	0.38	0.31–0.44
z	0.37	0.30–0.44		
Control 1	0.13	0.06–0.19	0.12	0.05–0.19
Control 2	0.29	0.23–0.35	0.28	0.22–0.35
Observations	1000		1000	
R^2	0.266		0.184	

I show the modeling results in Table 11.1. The true model includes both x and z, and the model correctly recovers a 0.25 estimate for x and a 0.37 estimate for z. The naive model omits z, and we see the impact of endogeneity—the estimate for x increases 52 percent to 0.38, and the confidence interval suggests a parameter as high as 0.44, 75 percent larger than the true estimate.

Bayesian specification
I estimated the naive model—omitting z—with a Bayesian linear model. I used the rstanarm package for R (Goodrich, Gabry, Ali, & Brilleman, 2018), although any software capable of estimating the Bayesian model will yield similar results (e.g., Stata, SAS, Python, and so forth). A defining feature of Bayesian modeling is the ability to set a prior specification for each estimated parameter in the model. In the case of our multiple regression model, $y = \alpha + \beta x + \beta c1 + \beta c2 + \varepsilon$, we may specify different priors for the intercept and for each coefficient estimate. A key consideration is the use of conjugate priors, wherein the distribution used for the prior is the same as the distribution expected for the resulting parameter (Gelman et al., 2013). In this case, I expect the parameter estimates to follow a normal distribution, and so choose a normal (Gaussian) distribution for the prior.

I show the results of two Bayesian models in Table 11.2. In the first model, I use a weakly informed prior, with mean 0 and standard deviation 10. Recall that the "true" effect of x on y is 0.25. This distribution centers the mean of the prior around 0, but allows for extremely large values of βx—well outside what we would expect in practice. As discussed previously, weakly informed priors are helpful for parameterization and regularization, and can be perfectly appropriate for modeling (Gelman & Carlin, 2014; Gelman et al., 2013). That said, a weakly informative prior is simply that—only marginally, if at all, expected to influence the posterior estimate. As seen in Table 11.2, the weakly informative prior yields a parameter estimate (median posterior estimate) roughly identical to the naive least squares model. This is a critical point—while Bayesian estimation provides several benefits over frequentist methods, it is still subject to endogeneity problems and other threats to consistency.

For the informative prior model, I kept weakly informed priors for the control variable and intercept parameters, but a much stronger prior for βx: mean 0.15, and

Table 11.2   Bayesian models

	Weak prior		Informative prior	
Coefficient	Est.	CI (95%)	Est.	CI (95%)
Intercept	−0.00	−0.07–0.07	−0.01	−0.07–0.06
x	0.38	0.32–0.44	0.23	0.19–0.27
Control 1	0.12	0.05–0.18	0.13	0.06–0.20
Control 2	0.28	0.22–0.35	0.29	0.22–0.36
Observations	1000		1000	
R^2 Bayes	0.186		0.124	

standard deviation 0.025. I selected 0.15 as a way to penalize the current literature—if the existing literature suggests, for example, an expected effect of 0.25, but that literature generally does not feature an endogeneity correction, then it may be appropriate to center the mean of the prior below that of the prior literature. Note that the mean of the prior is not 0. For a similar reason as the penalization, if there is little reason to expect the estimated parameter to be 0 or to take on a value below 0, then there is a reasonable argument for setting the mean above 0. I set the standard deviation to center most of the distribution around the mean, in this case, 0.025. This suggests a small probability of the posterior estimate to be more than .1 (four standard deviations) away from the mean, but as with all distributions allows for extreme values.

The choice of variance of the prior is a function of the level of specificity desired in the posterior, the researcher's understanding of the phenomena under study, and the number of sample observations. This is where the proportionality inherent to Bayesian estimation becomes central. The greater the amount of data used to estimate the likelihood function, the tighter the variance necessary in the prior to meaningfully influence the posterior (Kruschke & Liddell, 2018). There is, then, an inherent subjectivity to specifying the prior (Kruschke et al., 2012). As I will discuss, simulation and Bayesian stacking offer one way to evaluate the model and probe the prior specification. As shown in Table 11.2, the informative prior recovers a median posterior parameter estimate very close to the true value, 0.23, with a 95 percent credibility interval (the Bayesian alternative to a confidence interval) that includes the true effect size.

Using informative priors in practice
There are several important considerations for making use of informative priors, but I wish to highlight three specifically. The first is the importance of model checking (Gabry, Simpson, Vehtari, Betancourt, & Gelman, 2017). As with all model specifications, the researcher should be making use of post-specification tools to evaluate the model. In the case of Bayesian inference, that would include visualizations of the posterior distribution, evaluating convergence problems, and making out of sample predictions, among others (Gabry et al., 2017; Gelman et al., 2013). The second consideration is making use of multiple models and investigating multiple prior spec-

ifications. Bayesian model stacking, wherein a researcher evaluates multiple models and estimates a multilevel model to probe the variance across specifications, represents one, very useful, approach to estimate multiple models with varying informative prior specifications (Yao, Vehtari, Simpson, & Gelman, 2018). The intent would be to show how different prior specifications influence the model, while also estimating a single multilevel model to incorporate those differences into a single estimate (Yao et al., 2018). The final consideration is the concern over researcher degrees of freedom. While multiple comparisons are not necessarily a problem in Bayesian modeling, other choices made by the researcher in the design and analysis process may influence model results (Anderson et al., 2019; Gelman, Hill, & Yajima, 2012). As such, sharing data and code when using this method provides added transparency and the ability of other researchers to better understand the model and data generation process.

DISCUSSION AND CONSIDERATIONS FOR RESEARCHERS

There is a legitimate question as to whether strategic entrepreneurship progresses better with greater attention to theory construction, measurement, and exploratory analyses meant to uncover new patterns and new insights (Wennberg & Anderson, 2019). From this perspective, causal modeling and identification of causal effects is less important than developing new theoretical models, supported by appropriate empirics, that continue pushing the field forward (Bettis, Gambardella, Helfat, & Mitchell, 2014). We may argue that the success of the strategic entrepreneurship field owes much to the focus on identifying interesting and useful research questions, and the standard for research to make a novel contribution to the strategic entrepreneurship conversation as a condition for publication. As Anderson et al. (2019) noted, the desire to improve our empirics should not come at the expense of asking interesting and useful questions.

Another perspective is that research that is not empirically rigorous has little, if any, usefulness (Antonakis, 2017). Indeed, poorly conducted research, even if well intended, may do more harm than good to a field and to practice (Gelman, 2018). In this chapter, I argue a more nuanced perspective. Not all empirical work must address all forms of endogeneity and adhere to strict requirements for causal identification. Such a standard would likely stymie strategic entrepreneurship research and stultify our ability to inform practice with theory and empirical models. The field has much to gain from exploratory research that uncovers new insights and pushes theoretical boundaries (Wennberg & Anderson, 2019). Further, strict and conceptual replications of prior work, even in cases where the prior research may have been methodologically limited, is a key part of building cumulative knowledge (Bettis et al., 2016).

This chapter applies to another category of research—equally important to replications and exploratory analyses—and that concerns research explicitly meant to test theory and to derive predictable insights. This type of research, critical to building predictive theory, must be very rigorous, must address endogeneity, and must do so with special care and attention paid to threats to causal inference in a research design. Anderson et al. (2019) offer several best practices and practices to avoid in pursuing this type of research, and I do not expand on these here. I do wish to highlight, however, considerations for strategic entrepreneurship researchers and best practice recommendations to address those considerations.

Clarifying the Purpose of a Study

The first step in thinking through the challenges to causal estimation is to decide whether the study even needs to tackle a causal question to be useful. For example, research on the value of corporate venturing to the parent and to the venture entails numerous, and quite complicated, endogeneity threats (Dushnitsky & Lenox, 2006; Titus & Anderson, 2018). Truly establishing a causal effect of venturing activity on parent financial performance is a monumental challenge, and not one easily solved. That a substantial challenge to causal inference exists does not, however, mean that scholars should abandon corporate venturing research. Rather, it means that the nature of the research question and the phenomena under study limits the ability to make a causal claim, potentially to the point that causal inference is simply not realistic. As such, it may be inappropriate in these cases to demand sophisticated methodologies that may be more likely to exacerbate an endogeneity problem than solve the problem (Semadeni et al., 2014).

For the same reason, however, researchers must approach challenging endogeneity problems with humility, recognizing the inherent limitations of his or her ability to build a causal model. Just as reviewers may wish to avoid rigid standards for identification in situations where it is not feasible to adequately address the endogeneity problem, so too should researchers avoid sweeping claims and policy recommendations based on limited empirical evidence. If the researcher desires to build and test predictive theory, then higher standards apply from the outset (Pearl, 2009).

The Importance of Thinking Deeply

Finding a solution to multiple endogeneity problems requires thinking deeply about the research question, the data generation process, measures and measurement error, and how endogeneity enters a model (Angrist & Pischke, 2008). It is not enough to acknowledge endogeneity's presence—we know it exists for any study with an observational design. The material question for researchers is the source of the endogeneity problems impacting a study. This also requires deep conceptual knowledge of the research question (Anderson et al., 2019). For strategic entrepreneurship researchers, because of the complexity of our field, the diversity of predictor and outcome variables, and the shear breadth of the field's scope, it would be difficult to quickly engage with an observational study and derive a simple endogeneity "fix." Further, addressing threats to causal inference must occur before the researcher collects data. These considerations necessarily imply a longer runway for designing and collecting data for a study meant to build predictive theory.

Quantifying Bias and Uncertainty

Related to the preceding point is the necessity to quantify the sources of endogeneity and how they likely impact model parameters, which is not a trivial task. An analogy is helpful here. Under the null hypothesis testing framework, a researcher offering a hypothesis that x positively relates to y finds support for rejecting the null hypothesis whether the coefficient estimate is .001, or 100, or 1,000. Strictly speaking the magnitude does not matter, only the direction (Kruschke et al., 2012). Deriving a solution to the endogeneity problems in a model, particularly if the researcher desires to use an informative prior, requires making an informed guess at the magnitude of the problem. The researcher needs to have some notion of just how much a model parameter is likely to change depending on the level of endogeneity expected.

One overlooked approach in our field to begin quantifying potential endogeneity problems is to use simulations (Gelman et al., 2013; Imai, Keele, & Tingley, 2010). Not dissimilar to the approach used in this chapter, before collecting data the researcher conducts a series of simulations based on expected "true" parameters with different sources of endogeneity modeled at different values. The idea is to derive a range of plausible values where specific endogeneity problems are likely to materially influence model results and interpretation. The material influence standard is, however, very specific to the research question at hand, and the level of specificity the researcher desires.

For example, imagine evaluating whether the presence of a corporate venturing program results in a higher probability of forming future strategic alliances. Depending on the level of precision desired for the resulting probability, we might be concerned about how much endogeneity is biasing the result. If the desired prediction accuracy is low, and a wide uncertainty interval appropriate, say a 75 percent probability +/– 20 percent, then the amount of endogeneity bias necessary to influence this prediction parameter would likely be quite high. That is, there would likely need to be significant endogeneity bias to meaningfully influence the model result. Conversely, if the desired prediction accuracy is high, say a 75 percent probability +/– 3 percent, then it may not take much in the way of endogeneity bias to impact the model. A simulation can help, although only help, with exploring the sensitivity of the model to varying degrees of endogeneity.

Recognizing the Limitations of Empirical Approaches

Lastly, it is critically important for strategic entrepreneurship scholars to recognize that there is no methodological panacea for recovering causal effects in observational data (Pearl, 2009). Under the best of conditions—research design, high-quality measurement, and dealing with omitted variables—researchers *may* get close to identifying a causal effect (Angrist & Pischke, 2008). For example, while theoretically possible to include all possible covariates, the inability to do so requires researchers to integrate observable covariates with more robust methods to deal with endogeneity problems. Unequivocal causal estimation and prediction is therefore neither an appropriate, nor realistic standard for observational research. The informative prior approach described in this chapter, as with IV methods, difference-in-differences, propensity score matching, and other tools depends on assumptions that may not be appropriate for a given research question and design. The challenge for researchers is to understand those limitations and those assumptions, and to critically evaluate their validity and applicability. That is, the applicability of the method depends on the research design, measurement approach, and the nature of the endogeneity problem for a given study.

CONCLUSION

It is easy to build predictive theory; it is also inordinately difficult to provide empirical support for those predictions. For many strategic entrepreneurship questions, the usefulness of the answer depends on its applicability to practice, which often involves being able to make a prediction about a future outcome based on our causal understanding of a phenomenon. Unless specifically planning an exploratory study, it may be helpful to think about building a causal model as a default research design; each study begins with the goal of recovering a causal estimate. This perspective necessarily involves thinking through endogeneity and identification problems at the very beginning of the research design process. My hope is that this chapter facilitates that conversation, and if appropriate, the informative prior methodology provides another tool in the toolkit for strategic entrepreneurship researchers.

REFERENCES

Abadie, A., Diamond, A., & Hainmueller, J. 2010. Synthetic control methods for comparative case studies: Estimating the effect of California's tobacco control program. *Journal of the American Statistical Association*, 105(490): 493–505.
Anderson, B. S. 2018. *Endogeneity and entrepreneurship research*. Open Science Framework. https://doi.org/10.17605/OSF.IO/75TN8.
Anderson, B. S., Covin, J. G., & Slevin, D. P. 2009. Understanding the relationship between entrepreneurial orientation and strategic learning capability: An empirical investigation. *Strategic Entrepreneurship Journal*, 3(3): 218–240.
Anderson, B. S., & Eshima, Y. 2013. The influence of firm age and intangible resources on the relationship between entrepreneurial orientation and firm growth among Japanese SMEs. *Journal of Business Venturing*, 28(3): 413–429.
Anderson, B. S., Eshima, Y., & Hornsby, J. S. 2018. Strategic entrepreneurial behaviors: Construct and scale development. *Strategic Entrepreneurship Journal*: 1–22.
Anderson, B. S., Kreiser, P. M., Kuratko, D. F., Hornsby, J. S., & Eshima, Y. 2015. Reconceptualizing entrepreneurial orientation. *Strategic Management Journal*, 36(10): 1579–1596.
Anderson, B. S., Wennberg, K., & McMullen, J. S. 2019. Editorial: Enhancing quantitative theory-testing entrepreneurship research. *Journal of Business Venturing*, 34(5): 1–11.

Angrist, J., & Krueger, A. B. 2001. Instrumental variables and the search for identification: From supply and demand to natural experiments. *Journal of Economic Perspectives: A Journal of the American Economic Association,* 15(4): 69–85.

Angrist, J., & Pischke, J.-S. 2008. *Mostly Harmless Econometrics: An Empiricist's Companion.* Princeton, NJ: Princeton University Press.

Antonakis, J. 2017. On doing better science: From thrill of discovery to policy implications. *The Leadership Quarterly,* 28(1): 5–21.

Antonakis, J., Bendahan, S., Jacquart, P., & Lalive, R. 2010. On making causal claims: A review and recommendations. *The Leadership Quarterly,* 21(6): 1086–1120.

Bettis, R. A., Ethiraj, S., Gambardella, A., Helfat, C., & Mitchell, W. 2016. Creating repeatable cumulative knowledge in strategic management. *Strategic Management Journal,* 37(2): 257–261.

Bettis, R. A., Gambardella, A., Helfat, C., & Mitchell, W. 2014. Quantitative empirical analysis in strategic management. *Strategic Management Journal,* 35(7): 949–953.

Bollen, K. A. 1989. *Structural Equations with Latent Variables.* New York: John Wiley.

Boyd, B. K., Bergh, D. D., Ireland, R. D., & Ketchen, D. J. 2013. Constructs in strategic management. *Organizational Research Methods,* 16(1): 3–14.

Bun, M. J. G., & Harrison, T. D. 2018. OLS and IV estimation of regression models including endogenous interaction terms. *Econometric Reviews,* 38(7): 814–827.

Certo, S. T., Withers, M. C., & Semadeni, M. 2017. A tale of two effects: Using longitudinal data to compare within- and between-firm effects. *Strategic Management Journal,* 38(7): 1536–1556.

Clougherty, J. A., Duso, T., & Muck, J. 2016. Correcting for self-selection based endogeneity in management research: Review, recommendations and simulations. *Organizational Research Methods,* 19(2): 286–347.

Cohen, J., Cohen, P., West, S. G., & Aiken, L. S. 2003. *Applied Multiple Regression/ Correlation Analysis for the Behavioral Sciences.* Mahwah, NJ: Erlbaum.

Covin, J. G., & Miles, M. P. 1999. Corporate entrepreneurship and the pursuit of competitive advantage. *Entrepreneurship: Theory and Practice,* 23(3): 47–47.

Covin, J. G., & Slevin, D. P. 1989. Strategic management of small firms in hostile and benign environments. *Strategic Management Journal,* 10(1): 75–87.

Covin, J. G., & Slevin, D. P. 1991. A conceptual model of entrepreneurship as firm behavior. *Entrepreneurship Theory and Practice,* 16(1): 7–25.

Covin, J. G., & Wales, W. J. 2012. The measurement of entrepreneurial orientation. *Entrepreneurship Theory and Practice,* 36(4): 677–702.

Covin, J. G., & Wales, W. J. 2019. Crafting high-impact entrepreneurial orientation research: Some suggested guidelines. *Entrepreneurship Theory and Practice,* 43(1): 3–18.

Dushnitsky, G., & Lenox, M. J. 2006. When does corporate venture capital investment create firm value? *Journal of Business Venturing,* 21(6): 753–772.

Engelen, A., Neumann, C., & Schmidt, S. 2013. Should entrepreneurially oriented firms have narcissistic CEOs? *Journal of Management,* 42(3): 698–721.

Eshima, Y., & Anderson, B. S. 2017. Firm growth, adaptive capability, and entrepreneurial orientation. *Strategic Management Journal,* 38(3): 770–779.

Feller, A., & Gelman, A. 2015. Hierarchical models for causal effects. In R. Scott & S. Kosslyn (Eds), *Emerging Trends in the Social and Behavioral Sciences.* Chichester: Wiley.

Gabry, J., Simpson, D., Vehtari, A., Betancourt, M., & Gelman, A. 2017. Visualization in bayesian workflow. *arXiv [stat.ME],* September 5. http://arxiv.org/abs/1709.01449.

Gelman, A. 2011. Causality and statistical learning. *American Journal of Sociology,* 117(3): 955–966.

Gelman, A. 2018. Ethics in statistical practice and communication: Five recommendations. *Significance. Statistics Making Sense,* 15(5): 40–43.

Gelman, A., & Carlin, J. 2014. Beyond power calculations: Assessing Type S (Sign) and Type M (Magnitude) errors. *Perspectives on Psychological Science*, 9(6): 641–651.

Gelman, A., Carlin, J. B., Stern, H. S., Dunson, D. B., Vehtari, A. et al. 2013. *Bayesian Data Analysis*, Third Edition. Boca Raton, FL: CRC Press.

Gelman, A., Hill, J., & Yajima, M. 2012. Why we (usually) don't have to worry about multiple comparisons. *Journal of Research on Educational Effectiveness*, 5(2): 189–211.

Gelman, A., & Imbens, G. 2013. *Why ask why? Forward causal inference and reverse causal questions*. National Bureau of Economic Research, November. https://doi.org/10.3386/w19614.

Ghoshal, S. 2005. Bad management theories are destroying good management practices. *Academy of Management Learning and Education*, 4(1): 75–91.

Goodrich, B., Gabry, J., Ali, I., & Brilleman, S. 2018. rstanarm: Bayesian applied regression modeling via Stan. http://mc-stan.org/.

Greenland, S. 2017. For and against methodologies: Some perspectives on recent causal and statistical inference debates. *European Journal of Epidemiology*, 32(1): 3–20.

Hainmueller, J., & Hazlett, C. 2014. Kernel regularized least squares: Reducing misspecification bias with a flexible and interpretable machine learning approach. *Political Analysis*, 22(2): 143–168.

Imai, K., Keele, L., & Tingley, D. 2010. A general approach to causal mediation analysis. *Psychological Methods*, 15(4): 309–334.

Ireland, R. D., Covin, J. G., & Kuratko, D. F. 2009. Conceptualizing corporate entrepreneurship strategy. *Entrepreneurship Theory and Practice*, 33(1): 19–46.

Jarvis, C. B., MacKenzie, S. B., & Podsakoff, P. M. 2003. A critical review of construct indicators and measurement model misspecification in marketing and consumer research. *Journal of Consumer Research*, 30(2): 199–218.

Ketokivi, M., & McIntosh, C. N. 2017. Addressing the endogeneity dilemma in operations management research: Theoretical, empirical, and pragmatic considerations. *Journal of Operations Management*, 52(Supplement C): 1–14.

Kreiser, P. M., Marino, L. D., Dickson, P., & Weaver, K. M. 2010. Cultural influences on entrepreneurial orientation: The impact of national culture on risk taking and proactiveness in SMEs. *Entrepreneurship Theory and Practice*, 34(5): 959–983.

Kruschke, J. K. 2010. What to believe: Bayesian methods for data analysis. *Trends in Cognitive Sciences*, 14(7): 293–300.

Kruschke, J. K. 2014. *Doing Bayesian Data Analysis: A Tutorial with R, JAGS, and Stan*, Second Edition. London: Academic Press.

Kruschke, J. K., Aguinis, H., & Joo, H. 2012. The time has come: Bayesian methods for data analysis in the organizational sciences. *Organizational Research*, 15(4): 722–752.

Kruschke, J. K., & Liddell, T. M. 2018. Bayesian data analysis for newcomers. *Psychonomic Bulletin and Review*, 25(1): 155–177.

Lohrke, F. T., Holloway, B. B., & Woolley, T. W. 2009. Conjoint analysis in entrepreneurship research. *Organizational Research Methods*, 13(1): 16–30.

Loken, E., & Gelman, A. 2017. Measurement error and the replication crisis. *Science*, 355(6325): 584–585.

Lumpkin, G. T., & Dess, G. G. 1996. Clarifying the entrepreneurial orientation construct and linking it to performance. *Academy of Management Review*, 21(1): 135–172.

McNeish, D., & Kelley, K. 2018. Fixed effects models versus mixed effects models for clustered data: Reviewing the approaches, disentangling the differences, and making recommendations. *Psychological Methods*, 24(1): 20–35.

Miller, D. 1983. The correlates of entrepreneurship in three types of firms. *Management Science*, 29(7): 770–791.

Miller, D., & Friesen, P. H. 1982. Innovation in conservative and entrepreneurial firms: Two models of strategic momentum. *Strategic Management Journal*, 3(1): 1–25.

Morgan, S. L., & Winship, C. 2014. *Counterfactuals and Causal Inference: Methods and Principles for Social Research*, Second Edition. New York: Cambridge University Press.

Pearl, J. 2009. *Causality: Models, Reasoning, and Inference*, Second Edition. New York: Cambridge University Press.

Pearl, J. 2018a. Does obesity shorten life? Or is it the soda? On non-manipulable causes. *Journal of Causal Inference*, 6(2): 688.

Pearl, J. 2018b. *The Book of Why: The New Science of Cause and Effect*. New York: Basic Books.

Podsakoff, P. M., MacKenzie, S. B., & Podsakoff, N. P. 2016. Recommendations for creating better concept definitions in the organizational, behavioral, and social sciences. *Organizational Research Methods*, 19(2): 159–203.

Rauch, A., Wiklund, J., Lumpkin, G. T., & Frese, M. 2009. Entrepreneurial orientation and business performance: An assessment of past research and suggestions for the future. *Entrepreneurship Theory and Practice*, 33(3): 761–787.

Rocha, V., van Praag, M., Folta, T. B., & Carneiro, A. 2018. Endogeneity in strategy-performance analysis: An application to initial human capital strategy and new venture performance. *Organizational Research Methods*, 22(3): 740–764.

Rohrer, J. M. 2018. Thinking clearly about correlations and causation: Graphical causal models for observational data. *Advances in Methods and Practices in Psychological Science*, 1(1): 27–42.

Rosenbusch, N., Rauch, A., & Bausch, A. 2013. The mediating role of entrepreneurial orientation in the task environment–performance relationship: A meta-analysis. *Journal of Management*, 39(3): 633–659.

Rosseel, Y. 2012. lavaan: An R package for structural equation modeling. *Journal of Statistical Software*, 48(1): 1–36.

Rubin, D. B. 2005. Causal inference using potential outcomes. *Journal of the American Statistical Association*, 100: 322–331.

Semadeni, M., Withers, M. C., & Certo, T. S. 2014. The perils of endogeneity and instrumental variables in strategy research: Understanding through simulations. *Strategic Management Journal*, 35(7): 1070–1079.

Shadish, W., Cook, T. D., & Campbell, D. T. 2002. *Experimental and Quasi-Experimental Designs for Generalized Causal Inference*, Second Edition. Boston, MA: Houghton Mifflin.

Shaver, J. M. 1998. Accounting for endogeneity when assessing strategy performance: Does entry mode choice affect FDI survival? *Management Science*, 44(4): 571–585.

Smid, S. C., McNeish, D., Miočević, M., & van de Schoot, R. 2019. Bayesian versus frequentist estimation for structural equation models in small sample contexts: A systematic review. *Structural Equation Modeling*, 27(1): 1–31.

Titus, V. K., & Anderson, B. S. 2018. Firm structure and environment as contingencies to the corporate venture capital–parent firm value relationship. *Entrepreneurship Theory and Practice*, 42(3): 498–522.

Wales, W. J., Patel, P. C., Parida, V., & Kreiser, P. M. 2013. Nonlinear effects of entrepreneurial orientation on small firm performance: The moderating role of resource orchestration capabilities. *Strategic Entrepreneurship Journal*, 7(2): 93–121.

Wennberg, K., & Anderson, B. S. 2019. Editorial: Enhancing the exploration and communication of quantitative entrepreneurship research. *Journal of Business Venturing*, 35(3): 1–11.

Westfall, J., & Yarkoni, T. 2016. Statistically controlling for confounding constructs is harder than you think. *PLoS One*, 11(3): e0152719.

Wiklund, J., & Shepherd, D. A. 2011. Where to from here? EO-as-experimentation, failure, and distribution of outcomes. *Entrepreneurship Theory and Practice*, 35(5): 925–946.

Wooldridge, J. M. 2010. *Econometric Analysis of Cross Section and Panel Data*. Cambridge, MA: MIT Press.

Wright, M., & Hitt, M. A. 2017. Strategic entrepreneurship and the SEJ: Development and current progress. *Strategic Entrepreneurship Journal*, 11(3): 200–210.

Yao, Y., Vehtari, A., Simpson, D., & Gelman, A. 2018. Using stacking to average Bayesian predictive distributions. *Bayesian Analysis*, 13(3): 917–1007.

Yarkoni, T., & Westfall, J. 2017. Choosing prediction over explanation in psychology: Lessons from machine learning. *Perspectives on Psychological Science*, 12(6): 1100–1122.

APPENDIX: CODEBOOK

```
# Informative Prior Illustration -- R Script
# Authored by Brian S. Anderson, Ph.D.
# Current as of 24 February 2020

# Description
## This code demonstrates using an informative prior to shrink a parameter
## estimate closer to zero in response to an endogeneity concern. The model
## assumes that a single omitted variable captures multiple sources of
## endogeneity, and that the cumulative effect of these sources is to bias
## the estimate upward.

# Libraries
## Creating the data: https://cran.r-project.org/package=lavaan
library(lavaan)

## Bayesian modeling: https://cran.r-project.org/package=rstanarm
library(rstanarm)

## Creating HTML tables: https://cran.r-project.org/package=sjPlot
library(sjPlot)

# Data Generation
## Define the simulation model
## We assume the true effect of x --> y = .25; c1 and c2 represent exogenous
## covariates. The model simulates cross-sectional, observational data with
## a normally distributed continuous y and continuous x. The model assumes a
## continuous additional predictor, z, which simulates an omitted variable.
## The simulation assumes a .4 true effect of z on x and y.

sim.model <- "# Structural model with covariates
        y ~ .25 * x + .1 * c1 + .2 * c2
        # Omitted variable covariances
        x ~ .4 * z
        y ~ .4 * z"

## Create the simulated data with N = 1,000
set.seed(123)
```

```
sim.df <- simulateData(sim.model, sample.nobs = 1000)

# Models
## True Model -- Includes z
true.model <- lm(y ~ x + z + c1 + c2, data = sim.df)

## Naive Model -- Exclude z
naive.model <- lm(y ~ x + c1 + c2, data = sim.df)

## Weak Prior -- Mean 0, standard deviation 10 for each predictor
weak_prior <- normal(location = c(0, 0, 0), scale = c(10, 10, 10),
            autoscale = FALSE)
weak.model <- stan_glm(y ~ x + c1 + c2, data = sim.df, prior = weak_prior,
            seed = 123, refresh = 0)

## Informative Prior -- Mean .15, standard deviation of .025 for x
## Weakly informative priors for each remaining term
inf_prior <- normal(location = c(.15, 0, 0), scale = c(.025, 10, 10),
            autoscale = FALSE)
inf.model <- stan_glm(y ~ x + c1 + c2, data = sim.df, prior = inf_prior,
            seed = 123, refresh = 0)

# Tables
## Table 1. Regression
tab_model(true.model, naive.model, show.p = FALSE,
        dv.labels = c("True Model", "Naive Model"),
        pred.labels = c("Intercept", "x", "z", "Control 1", "Control 2"),
        string.est = "Est.",
        string.pred = "Coefficient",
        string.ci = "CI (95%)")

## Table 2. Bayesian
tab_model(weak.model, inf.model,
        dv.labels = c("Weak Prior", "Informative Prior"),
        pred.labels = c("Intercept", "x", "Control 1", "Control 2"),
        string.est = "Est.",
        string.pred = "Coefficient")
```

Index

Abadie, A. 243
absorptive capacity 3, 8–23
    attributes 11–12
    evolution over time 9
    knowledge decomposability and 13–18
    knowledge structures 12–13
    potential 8
    realized 8
Academy of Management, entrepreneurship
    and strategy divisions 1
Academy of Management Journal 87
ACAP *see* absorptive capacity
accelerator programs 82–3, 91–2
    academic research on 4
    entrepreneurial experience 97
    entrepreneurial need 97–8
    future research on 98–100
    literature review of 87
    performance and success of 100
    practice, implications for 96–7
    program fit 98
    research, implications for 94–5
    scopes of 94
    selection process and criteria 91
    support services 91
    teaching, implications for 95–6
    trends in articles published about 94
    types of entrepreneurs who use 94
    value in 84–6
    see also university-affiliated incubator
        and accelerator programs
accountability 148
advanced algorithmic text analysis 209–10
age, of firms 115, 135
anarchism 26, 27, 28, 29, 30, 32, 34, 35, 36,
    42
Anderson, B. S. 255, 256
Anderson, Brian 5
angel investors 68, 187
anti-smoking legislation, effect on cigarette
    consumption 243
Antonakis, J. 241
Armstrong, C. E. 4
arousal
    emotional 182, 183, 189
    level of 186

Ashby, N. J. S. 166
associational research 235–6
attentional bias 184, 186
Audretsch, D. B. 172
automated content analysis 207

Barney, J. B. 43
Baron, R. A. 134
Bátiz-Lazo, B. 132
Baumer, E. P. S. 218
Bayer, Florian 3
Bayesian inference
    criterion 179
    introduction to 247–8
    limitations of 251–2
    post-specification tools 254
Bayesian linear model 253
Bayesian model stacking 255
Bayesian modeling 5, 234, 253–4, 255
Bhawe, Nachiket 3
bias 166, 214, 250–51
    attentional 184, 186
    entrepreneurial 134
    quantification of 257
    survival bias problem 241
Bingham, C. 91
Biopolis (Singapore) 20
BioValley (Malaysia) 20
boxologies 173, 186
brain, the, connections between the body
    and 173
Brettel, M. 51, 62
Burridge, L. 187
business plans 204
    placement of information in 185
Bylund, P. L. 32, 43
Bylund, Per 3
Bylund, Susanne 3

Camp, S. M. 2, 25, 172
Campbell, Betsy 4
Campbell, D. T. 237
Cardon, M. S. 186
career motives
    expert (occupation orientation) 68
    linear (hierarchy orientation) 68

Printed and bound by CPI Group (UK) Ltd, Croydon, CR0 4YY

16/04/2025

14658377-0002